NIETZSCHE AND ZION

NIETZSCHE AND ZION

JACOB GOLOMB

CORNELL UNIVERSITY PRESS
Ithaca and London

First published 2004 by Cornell University Press

Printed in the United States of America

Library of Congress Cataloging-in-Publication Data

Golomb, Jacob.
  Nietzsche and Zion / Jacob Golomb.
    p. cm.
Includes bibliographical references and index.
  ISBN 0-8014-3762-8 (cloth : alk. paper)
  1. Zionism—Philosophy.   2. Nietzsche, Friedrich Wilhelm, 1844–1900—Influence.   3. Philosophy, Jewish.   I. Title.
  DS149.G5492 2004
  320.54'095694—dc22

                                                      2003019238

Cornell University Press strives to use environmentally responsible suppliers and materials to the fullest extent possible in the publishing of its books. Such materials include vegetable-based, low-VOC inks and acid-free papers that are recycled, totally chlorine-free, or partly composed of nonwood fibers. For further information, visit our website at www.cornellpress.cornell.edu.

Cloth printing   10 9 8 7 6 5 4 3 2 1

For Margit

Contents

Acknowledgments

No man is an island, and surely no one is an *Übermensch*. This is certainly true of the present writer. The list of colleagues, friends, and benevolent spirits who have advised, assisted, and encouraged this research is too long to give in full here. However, some individuals were so valuable that it would be a sign of bad taste and *ressentiment* (to use the Nietzschean term) not to give them their due.

I have the pleasure of mentioning the untiring assistance and encouragement of Roger Haydon, senior editor of Cornell University Press. From the day he first heard about this project, he was more than enthusiastic and provided the kind of support and insightful comments without which this book would have never been written in its present form. When the terrorists were inflicting their deadly attacks all around Jerusalem and I was struggling to complete this book, his unfailing support and warm words gave me the stamina to stick to my conviction that when the cannons are firing, the Muses ought not to become silent but, on the contrary, must raise their voices even more vigorously. I am especially grateful to John G. Ackerman, director of Cornell University Press (CUP), for initially recognizing the potential significance of this book, and would also like to acknowledge the professionalism and acumen of the other staff at CUP—especially Karen Laun, who saw this book through to its happy conclusion.

Some renowned scholars and friends with whom I have discussed this study and who have shown great interest include Stanley Corngold and Alexander Nehamas, both of Princeton University, Berel Lang of Trinity College, Hartford, and my dear colleague Robert Wistrich of the Hebrew University of Jerusalem, who generously provided me with helpful remarks on the chapter on Herzl.

I also thank Gavin Lewis, who worked so hard to render a difficult manuscript into readable form.

In addition, I should mention the kind assistance of the Fritz Thyssen Stiftung for their research grant.

Finally, I thank Margit, my beloved wife, who taught me more of the history of Zionism than these pages can testify, and who bestowed upon me a heartfelt dedication without which this book would never have been written or even conceived.

NOTE ON SOURCES AND LIST OF ABBREVIATIONS

I have, wherever possible, followed the most accessible English-language translations and editions of Nietzsche's major works—those by Walter Kaufmann and R. J. Hollingdale. All quotations from Nietzsche's writings are given in the text and identified by abbreviations of their English titles. Arabic numbers not identified as page numbers indicate the paragraphs or sections in which the passages appear. Where appropriate, Roman numerals are used to indicate the parts of the works in which they are to be found.

Citations from Nietzsche's other works are based on the texts as they appear in the Colli-Montinari *Kritische Studienausgabe* (*KSA*), and their *Sämtliche Briefe: Kritische Studienausgabe* (*KGB*). All translations are mine, unless otherwise noted. The transliteration of Hebrew titles of journals is according to "Newspapers and Periodicals, Hebrew," in *Encyclopedia Judaica*.

A	*The Antichrist.* In *The Portable Nietzsche.* Translated and edited by Walter Kaufmann. New York, 1954.
BGE	*Beyond Good and Evil.* Translated by Walter Kaufmann. New York, 1966.
BT	*The Birth of Tragedy.* Translated by Walter Kaufmann. New York, 1967.
CW	*The Case of Wagner.* In *The Birth of Tragedy.*
D	*Daybreak.* Translated by R. J. Hollingdale. Cambridge, 1982.
E	*Ecce Homo.* Translated by Walter Kaufmann. New York, 1967.
GM	*On the Genealogy of Morals.* Translated and edited by Walter Kaufmann. New York, 1967.
GS	*The Gay Science.* Translated by Walter Kaufmann. New York, 1974.
HH	*Human, All Too Human.* Translated by R. J. Hollingdale. Cambridge, 1986.
HL	"On the Uses and Disadvantages of History for Life." In *Untimely Meditations.*
KGB	*Sämtliche Briefe: Kritische Studienausgabe.* Edited by Giorgio Colli and Mazzino Montinari. 8 vols. Berlin, 1975–1984.
KSA	*Kritische Studienausgabe.* Edited by Giorgio Colli and Mazzino Montinari. 15 vols. Berlin, 1967–1977.

NCW   "Nietzsche contra Wagner." In *The Portable Nietzsche.*
NFP   *Neue Freie Presse.*
SE   "Schopenhauer as Educator." The third of the *Untimely Medita-tions.*
TI   "Twilight of the Idols." In *The Portable Nietzsche.*
UM   *Untimely Meditations.* Translated by R. J. Hollingdale. Cambridge, 1983.
WP   *The Will to Power.* Translated by Walter Kaufmann and R. J. Holling-dale. New York, 1967.
Z   "Thus Spoke Zarathustra." In *The Portable Nietzsche.*

In addition, the following editions of works by Nietzsche are occasion-ally cited.

Basic Writings of Nietzsche. Translated by Walter Kaufmann. New York, 1968.

Kritische Gesamtausgabe der Werke Nietzsches. Edited by Giorgio Colli and Mazzino Montinari. 33 vols. Berlin, 1967ff.

Philosophy in the Tragic Age of the Greeks. Translated by Marianne Cowan. Chicago, 1962.

NIETZSCHE AND ZION

Introduction

NIETZSCHE AND ZIONISM?

The reader may be forgiven at the outset for wondering what Friedrich Nietzsche could possibly have had in common with Zionism. Indeed, "Nietzsche and Zion" might appear to be a contradiction in terms, a coupling of two diametrically opposed ideological forces.

Granted, the main thrust of Nietzsche's philosophy was the freedom of the individual to authentically shape his own self and destiny. He was frequently described as the "radical aristocrat" of the spirit, because he abhorred mass culture and socialism, and strove to cultivate a special kind of human being, the *Übermensch,* endowed with exceptional mental qualities. What, then, can this thinker have had in common with a movement for national liberation that mobilized individual Jews to attain national aspirations and to establish, among other institutions, socialist communities in *Eretz Israel*? Can we ignore Nietzsche's claim that selfhood is primary to nationhood? Wasn't Nietzsche the most hostile critic of the Judeo-Christian ethos that originated in Zion? So how could he occupy a proper, even a respectable, place among Zionists?

This book, part of a larger project, attempts to answer these questions, in part by making use of material that heretofore has not been widely available. The results show that Nietzsche's ideas were widely disseminated among and appropriated by the first Hebrew Zionist writers and leaders.[1] It seems quite appropriate, then, that the first Zionist Congress was held in Basle, where Nietzsche spent several years as a professor of classical philology. This coincidence gains profound significance when we see Nietzsche's impact on the first Zionist leaders and writers in Europe (discussed in this book) as well as his presence in Palestine and, later, in the State of Israel (to be explored in future work).

This book, however, is not just another exercise in cultural history or a report on Nietzsche's reception within a certain intellectual-sociological universe. It aspires to do more than merely delineate the history of Zionist ideas, their confrontation with Nietzsche's thought, and their subsequent transmutation among the most influential writers and intellectual leaders of the Zionist revolution. It also attempts to fill a gap in modern Jewish history in general and in the history of Zionism in particular. The prevalent accounts of Zionism emphasize the national and social objectives of Zionism, that is, the establishment of a Jewish egalitarian society in Palestine. Thus they tend to overlook some of Zionism's more implicit ideological aspirations: for example, the attempt to foster a new image of an authentic Jew or Hebrew.

When seen through a Nietzschean prism, therefore, the current historiography of the Zionist movement must undergo a significant revision. The cultural import, less tribal, more universalistic and enlightening, will come to the fore. Most of the existing literature concentrates on the nationalist and collectivist impulses of Zionism, and on its goal of providing a national haven for European Jewry. It thereby ignores the aspirations of the movement's leaders and ideologues, its writers, philosophers, and politicians qua persons—to forge for themselves authentic new identities and to cultivate a new image of the Jew—as an Israeli who is also a Jew. This existential transfiguration from the "last Jews to the first Hebrews" (as Berdichevski put it) was effected, in no small measure, by adapting Nietzsche's views on the fossilizing antiquarian historical consciousness, on authenticity, and on the will for genuine creation and self-overcoming.

This does not mean, of course, that the objective of the Zionist movement to secure a haven for European Jews, especially after the horrors of the Holocaust, was not pressing and important. However, the official historiography of Zionism does not heed the personal objectives of Zionists *qua individuals*. Amid the waving of ideological banners and the thunder of cannons, the voices of these individual people were ignored. By listening to them with Nietzsche in mind we will be able to evaluate them for their merits or flaws. Hence the present research attempts to provide an "existential corrective"[2] that the official Zionist historiography urgently needs.

This "corrective" applies also to the so-called New Historians of postmodernist bent[3]—in particular to many of their simplistic generalizations. There is a considerable and growing literature in the United States as well as Israel that is critical of Zionism's idea of the "new Jew" as a lamentable misstep in Jewish history.[4] The "New Historians," accused by Efraim Karsh as suffering from what Nietzsche termed "*Selbsthass*" (self-hatred),[5] wished to *deconstruct* the more or less official Zionist narrative and its normative historiography by employing the Palestinian narrative.[6] In contrast, this book shows how, by using the Nietzschean prism, one may *reconstruct* the Zionist narrative by, among other things, dwelling on the persistent Zionist call for the cultivation of an authentic "new Hebrew."

By using the key Nietzschean notion of personal authenticity—absent from most of the New Historians' accounts which barely refer to Nietzsche)—this book throws into sharper relief motifs and aspirations mostly ignored by both the normative historians of Zionism and the New Historians. Both sides have been too preoccupied with the "right" and "objective" narratives of recent Israeli history. The New Historians are contesting the official narrative of the Israeli war for independence. Their post-Zionist research, however, has been conducted within the widely accepted consensus about the legitimate claim of the Jews to their land (or to a part of it). They have assumed that the *sole or principal* objective of the Zionist revolution was to secure a national haven for European Jewry. Thus both sides have chosen to ignore the Nietzschean warning that there are "no facts, only interpretations" and hence no objective and absolutely valid history can be ever written.

"*Eretz Israel* is not California," wrote a Zionist Socialist writer in a Socialist Party organ in 1920. "We do not celebrate its land because it contains golden nuggets but because on its ground we hope to mend *the flaws of our souls*."[7] The personal flaws of individual Jews that Zionism purported to correct were mainly existential, though some emerged because these individual Jews subsisted (sometimes barely) in perilous circumstances. Several of these flaws were the unwelcome outcome of the peculiar geopolitical and historical circumstances of the Jewish people as a whole in the Diaspora. But since Nietzsche appealed mainly to individuals and not to nations as such, the personal repercussions of the existential anomalies in the life of European Jewry are the focus here.

The ardent wish to overcome these flaws drew the Jewish authors examined in this book to Zionism. However, before attempting to solve their individual existential distresses by means of Zionism, they tried to overcome them by turning to Nietzschean philosophy. Thus, what attracted the most influential Zionist leaders and the first modern Hebrew writers to Nietzsche attracted them to Zionism as well—so much so that Zionism was for them the natural continuation of their fertile encounter with Nietzsche.

But what exactly were these "flaws in their souls" that they tried to mend, first through Nietzsche and then through Zionism? What exactly did they hope to correct by becoming Jewish Nietzscheans or by introducing Nietzschean motifs to the Zionist agenda?

NIETZSCHE AND JEWISH MARGINALITY IN FIN-DE-SIÈCLE EUROPE

Virtually all the individuals discussed in this book were impressed by Nietzsche's thought relatively early in their lives. They were young, sensitive, and highly impressionable Jews in the midst of acute personal crises that involved existential agonies concerning their personal identities. All of them, most notably Theodor Herzl and Max Nordau, suffered from what is now customarily labeled "the syndrome of marginality."

To these *Grenzjuden* (marginal Jews) or "stepchildren"[8] belonged prominent Western European Jewish intellectuals such as Else Lasker-Schüler, Arthur Schnitzler, Jakob Wassermann, Stefan Zweig, Franz Kafka, Franz Werfel, Kurt Tucholsky, Walter Benjamin, Carl Sternheim, Karl Kraus, Ernst Toller, Gustav Mahler, Sigmund Freud, Theodor Herzl, Max Nordau, and many others. They were *Grenzjuden* in that they had lost their religion and traditions, but had not been fully absorbed into secular German or Austrian society. For some, hatred of their ancestral roots led to self-destruction and breakdown. These doubly marginal individuals tragically lacked an identity: they rejected any affinity with the Jewish community but were nonetheless unwelcome among their non-Jewish contemporaries. Jakob Wassermann penetratingly describes them from within as "religiously and socially speaking floating in the air. They no longer had the old faith; they refused to accept a new one, that is to say, Christianity. . . . the physical ghetto has become a mental and moral one . . ."[9]

According to Gershom Scholem, "Because they no longer had any other inner ties to the Jewish tradition, let alone to the Jewish people," these marginal Jews "constitute[d] one of the most shocking phenomena of this whole process of alienation."[10] Yet despite their desperate attempts to be accepted as Austrians and Germans, most recognized the traumatic truth that, as Herzl's friend Arthur Schnitzler put it, "for a Jew, especially in public life, it was impossible to disregard the fact that he was a Jew."[11]

Central European Jews attempted a wide spectrum of solutions to their unbearable state of uprootedness, from full assimilation, including even conversion to Christianity (as the young Herzl wished for), to identification with some definite ideological or political cause such as socialism (Ernst Bloch, Kurt Tucholsky, Ernst Toller) or Zionism (Herzl, Nordau, Buber). My concern here, however, is limited to this last group—namely to those marginal Jews who opted to solve their marginality first by trying, under Nietzsche's influence, to become "free spirits" and then by embracing Zionism.[12]

Nietzsche was initially attractive to this group because he urged his readers to create their own selves and their own personal authenticity, just as an artist creates his own works of art.[13] As they solved their identity problems by means of Zionism, Herzl, Nordau, Buber and others gradually freed themselves from Nietzsche's spell. But at the beginning of their tortuous searches for personal authenticity, many young, sensitive, and vulnerable Central European Jewish intellectuals were excited by the possibilities Nietzsche held out to them. In their *Gymnasium* or university years, these marginal Jews were often euphoric about Nietzsche, whom they saw as a companion in their existential search. A case in point is Martin Buber, who admits in his writings that he felt Nietzsche's influence very strongly in his youth, so that even after adopting a kind of pacifist Zionism and existential Judaism, he had to make strenuous efforts to free himself from it.

Many of the Zionist Nietzscheans understood the main insight that a genuine Nietzschean should follow: to be really Nietzschean one has to get rid eventually of Nietzsche's influence as well. To succeed fully in creating one's own self, one has to overcome "Nietzsche's invasion" (a phrase coined by Buber) into this very self. Accordingly, those Zionist leaders and men and women of Hebrew letters who opted to uphold Nietzsche's ideas and then to abandon them were actually more Nietzscheans than those who blindly clung to his views throughout their lives.

NIETZSCHE AND THE COLLAPSE OF JEWISH SELFHOOD IN EASTERN EUROPE: THE "RENT IN ONE'S HEART"

Micha Josef Berdichevski, the first and foremost Hebrew Nietzschean, and his polemical opponent and friend Ahad Ha'am suffered from a different syndrome than sheer marginality. As the leading Eastern European Jews acculturated to the West, they experienced the acute affliction of what Berdichevski aptly described as the "rent in [their] hearts."

Nietzsche's reception among Eastern European Jews was different from that in Central Europe because of their unique cultural predicament. Eastern European Jews were not "marginal" from the perspective of their rich

Jewish culture. The German-speaking Jews, especially the second generation whose parents had already estranged themselves from Jewish heritage and religion, wanted to assimilate into the main currents of secular German culture, which they regarded as superior to their own. Eastern European Jews, on the other hand, regarded the culture of the Polish and Russian peasants as inferior to their own. Thus the rent in their hearts was not merely a superficial one but was both deeper and more acute, since it involved an internal schism between their *own* religious past and their present secular circumstances, to say nothing of their secular future aspirations.

Berdichevski and Ahad Ha'am revolted against their own fathers. As a result, they experienced a deep rift between their shaped secular identity and their religious background as well as guilt feelings that they had betrayed their fathers and deserted their homes in a time of great need. With the murder of God in their hearts, they also slaughtered their fathers' heritage and tradition. Nietzsche became for them the great healer who assisted them in creatively accepting the traumatic experiences of their torn hearts and spiritual agonies. As an archenemy of any kind of guilt, Nietzsche showed them how to overcome such feelings and go their *own* ways, as did Ahad Ha'am and Hillel Zeitlin, the former by adopting Jewish ethics and the latter by turning to Kabbalah and mysticism. Naturally their particular solutions to the problem of retaining their authentic *individuum* and mending their torn hearts also involved overcoming Nietzsche's powerful enticements. However, during the very process of their struggles for harmony and authentic identity, they employed Nietzsche's teaching more intensively than their Western brothers since they were in much greater need of his instructive prescriptions for attainment of solid identities.

AUTHENTICITY

It is one of my central theses that despite cultural and existential differences, both Western and Eastern Jewish luminaries were especially attracted to Nietzsche's ideal of authentic life and to his plea to overcome their built-in *dividuum* and attain the status of a harmonious *individuum*. But what exactly was it that these Jews found in Nietzsche that so echoed their longing for authenticity?

Nietzsche did not use the term "authenticity" explicitly, but it is possible to detect its presence in the recurrent distinctions he makes between *Wahrheit* (truth) and *Wahrhaftigkeit* (truthfulness) (see *D* 73, *GS* 357, *BGE* 1). One of the basic intuitions of Nietzsche's thought is the concept of complete immanence, formulated in sections 108–25 of *The Gay Science*. There are no transcendental entities or supranatural powers, no "pure reason," no other world, no domain different from or superior to our own. After the "Death of God" one must adopt for oneself the God-like role of originator of truth and of one's own self. The absence of a "preestablished harmony" between our cognition and reality permits us to shift our attention to the creation of our own genuine selves.

Nietzsche employs the metaphor of art and artistic creation. The search for authenticity is the wish to express one's indeterminacy by spontaneous choice of one of many possible ways of life. The individual is akin to the artist who freely shapes his self as a work of art. To become what we are is not to live according to our so-called "innate nature," but rather to create ourselves freely. To that end we must know ourselves, in order to distinguish what we can change in ourselves and the external circumstances that have shaped us from that which we have to accept as inevitable. This we must do in the heroic manner of *amor fati* and of "self-overcoming."

This teaching appealed to the Western "marginal" and Eastern "torn" Jews who sought to shed their traditional Jewish heritage to become authors of their new lives. They were drawn by Nietzsche's ultimate vision of a creative and authentic life in a world without dogmatic beliefs. The death of dogmas does not lead to disintegration of the self, but rather liberates the individual's creative resources. It opens up new horizons that function as life-enhancing "perspectives." Thus most of the protagonists of our story regarded Nietzsche's philosophy as he himself had regarded it: as a means, "a mere instrument," to entice them into forming their personal authenticity.[14]

However, Nietzsche's basic idea of the "transfiguration of all values" does not call for radical abolition of all inauthentic life patterns, but for a gradual approximation of authenticity. This process is constantly taking place "within a *single* soul" (*BGE* 260), vacillating between opposed modes of living. Nietzsche thus actually describes the internal pathos of both Western *and* Eastern Jews at the end of the nineteenth century, who experienced such fluctuating sentiments.

DESPIRITUALIZATION

In order to create for themselves new scripts of their lives and effect a considerable reevaluation of their ancient values, Eastern European Jews had to overcome their intensive immersion in traditional holy texts. From this point of view, Nietzsche was conducive to the liberating process of shedding

the burden of antiquarian consciousness, by acting as a heuristic catalyst for
what Buber termed "despiritualization." Under Nietzsche's inspiration,
Eastern Jews underwent a far-reaching liberation from the repression of instincts and natural drives, and attained the guilt-free ability to be creative in
the secular domain. What Buber initially was trying to foster under the
name of "Jewish Renaissance"[15] and "despiritualization" became, under the
auspices of Nietzsche in Israel, a Hebrew Renaissance, though not before a
certain transfiguration of characters and beliefs took place.

For modern Jews to overcome their fossilization within the ghettoes and
to become effectively active agents, to create their own history vis-à-vis that
of gentile Europeans, they had to overcome their traditional Talmudic patterns of learning, which could not be incorporated within secular Zionist
culture. The Jewish or, more precisely, Zionist Renaissance demanded that
the Jews overcome their antiquarian-rabbinic consciousness, around which
they had structured their Jewish identity in the Diaspora, and instead adopt
a "monumental" approach centering around the grandeur of their glorious days in ancient Israel. This incitement to "monumental history," which
the Zionist revolution aspired to foster, is expressed in Nietzsche's essay on
history in which he asserts that "monumental" historical consciousness
lends support to the creative and powerful individual who seeks an existence that expresses his inner power. It makes possible an empathetic identification with exemplary figures, and reassures those who aspire to greatness
by showing them that "the greatness that once existed was in any event
once *possible* and may thus be possible again" (*UM*, p. 69). The ambitious
person is encouraged to reject any gnawing uncertainties and to pursue
the path of glory and creation. And who among these Zionist leaders and
writers did not harbor such ambitions? It is small wonder, then, that the
better-known historical novels and dramas of many of these writers described the glorious past of their people and tried to foster in their readers the aspiration to recover their "monumental" ancient history. These
ambitions were expressed in Israel by David Ben-Gurion's thrust to turn
from the predominance of Talmudic learning to the studies and knowledge of *Tanach* (the Hebrew Bible) as the yearly International Contest of
Tanach Knowledge plainly testifies.

LEGITIMIZATION FOR ATHEISM

In order to leave behind divine history, to enter the world-historical stage
effectively, and to forge a new focus of identity and personal authenticity,

the overcoming of antiquarian consciousness was not enough. Eastern as well as Western Jews had to kill in their hearts their belief in the Jewish God, or the residue of such belief, and also had to courageously overcome his "shadows."

Surely, for religiously uprooted Jews in the midst of the process of secularization, the problem of faith and direction in matters of belief became acute.[16] The simplicity and difficulty of Nietzsche's atheistic solution fascinated them. His plea to embrace the idea of complete immanence and to do away with all Gods appealed to marginal Western Jews and to Eastern Jews who desperately needed support in their journey away from ancient tradition. The impotence of metaphysics and religion, felt so keenly by Jewish intellectuals at the turn of the century, attracted them to Nietzsche, who against transcendental doctrines of salvation from the hardship of life posited their antithesis: salvation from these doctrines themselves by inciting readers to live a creative and healthy atheistic life.[17]

NIETZSCHE'S PSYCHOLOGY, SELF-HATRED, AND ANTI-SEMITISM

The new psychology in Nietzsche's work was another important aspect that attracted both Western and Eastern Jews. To help them cope with their extreme identity crises, many needed considerable self-analysis. They sought consolidation of their souls and reactivation of the inner cores of their personalities, which had been lost in the tug of war between their double identities. Many of the Jewish writers were immersed in self-analysis. Hence the intimate bond between the psychoanalytic movement and marginal Jews: the first Psychoanalytic Society in Vienna, apart from Jung, consisted primarily of Jewish intellectuals and physicians. The prospect of therapy offered by psychoanalysis had great appeal for those Western *Grenzjuden* who wavered between the German culture and the Jewish traditions of their forefathers.

The Jewish psychoanalysts (and Herzl as well, as we shall see) were especially attracted by Nietzsche's genealogical methods of unmasking. Nietzsche proclaimed these as a way of freeing oneself from religious, metaphysical, and social ideologies that had previously provided ready-made and inauthentic identities, and thereby attaining a solid sense of selfhood and individual identity. The death of the divine Father—the Jewish God—and the decline of the authority of the human father were responsible for bringing the sons to the schizophrenic state they were now in.

Both Western and especially Eastern Jews sought to establish firm and authentic identities that would not draw their content from faith and tradition, but from their *own* individual mental resources. Nietzsche encouraged this process by showing how psychologizing could liberate the individual from dependence on mechanical internalizations, long-standing habits of thought, and established conventions.

Nietzsche served as a model of penetrating self-analysis of an acute neurosis, and also demonstrated, before Freud, the therapy needed to overcome this neurosis. According to Nietzsche's testimony, his neurosis, to which Freud frequently referred,[18] facilitated his psychological insights and helped him grasp such contrasts as that between good and evil, as opposed to that between good and bad. Many marginal Western and "torn" Eastern Jews, who had experienced and overcome such neuroses, possessed an "inborn fastidiousness of taste with respect to psychological questions" (*GM*—Preface 3) and were able to "go inside" themselves. This ability to "go inside" and overcome states of negative pathos was regarded by Nietzsche as indicating the individual's positive power. Many of creative *Grenzjuden* dared "go inside," and used such self-overcoming to produce masterpieces that were informed by this psychological enlightenment.

Moreover, the fascination Nietzsche had for the marginal Jews was also fueled by the fact that his psychology helped them understand one of the most troublesome phenomena they experienced in their daily lives: their own *Selbsthass* and the hatred of gentile anti-Semites. Constantly exposed to negative images of Jews, some of them began to look upon themselves just as the anti-Semites did. The result was a poisonous self-hatred toward their Jewish characteristics.

Theodor Lessing (1872–1933), a German Zionist and a disciple of Nietzsche who dedicated several writings to his philosophy,[19] wrote a comprehensive treatise, *Der jüdische Selbsthass,* in which he tried to understand this phenomenon using the Nietzschean concepts of *ressentiment* and *Verinnerlichung.*[20]

In this book, Lessing describes the Jews in the Diaspora as people who have been forced to live unnatural lives. After separation from their land, they turned to an excessively spiritual life in which they live "together with their dead ones." Lessing claims, in language that is definitely Nietzschean, that in their internalized lives—as a result of external pressure and out of fear of their hostile surroundings—the Jews directed their spiritual resources against themselves, manifesting self-doubt, insecurity, and self-torture. This agonizing state of affairs was so unbearable that they attempted to liberate themselves from it by despising anything that had to do with Judaism, especially themselves. Lessing ends his essay with a call to these Jews: "Sei was immer du *bist*" (p. 51). We should recall the existential motto of Nietzsche's autobiography, *Ecce Homo,* which also appears in its subtitle: "Wie man wird, was man ist." In Nietzschean terms, Lessing is calling upon these Jews not to betray their fate, but to love it in the manner of *amor fati,* that is, not through resignation and passive submission to wretched conditions, but by accepting their genuine selves and approving their historical roots.

Furthermore, in the second part of Nietzsche's *Genealogie der Moral* he deals with the phenomena of *ressentiment* and *Verinnerlichung*—the powerful "masters" that are responsible for the phenomenon of "internalization," in which most of man's instincts are turned "inward" against "man himself." They evoke in the "weak" the feeling of *ressentiment* that characterizes the first stage of the "slave morality"; in the second stage, when the "instinct for freedom [is] pushed back and repressed . . . [and is] finally able to discharge and vent itself only on itself" (*GM* II-17), they become "bad conscience." As a result, the intimidated individual becomes a schizophrenic personality in constant internal strife, fighting himself out of sheer self-hatred and being prevented from attaining inner harmony by this struggle.

This explanation can, of course, also be applied to the anti-Semite, who is a weak and psychologically unstable individual, with the character of a "slave." The phenomenon of anti-Semitism can be partly elucidated with reference to the psychological patterns of the weak and impoverished personality described in Nietzsche's main writings, beginning with *The Gay Science*.[21] Lacking personal power, and as a result of *ressentiment* and mental impoverishment, the anti-Semite is dependent upon external surroundings for self-determination. He needs acts of violence and cruel exploitation of others to enhance his feeble sense of power (GS 359). He is a vengeful and reactive person who uses his hatred, a hatred in which "there is *fear*" (GS 379), to attain some sort of security and self-identity. It follows that the anti-Semite is actually the "slave" and not the "master." This insight too, of which the marginal Jews were in tremendous need, encouraged them to adopt Nietzsche's attitude.[22]

SUBLIME MISSION

Nietzsche not only supplied the European Jews with the conceptual means to understand their self-hatred and to regard anti-Semitism as a manifestation of inferior mentalities. He also assigned them a practical and sublime mission in his agenda for rejuvenation of European culture, a mission that was a kind of a balm for their feeling of deficiency and inadequacy vis-à-vis the secular gentile culture.

Nietzsche appealed to the intellectual elite of the *Grenzjuden* by calling and bestowing upon them a vital role in the Europe of the future. In view of the positive psychological qualities Nietzsche found in the Jews, especially their "strong instinct" and abundance of spiritual power, he predicted that the Jews and the Russians will be "the provisionally surest and most probable factors in the great play and fight of forces" (*BGE,* 251). He does not imply Jewish political domination over Europe, but rather alludes to the Jews' spiritual role in the future when their creative resources will flow "into great spiritual men and works . . . into an eternal blessing for Europe" (*D* 205).

Echoing the biblical prophecy about Israel's magnificent future and its spectacular salvation, Nietzsche claims that the Jews will once again become the "founders and creators of values." The creation of values is the most significant task in Nietzsche's philosophy, which always returns to the "transfiguration of values" and the transfiguration of the nature of our culture, in which the Jews are to play the major role as well as to serve as catalysts. Nietzsche's hope of mobilizing European Jews to assist him in this transfiguration of values is the background for his emotional exclamation: "What a blessing a Jew is among Germans!" (*WP,* 49)

These words, and the mission entrusted by Nietzsche to the German *Grenzjuden* and to the acculturated Eastern European Jews, came at the right time. Godless Jewish intellectuals responded eagerly, helping to bring about what is still considered to be one of the most creative periods in German culture. Nietzsche's philosophy provided them with legitimization to participate in and contribute to the broad framework of German humanist culture. If Nietzsche killed God—and incidentally, he adopted the leitmotif of the "Death of God" from Heinrich Heine, one of the greatest Jewish *Grenzjuden*—and if he attempted to foster the *Übermensch,* so too the *Grenzjuden,* having put an end in their hearts to their religion, sought, in a sense, to become *Überjuden.* Herzl and Nordau took this challenge upon themselves and spoke of the future Jewish state in Zion as a reservoir for cultural values and treasures that would be imported to Europe. However, this last aspect seemed to stand in stark contrast to the official program of Zionism, namely, the relocation of European Jewry to Zion and building a flourishing society there. But wasn't Nietzsche's agenda to call upon those Jews to stay in Europe and assist him in creating or recreating a rejuvenated Dionysian culture there?

This brings us to four obstacles that might have hindered any bona fide attempt of Zionists to embrace any sort of Nietzscheanism. To some scholars, these obstacles have seemed so overwhelming that they have argued against the possibility of any relationship between Nietzsche and Zionism.[23]

The least important of these obstacles is Nietzsche's call to European Jews to mingle among the gentiles and even to marry them, and thereby to create from within a new European culture, whereas clearly the European Zionists thought of Zion and not Europe as the last resort for solving what they called "the Jewish problem." A related problem originates from Nietzsche's so-called "antinationalistic" attitude, which seems to contradict the aspiration of Zionists to found a national haven for European Jewry. The third and most crucial problem lies in the basic antipathy any Zionist, whether socialist or cultural, and certainly also religious, might be expected to feel toward the Nietzsche's asocial attitude—his elevation of the individual and his or her solitude to the primary factor in his existentialist philosophy. Furthermore, most of the figures discussed here seem to have believed in the values of progress and enlightenment. But what about Nietzsche's notorious opposition to progress and his attacks upon the Enlightenment? If the depth of Nietzsche's influence on Zionism is to be truly appreciated, solutions to this fourfold problematic must be found.

There is no question that there were some elements of Nietzsche's thinking that Zionists could not accept. Despite their longing for personal authenticity and identity, all the figures discussed here were profoundly sensitive to the misery of their fellow Jews whom they sought to represent. Hence they could not follow Nietzsche's pronounced elitism and his prescription to transcend "man" and "mob" on the way to the *Übermensch*. Zeitlin, for example, who was deeply alarmed by the ominous signs preceding the Holocaust, could not keep the Nietzschean elitist "pathos of distance" and tried (like Buber and Ahad Ha'am) to Hebraize the ideal *Übermensch* into the Hasidic tzaddik (righteous sage). At the time all three disregarded the crucial fact that whereas the Nietzschean *Übermensch* stands "beyond good and evil," i.e., beyond the prevailing ethos, the Jewish tzaddik became such an exalted figure precisely because he perfectly embodied the Jewish ethos of the shtetls. But their very attempts to identify the *Übermensch* with the tzaddik, strongly attests to their burning wish to assimilate Nietzsche into their own traditional frames of references, despite this and other conceptual difficulties.

Furthermore, a closer look at the Nietzsche's thinking on the future role of the Jews in Europe suggests that it was not so alien to the aspirations of Zionism as it might first appear. True, he was mesmerized by the example of the Jews in the Diaspora and their ability to establish an effective spiritual-cultural island in Europe without any state or territory. Despite this and other adverse conditions, they had manifested a "plenitude of power *without equal* to which only the nobility had access" (*GS* 136). Nietzsche's reference to the Jews as the most "powerful race," in spite of their obvious political and physical weaknesses, clearly showed that there was nothing physical in the sense of brute force (*Kraft*) in the Nietzschean concept of power (*Macht*). One might even claim that Nietzsche's vision of a new Europe devoid of national boundaries, and united not only by common economic interests but *also* by the wish to foster a genuinely creative culture was partially inspired by the example of European Jewry. Moreover, Nietzsche stressed the fact that even in the most adverse circumstances, the Jewish people "have never ceased to believe in their calling to the highest things" (*D* 205). This abundance of spiritual power could function creatively without national institutions. Hence Nietzsche bestowed on the Jews a vital role in the supranational Europe of the future when their plentiful power would flow "into great spiritual men and works . . . into an eternal blessing *for Europe*" (ibid., my emphasis).

Yet, Nietzsche's notion of a "Jewish calling" did not in fact contradict Zionist political aspirations. There exists a record of Nietzsche's conversations in the winter of 1883–84 in Nice with Joseph Paneth—an Austrian Jewish intellectual and a marginal Jew *par excellence* who was also a good friend of Freud. We know that Nietzsche and Paneth discussed the possibility of the revival of the Jewish people in Palestine and their "regeneration" there. Nietzsche was apparently not at all happy about the prospect that the Jews would estrange themselves from their Jewish tradition and history to become completely assimilated within the European nations, since such "free spirits (*freie Geister*) detached from anything are dangerous and destructive." He added that one should not ignore the "impact of nationality" and, according to Paneth, was "quite disappointed that I did not wish to hear anything about the restoration of a Palestinian state."[24]

It is even possible to hypothesize that Nietzsche might have supported the idea of a return of the Jews to the land of Israel and statehood there, which, especially in the times of the ancient Hebrews, had provided the earthly sources for their spiritual power and legacy. This hypothesis is in a sense implied by Nietzsche's statement that "in the hands of the Jewish Priests the great age in the history of Israel became an age of decay; the Exile" (*A* 26). Logically, one way out of this state of "decadence" would be the reestablishment of a Jewish state that would revive the kingdom of the ancient Hebrews in Zion.

Such a development would also serve Nietzsche's project of European cultural rejuvenation, since it would be quite possible to enlist the "new Israel" and its revival for the purposes of the "new Europe." Hence Nietzsche did not see any tension or contradiction between his plan for enlisting Jews for the sake of his new Europe and the Zionist program. And though he had heard about and was quite aware of the Zionist sentiments awakening among European Jewry in the last years of his lucidity, he never gave any vent to his disapproval as he did so loudly against many other trends of his time, including the extreme nationalism of his former friend and mentor Wagner and his followers.

Nonetheless, almost all the figures discussed here were acutely aware that for the majority of the Jews the uncompromising adoption of the Nietzschean ideal of the "free spirit" would bring only personal turmoil, as well as national disaster. Hence one of the main findings in this study is that there were in reality no Jewish Nietzscheans *par excellence*. In the middle of their tortuous way to their own selfhood, they quite prudently followed Nietzsche advice to Paneth and returned to their people and to the historical and religious identities with which their rich Jewish lore had endowed them.

We also have to bear in mind that even Nietzsche was not a pure Nietzschean. His ideal type, the ahistorical free spirit or *Übermensch,* was only a regulative ideal, which, among other things, was an antidote to the tendency of the Germans in his time to fill up the existential void incurred by the "death of God" by embracing extreme ideological and political substitutes. By this ideal he strove to fight the dangerous overemphasis prevalent in contemporary German culture on historicism and on the Hegel-inspired "mighty historical movement" (HL, p. 59). In his essay "On the Uses and Disadvantages of History for Life," though he opposed the German tendency to make history into a scientific and objective enterprise, he did not object to the use of the past in the service of life in the present. He argued only against a past that overpowers the present and annihilates any of its novel and vital elements, so that inter alia it also destroys the future. More vitality and less historicity was his slogan in this essay, but his "free spirits" did not act in an ahistorical vacuum, nor were they a kind of existential *tabula rasa* without memories, identities, and sensibilities rooted in their culture, heritage, and people. Nietzsche did not believe that one may succeed in severing all linkages with his or her historical background.[25] On the contrary, he attacked the illusion that it was possible to sever oneself completely from tradition, to become a "free spirit" by indiscriminately rejecting the past. Nietzsche did not believe that such a "liberation" was even feasible, let alone desirable. True, he was not at all reluctant to oppose either the metaphysical traditions of the past or the accepted Christian ethic. But even here he acknowledged that he drew his "fire, too, from the flame lit by a faith that is thousands of years old, that Christian faith" (*GS* 344; and see *GS* 377). He did not profess to be a nihilist, nor did he seek a complete break with the past and its values. Neither was he a radical revolutionary, freed of the restraints of tradition and descending into the historical arena from some ahistorical pinnacle. Nietzsche's commitment was to a path of self-transformation that was arduous and painstaking; for him, the rigors of self-education and the anguish of self-conquest constituted a process of slow and difficult evolution. He believed in a steady educational advance, devoid of grand illusions, which only gradually leads one to new patterns of life and thought.[26]

But is the state of an absolute free spirit really attainable? Even Nietzsche was far from being such a spirit, since he did not advocate obliteration or repression of all one's memories. Can one live in a linguistic vacuum? Surely not, and hence one is necessarily talking or writing or philosophizing in some specific language with all the connotations and associations that this language evokes. But even more important, can one completely overcome one's most personal feelings and inclinations, one's deep attachment to one's own people, as manifested by Hillel Zeitlin and Micha Josef Berdichevski?

Moreover, if one cannot overcome one's most cherished memories and sentiments, one cannot ipso facto free oneself completely from one's personal and national history. Here it is pertinent to quote the sharp criticism that one of Berdichevski's opponents launched against him. Berdichevski, as we will see, was perhaps the most Nietzschean modern Hebrew writer in Europe. Following Nietzsche, he advocated that the Jewish people try to forget their long history and embark upon the cultivation of an individual Jewishness whose connections with the past would be less compelling. But could one put aside four thousand years of Jewish history as if it were an old garment to be replaced by a new one? Surely this was not possible for people who were so profoundly versed in Jewish history and its literary achievements. And yet Nietzsche's ideals served as springboards for liberating themselves from the ruins of the "old temples" in order to replace them with the "new ones" (to use Nietzsche's famous saying).[27] The specific content of these "new temples" will be presented in the following pages.

As regards Nietzsche's well-known abhorrence of statehood and nationalistic sentiments, his indictment of the official *Machtpolitik* and its consequences for German culture was unequivocal. Once Nietzsche had thrown off the romantic nationalism of his early days, his devastating critique of Wagner—prophetic in many ways of what was to come—reveals with what penetrating insight he saw through nationalism's dangerous illusions.

But it does not necessarily follow that since Nietzsche detested German and other nationalistic attitudes, his teaching was essentially a nonpolitical one. It is noteworthy that many contemporary scholars—which has been less vulnerable to the atmosphere of suspicion that loomed over Nietzsche by the end of the Second World War—has tended to emphasize the significance of politics in his philosophy. They sensibly concede that even if one cannot find in Nietzsche's antisystematic writings any definite political thought, his radical discussions of morality and his concept of the "modern man" had far-reaching political significance. It was in a certain cultural and political context that Nietzsche sought to attain his ideal of a unique and authentic individual cultivating Dionysian values.[28]

Nietzsche did, however, reject the view that one can justify or rationally derive a political order from universalistic principles. It is also true that during his life Nietzsche did not publish anything comparable to Spinoza's *Tractatus Politicus,* which was specifically dedicated to political issues. Of course, there were always political implications in writings like his *Genealogy of Morals* which examined critically the moral values prevalent in modern society. Moreover, there is an early unpublished work by Nietzsche that analyzes the "Greek State," and we also have many long passages from his published works that specifically deal with politics.[29]

It is worthwhile in this context to examine closely Nietzsche's confession in *Ecce Homo* that he was the "last *antipolitical* German," and as a result "perhaps more German than present-day Germans, mere citizens of the German *Reich,* could possibly be." He thereby admits to belonging to the German nation even while he clearly distances himself from the German *Reich* of Bismarck. The German word *antipolitisch* is different from *unpolitisch*—referring to somebody who is utterly indifferent to politics. Likewise, in a section of his *Twilight of the Idols* entitled "What the Germans Lack," Nietzsche distinguished between these attitudes toward politics by contrasting the Bismarckian modern *Reich* which embodies a strong political power (*Grossmacht*) with a society that is essentially *antipolitisch*—that is, one that objects to using political force (*Kraft*) to promote its culture. Nietzsche gives as an example France, which he calls a *"Kulturmacht."* We will see that many of the Zionist ideologues, especially the cultural Zionists, explicitly adopted this stance.

Thus, Nietzsche was not unpolitical, let alone an anarchist. On the contrary, as a great advocate of human creativity he could see the need for statehood and a civil society in whose framework creativity might take place and flourish. Nietzsche distinguished sharply between the more sublime spiritual and mental powers of individuals (or entire peoples) which generate and produce sublime cultures, and the physical or political force which is an overpowering *Kraft* or *Gewalt*. Possibly in opposition to Hegel, who regarded the Prussian state of the nineteenth century as the highest rational manifestation of the universal *Geist*, Nietzsche felt particularly driven to attack this idea of statehood that so attracted his contemporaries.

In fact, Nietzsche was an antipolitical thinker for political reasons and a political thinker for philosophical reasons, among them his attempt to foster the existential ideal of personal authenticity. In other words, Nietzsche adopted an antipolitical attitude for reasons that had to do with the future of human culture. For Nietzsche, politics actually becomes "great"—*grosse Politik*—when it sustains and assists in cultivating human greatness and cultural grandeur. This "great politics" is exactly what the cultural Zionists discussed here were hardly trying to cultivate. And if we broadly define politics as an organized mobilization of human resources for the sake of a group or nation, Nietzsche was indeed deeply engrossed with a politics that would embark on the cultural engineering of the entire society. So were Ahad Ha'am, Buber, and others. We should also recall that like Plato, Nietzsche envisaged the philosopher as a legislator (as did Herzl in his *Altneuland*). Hence Nietzsche is no less political than he is an "immoralist"—in a very moral and political sense.

Nietzsche abhorred the state only insofar as it became a goal in itself and ceased to function as a means for the advancement and education of autonomous and creative human beings. His preferred and most admired models to achieve the latter ideal were the Greek *polis*, ancient Rome, and the city-states of the Italian Renaissance—cultural patterns that had never made national supremacy the cornerstone of their ideal, or regarded the ethnic attributes of their citizens as a mark of creativity or superiority. But there was nothing in his writings to suggest that Nietzsche objected in principle to the political organization of statehood (as in national Zionism), so long as it did not repress genuine culture and persons.

Nietzsche did not reject the state if it was conducive to life's aspirations—a vital element in his philosophy. But once this legitimate creation changed its nature and became a manifestation of extreme nationalism that hindered free and spontaneous creativity, Nietzsche vehemently opposed it and wished to curb its destructive effects. Perhaps under the influence of Hobbes's *Leviathan,* Nietzsche called this kind of state "the cold-est of all cold monsters."[30] However, where it encouraged individuals to shape and form their cultural identity in an authentic way, Nietzsche re-garded the state as a "blessed means." Hence, if he could have realized that this was exactly one of the main driving forces and goals of most of the Zionist thinkers and writers presented here, he would have gladly partici-pated, at least in writing, in their struggles for cultivating a new, authentic Jewish image, that of an Israeli Hebrew.

Two significant motifs stand in tension with one another in the lives and thought of the Jewish Nietzscheans. On the one hand they apologize for their former attraction to Nietzsche as a "foreign" (though not new) source of inspiration. On the other, Nietzsche remains deeply and perva-sively present in their world, even once they embrace the Zionist solution to the problem of consolidating and affirming their new or renewed iden-tities and selves.

These two elements were present in most of the thinkers and writers we will deal with below. At a later date, the apologetic element becomes scarce and disappears altogether in Zion, while the second element remains strik-ingly influential. Perhaps the openness of the secular Israeli to Western lit-erature and thought, and their hard-won confidence in their national/ cultural identities, has made the apologetic aspect less relevant.

In any case, as claimed above, this book stands somewhat at odds with the official presentation of Zionism as a national movement that aspired to provide a peaceful haven for the politically and culturally oppressed Eu-ropean Jews. When one highlights the motif of security using political-national categories, one necessarily clashes with other people's needs for self-determination and national aspirations. When one stresses (using Nietzsche) cultural aims and existential objectives, the clash may seem less pertinent and unavoidable. Spiritual *Macht* (power) and not physical *Kraft* (force) was Nietzsche's consistent preference. Perhaps with his inspiration, Jewish and Palestinian states and cultures may one day be able to co-exist peacefully together.

Be that as it may, the question that should be raised is not whether Nietz-sche had a formative impact on the rejuvenation and content of modern Hebrew culture and on its most influential and active writers and ideo-logues. Rather, the question is why, despite the overwhelming and abun-dant evidence of his presence in Zion, there has been so little written on his reception among Zionist leaders and writers. The present study strives to fill this lacuna. Perhaps those who follow this book's explications of Nietzsche's presence among non-Israelis and Israeli Jews will gain deeper insight into who the European Jews were and who the Israelis are—or at least what they would like to become.

One thing is certain: all the figures presented here dared to look into Nietzsche's abyss. This book tells us what they found.

PART I

NIETZSCHE AND POLITICAL ZIONISM

CHAPTER 1

"Thus Spoke Herzl"

NIETZSCHE'S PRESENCE IN
THEODOR HERZL'S LIFE AND WORK

In a diary entry of 28 June 1895, Theodor Herzl reported a conversation with Leo Franckel:

> I explained to him why I am against the democracies. "So you are a disciple of Nietzsche?" he said. I: "Not at all. Nietzsche is a madman. But one can only govern aristocratically." Franckel: "How are you going to establish this aristocratic government?" I: "There are all kinds of ways. Here is just one example. . . . The French Academy constitutes an elective aristocracy." Franckel: "That way everything can be arranged *collectivistically*." I: "By no means. The *individual* must not be done away with."[1]

This passage illuminates a paradox: whereas Nietzsche's philosophy focuses on the individual and is largely concerned with enticing the reader to embrace subjective patterns of personal authenticity, the main ideologues of Zionism were mainly focused on establishing a Jewish state and securing a safe shelter for the Jewish people. Many of Zionism's founding fathers were also preoccupied with the creation of socialist institutions in *Eretz Israel*.

In Herzl's case, the paradox is only an apparent one: he rejected the collectivist ideology and elsewhere vehemently objected to socialism.[2] Unlike his Eastern European Jewish followers, who were profoundly influenced by socialist and Marxist movements, Herzl's sociopolitical thought was primarily based on the liberal British paradigm and was open to the needs of individuals to express their personal identities.[3]

Herzl's vision of the Jewish state purported to foster an authentic identity for those Jews who were unwilling to assimilate or to embrace Christianity. Indeed, Herzl was interested in the effect of Zionism on the individual, namely in the ways Zionism might reshape the image of the Jew. Thus, by embracing a new ideology and a secular way of life, the Jew could replace the traditional religious frame of reference. This existential relevance of Nietzsche to "marginal" Zionist intellectuals[4] was one of the crucial factors that attracted Herzl to his philosophy before he wrote *Der Judenstaat* (The Jewish State) in 1895, and before he succeeded in forging his identity as a secular Zionist Jew. In that pre-Zionist period, Herzl epitomized the class of the German-speaking *Grenzjuden*. He realized that despite his untiring attempts to be accepted by the Austrians as Austrian he could not disregard the fact that he was a Jew. Hence he wrote bitterly that all the political experience he had gained while working as a correspondent for the *Neue Freie Presse* in France had been for nothing. "It will only benefit those who have the opportunity to enter political life. But for myself? A Jew in Austria!"[5]

Herzl's reference to Nietzsche as what is rendered in the English translation as "a madman" is undoubtedly derogatory. However, the German original reads: "Nietzsche ist ein Irrsinniger" (*HBT* 2:206). An Anglo-German dictionary of 1900 defines *irrsinnig* as "mentally deranged," indicating an actual mental illness and not, therefore, what Germans, referring to a state of mind or behavior, would call *verrückt* or *wahnsinnig* (crazy).[6] Herzl's close friend and collaborator Max Nordau uses this latter term when he writes that Nietzsche is "von Geburt an wahnsinnig und seine Bücher tragen auf jeder Seite den Stempel des Wahnsinns" ("insane from birth, and his books bear on every page the complaint of insanity").[7] In striking contrast to Nordau, Herzl uses a term that quite correctly describes Nietzsche's mental state in 1895. Nietzsche spent the last ten years of his life (1890–1900) suffering from a general paralysis, some of its symptoms being prolonged unconsciousness and mental derangement. It is therefore quite reasonable to assume that Herzl meant to imply that he could not follow a man who was then (at the time of Herzl's conversation with Franckel) functioning neither mentally nor physically. If correct, this shows that Herzl was quite aware of Nietzsche's state and was far from deriding him as Nordau had. Indeed, there were numerous volumes by Nietzsche in Herzl's private library; hence, if Herzl really believed that Nietzsche was a "madman" or "insane from birth," why would he have purchased so many of his books, some published after his conversation with Franckel? There is ample historical evidence to contradict the view that Herzl was ignorant of Nietzsche's philosophy and legacy, such that the issue is not whether Herzl knew Nietzsche's work but how he could not have known it and what concrete influence it had on him.

THE HISTORICAL TESTIMONY

Most of the books from Herzl's private library in Vienna are now located in Jerusalem, in the Central Zionist Archives and in the Herzl Museum. Even a cursory glance discloses Herzl's preference for philosophy in general and Nietzsche in particular.[8] Almost all of Nietzsche's works are to be found here, and their expensive leather bindings suggest the owner's willingness to invest significantly in Nietzsche's writings.[9] In addition, references and quotations in Herzl's own diaries, letters, and other writings provide copious testimony to his knowledge of Nietzsche. In a letter to an unidentified theater critic, Herzl invokes Nietzsche's "explanation" of the desire to be "modern": "Nietzsche would probably explain this by saying that people do not yet know what kind of comedy they have to play for their new acquaintances."[10] Another reference appears in a letter Herzl wrote to Nordau in which he apologizes for not including Nordau's essay on Nietzsche in a recent issue of the *Neue Freie Presse*.[11] Nordau's article eventually appeared after the philosopher's death, on 3 October 1900.[12] It is significant, too, that under Herzl's editorship, seven consecutive issues of the *Neue Freie Presse* were dedicated to obituaries of Nietzsche. A telling remark about Nietzsche appeared in the final sentence of Herzl's essay "Frankreich im Jahre 1891": "However, the 'European man,' the new type that Nietzsche sees coming closer and closer to us, is still a very remote figure."[13] The Nietzschean ideal of the "new European man" is close to Herzl's ideal of the "new Jew," and the resemblance between these types should not surprise us. Neither should Herzl's belief that the "new man" was more likely to materialize as the "new Jew" in Zion, namely as the creative and authentic Jew who, like the Nietzschean *Übermensch*, would become the father of his own destiny and would freely shape the course of his life and the history of his people.

During Herzl's early days at the University of Vienna, it was not necessary to have studied Nietzsche directly to be permeated with his thought, given that he was quoted, reviewed, and discussed in every circle (especially in those to which Herzl belonged) and in every journal and newspaper.[14] Nietzschean concepts and ideas were widespread among Jewish intellectuals. If some of them were rather critical of his teaching, they were at least familiar with it and were even emotionally stirred by it, as Nordau's case clearly indicates.

In his freshman year, Herzl joined the *Akademische Lesehalle,* the original membership of which comprised an eclectic mix of German, Slav, Hungarian, and Jewish students. It was politically neutral and dedicated mainly to social and cultural affairs.[15] From the start Herzl was active on committees, organized literary meetings, and participated in debates. Moreover, he was quite close to some of the leading members of the Pernerstorfer circle, which comprised some of Nietzsche's first influential admirers and was nicknamed "Nietzsche's Society in Vienna."[16] Among the members of the Pernerstorfer circle were the Socialist leader Victor Adler, Hermann Bahr, the Socialist Heinrich Braun, Joseph Ruben Ehrlich (the Austrian journalist who wrote an idolizing letter to Nietzsche in 1876 and signed it as "his most devoted admirer in Vienna"),[17] Siegfried Lipiner, Josef Paneth, and Arthur Schnitzler.[18] It is absurd to assume that while these men were so preoccupied with Nietzsche, Herzl was not.

Herzl aspired to be more than just a serious dabbler in philosophy. In his *Jugendtagebuch 1882–1887,*[19] he refers to Plato, Aristotle, Kant, Feuerbach, Schopenhauer, Fichte, Hegel, Schelling, and Brentano. In a diary entry of 21 March 1897,[20] he notes that he has sent *Der Judenstaat* to Herbert Spencer with a short letter in which he called Spencer a "great spirit." Admittedly, Herzl, not satisfied to approach only businessmen and politicians, was eager to ensure the support of the leading philosophers of his time for his Zionist project. Elsewhere in his diary, he is critical of Rousseau and quotes from works by Kant, More, and Voltaire that can be still found in his private library.[21] Furthermore, after Herzl moved with his family from Budapest to Vienna in 1878 and began studying at the law faculty of the University of Vienna, he attended Brentano's lectures on practical philosophy. Sigmund Freud, whose interest in Nietzsche's philosophy is well known,[22] also attended Brentano's lectures while studying medicine at the university as a contemporary of Herzl. It may well be that these two great Jewish figures met—they were actually neighbors—without, however, becoming friends.

The publication of the first edition of Nietzsche's collected works in 1892 was a major intellectual event in the German-speaking world.[23] Two years later, a study of Nietzsche by his intimate friend Lou Andreas-Salomé was published in Vienna,[24] and in 1895 Elisabeth Förster-Nietzsche published the first volume of her biography of her brother.[25] The same year saw the first publication of Nietzsche's most provocative works, *Der Antichrist* and *Nietzsche contra Wagner.*[26]

In his capacity as the chief features editor of the *Neue Freie Presse,* Herzl was exposed to many articles on Nietzsche[27] and collaborated with many Nietzschean writers and intellectuals. He became the features editor of the newspaper in September 1895, having worked on it for four years. Nietzsche's fame began to soar in the early 1890s, when Herzl was the newspaper's Paris correspondent, and the period between 1895 and 1902 is the most crucial for determining Nietzsche's impact on Herzl.

All these facts indicate that Herzl was operating under the influence of a *Zeitgeist* permeated by Nietzsche's presence. However, the most conclusive firsthand evidence that Herzl was familiar with Nietzsche's work and thought is provided by Herzl's cousin, the playwright and novelist Raoul Auernheimer (1876–1948). Auernheimer, who also specialized in literary journalism, was associated together with Herzl with the "Young Vienna" circle, to which Arthur Schnitzler, Hermann Bahr, and Stefan Zweig also belonged.[28] In a memorial tribute he claimed that his cousin was more than just a feuilletonist but "a thinker and a philosopher. . . . He not only, like the other feuilletonists, read Schiller, Heine, but was also familiar with Nietzsche, whose influence inaugurated a new era in German publicistic writing; and he . . . *absorbed his style.*"[29]

These remarks from an expert who was so intimate with Herzl's work and background corroborate the intuition of many of Herzl's readers that he was, like Nietzsche, a master of the aphorism. It is no coincidence that some of Herzl's editors could not resist giving several collections of his aphorisms titles that bear a direct association with Nietzsche's *Thus Spoke Zarathustra*—most notably, the Hebrew collection of Herzl's aphorisms published in Palestine by Herzl's secretary, A. Pollack, under the title *Ko Amar Herzl "Thus Spoke Herzl."*[30]

FROM THEATER TO AUTHENTICITY: HERZL'S TRANSFIGURATION

While engaged in his search for personal authenticity and identity, that is, while still living in the limbo of identity of a *Grenzjude,* Herzl evoked Nietzsche's name and played with his philosophical ideas using ironic posture, dissimulation, and distance. These years—from the beginning of his studies at the University of Vienna to his growing preoccupation with Zionism—were marked by marginality and estrangement. Herzl, at that time, was still the *Grenzjude* who had sought success and fame within European culture by trying to distinguish himself in belles-lettres. At the same time

Herzl disguised his personal search for authentic identity with irony and with what Nietzsche called the attitude of *la gaya scienza.*[31]

During that period, Herzl found many aspects of Nietzsche conducive to his aspirations. He and other early Zionists realized that they were torn between their secular aspirations and their own Jewish religious tradition. As a result, they could not form harmonious selves; and, living on the margins of all identities, neither could they feel authentic. Sensitive and proud, Herzl could not bear such a schizophrenic existence. Assimilation brought him only to a dead end. His inability to reject his Jewish origins altogether, his unwillingness to return to the "Old Ghetto" with its Orthodox Jewish lore, and above all his proud rejection of the fact that he did not belong on equal terms within gentile Viennese society had a destructive potential (as the suicide of Otto Weininger, among others, testified) and drove him to find a solution.

Initially, Herzl considered solving the problem of his own marginality by calling for mass conversion to Christianity—he himself would help the pope to conduct the baptismal ceremony on the steps of St. Stephen's Cathedral in Vienna.[32] Then he tried to assimilate into Austrian society, to follow in the footsteps of the best Viennese artists and playwrights, without striving to attain a separate personal identity. During this period Herzl became part of the frivolous world of Vienna's fin de siècle, not merely as a passive spectator but as an active contributor. However, Herzl turned away from the Vienna stage *before* the Dreyfus affair. It was not the Dreyfus affair, traumatic as it was, that drove Herzl to Zionism, but his gnawing feeling that he could not bear any more the distressing predicament of marginality and the existential cul-de-sac that advanced assimilation had brought upon him and his fellow Jews.[33]

In November 1894 Herzl wrote *Das Neue Ghetto* (The New Ghetto), a semi-autobiographical play about the wounded honor of Dr. Jacob Samuel, a lawyer in Vienna (like Herzl himself), and a marginal Jew who regains his honor by fighting a duel with an anti-Semite. The play describes the existential vulnerability of a proud Jew who strives to overcome his marginality after realizing that he has "betrayed his own self" by shaping his personal identity solely by imitating his gentile friends. This attempt to assimilate has not succeeded because his friend "simply abandons me after I made him my example, absorbed his habits, spoke his language, thought his thoughts."[34]

Das Neue Ghetto expressed Herzl's realization that assimilation was an illusion, and that the Jews' estrangement from themselves was fruitless. The play's conclusion is that European Jews should authentically shape a new image of the Jew who is proud of his or her historical past but will not necessarily express this identity by observing the traditional religious rites. *Das Neue Ghetto* was written before *Der Judenstaat,* hence its importance to Herzl's goal of attaining personal authenticity that required him to overcome his existential marginality. This was a stage of his transfiguration that exposed him to a significant dialogue with Nietzsche. We should also note that fiction, according to Nietzsche and other more recent advocates of authenticity, is the most appropriate medium to express the subjective pathos of authenticity, which can be neither defined nor communicated by direct language nor prescribed by rational persuasion.[35]

The play portrays three negative reactions to marginality: conversion to Christianity, as represented by a character who confesses that "nothing was solved this way"; the reaction of traditional Judaism, namely, to return to the old ghetto with its traditional values and faith; and the popular reaction of the uneducated Jewish masses, personified by the crude figure of the stock exchange Jew Wasserstein, who shrewdly adjusts to the prevalent anti-Semitic image of Jews as materialistic and greedy by acting accordingly and amassing a fortune. This hard-working and despised Jew, however, recognizes a fourth reaction to marginality. Though he claims that "everything revolves around money," he admits that honor is equally important. Wasserstein regards Jacob Samuel as far superior to himself, an individual who "soars above us like a bird." Samuel transcends the existential limits of marginality over the walls of the new ghetto, and becomes, then, a kind of a new type of a Jew—the fourth, and only acceptable, solution to the problem of marginality, according to Herzl's narrative.

Jacob resembles Zarathustra's eagle, the authentic and unique individual who does not belong to the herd but soars alone high above the new (and the old) ghettos. He manifests many of the character traits and spiritual power with which Nietzsche endowed his authentic hero. Jacob is a masterful figure who behaves nobly and proudly with no *ressentiment.* He despises the stock exchange, but that does not lead him to shun Wasserstein, whom he prefers to Franz, the gentile who "did not feel comfortable in the society of such people." "It is not his fault," Jacob claims, referring to Wasserstein's occupation. "It was not even nature that made us what we are, but history. It was your people who rubbed our noses in money—but now we are told to despise it."[36]

Jacob, like Nietzsche's Zarathustra, strives to create new norms and values. He seeks to form the "moral element" and embarks upon the journey of self-overcoming by "overcoming" his old marginal self. He no longer wishes to live passively within gentile history but prefers to initiate a new history—of his own making. Although at the beginning of his existential journey, at the stage of his assimilation, he internalizes and imitates the behavioral patterns and ethos of his gentile neighbors, this was, as he admits now to Franz, "only a transitory period on my way to becoming a free citizen." "Now I can continue my journey by myself," he says to Franz. In so doing, he obeys Zarathustra's prescription that if his followers wish to stay loyal to his teachings, they must abandon him and go alone on their *own* ways—even if this means attempting to overcome their master, as Jacob is trying to do vis-à-vis Franz and the Western European culture that had brought upon the Jews the unbearable predicaments of marginality and estrangement.

However, is not Jacob's emphasis on the honorable duel an indication of his strong dependence on gentile values? Not so, since the dignity of human beings and their authentic spiritual power are not Christian inventions. As Nietzsche used to stress, freedom, pride, and nobility are ancient Hebrew values.[37] Hence Jacob returns here to the origins of personal power, pride, and dignity. Nietzsche elevated these above the Christian values of pity, meekness, and humility. Likewise, Herzl does not seek to foster here a Christian European set of values but the free, powerful, and creative individual capable of defining his own values and norms. It was honor in this sense that was prevalent within the "Old Ghetto," the origins of which are to be found in biblical Zion.[38] In Nietzsche's *Zarathustra* the journey to personal authenticity, to the state of a "child's innocence," passes a second stage: that of the "lion" overcoming the hump of the "camel" that bears all the values and norms of the old tradition and teachings.[39] Although Herzl overcame most of the Jewish tradition, he (and his contemporary Western and Central European Jews) were afflicted by the curse of marginality in the "New Ghettos," which prevented them from attaining genuine self-liberation. To overcome the agonies of such a marginality is for Herzl already a positive way out that will lead him to the third and more constructive stage of liberation of his self: Zionism.

The play does not propose a way out of the "New Ghetto." Jacob's final sentence before his heroic death in the duel ends in ellipsis, and the outcome is destructive for someone who has dared to soar like an eagle above the walls of the "New Ghetto." For Herzl, this negation of a negation pointed to a concrete solution: the land in which the values according to which Jacob aspired to live were originally manifested and genuinely invented for the first time. The journey toward personal authenticity will also include negative ramifications, according to Nietzsche's well-known statement: "If a temple is to be erected, a temple must be destroyed" (*GM* II—24). Interestingly, Herzl used almost the same version in *Der Judenstaat:* "If I wish to substitute a new building for an old one, I must demolish before

I construct."[40] Nietzsche proclaimed the dialectic of suffering under the dictum "What does not destroy me makes me stronger." Herzl's struggle was not waged with a sword but with words and with the exhausting political activity that eventually killed him, but not before liberating him from his most hated role: that of the despised *Grenzjude*.

This dialectic of suffering is effectively expressed in another of Herzl's plays, *Solon in Lydien*.[41] The play, written in 1900, belongs to the Zionist period of Herzl's life, during which the Nietzschean motifs were not altogether discarded. The hero of the play is Solon of ancient Athens, who represents Herzl. When Eucosmos, an ambitious young man, discovers a way to produce wheat without toil, Solon becomes worried. Solon, according to his declaration, "glanced beyond the veil that disguises things," and he seeks to expel or to kill Eucosmos because the latter's invention, the elimination of poverty and of existential anxiety, will bring about only chaos and the end of human culture. Solon claims that Eucosmos is striving to take from people "the most precious thing they are blessed with—hunger," and, as a result, "the fundamentals of culture will disappear as well." Solon believed in the Nietzschean principle of the sublimation of Dionysian instincts through creative work. Echoing Nietzsche's statement about the ancient Greeks ("How much did this people have to suffer to be able to become so beautiful!"), Herzl writes: "They need poverty! It urges them to create and invent. . . . Work flourishes sublimely to the level of art, as much as thinking about the private advantages of human beings is raised to the level of sublime philosophy." Herzl mentions Apollo several times, thereby enhancing the impression that we have here the dramatization of Nietzschean insights expressed in his *Birth of Tragedy*. It becomes obvious by now that Herzl's search for personal authenticity did not take place in a vacuum but was pursued in an atmosphere saturated by Nietzsche's ideas.

Zionism, as envisioned by Herzl, would foster the emergence of a new and unique (that is, authentic) image of the Jew in a society without God, dogmas, or "isms." This antidogmatic and Nietzschean libertarianism was sometimes narrowly regarded by Herzl's historians as shrewd pragmatism. But examining the father of political Zionism through the Nietzschean prism reveals him as the pioneer of a historic experiment of fostering personal authenticity by creating it for the whole nation. This perspective shows that *Der Judenstaat* was not written solely as a reaction to the failures of emancipation and assimilation, but also as an attempt to provide a constructive solution to the syndrome of marginality that at the individual level was the most hideous symptom of this failure.

This brings us back to Herzl's view that the Nietzsche's "European man" was still "a very remote figure,"[42] and that the European Jew could not shape his character in Europe because Europe did not want the Jews. From this perspective, Jewish emancipation had failed. Herzl's personal experience of marginality and estrangement prevented him from adopting Nietzsche's European ideal, and he sought to transfer it to more fruitful soil. Herzl believed that the free, creative, and authentic Jew would be more likely to evolve in Zion, on virgin ground unstained by what his friend Max Nordau called European "degenerated culture." Thus, under Nietzsche's influence, Herzl arrived at the ideal of the authentic human being and sought to apply it first of all to himself and then to other European *Grenzjuden.* In his eyes, the Zionist solution was more authentic than the continuation of assimilation, dissimulation, and the prolongation of the dangerous game of being a "free spirit" in Europe. And this at a historic point, when European national and anti-Semitic repression had inflicted upon the Jew the crisis of identity that had brought many, including Herzl himself, to the desperate search for authenticity.

It is therefore possible to delineate Nietzsche's impact upon Herzl according to Herzl's existential stages of assimilation, marginality, and Zionist identity. If we adopt Nietzsche's formula for authenticity, then Herzl "becomes what he is" by overcoming what he is not: neither an Orthodox Jew, nor a Christian, nor, finally, a marginal Jew. He overcame these potential identities until he became what he wanted to be: a free secular Zionist and an authentically creative Jew, who proudly belonged to his people according to his own definition of the Jewish nation in *Der Judenstaat*: "a historic group with unmistakable characteristics common to us all."[43] Thus the Zionist journey intended to assist the *Grenzjuden* in overcoming the syndromes of marginality and split personality; and only Zionism, Herzl believed, would shape them into genuine individuals and help them to overcome their socio-psychological duality. Nietzsche claims that in the prevalent European scheme of morality, "one is splitting one's essence and for part of it one sacrifices all the rest"; and thus European man "treats himself not as *individuum* but as *dividuum*" (*HH* I-57). These words were especially applicable to the complex existential predicament of the German-speaking marginal Jews who were obliged to suppress some of their most vital elements. By doing so, they were prevented from attaining personal harmony and from spontaneously expressing their genuine nature, as Herzl, the herald of Jewish authenticity, claims: "The very act of going this way will change us into different people. We regain once more our inner unity that we have lost and together with it we also gain a definite character, namely our own, not the false and adopted character of the *marranos*."[44]

By the time he left Paris in 1895, Herzl had abandoned his dream of becoming a famous writer and had ceased to live in the existential state of the "New Ghetto," which he found unbearable. With *Der Judenstaat,* Herzl committed himself to a Jewish-Zionist identity. Thereafter, as with Martin Buber after his arrival in Palestine,[45] Nietzsche ceased to be the catalyst in Herzl's life: his function as a temporary scaffold for climbing to the highest ladder of genuine authenticity had been fulfilled. Nevertheless, the posture of ironic disguise and narrative distance is quite conspicuous in the *Philosophische Erzählungen* (Philosophical Tales), the title Herzl insisted on giving to his collection of short stories—a fact that reveals his aspiration to be considered a thinker, not just a capable minor journalist.

THE "UNMASKING" OF THE "HUMAN, ALL-TOO-HUMAN"

Herzl was attracted by Nietzsche's genealogical method of "unmasking" the human psyche. Nietzsche used this method to attain selfhood by freezing the motivation to uphold any religious, metaphysical, or social ideologies that had previously provided ready-made identities. Following the death of the Father—the Jewish God—and the decline of the authority of the father, *Grenzjuden* (such as Herzl) sought to establish an identity that would draw its content not from the faith and tradition of their fathers but solely from their own mental resources. Nietzsche encouraged this process by showing how one could liberate oneself from dependence on habits of thought and conventions. Yet Herzl had to come to terms with his own paralyzing "human, all-too-human" elements. Nietzsche becomes a model of such self-knowledge since he delineates the basic conflict between the negative, weak, reactive, sick, and decadent and the positively powerful, vital, active, and dynamically creative expression of personal spiritual power.[46] Such neurotic fluctuations between two mental kinds of pathos are frequently described by Herzl: "I do not contemplate death, but think of life full of heroic deeds that overcome anything low, wild and complicated that perhaps once was within myself. . . . In these days I am frequently afraid that I will completely lose my mind."[47] Nietzsche assists Herzl in expressing the gap between the optimal authentic power of the *Übermensch* and the depth of weakness that looms beneath the "human, all-too-human," and which must be overcome if the authority and dignity of the free Jew is to be attained. Indeed, careful reading of Herzl's writings shows that most of the traits he attaches to the marginal Jews in the Diaspora belong to the patterns of negative power ascribed by Nietzsche to the "morality of slaves" and the "crowd," whereas the main objective of Herzl's Zionist revolution is to strengthen and solidify the powerful patterns of "nobility" and "morality of masters" (to use the enticing and provocative Nietzschean terms). Herzl's disdain for the Jewish uneducated masses, and his will to transform them into something more sublime and noble, are well known. His revolution aimed to foster in the life of the marginal Jew moral patterns and qualities once prevalent among the ancient Hebrews: "In order to remain in its place and also to wander the race should be first improved. It is necessary to strengthen its power for war, to instill in it the joy of working and all good virtues."[48]

The Zionist revolution would enable the "new Jews" to decide whether to go to Zion or stay in Europe. However, for such a mental transfiguration, Herzl needs the kind of psychology that Nietzsche called the "bitter psychology," which unmasks weaknesses that must be overcome. Herzl frequently conducts these psychological examinations: "I found out that the great are petty, as petty as myself." However, Herzl's "petty self" aspired to attain the greatness of a Bismarck, who was, like Nietzsche, an "active psychologist who read individual souls as well as of the soul of the crowd."[49] Such a reading of the human soul is manifested in the *Philosophische Erzählungen*. These stories, written not long before and after Herzl's transfiguration into the new figure of a Zionist Jew—indeed, the very act of writing them assisted him in this painful process—express some characteristic Nietzschean notions: the search for an authentic existence beyond the dissimulation and deceit of some of the characters in these stories, as well as that of their author; the transfiguration of one's character from its low level of passive and feeble existence to active, proud, and vital patterns; insights into the nature of human beings and their "human, all-too-human" elements.

What is more, the stories are impressionistic and unstructured, with a flow of spontaneous associations that evidence more concern with aphoristic brilliance than with systematic consistency. All these literary characteristics corroborate Raoul Auernheimer's observation that Herzl owed a large debt to Nietzsche's style and literary genius.[50]

More important, however, the content of these stories also bears a distinctive Nietzschean imprint. One of Herzl's stories, "The Mind Reader,"[51] written in 1887 at the beginning of his Zionist period, depicts the search for authenticity and the rejection of falsehood, in a kind of Nietzschean thought-experiment. It plays with a man who "sees the falseness everywhere," who observes the shifts in behavior patterns from "*echt*" (genuine) to "*unecht*." This example was probably influenced by Nietzsche's hypothetical construct of *homo Heraclitus,* who "did not possess the power of forgetting at all and who was thus condemned to see everywhere a state of be-coming: such a man would no longer believe in his own being, would no longer believe in himself . . . and would lose himself in this stream of be-coming: like a true pupil of Heraclitus, he would in the end hardly dare to raise his finger" (HL, p. 62). Similarly, Herzl's hero claims that "it is a dis-aster to know how to read our thoughts." The term *echt*, as used by Herzl, is synonymous with Nietzsche's term for "authentic," *wahrhaftig*. However, fully authentic life is not possible in European society, as Nietzsche also claimed, locating his hero of optimal authenticity, Zarathustra, in a cave far removed from human society. In contrast to Nietzsche's hero, the hero of Herzl's story has "social inclinations" and is married (though, like Herzl, not happily). Herzl, who at that time was also preoccupied in finding a po-litical solution to the problem of Jewish authenticity, could not entertain Nietzsche's idea of the splendid isolation of the authentic *Übermensch*, hence he had not severed authenticity so radically from the social sphere. The problem of identification between authentic and inauthentic personalities, and the problem of recognizing authentic human beings—both problems that had not found an adequate solution in Nietzsche's thought—were solved by Herzl through a kind of deus ex machina, since he believed that in principle every human being is born a good and truthful person who be-comes untruthful only later on.

But Herzl, unlike Nietzsche, does not attempt to uncover the various mechanisms that change us into inauthentic beings and he does not aspire to answer the crucial question asked by the Scottish poet Edward Young: "Born originals, how comes it to pass that we die copies?"[52] It is significant that during his intensive search for a political solution to the Jewish ques-tion, Herzl was also deeply preoccupied with the issue of authenticity that had bothered him as a *Grenzjude*. He deals with this existentially crucial problem by a conscious use of Nietzschean formulae. For example, the key formula of Nietzschean authenticity—"How does one become what one is?"—is phrased by Herzl in "The Mind Reader" in a similar version: "This is the question of experiences that make me what I am." Herzl adopts also the psychologizing attitude when he embarks, with the hero of his story, upon "all the ugliness and filth that stirs and lives in the soul." These Nietz-schean motifs reappear in two other philosophical stories: "The Dressing-Room" and "Pygmalion," but this time another Nietzschean leitmotif is added: the belief in our ability to transfigure ourselves so that we become what we are. A fateful change takes place in the heroine of "The Dressing Room" behind the mask of make-up in the theater, and she becomes "com-pletely different from what she was." In "Pygmalion" it appears that Herzl, like Nietzsche and other existential thinkers such as Sartre, does not believe in a rigid and permanent human essence. Instead, he adopts the dynamic-evolutionary view of the free creation of personality. The impresario who is the chief character of the story, and who probably represents Herzl himself, undergoes a significant transformation from playwright to political director on the stage of the reborn nation. In other stories, estrangement is prevalent, and their wandering heroes manifest syndromes of marginality and fluctuate from one definition of identity to another. Herzl himself, from the dubious status of an assimilatory *Grenzjude*, underwent "a fateful shift" and "a full transfiguration of the spirit" (as Nietzsche would put it) to become a proud statesman with a definite vision and identity.

Such an aesthetic staging of identity is conducted by Herzl under the ironic disguise of the figure of an impresario, also the narrator and hero of the 1888 story "The Riot in Amalfi." Herzl's theatrical experience is applied in this story to arouse the dormant Jewish masses for a significant move from the "New" and "Old Ghettos." "The real impresario is capable of staging street-shows" and political theater, at which Herzl excelled. Thus the impresario of this story, who adopts a condescending, paternalistic, and aristocratic tone toward the "mob," arranges an ecstatic mass orgy in which the "mob" wants to tear the impresario apart as a result of "the crazy and wild drives that erupted" (*Philosophical Tales*, p. 91.). Nietzsche's descriptions of the "Dionysian barbarian . . . mixture of sensuality and cruelty" (*BT*, p. 39) are echoed here, as are his insights about our "human, all-too-human" souls. Herzl deals in this story with the lowest driving force: unrestrained greed. He uncovers this region of the psyche and immediately translates it into political activity. His writings become a kind of a psychological laboratory whose findings he applies in life itself: "The market place in Amalfi is the world with its ugly life of rioting" (p. 93).

Herzl also expresses the inner pathos of his protagonists, their reflections and introspection, in their attempts to comprehend their "roots" and their existential experiences. In "Beautiful Rosalinde," Herzl presents the extreme experience of a character who sees his own skeleton and draws existential conclusions from this encounter with finality and death (p. 177).[53] Another Nietzschean motif appears here: overcoming sickness to attain psychological insights. "The sickbed made more than one person into a philosopher" (p. 179). The same truly Nietzschean spirit is also expressed in a reference to the "birth-pangs of a self-knowledge" by a character who wishes to return from his inauthentic "escape" from himself (ibid.). In this context Herzl mentions the search by the "modern man" for "a remedy" and meaning, and reflects about "philosophy" and "true poetry" and about the disabling effects of reflection with which Nietzsche dealt specifically in "On the Uses and Disadvantages of History for Life."

The "small letters" of the "human, all-too-human" soul, our most secret driving forces, appear as a motto in "A Good Deed." The epigraph reads: "You have done a good deed, be careful to conceal its reasons" (p. 221). This aphorism and the theme of the story show a deep suspicion of our conscious motives for our actions. The motif finds its expression in the aphorism that so excited Freud who, like Herzl, was deeply influenced by Nietzschean psychology: "'I have done that,' says my memory. 'I cannot have done that,' says my pride, and remains inexorable. Eventually—memory yields" (*BGE* 68, p. 80).[54] This last motif recurs in several stories, conspicuously in "The Caterpillar," in which the hero, Fritz, reads a chapter from Hyppolite Taine's *De l'intelligence* on the "metamorphosis of the caterpillar into a butterfly" (p. 214). "The Aniline Inn," written the same year *Der Judenstaat* was published, expresses the belief that a new image of man can be created and shaped by sublimating despair. This Nietzschean story focuses on the sublimation of "the most offensive material" (p. 263), where Herzl uses chemical terms that lie at the root of the concept of *Sublimierung*, and proclaims the existential significance of death for self-overcoming on the way to greatness since "one cannot reach philosophical height if one has not squarely faced death"(p. 264).

Herzl deals in most of these stories with the "attractive power of the abyss" and returns to the fundamental idea of his play *Solon in Lydien*, namely that "we human beings cannot live without distress."[55] These Nietzschean motifs of sublimating our more basic drives to create artistic artifacts of aesthetic and cultural value and of the "metaphysical comfort" of art (the leitmotif of Nietzsche's *Birth of Tragedy*) reappear in the story "Sarah Holzmann" about "a little Jewess" who sings and plays music to sublimate her sufferings, since "our best achievements were reached out of our torments" (p. 45). This idea is nicely expressed by Nietzsche: "The beast that bears you faster to perfection is suffering" (SE, p. 158). The conclusion of this story is presented directly by the narrator, who confesses: "Art has always been a great comforter in my life, because it is capable of turning pain into flowers that give joy to other people, especially to those who are troubled and oppressed"(p. 55). This remark is clearly autobiographical. Herzl, with his own troubled personal life, sublimates his marginality through creative writing and overcomes it through political activity. The main aim of this activity is to provide the right conditions for the creation of a new image of a Jew who sublimates his sufferings as the marginal "slave" to become a "master."

Although Herzl cites Schopenhauer in his story "The Good Things of Life," written in 1898, and calls him "the great pessimist,"[56] he emphatically rejects Schopenhauer's metaphysical pessimism. Instead he opts for Nietzsche's optimistic worldview. Indeed, the first sentences echo formulations found in Nietzsche's "Schopenhauer as Educator." Nietzsche demands from us that we should be "responsible to ourselves for our own existence; consequently, we want to be the true helmsmen of this existence and refuse to allow our existence to resemble a mindless act of chance" (SE, p. 128). Herzl follows this prescription: "No longer does chance toss us this way or that. We ourselves are at the helm of the ship."[57] Nietzsche raises in his essay penetrating existential questions—"Why do I live? What lesson have I to learn from life? How have I become what I am?" (SE, p. 154)—which Herzl tries to answer: "I know what I am after, though I don't know whether I'll reach it."[58] Nietzsche deals with the crucial issue of authenticity: how to arrive at the nucleus of one's personality beyond the layers of cultural and social conditioning. To reach this nucleus, Nietzsche does not employ self-analysis and direct introspection because, as a sober psychologist, he does not consider them reliable; instead, he adopts the indirect way to self-knowledge: "Let the youthful soul look back on life with the question: what have you truly loved up to now, what has drawn your soul aloft, what has mastered it and at the same time blessed it? Set up these revered objects before you and perhaps their nature and their sequence will give you a law, the fundamental law of your own true self" (SE, p. 129).

This is exactly what Herzl does in this story about a literary-philosophical experiment—the prearranged meeting of four friends twenty years after they have graduated, each of whom has followed his own path to find meaning and value in life. Three of them depict their disappointment with the materialistic value of wealth, the shallow and illusory value of honor, and the emptiness of the values of family and subsistence. Only the fourth friend, Wilhelm, who asked at the start of his existential journey for "that which fulfills a man,"[59] succeeds in gaining the "internal results of the success" in "this philosophical wager," in which appearances and external layers are illusions and there are no guarantees for attaining a truthful life or a meaningful answer to the existential question of "why" and "what for." Wilhelm, like Herzl himself, "when he finished his studies at the university tried for a while to be a writer." He went "on trips to England and France" to learn "about modern movements of social welfare."[60] This was undoubtedly Herzl's hint at the nature and the objectives of his Zionist project.

Important, however, is the fact that in sharp contrast to Schopenhauer's view of "blind Will" and its manifestations as the pure evil, Herzl empha-sizes the sober optimism that values the very act of willing and of hope as ends in themselves, since belief in the future "is the only thing in which one is never disappointed because the future is never here."[61] Thus Herzl adopts the attitude expressed in most of Nietzsche's writing, that the way is the goal. A similar idea is presented here by Herzl: only Wilhelm, who sought an existential goal that cannot be fully reached, namely personal authenticity, attained his goal. This existential insight is expressed politi-cally by Herzl's famous claim: "Zionism is the Jewish people on the road."[62] Herzl, who according to the popular simplistic perception was a romantic dreamer or a naïve prophet, appears here as a cautious, realistic optimist.

Although Herzl ends most of these stories with moralistic lessons, we cannot avoid the impression that the writer is floating above Nietzschean insights, as it were, and is not seriously involved with them. It is likely that Zionism, which engrossed Herzl during the writing of these stories, and which sealed his troubled journey to shape his own authentic identity, is what prevented him from becoming seriously engaged with psychological philosophy. His distance from Nietzsche was actually an indication of the philosopher's positive impact on him. As a genuine "impresario" or com-poser of his own life, Herzl managed to transfigure it, and in doing so to attain his own authentic identity. It may well be that Herzl was even more optimistic than Nietzsche. Perhaps Nietzsche's optimism was too weak and restrained for Herzl. We should not forget that Herzl sought to advance the Jewish people and their culture to the sublime achievements repre-sented in "The Good Things of Life," in which he expresses his enthusi-asm for "our great cultural achievements. For we live in a time that reminds one of the glorious age of the Renaissance and the Reformation"(p. 128).

HERZL ON TECHNOLOGY AND ENLIGHTENMENT

Was not Nietzsche's skepticism toward such technological and cultural "progress" the main factor behind the cooling of Herzl's attraction to a thinker who had been so formative in shaping his worldview? In fact, the common belief that Herzl believed unreservedly in progress and in the "heaven" that science and technology would bring to humankind and to Zion is far from exact.[63] In "The Dirigible Airship," one of his "techno-logical" stories and also a fable about Zionism, Herzl tempers his enthusi-asm for this revolutionary invention. Employing a Nietzschean tone, he asserts that "people are not worthy of flying. As they now are—crawling is still good for them." There is therefore a good chance that they will misuse this invention for evil deeds and thereby "bring new forms of misery" (p. 38). He repeats his warning against technological progress elsewhere: "The scientific revolutionaries prepare salvation from known distresses, thereby immediately instigating new miseries."[64] It appears that Herzl's faith in technological progress stemmed solely from pragmatic Zionist needs and that, like Nietzsche, he harbored no illusions about it. Such an attitude is incompatible with the optimistic outlook of someone who fully believed in Enlightenment, progress, education, human reason, and the moral improvement of humankind resulting from the advancement of science. Still, it seems that despite these reservations about our "human, all-too-human" nature and about the increasing gap between ever-improving technological knowledge and deteriorating morality, an element of optimism does appear, since these technological inventions will bring "an improvement in the welfare and mores" of humankind.[65] Thus, as Nietzsche's optimism clashes with his metaphysical doctrine concerning the conservative and static elements of the "eternal recurrence of the same" expounded in his later works, so also Herzl's optimism is tempered by "human, all-too-human" nature, which could turn technological and scientific progress into a moral nightmare.

Moreover, Herzl's revolutionary Zionism was nourished by the collapse of religious and secular linear historical narratives that believed in teleological or rational progress. Under Nietzsche's influence, historical time and consciousness became open to any kind of "monumental" adventure or intervention without any clear course, and without commitments to earlier eschatological stories of coming salvation and deliverance.[66] Herzl had arrived on the European scene in an age when belief in God was declining, and when the prevalent ethos derived from the Enlightenment's metanarrative of progress was in an accelerated process of what Nietzsche called a "*décadence.*" Like Nietzsche's philosophy, Herzl's Zionist ideology celebrated the Jewish people's capacity to begin something completely new where nothing had existed before but the relics of the "destroyed Old Temple." These historic "infinite horizons" and opportunities, which Nietzsche evoked, became open to fresh cultural and social experiments that Nietzsche was enticing people "to experiment with." Herzl, with his determination, imagination, and personal courage, was exactly the right man at the right time to follow this Nietzschean call to overcome the "old" time. In so doing he would begin a radically new history that would sweep away the maladies of the new and old ghettos and overcome the syndromes of marginality and tradition.

Nietzsche's doctrine of the "eternal recurrence of the same" provided Herzl with the positive consequences of the notion of cyclicity and recovery of the ancient language, land, and values, which necessitated a move backward to the point of origin where authenticity and harmony had resided. These positive dimensions made Zionism into a viable ideology and successful mass movement without which the present state of Israel would have been inconceivable. Despite the inherent tension between negative and historically open dimensions and positive, past-related values and legacies, both were needed by Herzl in his Zionist program. However, for the practical implementation of his vision he also needed to employ pragmatic tools such as technology and scientific advance.

It seems that Herzl accepted technological advance as a lesser evil out of the sober and affirmative Nietzschean attitude of *amor fati,* for "there is no way to salvation but by giving up what is already lost." This development, therefore, "cannot be restrained and halted,"[67] and Herzl, as a genuine liberal pragmatist, sought to use it for the well-being and freedom of the individual.[68] But Herzl is well aware of the Enlightenment's flaws and of the price to be paid for them, hence his cautious and sometimes ironic attitude. This irony reaches a pinnacle in his story *Das Automobil,* written in 1899: "The machine has, as it were, the capacity to be improved, which cannot be said with the same certainty about living creatures."[69] Here, Herzl ironically terms the crisis of modernity, pace Hobbes, "Bellum omnium contra omnibus." Given all this, one can certainly detect that Herzl's psychology softened his pragmatic "technological" inclinations. "How quick becomes our driving . . . how slow is our wisdom," he declares in a Nietzschean aphorism characteristic of the period of his life when he began his transfiguration from "caterpillar" to authentic "butterfly," from marginality to Zionism. Under Nietzsche's influence, Herzl downgraded ideas of Enlightenment and progress. This influence increased even further because Nietzsche's psychology enabled him to understand one of the most despicable phenomena from which marginal Jews, Herzl among them, suffered: anti-Semitism and its analogue, Jewish self-hatred.[70]

Nietzsche's insights on these themes provided Herzl with the conceptual framework to understand the mental mechanism that gives rise to anti-Semitism. Equally important, he used it to grasp the roots of his own self-hatred: "There is no other nation about which so many widespread prejudices are spread" as the Jewish people. Indeed, due to our historical distresses we have become so depressed and broken-hearted that we ourselves repeat these prejudices and begin to believe them as [anti-Semites] do."[71]

Already in his *Jugendtagebuch 1882–1887*, Herzl analyzes the anti-Semitism expressed by Dühring in his popular book on the Jewish question.[72] He employs a Nietzschean psychological dissection of the motives for Dühring's anti-Semitism, describing him as a weak person with a "slave mentality," vengeful and frustrated because of his personal failures—in short, as a man driven to anti-Semitism by the instinct of *ressentiment*: "This professor, who was dismissed from his teaching position, is overwhelmed by a revengeful and impotent rage."[73] On the next page, Dühring is compared to a "dismissed servant." He and other anti-Semites are afraid of Jewish competitors; hence they want them "out!"—acting hypocritically like the Jesuits.[74] Already in 1882, Herzl describes Dühring's personality and his outlook in distinctly Nietzschean terms.[75] Herzl also employs Nietzschean psychological tactics, which can be summed up as "Show me who your enemies are, and I will tell you who you are," and derives some positive conclusions about the Jewish people from the hatred of anti-Semites: "We are hated in no lesser degree for our virtues than for our vices."[76]

Despairing at pervasive anti-Semitic sentiments, Herzl suggests a proud inversion of values and calls upon his brothers: "The nickname *Judenjungen* has been up to now an insult. Reverse the order and it will become a term of honor: *junge Juden*."[77] And as another term of honor I would add "*new* Jews," who, following Nietzsche's inspiration, dared to embark on a brave journey for the sake of their transfiguration. Interestingly, Herzl does not discuss this issue in religious terms—he does not refer to Judaism in his attacks against the anti-Semites because he has lost his religious faith. However, it was precisely Nietzsche who legitimized Jewish atheism and sheer immanence devoid of transcendental and divine intervention. His model allowed liberation from the various doctrines of metaphysical salvation, and was therefore utterly relevant to Jews' existential concerns.

CONCLUSION

The old ghetto's traditional Talmudic patterns of learning could not be incorporated in the new ghetto. Marginal Jews, therefore, considered Orthodoxy, in the words of one of their eloquent spokesmen, Franz Werfel, to be the "holiest fossilization."[78] Herzl's image of the "new Jew" demanded that the Jews overcome their rabbinical consciousness, around which they had structured their Jewish "antiquarian" identity in the Diaspora. Herzl stipulated that instead they adopt a "monumental" approach centered around the grandeur of their glorious days in ancient Israel. This incitement to "monumental history," which focuses on dramatic historical events, disregarding everyday life, is expressed in Nietzsche's essay "On the Uses and Disadvantages of History for Life," in which he asserts that "monumental" historical consciousness lends support to creative and powerful individuals. It makes possible an emphatic identification with exemplary figures, and reassures those who aspire to greatness by showing them that "the greatness that once existed was in any event once possible and may thus be possible again" (HL 69). The ambitious individual is encouraged to reject uncertainty and to pursue the path of glory and creation. Thus Herzl's project for the vital regeneration of the Jewish people, and his insistence that they recreate their ancient glory, could be seen as an adoption of Nietzsche's attitude toward "monumental history." Herzl, who returns "home," insisted upon returning to the historical and authentic sources of the Jewish people: "Zionism is a return to Israel before the return to *Eretz Israel*," and "though we had to become a new people, we will not deny our ancient race."[79]

Nietzsche believes in the slow but more reliable process of education, cultivation, and development of habits of thought and living, that is, in the creation of a "second nature." Here also lies the relevance of his teaching for Jews fluctuating between the traditional *Yeshiva* and secular university education. To them, Nietzsche would recommend adopting "monumental" historical consciousness, which would assist them in withstanding the torments of transfiguration and help them to attain their glorious future. The necessary condition for assistance from "monumental" consciousness is the aspiration and the will to make an imprint upon human history—or at least Jewish history. Herzl nurtured such a "monumental" mission and distinguished between "mundane history" and "glorious history": "All these petty, unknown, noisy and insignificant men, who plot plots, overturn governments, and do not feel where they are directed . . . act in history . . . without any objective and choice."[80] Herzl stresses his own "monumental" vocation: "I feel within myself a great power which is ever-increasing toward the splendid mission." He looks to the past of the Jewish people through the selective prism of "monumental" consciousness and asserts that "owing to all our troubles we became decadent and the opposite of what we have once been: a nation gifted with tremendous talent."[81] He refers to heroic ages and seeks to revive their greatness: "I believe that on this earth will grow a generation of wonderful Jews. The Maccabees once more will come into being." As the leader of a national revival of the glorious past, Herzl sees himself and his companions from the monumental historical perspective: "I will fight courageously. But all these who are accompanying me will become great historical figures."[82] He reflects on the fate of an eminent leader vis-à-vis the pettiness of the masses: "I know that the highest objective of democracy is to get rid of singular individuals for the sake of the common good. . . . Great men of spirit . . . are estranged from their people just as well as the people are strangers to them. . . ."[83]

Herzl does not shun greatness, because "it is he who seeks greatness that is in my eyes a great man—not the one who has attained it." He draws the strength for his determination and his aspirations for greatness from the splendid past of his people. Zionism is a political-practical materialization and revival of this "monumental" past: "I am not presenting to you a new ideal; on the contrary it is a very old one. This is the idea that dwells in each of us, it is as ancient as our people, who never have forgotten it." Therefore "we need Maccabees who know how to work: to work with their spirits and their hands."[84] Indeed, the provision of role models is, for Nietzsche, the main function of monumental consciousness for the active and ambitious man, "the man of deeds and power, for him who fights a great fight, who needs models, teachers, comforters and cannot find them among his contemporaries" (HL, p. 67).

In the *Birth of Tragedy* (which, as we have seen, Herzl read quite closely) Nietzsche claimed that the dominance of the Apollonian-rational element over Dionysian drives diminished the vitality of human creative powers. This spiritual asceticism, he stated in the *Genealogy of Morals,* is caused by excessive repression of instincts and "spiritualization" (*Vergeistigung: GM* II-16.) To reverse these destructive tendencies, Nietzsche advocated a return to the vitality of the senses and a full sensual life. Marginal Jews, acutely aware of their anomalous existence and longing for healthy and natural life, responded enthusiastically to this injunction. In his speeches and writings, Herzl emphasized the "normal" work that "new Jews" would undertake in their new-old state. To arrive at this, of course, he had to align himself with the Jewish masses in the Diaspora.

Despite his aristocratic aversion to them, Herzl was well aware that his Zionist revolution needed the Jewish masses. Like Nietzsche, Herzl sought to entice his people, using symbolic rituals to enable them to uncover in themselves personal and national powers that had lain dormant in the Diaspora. Herzl posited the flag as a means of enticement: "With a flag we are leading the people to a place we want to, even to *Eretz Israel.* For the flag they live and die, it is also the only thing for which they die in masses if they are trained to do so."[85]

The masses also needed slogans,[86] so this charismatic man supplied the Jewish masses with slogans and phrases in his attempt to entice them to re-

new themselves. However, Herzl did not employ the most decisive enticement to self-transfiguration and to the attainment of personal authenticity; rather, he engaged himself in a fruitful, mostly hidden, dialogue with
Nietzsche, the teacher of personal transfiguration. He confined his personal journey to authentic life to a journey of overcoming the mental
"ghettos" within his subjective life. This took place in the deepest mental
recesses of Herzl's soul, since "we ourselves want to advance to a new
morality,"[87] and "one who wants to attain to greatness has first of all to conquer his own self."

CHAPTER 2

Max Nordau versus Nietzsche

THE STRUCTURE OF AMBIVALENCE

There are books that have opposite values for soul and health, depending on whether the lower soul, the lower vitality, or the higher and more vigorous ones turn to them: in the former case, these books are dangerous and lead to crumbling and disintegration; in the latter, herald's cries that call the bravest to their *courage.*

(*BGE*, 30)

Did Max Nordau admire Nietzsche and his work as did Herzl, his closest friend, or did he genuinely detest him? Among the first Zionist leaders, Nordau was the most striking example of a marginal Jew. As such he felt, on the one hand, that Nietzsche's philosophy presented dangers for him, but, on the other, that it challenged him and had vital relevance for his life. Nordau's marginality was thus the main reason for his ambivalence toward Nietzsche. Nietzsche called his readers to create for themselves harmonious and authentic selves, but Nordau's inability to do so led him into unbridled attacks on Nietzsche, unmatched in ferocity even by today's standards, that occasionally vulgarized his thought.

Nordau's vicious ongoing attack on Nietzsche was actually the first detailed criticism that Nietzsche received. It reached its climax in his book *Degeneration* (1892). Nearly all of Nordau's attacks on Nietzsche in the book are *ad hominem*, scarcely mentioning his ideas. One can discern here a conspicuous genetic fallacy that judges the validity and value of Nietzsche's thought by the sole fact that by the end of his creative life, he suffered from a mental disease and paralysis of the nerves. "From the first to the last page of Nietzsche's writings the careful reader seems to hear a madman, with flashing eyes, wild gestures, and foaming mouth . . . a series of constantly reiterated delirious ideas, having their source in illusions of sense and diseased organic processes."[1] Likewise, Nordau claims that though "Nietzsche wrote his most important works between two detentions in a lunatic asylum . . . He is obviously insane from birth, and his books bear on every page the imprint of insanity" (p. 453). To explain the bizarre (in his eyes) fact that despite Nietzsche's lifelong "madness," his books and ideas enjoyed such enormous popularity, Nordau does not hesitate to call Nietzsche's prominent followers by the same vicious names he gives to Nietzsche. For example: "without doubt, the real Nietzsche gang consists of born imbecile criminals, and of simpletons drunk with sonorous words" (p. 469). And this is sonorously stated despite the well-known fact (known also to Nordau) that most of the most brilliant contemporary intellectuals and thinkers, among them the most creative German-Austrian Jews, were strongly attracted to Nietzsche's words and ideas. Nordau ends this chapter with a no less startling statement: "it still ever remains a disgrace to the German intellectual life of the present age, that in Germany a pronounced maniac should have been regarded as a philosopher, and have founded a school" (p. 472).

Nordau saw in Nietzsche his most dangerous enemy, since the increasing influence of his teaching throughout Europe threatened to disintegrate Nordau's intellectual credo, namely the ideas of the Enlightenment fostered by the French Revolution. The old order of "reason" that granted Nordau his identity card as an assimilated European Jew began to collapse under Nietzsche's forceful critique. After his death, Nordau's daughter and wife wrote that *Degeneration*'s ruthless attacks against artists and writers whom Nordau regarded as degenerate persons reflected "no personal motive" on his part, and that his "diagnoses were the impersonal ones of a physician."[2] Nonetheless, reading *Degeneration* one can feel a deliberately vicious condemnation of Nietzsche. Nietzsche had not only opened the Pandora's box of Nordau's intellectual prejudices but also deeply touched his acute problem of personal identity.

Nordau's vehement opposition to Nietzsche, both before and in the early years of his Zionist activity, is the first telling example of an anti-Nietzschean bent among Zionist thinkers and writers. These intellectuals tended to believe that in several important respects—his abhorrence of nationalism, statehood, and collective enterprise—Nietzsche's thought contradicted Zionism. From this point of view, Nordau was the first Zionist who recognized the latent tensions between Nietzscheanism and political Zionism. But can all these intellectual disputes adequately account for the emotional intensity of Nordau's attacks on Nietzsche?

Nordau's biographers testify that he refrained from any personal contact with the figures that he had attacked in his book, in order not to diminish the 'objectivity' of his judgments and analyses. All the same, they mention the fact that in the year Nordau wrote *Degeneration* "the friend and critic of Nietzsche . . . Lou Andreas-Salomé" used to come to his office as a patient.[3] It is likely that Nordau learned a great deal about Nietzsche from Andreas-Salomé, just as Freud himself did.[4]

Nordau's ambivalent feelings about Nietzsche are apparent precisely from the space he dedicates to destroying Nietzsche's legacy, as if he wished to eliminate some disturbing part of his own personality. This is clear not only from the chapter on Nietzsche in *Degeneration*, one of the longest in the book, but also from the fact that he bothered to write about Nietzsche even during his Zionist period. Following the philosopher's death in 1900, for example, Nordau wrote an essay extolling Nietzsche in the *Neue Freie Presse*—which, not incidentally, was edited by Theodor Herzl.

To understand Nordau's complex relationship with Nietzsche, one must distinguish between Nordau the cultural critic, who saw Nietzsche as a disturbing cultural phenomenon that undermined the European Enlightenment, and Nordau the Zionist, who was deeply disappointed with the European Enlightenment. At the beginning of his literary career, Nordau reacted in extreme fashion to Nietzsche because Nietzsche challenged his attachment to Enlightenment values, despite the curious fact that he paralleled Nietzsche's language and concepts in unexpected ways. In later life, however, Nordau became less emotional in his opposition to Nietzsche's legacy and was significantly less hostile toward him, because he understood Zionism as a Jewish reaction to disappointment with the meager practical results of the emancipation of European Jewry—an emancipation largely derived from the core Enlightenment values of European civilization.

Be that as it may, even within the framework of Zionist ideology, Nordau's critique of Nietzsche had a quiet but significant impact upon the Revisionist movement established under the leadership of Zeev Jabotinsky, whose spiritual mentor was none other than Nordau. Ironically enough, as we shall see, the Zionist Revisionist movement emerged from, among other sources, Nordau's misreading of Nietzsche.

One must ask, however, if Nietzsche's books were so "dangerous" for Nordau (to quote once more Nietzsche's saying about his more "problematic" readers), why did he bother to deal with Nietzsche even in his

Zionist period? And how can one explain Nordau's unrestrained attacks against one of the most influential thinkers of the twentieth century?

THE MARGINALITY OF MAX NORDAU (ALIAS SIMHA SÜDFELD)

Nordau's biographers give us a moving picture of his marginality: "Nordau himself passed his mature life in Paris, everywhere at home and yet everywhere a stranger. . . . and so pride and reserve made him withdraw within his own shell."[5] Nordau, like Herzl, was born in Budapest. He assimilated into the German culture and became a writer and a journalist. He spent the majority of his life in Paris. Nordau's practice as a physician was quite secondary to his many other occupations. He tried to write plays and, like Herzl, failed. But Nordau's starting point was much more Jewish than that of Herzl. Herzl was already born into an assimilated family, whereas Nordau was born into a Jewish-Hungarian home that observed the Orthodox tradition. His father, Gavriel Südfeld, was an ordained rabbi. Since Nordau belonged to the first generation of assimilators, his identity crisis was much more distressing than that of Herzl. Nordau married a gentile woman who was a "Danish Protestant and a descendant of a long line of gentlemen farmers and army officers. She had known no Jews except through the medium of the Bible."[6] Aside from Nordau's affectionate relations with his mother and sister (both religiously Orthodox), he detached himself completely from the Jewish people. Following the death of his father, he changed his name from Südfeld ("southern field") to Nordau ("northern meadow"). This name change indicated Nordau's wish to become fully assimilated into German secular society. And though one scholar has warned us against seeing this action too simplistically, as expressing some kind of yearning to attain a status of a pure Aryan,[7] it is quite tempting to speculate that Südfeld symbolizes the southern pole of the young Nordau's identity—the ancient Israel where his people shaped their original identity before dispersing into the Diaspora—whereas Nordau represents northern Europe, namely Germany and Austria, where Nordau underwent his rapid assimilation.

Such a life history may account for Nordau's ambivalence toward Nietzsche. Nietzsche's plea to create an authentic and harmonious self threatened Nordau's schizophrenic world more than it threatened Herzl's less divided self. Thus, Nordau was more ambivalent toward Nietzsche than Herzl.

DEGENERATION

The term "degeneration" was coined in 1857 to characterize people suffering from mental breakdown due to consumption of various toxins like alcohol or opium, or from various hereditary physical defects. It also referred to those who deviated from common moral norms. Accordingly, this mixture of biological, clinical, and ethical connotations did not pertain solely to organic sickness but also, and mainly, to deviant life patterns.[8] The lack of any objective criterion enabled Nordau to pronounce a number of subjective judgments in his book that were, for most part, projections of his syndrome of marginality, including his Jewish self-hatred.

The motif of self-hatred is clearly present in *Degeneration*. Some of the features of degeneration that Nordau finds in contemporary geniuses— Ibsen in the theater,[9] Wagner in music, Zola and Tolstoy in literature, Baudelaire in poetry, and Nietzsche in philosophy—are the same features that could be attributed to marginal Jews. Thus his attack against the patterns of degeneration is simultaneously a critique of such Jews, containing in no small measure the element of deeply rooted self-hatred.[10] Hence Nordau is absolutely right in claiming that "it is a habit of the human mind to project externally its own subjective states" (p. 2). Indeed, this description applies also to Nordau, who projects onto others his own symptoms of degeneracy, such as uprootedness, alienation, and itinerancy, though he does not admit that he too is afflicted by the same complaint.

According to Nordau, some of the most serious signs of degeneration are personal inauthenticity, dissimulation, pretense—the artificial masks people wear in order to be or to "present something that they are not" (p. 9). But was this not exactly the case with so many marginal Jews? Nordau's reluctance to analyze himself can partially explain his aversion to Nietzsche's thought where the psychological element is so dominant.

Yet Nordau's writings were heroic struggles against his time and its most prevalent outlooks. Like Nietzsche, Nordau too was thinking and acting "untimely."[11] Like Nietzsche with his ideal of classical Greek culture, Nordau too looked to the past—to the classical period of the European Enlightenment, namely to the French Encyclopedists, to Heine, and to Goethe. But in contrast to Nietzsche, who encouraged the revolutionary spirit and sought original and authentic innovation, Nordau sought to strengthen the values of the Enlightenment and did not wish, like Nietzsche, to "reevaluate all values."

Thus, it is no coincidence that one of the first figures mentioned by Nordau in his book is Wagner. Wagner is depicted as the great enemy of progress and as the representative par excellence, in the field of music, of degeneration. Nordau read Wagner's anti-Semitic treatise, *Das Judentum in der Musik* (1850), which significantly contributed to the rise of German Nazism in the twentieth century. By referring to this tract and to Wagner's "furious anti-Semitism" (p. 172), and by describing the composer as a figure who suffers from "a greater abundance of degeneration than all the degenerates put together" (p. 171), Nordau tries to counterattack these vicious anti-Semitic views, degrading their author to the rank of degenerate and taking from him any status of respectability. In his chapter on Wagner, Nordau sheds for a moment his character as a self-hating Jew and, as a proud Jew, attacks one of the worst enemies of the Jewish people.

Nordau uses Nietzsche's writings extensively to justify his views on Wagner. This should not surprise one who knows Nietzsche's attitude toward his ex-friend and ex-mentor, whom he calls "my antipode" and who "had condescended step by step to everything I despise—even to anti-Semitism."[12] Nietzsche blames Wagner for being "the artist of decadence . . . its protagonist, its greatest name" (*NCW*, pp. 164, 165). Nordau, continuing Nietzsche's accusations, refers to the Wagner festival in Bayreuth as a phenomenon of German degeneracy. In this way, Nordau seeks to overcome the dissonance between his personality and his worldview. As a Jew, he was constantly threatened by the society and the culture which he wanted to belong to and identify with.[13] By presenting the cultural sources of anti-Semitism as manifestations par excellence of degeneration and anomaly, Nordau wished to convince his readers, and especially himself, that anti-Semitism was shared only by a minority, though a dangerous one. It was a minority that suffered from severe mental disturbances and thus was but a deviation from the great path of the European Enlightenment. This was the personal background for Nordau's statement that anti-Semitism too was a manifestation of "German hysteria," "persecution-mania," (p. 209) and degeneration.

In their references to Wagnerian anti-Semitism, there is a striking similarity between Nordau and Nietzsche. Both saw in anti-Semitism a manifestation of decadence and weakness. Nietzsche sought to overcome this, in his eyes, abominable phenomenon by showing, via his genealogical-psychological investigations, that its sources lay in the mental patterns of a "slave" who out of impotency exhibits a weak, "negative," and resentful power. Nordau, too, preferred to fight this phenomenon by making its acknowledged leader and main initiator none other than the king of degenerates in a field so dear to the German heart—music.

Be that as it may, from the first definition of the notion of degeneration onward we can discern a strong relativistic and subjective meaning:

> The clearest notion . . . of degeneracy is to regard it as a *morbid deviation from original type* . . . anyone bearing in him the germs becomes more and more incapable of fulfilling his functions in the world . . . When under any kind of noxious influences an organism becomes debilitated, its successors will not resemble the healthy, normal type of the species, with capacities for development, . . . fortunately [they] are soon rendered sterile, and after a few generations often die out before they reach the lowest grade of organic degradation. (p. 16)

On the surface, this definition is formulated in terms of biological concepts characteristic of the Darwinist period, but since it includes the phrase "healthy, normal type," it clearly involves a value judgment.

Nordau applies his notion of degeneracy to culture and distinguishes between degenerate geniuses and the "true and original talent" (p. 32). However, he does not provide us with any valid distinction between a positive genius who "healthily" advances the culture, and a "degenerate" and "regressive" genius who makes it "sick." Nordau claims that the degenerate genius is "indifferent" to "the opinion of the majority" (p. 31), but all genuinely creative spirits must be indifferent in this respect; otherwise they would not be able to create originally, and to have a significant impact on their generation—they could not become geniuses.

The subjective, relativistic, and judgmental character of Nordau's definition[14] is also conspicuous in his treatments of, for instance, decadence and egomania. Today we are quite well aware that terms like "decadence" are relative and dependent on the political and ideological perspectives of those who use them. Recall that the commissar for culture in Stalin's Soviet Union, Andrei Zhdanov, called all the "bourgeois" literature and art of the West decadent, and censored it because it did not portray in positive and realistic terms the Socialist "heaven." Here, however, it is more relevant to compare "degeneration," the key notion of Nordau's work, to the central notion of Nietzsche's philosophy, that of negative power. This comparison shows the magnitude of Nordau's debt to the same Nietzsche he attacked so bitterly in this very book.

Just as phenomena like egomania, hysteria, mysticism, and decadence are but subdivisions of the wider syndrome that Nordau called "degeneration," so in Nietzsche decadence, nihilism, and asceticism are mere cultural and individual phenomena forming what Nietzsche describes as pattern of negative power.[15] But what about the very term "degeneration"? Is it referred to as such by Nietzsche? In his essay "Schopenhauer as Educator," Nietzsche discusses Rousseau's "image of man" and, like Nordau, sees in the tendency to return to nature a degenerate tendency, since it withholds the creative processes of sublimation. It is noteworthy that Nietzsche sees in "self contempt," that is, in self-hatred, a clear symptom of degeneration. Thus by his standards, Nordau, who suffered acutely from this, is a degenerate person.

Generally speaking, for Nietzsche degeneration, decadence, and nihilism have one central meaning: the impoverishment of human vitality, the will to end, the inability to grow, to create, and to realize all our potentiality. Nietzsche's diagnosis of the cultural situation by the end of the nineteenth century is quite similar to Nordau's, and their respective etiologies of degeneration are almost identical.

Nietzsche's key notion of his mature philosophy is the concept of power (*Macht*). He distinguishes its two central manifestations: the positive, which I take to be the authentic, and the negative, or inauthentic. A comprehensive elaboration of this distinction cannot be given here,[16] but to show the resemblance of this doctrine to Nordau's views, I present it in brief. Negative power is symptomatic of a weak personality, lacking in power but incessantly attempting to obtain it. It is an insecure personality that depends on external circumstances to secure an intrinsic sense of power. Such people tend to acts of violence and abuses of others as means to fortify their weak sense of power and out of sheer resentment and desire for vengeance. They need metaphysical and religious consolations, hold fast to various dogmas, and suffer from passivity, repression, and depression. They shun any innovation and always seek to conserve their being, but not to enhance it. They suffer from lower vitality and creativity. They have a tendency to nihilism and to anarchism.

Many symptoms that Nordau assigns in his book to the degenerate type are amazingly parallel to Nietzsche's descriptions of persons with negative power, so we may assume Nietzsche's imprint here. And indeed, Nordau frequently refers to Nietzsche when he describes the degenerate patterns of Wagner, and even quotes from *The Case Against Wagner*, where Nietzsche returns to his basic distinction between the patterns of positive and negative power. Nordau's familiarity with Nietzsche's works is especially noticeable when he argues his case against degenerate geniuses while using Nietzschean phrases and slogans like "beyond good or evil" (p. 275).

In Nordau's typology, most of the characteristic traits of Nietzsche's notion of negative power reappear. For example: "the degenerate . . . shuns action, and is without will-power (*Der Wille zur Macht*); has no suspicion that his incapacity for action is a consequence of his inherited deficiency of brain" (p. 20). When we ignore the physiological reductionism of Nordau, which has no parallel in Nietzsche, and address ourselves solely to Nordau's descriptions of degenerates as neurasthenics who suffer from nervous exhaustion, we realize that these are exactly Nietzsche's descriptions of Wagner's decadence—that he has "diseased nerves" and is hysterical. Nietzsche claims against Wagner's followers that they are "immature, *blasé*, sick and idiots" (*NCW*, p. 667). Ironically these are the same features that Nordau attributes to the followers of Nietzsche!

At this point a perplexing question poses itself: why, despite all these (and many other) similarities between Nietzsche's and Nordau's typologies, does Nordau not admit that he follows Nietzsche's diagnosis of European decadence and degeneration?

The easy explanation that comes to mind is a psychological one. Nordau's identification with Nietzsche was so strong that by writing *Degeneration,* he sought to liberate himself from Nietzsche's influence. However, the main and, perhaps, deeper, reason has to do with the essential difference between the two thinkers as far as their views on morality are concerned. What characterizes the egomaniac, according to Nordau, is his "egoism" (p. 244). Nordau emphatically prefers altruism and declares, in opposition to Nietzsche, that the altruist is "the highest achievement of living matter . . . the highest degree of development of the 'I' " (p. 252). He defines the "sane man" as a person whose "thoughts and actions are determined by knowledge of Nature and his fellow-creatures, and by the consideration he owes to them" (p. 253). All these are far from the Nietzschean morality of optimal power, personified by the ideal of the *Übermensch*. Against the background of Nordau's descriptions and prescriptions, the figure of the Nietzschean *Übermensch* emerges as that of a solipsistic and psychopathic personality. Nordau stresses in this context the figures of Caesar Borgia and Napoleon as the typical egomaniacs who were morally deranged (p. 260). But these, together with Goethe, also constitute Nietzsche's few examples of historical figures that came close to personifying the *Übermensch*.[17] Is it sheer coincidence? From the text it is quite apparent that Nietzsche's examples were before Nordau's eyes since he refers on the same page where he speaks of Caesar Borgia and Napoleon to certain "philosophic systems" that "justify this depravity, or . . . employ an accommodating rhetoric in verse and prose to celebrate it . . . and present it under as seductive a form as possible" (p. 260)—a description that best fits Nietzsche's poetic presentation of the ideal *Übermensch* in *Thus Spoke Zarathustra*.

Be that as it may, there is a certain perplexing paradox in Nordau's relation to Nietzsche. It has to do with Nietzsche's recurrent statement that he and Richard Wagner are "antipodes."[18] But according to Nordau, Wagner is the greatest degenerate, so how is it possible that Nietzsche is on the same par with Wagner, as Nordau claims he is? Either Nietzsche misjudges his own position vis-à-vis Wagner, or Nordau is entirely mistaken—which is quite natural given his strong ambivalent feelings toward Nietzsche. To prove the second alternative, I turn now to Nordau's chapter on Nietzsche.

Immediately we feel a highly emotional tone that comes to the fore in a passage where Nordau confesses that he has "devoted very much more space to the demonstration of the senselessness of Nietzsche's so-called philosophical system than the man and his system deserve" (p. 452). And indeed, if Nietzsche's "system" is so absurd and valueless, why spend so much time, space, and energy on it? Is this not a decisive symptom of Nordau's strongly ambivalent relation to Nietzsche?

These overtones and undertones of Nordau's personal relation to Nietzsche are prominent in Book III of *Degeneration,* dedicated to "Ego-Mania"— which, according to Nordau, is a derivative phenomenon of degeneration. Without any hesitation, Nordau labels Nietzsche an egomaniac, though from his own definitions it is far from clear that Nietzsche indeed deserved this label.

In any case, when Nordau describes Nietzsche as a writer who sputters "expressions of filthy abuse and invective" against his opponents (p. 416), he is projecting a great deal of his own treatment of Nietzsche onto his subject. Apparently Nietzsche functions for Nordau as his alter ego with whom he identifies and whom he seeks to become. But due to his identity problems he tries to remove Nietzsche from his own life. It was in that manner that Wagner functioned for Nietzsche. If the object of adoration is destroyed, it opens the way to spiritual autonomy and a complete self.

In his chapter, Nordau tried to undermine Nietzsche's impact not solely by an ad hominem, genetic approach (and fallacy), but also by some more substantial and concrete arguments against his philosophy. These can be arranged under five headings: (1) Criticism of Nietzsche's style and his lack of a system;[19] (2) Moral criticism;[20] (3) Criticism of Nietzsche's notion of the will to power;[21] (4) Rejection of the Nietzschean ideal of the *Übermensch;*[22] (5) Rejection of the image of the "blond beast";[23] and (6) Attacks against the irrational and anti-Enlightenment ramifications of Nietzsche's thought.[24] What is amazing, however, is that Nordau's criticisms actually anticipate some of the Nazi misappropriations of Nietzsche's philosophy.[25] And though it is not my purpose here to defend or criticize political and historical appropriations or misappropriations of Nietzsche,[26] one comment seems to be relevant.

Nordau, in his pre-Zionist period, believed in the narrative approach to history, according to which human existence in time is governed by unfolding reason and by the rational progress of freedom, equality, and fraternity posited by the Enlightenment. However, Nietzsche attempted to free us from unconditionally upholding such a narrative history and wished to open our horizons to "infinite perspectives" and fresh cultural "experiments."[27] Nordau's friend, Herzl, introduced a revolutionary Zionism nourished by the collapse of the religious and secular linear historical narratives that believed in teleological or rational progress. Under Nietzsche's influence, historical time and consciousness became open for any kind of monumental adventure without any clear course or commitments to earlier eschatological stories of coming salvation and deliverance. Herzl arrived on the European scene in an age when the prevalent ethos that permeated the Enlightenment's metanarrative of progress was collapsing, having found itself in decline or in an accelerated process of what Nordau calls "degeneration." In the previous chapter we saw that, like Nietzsche's philosophy, Herzl's Zionist ideology celebrated the Jewish people's capacity to begin something new where nothing had existed before but the relics of the "destroyed Old Temple" and memories from the "Old Ghetto." These historic "infinite horizons" became open to fresh cultural and social experiments that Nietzsche was enticing us "*zur versuchen*" ("to experiment with"). Before his conversion to Herzl's Zionism, Nordau made a desperate effort to defend the crumbling metanarrative of the Enlightenment by attacking Nietzsche. When he adopted the Zionist program, however, Nietzsche ceased to be such a threat to him. Consequently, he tried to establish a kind of intellectual alliance with Nietzsche and his legacy. But even in his pre-Zionist stage, Nordau did not successfully liberate himself entirely from Nietzsche. He continued to use Nietzschean expressions and ideas quite frequently. For example, he speaks about the "revolt of slaves into literature" (p. 533), admitting that it is "Nietzschean expression."

On the last page of his work, Nordau declares that he wants to "spread enlightenment" and defend "progress" (p. 560). He wants to move the frozen wheels of "emancipation" and strengthen the power of judgment and the validity of reason and education. It is quite characteristic of a marginal Jew such as Nordau that at the end of his book he quotes from the New Testament (*Matth.* 5:17) and once again mentions the "emancipation" by means of which he dreamed (together with many other marginal Jews) of solving the identity problems of his marginality. And it is quite ironic that five years later, exactly this emancipation would become the main object of his attack in his famous speech before the First Zionist Congress in Basle.

THE ZIONISM OF MAX NORDAU

Since Nordau experienced the predicament of Jewish marginality, it was only natural that he was the one to express it most poignantly in Basle in 1897: "The emancipation of the Jews was not the consequence of the conviction that grave injury had been done to a race . . . and that it was time to atone for the injustice of a thousand years; it was solely the result of the geometrical mode of thought of French rationalism . . . of pure logic, without taking into account living sentiments. . . . The emancipation of the Jews was an automatic application of the rationalistic method."[28] Because they were merely "mathematically" accepted among the nations, the European Jews remained strangers in Europe. This formal emancipation, which granted the Jews rights only on paper, was the main reason for the gradual growth of the phenomenon of marginal Jewry.

Nordau was not content just to get rational justice but also wished to see a change of heart in his gentile neighbors. However, his personal experience with anti-Semitism denied him any hope. His speech raises the issue of Jewish authenticity. In contrast to authentic Jewish experience in the "Old Ghetto" were the nightmare of marginality, the self-hatred, and the self-denial of the new Jews who lived outside the walls of their former ghettos, referred to by Nordau as "new Marranos" (p. 72). Nordau describes these "new Marranos" using Nietzsche's attributes of negative power. They are people unwilling to employ their own "powers for the development of their real being." They also suffer from tormenting self-hatred, "suppression and falsification of self" (ibid.).

Nordau's speech against the illusions of emancipation is typical rhetoric of a marginal Jew who is frustrated in his attempts to solve the problems of his split identity by means of universal values. Nordau understood, and deeply felt, that legal rights could not solve the existential conflict involving personal and national identity. Could Zionism do the trick?

Nordau tended at the beginning of his Zionist career to answer this question in the affirmative and to complete the radical transfiguration from a marginal, assimilated, and enlightened Jew into an enthusiastic Zionist. This transfiguration into national Zionism was indeed radical since Nordau adhered more steadfastly than Herzl to the ethos of the Enlightenment, which believed in universal solidarity. But Zionism could not base itself solely on the Enlightenment since it was a particularist movement. From the perspective of the Enlightenment it had too many religious and tribal components. For this reason, Nordau's attempt to overcome his split identity by means of Zionism eventually failed, since it fostered another unbearable tension in place of the original one: the tension between the Enlightenment and Zionism.

Nordau's marginality was so pervasive that even after he became a Zionist, the duality within his person between European liberalism and national Zionism did not disappear. As a Zionist he was a liberal, and as a liberal he was a Zionist. Eventually he could not withstand such an internal schism. His initial enthusiasm for Zionism significantly chilled after Herzl's death (in 1904), and though he did not formally leave the movement, he considerable restricted his activities, and his friends' attempts to push him into the leadership of the Zionist movement were to no avail. This indicates that Nordau's attempts to overcome his marginality and his basic duality ultimately failed. For that reason, Nietzsche became for him even more relevant and he was increasingly less ambivalent about him.

Certain Nietzschean motifs came to the fore in Nordau's Zionist thinking. Nordau came to recognize the syndromes of his inauthentic Jewish marginality, and his longing to return, by means of Zionism, to an authentic and harmonious self that would secure the wholeness of the *individuum* and the overcoming of the *dividuum*. In this context Nordau's disgust with any kind of fraud, duplicity, and self-hatred, and all other syndromes of the Jews in the Diaspora, became evident. He employed the criteria for degeneration and accused Western Jewry, especially in Germany, of being passive, weak, and in a state of constant inertia. Thus Nordau meant for Zionism to be his personal remedy against degeneration and marginality. In the moment of truth in his life, Zionism became for him the "why" whereas the search for personal authenticity is the spirit of this "why." In 1909 he asserted that "Zionism endowed me with meaning and [the] content of my life."

In his attempts to incorporate the Enlightenment into Zionism, Nordau was also guided by Nietzsche's call to European Jewry to take upon themselves a vital mission that had to do with the rejuvenation, enrichment, and expansion of European culture. In fact, Nietzsche claimed, the Jews had already helped Europe, not so long before: "in the darkest times of the Middle Ages, when the Asiatic cloud masses had gathered heavily over Europe, it was Jewish free-thinkers, scholars, and physicians who clung to the banner of enlightenment and spiritual independence in the face of the harshest personal pressures and *defended Europe against Asia.* . . . Judaism has helped significantly in . . . making Europe's task and history a continuation of the Greek."[29] Nordau, who wished to keep and guard the spirit of the Enlightenment also within the Zionist program, echoes these sentiments, saying in his address before the Eighth Zionist Congress at The Hague in 1907: "It was stupidity which described Zionism as a lapse into religious fanaticism, as a renunciation of modern European progress, culture and science; as the yearning for Asiaticism and the isolation of the Ghetto. . . . We intend going to Palestine as the standard bearers of civilization, with the mission of extending the moral frontiers of Europe to the Euphrates."[30] Another echo is provided by Jabotinsky, and before he reminded Nordau in Madrid during the First World War of what he had said at The Hague, he exclaimed: 'We, thank God, are sons of Europe, and also its builders for the last two thousand years."[31]

NORDAU, NIETZSCHE, AND JABOTINSKY

The figure of the "new Jew," envisioned by Nordau and personified by the protagonist of his play *Dr. Kohn,*[32] (like Herzl's Jacob Samuel), embodies not just a spiritual excellence but also a physical manifestation in the form of a duel, as a means to defend his wounded honor as well as uplift the image of his humiliated people. Nonetheless, Nordau himself stresses the view of Kohn's father, who refuses to be consoled by the fact that his son has acted chivalrously and died honorably. In contrast to his son who, though secular and proud, still vacillates between modern humanist enlightenment and the tradition of the "Old Ghetto," his aged father expresses the traditional Jewish ethos: "This is no consolation at all. Why should my son be chivalrous? He is no knight. We have learned from our forefathers to abhor brute force. Let others slay with bullet and fist. Our weapon is the mind."[33] Nordau rejects this approach and seeks to "normalize" the Jewish people by moving them toward the physical history of force and action (as opposed to the mere spiritual existence), and by stressing the importance of what he calls *"Muskeljudentum"* ("muscular Jewry").[34] The new Jew should be proud, brave, and militant, a fighter who had traded his excessive spirituality for the cultivation of the body. And thus, despite Nordau's rejection of what he wrongly perceived to be the physical ramifications of Nietzschean notion of power, he himself was strongly influenced by his own misrepresentation of Nietzsche. Here we approach one of the most exciting ironies of the history of Zionism, namely that Nordau's mis-

understanding and, at times, deliberate and vicious distortion of Nietzsche's philosophy of power was partially responsible for the emergence of
the Revisionist movement within the Zionist organization. The founding
leader of this movement, Zeev (Vladimir) Jabotinsky, under Nordau's decisive influence, adopted from him this distorted reading of Nietzsche and
began to admire Nietzsche for the wrong reasons.

Commemorating the tenth anniversary of Nordau's death, Jabotinsky
wrote in 1933 that Nordau had fulfilled an almost Nietzschean "function"
of fighting all the "conventional lies of our civilization."[35] In his tribute,
Jabotinsky stressed what was common to Nordau and Nietzsche and completely ignored Nordau's attack on Nietzsche in *Degeneration*. However,
Jabotinsky's intellectual integrity prevented him from being a blind admirer of Nordau, and despite his claim that "in 1890, Nordau's name became a symbol for the whole new generation," he also admitted that
"Nordau was not alone" and that his way to fame was paved by a long line
of great thinkers and men of spirit—giants like Nietzsche, Ibsen, and Berg-
son. The very fact that he mentioned Ibsen and compared Nordau to the
hero of Ibsen's famous play *An Enemy of the People* is an indication that he
did not agree with the one-sided rejection of Ibsen by Nordau in *Degeneration*. Jabotinsky asserted categorically that "Nordau was not endowed with
a creative talent like that of Ibsen or Nietzsche; but in one respect he was
the greatest of them all: as a writer who knew how to popularize things."

Significantly, despite Jabotinsky's admiration for Nordau, he rejected
his sweeping generalizations and attacks against most European revolutionary movements at the end of nineteenth century, and even had some
reservations regarding his mentor's negative evaluations in *Degeneration*.
He wrote positively about Nietzsche and saw in him "the most dominant
figure in the *fin-de-siècle* . . . the teacher and the prophet of all the instiga-
tors and revolutionary spirits."[36] Despite his admiration for Nietzsche,
however, Jabotinsky hardly referred to the philosopher's own writings; instead, he unquestioningly accepted Nordau's verdict in *Degeneration*: "Nordau's claim that Nietzsche was simply a decadent is one of the few very true
assertions in this book."[37] Be that as it may, for Jabotinsky, the notion of
decadence had a positive connotation, which he defined in almost a Nietzschean spirit as romantic-revolutionary heroism.[38]

Although Jabotinsky read Nietzsche in his youth,[39] he may have hesi-
tated to express his own views on philosophy, seeing himself as far from an
expert on the subject. Instead he deferred to Nordau, whom many ac-
claimed as a leading philosopher of the age, accepting his authority and
his interpretation of Nietzschean thought. This did not prevent him, how-

ever, from stressing, like Nietzsche, and in stark opposition to Nordau's ideal of solidarity, the primacy of the individual over the collective: "in the beginning God created the *individual*; every single person is a king equal to another. . . . it is preferable for one person to sin against the public than for society to sin against the individual; it was for the benefit of individuals that society was established—not vice versa."[40]

Jabotinsky accepted without hesitation Nordau's "militant" interpretation of Nietzsche's teaching, embracing it enthusiastically despite the fact that Nordau himself actually rejected it. It is little wonder that the focus of Jabotinsky's conversations and disputes with Nordau in Madrid was his project to mobilize "Hebrew regiments." When such military units were established he served in them as an officer fighting for the British in 1918 in their conquest of *Eretz Israel* from the Ottoman Empire.

Now, if indeed Jabotinsky also took his views about physical might from Nordau's distorted picture of Nietzsche's notion of the "will-to-power" and was not solely influenced by the spirit of nationalism that became a dominant force in Europe, then we can safely say that a misapprehension of Nietzsche's thought became a formative factor in the history of Zionism no less than a sound and sensible reading of his writings. An incorrect reception is still a reception. Its impact on the development of history can be quite significant, and certainly was so in the case of political Zionism and the ethos of "*hod ve-hadar*" ("Glory and Splendor")—force and muscles, which were in Jabotinsky's eyes the epitome of the authentic "true Jew" and made him the genuine son of the People of the Book. We should remember that Nietzsche also admired the Bible—the Old Testament, being very critical of the New[41]—since he found in the ancient Hebrews the same self-respect, pride, glory and splendor that were so dear to Jabotinsky.

It is important to note in passing that Nordau's ideas about "muscular Jewry" cannot be solely attributed to his misreading of Nietzsche's writings. Another possible factor can perhaps be located within the framework of sociocultural history, if we recall that the glorification of physical culture was actually a much broader Germanic phenomenon of the nineteenth century, as attested by the gymnastic club movement in Germany.[42] Be that as it may, however, since Nordau spent most of his life in Paris and not in the German domains, the dominant forces here were Nordau's attempts to overcome what he called the physical degeneration of contemporary European Jewry. He strove to overcome the syndromes of a person who "hangs in the air" (to use his language) by calling his people to develop their muscles (especially by gymnastic exercises). He believed that Jews had become degenerate, and by emphasizing the body and its cultivation he wanted to counterbalance the excessive spiritualization of Jewish life "in the narrow confines of the ghetto." Nordau was a strong supporter of the concept of *mens sana in corpore sano* (a healthy mind in a healthy body) and called upon his people to improve their physical health.[43] Nonetheless, we can see this an echo of Nietzsche's objection to the excessive abuse of our Apollonian inclinations that repress our vital and sensual (Dionysian in Nietzsche's language) elements. Nietzsche's call to adopt a healthier, more vital, and natural life met with a warm and enthusiastic reception from marginal Jews. Hence it is small wonder that Nordau also tried to absorb this plea and spoke in his Zionist speeches and essays about "Free, strong, happy, and life-loving people."

But beyond Nietzsche's impact on Nordau (and Jabotinsky) in this matter, one has the impression that a more personal element also played a significant role in Nordau's emphasis on physical *Kraft* rather than on spiritual *Macht*. Whereas Herzl emphasized the "spiritual transfiguration" that has to take place in the new Jew, Nordau displaced this struggle from the internal-mental domain to the external physical manifestation of sheer force. He did this because of his inability to overcome the basic schism in his life as a marginal Jew who wanted to become simultaneously a revolutionary Zionist and universal humanist of the Enlightenment, which he tried to plant into Zionism. Characteristic in this context is his address before the ninth Zionist Congress, where he made the following confession: "My ideal is to see a Jewish people in the land of its fathers, ennobled by a two-thousand-year-old firmness of character, respected on account of its honest and fruitful cultural work, an instrument of wise progress, a champion of justice, an apostle and personifier of brotherly love. Of this idea I will not surrender an iota. At this point there can be no concession. This ideal I would not exchange for all the treasure in the world."[44] The ideal of fraternity or "solidarity," to use Nordau's term, is that spiritual-social "treasure," that relic of the glorious Enlightenment which had to help Nordau to overcome his marginality. Hence he was attracted to it all his life long and tried to find some kind of synthesis between this ideal and Nietzschean individualism.

"INDIVIDUALISM" AND "SOLIDARISM?"

In October 1900, two months after Nietzsche's death, Nordau wrote about him much more moderately than before. This cannot be ascribed solely to the fact that this was an obituary, a way of saying farewell, a piece dedicated to Nietzsche's memory, but mainly to the fact that when Nordau became a Zionist, his commitment to the paradigm of enlightened Europe weakened slightly. Nordau sought at that time to solve the tension between the Enlightenment's universal values of his old and beloved Europe and the national Zionist particularism to which he was now so attracted. He now felt that by means of Zionism he would be able to overcome his problem of identity and succeed in forming a harmonious and authentic self. His effort to fuse national matters ("solidarism") with personal longings ("individualism") led him to attempt to form a synthesis between his enlightened solidarity and his feelings about the importance of personal authenticity, namely between the components of Enlightenment and of Nietzscheanism.

In his eulogy, entitled *"Individualismus, Solidarismus,"*[45] Nordau praised what he had cursed before—Nietzsche's "wonderful use of language." Though he mentioned Nietzsche's sickness, he did not do so as a means of refuting his entire thought, but rather with a restrained compassion for his "suffering," using the phrase *"den armen Toten"* ("the poor deceased"). What still threatened Nordau, however, was the fact that the enormous rise in Nietzsche's popularity in Europe, had strongly encouraged the tendency to emphasize individualism. This trend, Nordau thought, would bring the final collapse of the European Enlightenment. In order to defend the ethos of this Enlightenment and to slow down this "destructive" turn, he tried to show that there is no essential contradiction between solidarity and individualism, and that both are desirable and even capable of functioning together in a kind of mutual *Aufhebung* (to use the Hegelian term that denotes elevation, suspension, and removal). Nordau concluded: "we have to proceed not in the direction of Nietzsche and/or Tolstoy. In other words, individualism and Solidarism are not valid by themselves and thus the highest task that confronts any political theory and ethics is to find some compromise or a synthesis between these two opposing viewpoints. This is the highest mission of culture."[46] This is exactly what Nordau was trying to accomplish on the personal and national level by means of Zionism. I shall not discuss the quite intriguing issue whether such a synthesis is at all possible. It is sufficient to say here that this was Nordau's last serious attempt to unite within his own self the various basic contradictions in his person and in his intellectual world. He tried to attain a viable synthesis between Zionism and Nietzscheanism, between Enlightenment and Darwinism. He was struggling now to bring Nietzsche to the enlightened Zionist camp instead of banishing him from Europe and from Zion, as he had tried to do in *Degeneration*.

Toward the end of his creative life Nordau came even closer to Nietzsche, as evidenced by his last important book, *The Interpretation of History* (1909), which includes many central Nietzschean insights. Here Nordau eschews any reference to Jewish and Zionist issues but shows his debt to Nietzsche's essay on history[47]—thus becoming one of many Zionist writers to be inspired by it. Like Micha Josef Berdichevski (discussed in the next chapter), he also preferred the monumental consciousness in our relation to our past and criticized the conservative "antiquarian" elements of our historical consciousness. His preference for the monumental and heroic component was a natural outcome of his conversion to Zionism and an echo of Nietzsche's recommendation that the active person who aspires to accomplish a radical change in the world adopt for himself this monumental consciousness. Nordau recognized the importance of this perspective for the first Zionists, and thus he (together with Herzl and many others) wrote nostalgically about Moses and the glorious past of the Jewish people in ancient Israel.

In an important chapter of this work, "Society and the Individual," Nordau wrote: "man walks in fearsome loneliness throughout his life."[48] Nordau's view of solitude has a biographical background, but it is not only a bitter fruit of his disappointments with the Zionist movement and many of its leaders and activities. In my view it was also a sober realization at the end of his life (he died in 1923) that he had failed in his existential mission: to overcome the patterns of marginal Jewry and to become an individual with definite and harmonious identity. In contrast to Herzl, Nordau did not succeed in the task of transfiguration and of overcoming the patterns of pervasive marginality and detachment within himself.

Nordau's last words, as reported by his family, were quite touching: "I missed my life."[49] This personal confession indicates Nordau's sober awareness that he had failed in the Nietzschean mission of self-overcoming—in his case, of overcoming his sense of marginality: not Zionism and not even the Enlightenment assisted him in this formidable existential task. The greater Nordau's failure, the stronger became his ambivalence toward Nietzsche.

PART II

NIETZSCHE AND CULTURAL ZIONISM

Nothing is more complete than a broken heart.

—RABBI NAHMAN OF BRASLAV

Previous chapters have dealt with the first two leaders of political Zionism who belonged to the elite of acculturated "marginal Jews" in Central Europe. Their convoluted relation to Nietzsche was sustained by their attraction to his teaching on authenticity, to his rejection of the phenomenon of self-hatred, to his plea for transfiguration of the self, and to his staunch atheism. Through these elements of Nietzschean thought they sought to overcome their divided selves and attain the status of harmonious individuals. Following their disillusionment with the Western European Enlightenment, they sought, by means of national resurrection, to cultivate a new image of the Jew. They were attracted to Nietzsche's criticism of Europe's "decadent" institutions. Western "enlightened" society refused to accept the Jews; hence the Jews must reciprocate that rejection and establish a more vital society far away from decadent Europe.

But what about the Eastern European Jewish Zionists? Did they have any significant relation to Nietzsche? When we come to deal with their most influential representatives who spent their youth within the walls of the old ghettos, to use Herzl's expression, the reasons for Nietzsche's impact and its manifestations changed dramatically. Unlike their Western brothers, Eastern Jews were not marginal from the perspective of their rich Jewish culture. Western Jews, especially those living in the German *Sprachraum* (language area) and the German *Kulturbereich* (cultural sphere) wanted to assimilate into the main currents of secular German culture, which they regarded as more sublime and fruitful than their own. In striking contrast, their Eastern brothers regarded their gentile neighbors and the culture of the Polish and Russian peasants as markedly inferior to their own.[1] Consequently, those who lost their belief in the God of Israel and could not follow the Torah did not wish to assimilate into the surrounding environment but sought a new definition, or redefinition, of their heritage. While overcoming their historical "antiquarian consciousness," they were looking for new perspectives and for more natural relations with their heritage. For them, certain major questions were existentially relevant: What would be the concrete content of their new Hebrew secular culture? Following the "death of the Jewish God" and the deterioration of the authority of their fathers, what kind of relation would prevail between their old religious culture and their modern modes of living? Would it be a radical break and a new beginning, as Berdichevski wished, or rather a continuation of and a viable synthesis with the old Jewish heritage, as Ahad Ha'am wanted? What would be the nature of the relation between this new Hebrew culture and modern European culture, one of whose heralds was Nietzsche? Would they follow its temptations after the manner of their brothers in the West, or would they be satisfied to accommodate the Western cultural and secular treasures within their own reawakening Hebrew culture?

These urgent questions prompted a keen interest in Nietzsche, to such an extent that many passages of Berdichevski's polemical essays consist of paraphrases of "On the Uses and Disadvantages of History for Life," where Nietzsche emphasizes the value of the existential application of history for the revitalization of life. Clearly, the Eastern European Jewish intellectuals were attracted to Nietzsche's plea to overcome "antiquarian" history. Berdichevski, for example, claimed that "the yoke of the book" paralyzed Jewish vitality, meaning by the "book" or "scripture" the whole edifice of Orthodox literature: the Mishnah, Talmud, and all the later layers of exegetical writings. Berdichevski and Ahad Ha'am were attracted to Nietzsche's suggestion to adopt the "monumental consciousness" and revive the heroic past and deeds of the exemplary figures of the old Bible. Both belonged to notable rabbinic and Hasidic lineages and they left their shtetls for Central and Western Europe, where modern culture, especially Nietzsche's teaching, made a lasting impression on them. Thus we will see how both were struggling to assimilate Nietzsche (Berdichevski) or accommodate him (Ahad Ha'am) into their own Jewish legacy and their future national-cultural projects.

In the second half of the nineteenth century in the Russian-Polish Pale of Settlement, there were three distinct attempts by Jewish intellectuals to shape for themselves new foci of identity. These extended beyond and sometimes even against rabbinic-traditional hegemony in the old shtetls, where the intellectuals had left the *yeshivot* (Talmudic academies) for good.

There were the supporters of the *Haskalah,* the Jewish Enlightenment, which was informed by the values of Western culture. These intellectuals tried to incorporate the *Haskalah* into the dawning secular Hebrew literature and poetry, especially the values of reason and progress. Naturally, this quite large group did not produce any prominent Nietzscheans since they were quite aware of the basic tension between the ethos of the Enlightenment and Nietzsche's philosophical "hammers" that tried to erode and shatter these values.

The second group, the revolutionary intelligentsia,[2] were less Hebrew-oriented. They were eager to associate themselves with social and political groups of populist-slavophile *Narodniks* or with the more universal values of the various Russian socialist parties such as the Bolsheviks or Mensheviks. They believed that the Jewish problem together with Jewish national identity would evaporate after the great revolution due to assimilation into the cosmopolitan working class (the proletariat). In contrast, there were also hundreds of thousands of Jewish workers who joined the Bund, a socialist organization, but who wished to maintain the distinctive cultural Jewish identity and language (Yiddish) following the revolution. None of these social or national varieties of Populism encouraged any inclination toward Nietzsche, with his philosophy of elitism and his radical, spiritual, aristocratic posture, especially as his antisocialist stance was duly noted and rejected.

Most of the Eastern European Nietzscheans, because of their wish to attain a harmonious and authentic identity, were ardently interested in the transfiguration of man's inward heart and were much less preoccupied with the transfiguration of social conditions or political consciousness. Like Nietzsche, they aspired to change man (in their case the individual Jew), whereas the socialists wished first to change the social order. Thus, for example, Zeitlin's attacks against the Jewish Socialists echoed Nietzsche's reproaches against societal changes that would have little impact on the individual within society. This was one of Berdichevski's and Ahad Ha'am's reasons for rejecting Herzl's political Zionism which, in their eyes, would not suffice to foster a significant transfiguration of the Jewish character. Thus Berdichevski and his *Tzeirim* (the Young Ones), Ahad Ha'am, and many other Jewish Eastern European young intellectuals, belonged to a third group among the Polish- and Russian-Jewish intelligentsia.

This third group consisted of autodidactic, eclectic, impressionable Jewish intellectuals who, in Nietzschean terms, strove to become truly "free spirits," looking to create their individual identities without leaning on prevalent intellectual vogues or political-social ideologies. They were living in a sociological vacuum since, unlike their Western brothers, they were not allowed to study in Russian universities, and they did not wish to return to their "Old Ghettos." Suspended between the values of the West and their traditional Jewish heritage, as well as unwilling to assimilate into modern Russian culture, they tried to shape their life from within, namely, without completely assimilating to foreign beliefs and doctrines. Consequently, their tendency to follow Nietzsche's teaching on authenticity was quite understandable, and in their first period of their spiritual journeys and literary activities they became enthusiastic Nietzscheans. The "rent in their hearts" between their religious past and the secular future, or, in Berdichevski's language, between the ethical "tents of Shem" and the aesthetic values of the "tents of Japhet," exposed them to Nietzsche and prepared them for Zionism. Hence they were looking, like Ahad Ha'am, for some kind of synthesis between Nietzscheanism and Zionism or between individualism and their feeling of solidarity with the fate and future of Jewish people.

Unlike Herzl and Nordau, who attempted to define and shape their identity and who aspired, as outsiders to the Jewish experience, to attain a "transfiguration" of their characters, Berdichevski and Ahad Ha'am tried to redefine from *within* their relations toward their Jewish heritage. Such a redefinition or, to put it in Nietzschean terms, "reevaluation" of Jewish values, required a new evaluation of their own culture. More specifically, it needed, as a source of inspiration, Nietzsche's attitude toward history: its monumental and critical crutches and its radical disposal of antiquarian, conservative bondage. For Herzl and Nordau, the question concerning the content of their new Zionist identity and culture was set aside by pressing political exigencies and activities. When they touched upon it, it was in terms of European categories and frames of reference. Thus, for example, Herzl's Zionist utopia, *Altneuland,* is but an extension of Europe, complete with an imaginary opera house in Haifa that is depicted by Herzl as a copy of the one in Vienna—a vision that was ridiculed by Ahad Ha'am.[3] In contrast, Berdichevski and Ahad Ha'am were well versed in Hebrew and in its multifarious biblical and Talmudic styles, and they wrote predominantly in that language. They were estranged from Western European culture, contributed intensively to the revival of modern Hebrew, and could hardly be satisfied with the *Staatsoper.* They were not content to transplant Europe to Zion, but sought to revive Zion only partly by means of Europe. This was the meaning of Berdichevski's slogan: "We are the first Hebrews and we shall attend to our hearts."

However, this "heart" was bleeding from a deep emotional split. They had both left their homes and revolted against their own fathers and against their most intimate friends. As a result, they experienced a deep rift between their newly found secular freedom and their religious background, as well as guilt feelings that they had betrayed their fathers and actually deserted their homes.[4]

The sources of Herzl's and Nordau's *dividuum* were mainly intellectual: Enlightenment versus political Zionism, universal emancipation and European culture versus particularity and existential marginality. In their cases, the "betrayal" was more abstract because it had to do more with their intellectual credos. Though they acutely experienced the existential predicaments of marginality and were intellectually struggling against what Nordau termed "solely a mathematical emancipation," their main efforts were directed toward the intellectual polemics, pragmatic politics, and statehood. In the case of Berdichevski and Ahad Ha'am, however, their struggle was not directed solely against the external sources of their discontent, but also against their inborn values and patterns of life within the ghetto's walls. Consequently, they had to deal with predominantly emotional matters at great existential cost, at the price of torn hearts from which they suffered all their lives.[5]

However, Berdichevski and Ahad Ha'am differed in their reactions to what Hertzberg aptly translated as "the rent in the heart."[6] Berdichevski strove to keep the rent in his heart wide open. His perception of Jewish history (like Nietzsche's attitude toward history in general) did not follow essentialist lines. Hence he did not believe in the viability of the synthesis between the religious faith of the "Old Ghetto" and the secular values of modern European civilization. Instead he wanted to reject the "meek" culture of the Jews in the Diaspora and return to the monumental history of the Jewish people. For him, Zionism signified a radical beginning, a clean slate, and, to use his Nietzschean language, a "fundamental transvaluations in the whole course of our life, in our thoughts, in our very souls."[7]

Ahad Ha'am, on the other hand, wanted to overcome his torn heart and replace his religious vacuum by a kind of Hegelian synthesis (*"Aufhebung"*), where the religious dimension of his Jewish heritage would be discarded but the ethical and universal essence of Judaism would be distilled out so as to function as the fundamental evolving principle of the whole of Jewish history. For Ahad Ha'am, Zionism meant a continuation of Jewish antiquarian-cultural history in Zion with the significant addition of a secular perspective toward the religious past. This was the main issue at stake in the famous dispute between Ahad Ha'am and Berdichevski, which was con-

ducted in part in Nietzsche's shadow. Berdichevski used Nietzsche to attack Ahad Ha'am's more conservative attitude. The latter, to defend his
view about an immanent evolution of Jewish culture, responded by attacking part of Nietzsche's theses. Both, however, embraced Nietzsche's
secularism. In this respect Ahad Ha'am was less Hegelian than the German
philosopher: he rejected the divine element in the notion of *Geist* and replaced God in history with the universal dimensions of Jewish ethics.

But Ahad Ha'am's criticism of Nietzsche had deeper reasons than as a
sheer tactical move in a dispute against his worthy opponent. By the end
of the nineteenth century, especially during its last two decades, modern
Hebrew literature in Eastern Europe was still in its shaky beginnings, despite a proliferation of dozens of new journals, newspapers, and books
within the borders of the Russian Empire.[8] It was but natural that the first
significant steps in the birth of modern and revitalized Hebrew culture and
literature were accompanied by a growing sense of insecurity regarding
their external sources of inspiration. Once the new culture became se-
curely established and its character determined, it would no longer feel
that its originality was endangered by external influences and inspirations.
At this point we can sense certain puzzling paradoxes in the relations of
East European Zionists and intellectuals to Nietzsche: on the one hand,
the rejection of Western culture and the search for an authentic cultural
self-determination brought Nietzsche's teachings to their attention. On
the other hand, this very yearning for self-determination, together with the
accompanying insecurity as to the possibility of its attainment, brought
them to shun dominant external influences, including that of Nietzsche.
This paradox was quite conspicuous in Ahad Ha'am, who argued for an
immanence of Hebrew culture in terms and concepts taken, among others, from Western European thinkers and philosophers.

Nonetheless, Nietzsche's presence (despite the heated dispute over his
significance among the Eastern Jewish Zionist intelligentsia) was more
readily and explicitly acknowledged by those intellectuals who had deep
roots in their own Jewish-Talmudic culture than by the uprooted Western
Jews. The East European Jewish intellectuals, who were far from being marginal Jews, were more open to Nietzsche's influence and were not afraid
of freely and openly expressing their debt to or fascination with his writings. Their heritage endowed them with enough self-esteem, pride, and
confidence to change it from within. Hence despite the fact that geo-
graphically and culturally they were more remote from Nietzsche than
their German or Austrian brothers, they dared to come closer to Nietzsche's spirit.

The impact of Berdichevski and Ahad Ha'am on the young Jewish generation, especially on its future writers and Zionist activists, was tremendous. Nietzsche's legacy was directly disseminated by these two leading propagators of modern Hebrew culture. The young Jewish intelligentsia became saturated by Nietzscheanism and also by anti-Nietzschcanism. The spirit of rebellion and of radical transvaluation kindled by Berdichevski's Nietzschean stand, and the spirit of evolution and reform propagated by Ahad Ha'am were the strongest formative forces on the new Hebrew culture and literature. Thus, it is quite immaterial which happened first: Berdichevski's original insights or his relatively early discovery of Nietzsche's ideas and his selective adoption and transmutation of many of Nietzsche's intuitions and insights. It is enough if we show that Nietzsche's presence in the life and thought of this impressionable young man was one of his main sources of inspiration and encouragement. The exact extent of Nietzsche's impact will be evaluated in chapter 3 on the basis of Berdichevski's writings. Chapter 4 will present an analysis of the dispute between him and his formidable adversary, Ahad Ha'am, mainly from the perspective of the latter.

This dispute is still bubbling. Almost the same Nietzschean motifs and sensibilities that were prevalent among the first cultural Zionists are manifested today in Israel. Nietzsche's legacy is still echoed in the current cultural war that is being waged among many modern Israelis over the desirable image of contemporary Hebrew culture and the specific content of their identity as secular Israelis.

CHAPTER 3

Micha Josef Berdichevski

WAS THE FIRST MODERN HEBREW WRITER
A "TRUE NIETZSCHEAN"?

> *We wish to become "Hebrew human beings" at once . . . We feel a burning need to heal the . . . dreadful rent in our hearts. We should expand our borders and place the human culture in the same line with our ancient heritage, so that they will be seen as given by one shepherd. . . .*
>
> —Berdichevski, "At the Crossroads:
> An Open Letter to Ahad Ha'am" (1896)

> *These are the sayings of Rabbi Nietzsche, with which we are threatened, sayings that destroy in order to build.*
>
> —Berdichevski, "On the High Road" (1898)

Why was the first and most influential modern Hebrew writer so susceptible to Nietzsche's influence? Was it because his sensitive heart was so severely torn?

Micha Josef Berdichevski experienced the anxieties of an orphan who stands before open horizons and must choose a new personal identity and calling.[1] He needed a mentor, a guiding hand, an inspiring model. Nietzsche, being himself such an orphan, welcomed such kindred spirits and tried to encourage them on their way to spiritual autonomy. Berdichevski was in urgent need of Nietzschean crutches to become what he wanted to be: a proud modern Hebrew writer and cultural revisionist.

Berdichevski's journey in search of intellectual autonomy and a redefinition of his self began with the strict Orthodox teachings of his youth. He fled from the Eastern European shtetl and discarded his identity as a brilliant yeshiva student and Talmudic prodigy. In his escape to the West (partly voluntary and partly forced upon him) he was driven in some measure by his traumatic experience of complete abandonment (including separation from his beloved wife). Nietzsche became, at least in his formative years, the most conspicuous influence upon him because he was so deeply afflicted by the existential maladies that Nietzsche's philosophy attempted to address.

ON "THE THREE METAMORPHOSES" OF BERDICHEVSKI'S EXISTENTIAL JOURNEY

Of three metamorphoses of the spirit I tell you: how the spirit becomes a camel; and the camel, a lion; and the lion, finally, a child . . .[2]

Nietzsche was well aware of the strong conditioning forces exerted on the individual by historical heritage and culture, by social convention and educational systems. Consequently he thought that the road to personal authenticity requires at least two stages. The individual ("the lion," a metaphor for self-overcoming) must liberate oneself from "the camel," from all the external layers imposed by institutional conditioning and by the social circumstances of one's birth. Only then, after attaining a child-like state of "innocence," namely, a negative freedom from this spiritual burden, can one proceed to the second stage, in which one consciously adopts values and patterns of life and thought. These may well reflect the traditional values discarded in the first stage, since it is not their content that really matters but the unconstrained free manner in which they are adopted.

It seems quite instructive to present Berdichevski's spiritual development along the lines of this existential scenario and test Nietzsche's formulas for attainment of authenticity in a concrete case. How far can it be put into practice by a strong-willed individual for whom a success in such a journey seems the only way to overcome the rent in his heart and attain a viable existential equilibrium?

For Berdichevski, the "camel" stage lasted from his birth in April 1865, to December 1890. Born in Miedzyborz in Poland, the cradle of Hasidism, into a notable rabbinic lineage, Berdichevski was remarkably well-versed in Talmud and other texts of Orthodox Judaism, and from an early age was considered to be a brilliant scholar ("*ilui*"). He was attracted by Bratslav Hasidism but in secret also read secular Hebrew literature. When his rich father-in-law caught him reading such "profane" books, he expelled the twenty-year-old Berdichevski from his house and forced him to divorce his daughter. The process of Berdichevski's secularization was thus accompanied by personal crisis, with his spiritual journey paralleling the travails of his heart. His exile from the ghetto was inter alia also his forced divorce from his beloved.

After his expulsion from his father-in-law's house, he went to study in the famous yeshiva in Volozhin (1885–86). Thus he was the first Zionist figure to have studied the Talmud so intensively—unlike Herzl and Nordau. His dissatisfaction with rabbinic Judaism, however, is already expressed in his first essays and literary pieces on life in the yeshiva (1886–88). In the summer of 1889, he went to Odessa and over the next year and a half became acquainted with Ahad Ha'am and many other Jewish freethinkers. The main reason for his departure to Odessa, however, was his decision to study German and go to Berlin to attend university.

The stage of the "lion," of self-overcoming and of the great revolt against his religious heritage, extended from 1890 to 1902. This was the stage where Berdichevski tried to attain a transfiguration of his self along the aesthetic model of authenticity as delineated by Nietzsche, and began the "revaluation of all values." Naturally this was his most Nietzschean period. His Hebrew short stories written in these years[3] depicted the pathos of an individual who vacillates between different life scenarios. In contrast to the literature of the *Haskalah,* which mainly dealt with progressive and linear processes of *Bildung,* Berdichevski delineated in a quasi-autobiographical manner the personal crises and radical transformations of his young Jewish heroes.

In December 1890 Berdichevski left Odessa for Germany but instead of going to Berlin he remained for three years in the Silesian capital, Breslau, where he studied philosophy in the local university. He came to know David Frischman (who translated into Hebrew *Thus Spoke Zarathustra* in 1909–11). During these impecunious student years, he read voraciously (in German) such European literary luminaries as Heine, Tolstoy, Dostoevsky, Balzac, and Zola, and was also impressed by the philosophies of Rousseau and Kant. In April 1893 he moved to Berlin to continue his studies. It was there that he began to read Nietzsche and became profoundly attracted to his writings. He also began to attend the *Beith Hamidras Haelyon* (The Highest School of Learning) for *Hohmat Israel* (Wisdom of Israel), where several Jewish students from Eastern Europe were also strongly interested in Nietzsche, among them his friend David Neumark, who wrote the first Hebrew article on the philosopher.[4] Together with these enlightened young Jews, Berdichevski founded the circle of *Tzeirim* (the Young Ones) whose aim was to accomplish a turn, or rather a radical redirection of modern Hebrew literature and to fuse the values of European culture with Jewish secular culture. In 1893 he virtually ceased publishing his polemical essays and short stories in Hebrew and began his first attempts at writing German fiction. In October 1894 he left Berlin for Switzerland to study at the University of Bern, and under the supervision of the renowned Jewish philosopher Ludwig Stein, wrote his dissertation "On the Relation between Ethics and Aesthetics." In February 1896 he was awarded a Ph.D. in philosophy, and began writing an autobiographical novel in German. In August 1896 he accepted Ahad Ha'am's invitation to assist him in editing a new Hebrew journal, *Ha-Shilo'ah*. His close cooperation with Ahad Ha'am, according to his own testimony, helped him to return to Hebrew literature, having previously decided to leave it altogether. After touring several Jewish cultural centers in Eastern Europe, Berdichevski settled once again in Berlin in September 1897 and developed many connections with both Jewish and non-Jewish German writers, men of letters, and publishers (such as the famous publisher Samuel Fischer). In October 1898 he went once again to Weimar to be inspired by several German writers and especially by the spirit of Nietzsche. At that time Nietzsche was already paralyzed in body and mind. Berdichevski met Nietzsche's sister, Elizabeth Förster-Nietzsche, several times, and visited Nietzsche's archives and house. In 1899, in his polemical Hebrew essay "Zikna Vebaharurt" ("The Old and Young Age: A Reevaluation of Values"), containing a motto from Nietzsche's writings, Berdichevski used for the first time the pseudonym that later became his official name: Bin-Gorion. In Berlin he wrote prolifically in Hebrew and German. He planned to settle in Palestine, but ultimately did not do so because of the harsh conditions there.

At the beginning of the final stage of his existential metamorphosis, that of the innocent child, he remarried, visited Warsaw and the grave of Rabbi Nahman of Braslav in Uman, and settled in Breslau (until 1911) and finally in Berlin. In this period, Berdichevski returned to what may be described as the "camel" stage, readopting his previously discarded heritage, but he did so consciously and according to what Nietzsche called "critical consciousness." In his final years (he died in 1921), Berdichevski, besides writing many stories and essays in Hebrew, Yiddish, and German, produced collections of Talmudic and post-Talmudic legends and prepared a major study (part of which appeared posthumously) entitled *Sinai und Gerisim*. This historical research aimed at a reevaluation of the religion of the ancient people of Israel, which, he argued, was not ruled by monotheism but by a nature worship and idolatry.

The question that will be addressed below is whether Berdichevski really deserves the title that some of his opponents derisively gave him, "The Hebrew Nietzschean." Can he be fairly described as the most genuine case of the adoption of Nietzscheanism by modern Hebrew literature and culture? Berdichevski's various critics offered a variety of answers to this question. I survey their stormy reception of Berdichevski's Nietzscheanism, since it throws into sharper relief the whole problematic of Nietzsche's reception by subsequent Hebrew writers and Zionist thinkers. Then I analyze Berdichevski's main letters and writings where Nietzsche's ideas appear most frequently.

NIETZSCHE'S ROLE IN BERDICHEVSKI'S WORK

The exact nature and depth of Nietzsche's impact on Berdichevski was from the beginning a matter of heated dispute. Many Jewish intellectuals argued against the validity of Berdichevski's radical views on the direction and content of a new Hebrew culture and literature. Still, one must distinguish between the Berdichevski/Ahad Ha'am dispute, which reached its peak between the years 1898 and 1902, and the other, fiercer dispute between Berdichevski, his followers, and their opponents. In sharp contrast to the Berdichevski/Ahad Ha'am controversy, which was conducted in a gentlemanly way and addressed itself solely to issues at hand, the other, more virulent critics of Berdichevski resorted, like Nordau, to an ad hominem approach. They tried to invalidate his views by pointing to Nietzsche's madness and its negative influence on the no less "mad" Berdichevski. It is highly ironic that despite, or perhaps because of, the intensity and ambivalence of Nordau's treatment of Nietzsche, the latter became a central stimulating and inspiring figure among the first Zionists and Hebrew writers by the end of the nineteenth century and at the beginning of the twentieth. Not all of them read Nordau's chapter on Nietzsche in *Degeneration*, but many were aware of his terse onslaught against him in the introduction to the 1900 Hebrew translation of his book *Paradoxes*,[5] when, according to the translator's note, "Nietzsche's body was still alive."[6]

In his introduction to the Hebrew edition of *Paradoxes*, Nordau attacked Berdichevski for his Nietzscheanism. Without mentioning his name, he protested against the "chutzpah" of those who, "escaping from the yeshi-

vas," introduced Nietzsche "into Hebrew literature." They foolishly looked
to "this poor madman, who wrote lecherous books during his deranged
and confused years, as to the final epitome of European wisdom."[7] Nordau's attacks here, and in *Degeneration* on Nietzsche, inaugurated widespread and indignant condemnation of any trace of Nietzscheanism in
modern Hebrew literature. Naturally, the main target of this disapproval
was the first modern Hebrew writer to use Nietzsche so copiously.

The fiercest attackers of Nietzsche's presence in Berdichevski's work
were mainly admirers of Ahad Ha'am and followers of Nordau. They
claimed that his theory of "reevaluation of values" was but a cheap imitation of Nietzschean slogans and conceptions which are out of place within
the framework of Jewish history and Hebrew culture. An illuminating example of this approach is Simon Bernfeld's articles.[8] Bernfeld presents two
significant arguments against incorporation of Nietzsche into the nascent
Hebrew culture. First, Hebrew culture lacks territory to consolidate its
identity and to secure its future; thus it cannot sever its cultural-religious
and historical roots. Second, since the Jewish people want to revive their
sense of nationhood, Nietzsche's teaching about the *Übermensch,* which is
relevant to individuals only and never to the people as a whole, can be very
disastrous. Thus with Berdichevski "our national culture is at the mercy of
mentally sick young persons."

Besides Nordau, Moshe Leib Lilienblum (1843–1910), a famous Hebrew writer and critic, could not stomach Berdichevski's radical individualism and blamed Nietzsche for having negatively influenced this young
"pupil and friend of Nietzsche's *Übermensch.*"[9] The slogan "reevaluation of
all values" had no positive content but was rather a vicious attempt to "destroy Judaism." Hence Berdichevski's blind application of the thought of
"this philosopher from the madhouse" to Hebrew culture and history were
suicidal. Lilienblum's main argument was that Berdichevski's and other
young Jewish intellectuals' torn hearts were not caused by existentially
unbearable cultural predicaments but were solely another symptoms
of "decadent hearts," and the reason for the rift was the impossible
attempt to "unite fire and ice together . . . the Jewish Hasidic movement
with Nietzsche's theory." Following Nordau's example, Lilienblum used
quite abusive language against Berdichevski.[10] He accused Berdichevski
(and Nietzsche) of ethical relativism and nihilism, and claimed that
Berdichevski hated spiritual power and opted for an exclusive use of the
physical "fist."

In stark contrast to this widespread attitude were a small number of critics who agreed that Berdichevski was indeed a "Hebrew Nietzschean" but

who approved of and applauded him for it.[11] The dispute was quite emotional, since it touched the very core of the existential issue of the new identity and image of the Hebrew people in the making. Locked in cultural conflicts and preoccupied by hectic political-social activities, both sides lacked a cool and more objective perspective on this issue.

It goes without saying that those who supported Berdichevski's campaign of reevaluation of Jewish values—mainly "the Young Ones"—tended to be more sympathetic to Berdichevski's Nietzscheanism. Realizing, however, that Nietzsche was a lethal weapon in the hands of Berdichevski's opponents, they strove to minimize his role in the writer's career. Consequently, they argued that Berdichevski used Nietzschean terms, slogans, and phrases only on the rhetorical surface, but had never really internalized Nietzsche's theories which were alien to Jewish culture and heritage. In their eyes, Nietzsche's influence on Berdichevski was temporary and inconsequential.[12]

After Berdichevski's death, some of his devotees continued to discuss the issue of Nietzsche's presence in his writings. They tried to raise Berdichevski's stature by emphasizing his intellectual independence and, by the same token, to rehabilitate his memory in the eyes of the more conservative Jewish public. Some tried to minimize Nietzsche's impact on his writings,[13] while others tended to stress Nietzsche's role in Berdichevski's works.[14]

With the foundation of collectivist settlements in Palestine, the focus of the dispute revolved around Berdichevski's emphasis on the individualistic mode of life at the expense of the collective one. The new society of the *Halutzim* (pioneers), who tried to reclaim and rebuild the land in Palestine, saw in Berdichevski's extreme individualism, allegedly adopted from Nietzsche, a serious threat to the whole Zionist project.[15] Furthermore, any call (as made by Berdichevski) to transcend the collective frames of reference of the "Old Ghetto" in order to cultivate and express the individual self was regarded as a threat to the very existence of Jewish communities. The delicate social fabric and the inner cohesiveness of Jews, surrounded by often hostile gentiles, was guarded by the rich social and educational life of institutions such as the *heder, shul,* and yeshiva). Preservation of the antiquarian tradition kept intact the very identity of the Jewish people qua Jews. Hence the individualistic trends heralded by Berdichevski were perceived as disintegrating elements. Since Zionism still was not as yet as popular and victorious as religious and communal traditions, Nietzsche the gentile prophet of individualism, and his Jewish counterpart, Berdichevski, became the archenemies of the Eastern European Jewish communities and of the first Zionist settlers in Palestine, who were still fighting for their very existence.[16]

Berdichevski, and other Hebrew writers and Zionists who followed him, attempted to normalize Jewish life, among other means, by stressing the rights of Jewish individuals within the framework of their future state to express their own private concerns, wishes, and feelings. This, I think, was Berdichevski's main contribution to the development of Jewish-Hebrew "normal" life in the Diaspora as well as in the state of Israel. This normalization, or rather secularization, of Jewish existential predicaments was achieved to no small degree under Nietzsche's auspices. However, at the beginning of this process, individualistic tendencies were perceived as a cardinal danger looming from within. Hence even writers sympathetic to Berdichevski and to Nietzsche, could not accept this ramification of their thought.[17]

The tendency to cleanse Nietzsche from Berdichevski's work and life or to minimize Nietzsche's impact on him became even more pronounced during the Nazi regime and after the Second World War. Nietzsche was misused by the Nazis, who proclaimed him their spiritual *Führer*. Of course, the impact of such misinterpretations following the Holocaust shed a negative light on the reception of Nietzsche (and hence also of Berdichevski) by Zionist intellectuals and leaders. Consequently, Nietzsche was again portrayed through Nordau's distorted prism as a philosopher who rejected any kind of ethics: "Berdichevski, despite the fact that he embraced Nietzsche's solution for the problems of the modern man . . . could not draw the conclusion about 'a society without any moral restraints' where the 'blond beast' roams freely."[18]

From the postwar perspective of Zionists and literary critics who had settled in Israel, it was imperative to cleanse the influential first modern Hebrew writer from "Nietzsche's complex that had almost completely won him over," so much so that "his uttermost secret wish was to become a Hebrew Nietzsche."[19] However, as more time has passed since the Holocaust, more balanced accounts of Berdichevski's Nietzscheanism have been offered.[20] One of these commentators claims in reference to Berdichevski that "Nietzscheism as such did not conquer Jewish or Zionist life. There never was a 'pure' Hebrew Nietzscheism."[21] This, of course, is true. No Hebrew writer or Zionist leader from Eastern Europe could become a "pure Nietzschean" since they were deeply rooted within the history and tradition of their people. The crux of the matter, however, is the question of what exactly is meant by the term "pure" or "true" Nietzschean."

BERDICHEVSKI COULD NEVER BECOME A "PURE" NIETZSCHEAN

Everyone has his own Nietzsche in mind: there has never been a unanimous agreement as to who is the true Nietzsche. There is no canonical, authoritative Nietzsche, and being Nietzschean is, first of all, to acknowledge this very fact. However, if we take a "pure" Nietzschean to be a thinker who urges us to overcome our entire cultural upbringing and historical roots and to exist, as it were, in an ahistorical vacuum, then it goes without saying that no Zionist activist or writer who aspired to revive the glory of the ancient Hebrews in *Eretz Israel* could embrace such a Nietzscheanism. Neither could Berdichevski, a Hebrew writer who was deeply rooted and profoundly versed in the antiquarian tradition of his people. The reborn "innocent child," to borrow Nietzsche's metaphor, is in the case of Berdichevski (and other early Zionists and modern Hebrew writers) four thousand years old!

Jews in the Diaspora had no external history, no statehood; hence, as perceptively noted by Nietzsche, they suffered from "a complete lack of real aims, of real tasks. . . . The state took this work from their shoulders: these impudent people nonetheless behaved as if they had no need of the state" (*WP* 197). They did not need a state of their own because they lived within their own immanent religious sphere and, being contented with their ancestral lore, did not come forward to act within external history. Consequently, they did not instigate any processes that might or would significantly shape and alter their present. Berdichevski and his followers wished to change this state of affairs. His passionate appeals to his people to enter onto the stage of a mundane and external history were directed from within (unlike his Central European marginal brothers such as Herzl and Nordau). He urged his people to proceed from their books to life, to transcend the oppressive walls of their "Old Ghettoes," and to live and experience the here and now. He called upon them to reactivate and revitalize their dormant senses.

It should be clear, however, that he did not wish to completely abolish Jewish history, but to transform it. By "reevaluating" Jewish values he aspired to incite a shift from learning and memorizing to doing and experiencing. Thus for him, it was not a question of living without history in a suprahistorically suspended mode, as it were, but living within the framework of a monumental history. For him it was not a question of an absolute transfiguration and radical overcoming of oneself but a shift of emphases and values. More vitality and less historicity was his call to his brothers who

were, according to his opinion, slaves of their exclusively antiquarian consciousness and identities. Berdichevski's "lion" did not arrogantly rear and
roar, but was a sad and weeping lion who could not live solely within his
painful past nor live altogether without his past. In this sense, neither Berdichevski nor any of the other Zionist writers and leaders were "pure" or
"true" Nietzscheans.

For a modern Jew and an aspiring "new Hebrew" like Berdichevski, to
become an effective and creative agent of the Zionist enterprise he had to
overcome his traditional Talmudic patterns of learning, which could not
be incorporated within cultural and secular Zionism. The Zionist revolution demanded that the Jew overcome his antiquarian-rabbinic consciousness, around which he had structured his passive and mostly reactive
Jewish identity in the Diaspora, and instead adopt a more vitalistic and
"monumental" approach centering around the grandeur of his glorious
days in ancient Israel. This incitement to "monumental history" is expressed in Nietzsche's essay "On the Uses and Disadvantages of History for
Life," in which he asserts that "monumental" historical consciousness
lends support to the creative and powerful individuals who aspire to greatness by showing them that "the greatness that once existed was in any event
once *possible* and may thus be possible again" (*HL*, p. 69). Ambitious people are encouraged to reject any gnawing uncertainties and to pursue the
path of glory and creation.

This message attracted Berdichevski to Nietzsche's essay on history,
where he discusses the organic growth of life and character formation:
every process of growth and development contains a component that with-
ers and falls, to be replaced by a new element more suited to its task. In
this light, Nietzsche regards the historical and memorializing Apollonian
consciousness as life-preserving and the nonhistorical and forgetful Dionysian consciousness as life-enhancing. Thus he declares: "The unhistori-
cal and the historical are necessary in equal measure for the health of an
individual, of a people and of a culture" (*HL*, p. 63).

Within this wide spectrum between an attitude of complete nonhistory
(personified by the ideal *Übermensch*) and one of everything-is-history (as
manifested by the antiquarian consciousness of the "Old Ghetto"), we have
to look for Berdichevski's position. Nietzsche functioned for Berdichevski
as a kind of magnet that moved him to the vital pole. But Berdichevski's
life-affirming attitude was definitely his own even without Nietzsche's influence. Life is stronger than any opinion, eloquent and enticing as it may
be, put forward in some philosophy or expressed by some philosopher.
Thus Nietzsche could at most serve as a monumental catalyst and a kind

of Socratic-vitalizing gadfly that encouraged Berdichevski's hopes and legitimized his thirst for life. This thirst is vividly presented in his semiauto-biographical stories "From My Old Town,"[22] where Berdichevski empha-sized the vitality of the everyday life of the shtetl. Though these erotic and thirst-for-life components were manifested in a rather inhibited and timid way, they nonetheless could not be completely repressed and obliterated by the historical components. And since life-affirming values were inher-ent even within the walls of the "Old Ghetto," Berdichevski wished to re-vive them among his people, on their march to Zion.

This cry for a revitalization of these latent values and elements was strongly encouraged by Nietzsche. It would be pronounced by Berdi-chevski, though perhaps with a lesser intensity and tenacity, even if he had not been so strongly attracted to Nietzsche. The Jewish boy from the shtetl was greatly interested in the present and future of his people and con-tributed significantly to their culture. Thus, even had he seriously tried, he could not have attained a complete transfiguration of his nature. Neither could he have completely assimilated into the general gentile world.

Nonetheless, there are few who were (and are) critical of Nietzsche's im-pact on Berdichevski. On the one hand, most of these critics overestimated Nietzsche's influence on Berdichevski and, being strongly prejudiced against him, grossly misjudged its nature. But on the other, some of them adhered to the viewpoint that Jewish history is an entirely internal process of the Jewish people, who evolved solely due to their own dynamics and in-herent forces. For these critics, Nietzsche was only a passing episode involv-ing inconsequential external factors, and his role was utterly insignificant for Berdichevski's internal development. When we explicate Nietzsche's presence in Berdichevski's life and thought, we will see how far from the truth was this opinion. However, one can sympathize with their reasons for holding this view. A nation in the midst of perilous and frequently painful processes of redefining its own history, identity, and future (even today) is very much on its guard against any external sources of influence, which might undermine its stamina and its cultural autonomy—especially a na-tion countless of whose members immersed themselves deeply in the self-alienating processes of assimilation, self-hatred, and conversion. Nietzsche, the epitome of a foreign culture, a God slayer, a herald of modern secu-larization, was perceived as a potential threat to the inner cohesiveness and the future prospects of the Jewish people qua people. Hence, any voice that deviated from the shared consensus and accepted ethos—and such was the voice of Berdichevski—had to be suppressed. Yet we should recall that nei-ther Berdichevski nor his followers were living in a cultural vacuum, hermetically sealed from the winds of change that were so strongly blowing outside the ghetto's walls. Thus it would be wrong to ignore the positive impact Nietzsche might have on all the sensitive Jewish intellectuals who were not satisfied to limit their horizons only to their own holy writings and libraries.

Be that as it may, both critics and supporters of Berdichevski's Nietzscheanism enlisted Nietzsche in the heated disputes over the image of the new Hebrew culture. Consequently, they cannot assist us much in attaining balanced opinion on the exact nature of Berdichevski's relation to Nietzsche. We can arrive at a clearer understanding of this only after a diachronic exposition of Berdichevski's published as well as unpublished writings. However, we should note that one of the main obstacles for anyone who aspires to trace objectively Nietzsche's presence in Berdichevski's writings is the fact that during the period 1919–21, Berdichevski altered many of his essays and stories in the course of preparing an edition of his collected works.[23] Some of these changes included the removal of direct, sometimes quite extensive quotations from Nietzsche's works. Clearly, one of the reasons for this self-censorship was the unbridled attacks on Berdichevski's Nietzscheanism that, as we have seen, became the main means of discrediting the significance of his attempts to inspire a far-reaching reevaluation of Hebrew culture. By reducing Nietzsche's presence in his works, Berdichevski wished to overcome one of the main obstacles to his reception within the Zionist movement and the wider Jewish community.

Besides this censorship of Nietzsche, Berdichevski also suppressed many traces of his "torn heart." He now wanted to present himself before his readers as a mature and harmonious individual with a consistent and well-developed worldview. But the period of his earlier existential wondering and wanderings had been the most conducive to Nietzsche's impact on his life and work. Consequently, in order to gain an uncensored view of Nietzsche's presence in Berdichevski's writings, one has to analyze these as they appeared for the first time. All the same, Berdichevski's self-imposed censorship can be seen to have worked two ways. Those parts of his writings that were recognized by him as the official narrative of his intellectual-literary development can more validly attest to Nietzsche's impact on Berdichevski, especially those parts where Nietzsche's notions and slogans, or even direct quotations and paraphrases from his writings, remained intact.

Now, however, it will perhaps be worthwhile to offer a working definition of "Nietzscheanism." For my purposes here, a "Nietzschean" is simply one who at some point in his creative life admitted to having been influenced one way or another by Nietzsche and sought to give this influence some concrete expression in his oeuvre. Can we find any reaction by Berdichevski to the accusations or praises of his critics for his debt to Nietzsche? What does the accused himself have to say in reply to these charges or compliments?

BERDICHEVSKI ON HIS RELATIONSHIP TO NIETZSCHE

Berdichevski's first public explanation of his attitude to Nietzsche is found in his essay "On the High Road" of July 1898, where he responded to Ahad Ha'am's critique in *Ha-Shilo'ah* against the "Hebrew Nietzscheans," namely, Berdichevski.[24] Despite the apologetic tone, Berdichevski was far from denying his close affinity to Nietzsche and even called him "Rabbi," which in the Jewish tradition has the well-known connotation of a distinguished teacher and a spiritual guide. After referring his readers to his essay of July 1896 (quoted in the epigraph to this chapter), which adopts Nietzsche's slogan as its motto, Berdichevski once again repeats the slogan: "Our father in heaven knows that our hands and heart are clean. He knows how sadly we listen to our inner voice: *if a temple is to be erected a temple must be destroyed.*" Before that quotation he asserts: "You threaten us with the god of Zarathustra who in your eyes is a heresy against the God of Israel—but we say: better the god of Zarathustra than the god of Bernfeld" (an allusion to that critic's attack analyzed above and to the theological aspect of Bernfeld's attitude).

In this essay Berdichevski admits that his lifelong project of mending his "torn heart" and attaining a harmonious and authentic selfhood dated from the very beginning of his existential and intellectual journey. Nietzsche and other external influences only accelerated, consolidated, and finalized Berdichevski's journey. Such a journey is instigated in the majority of cases by personal predicaments and by the heart's strivings and longings, but during its stormy wanderings it needs reliable signposts. And thus Berdichevski used Nietzsche to arrive safely, by way of the "High Road," at the final goal. Therefore, according to Berdichevski's own admission, Nietzsche's impact on his life and thought was quite significant.

Berdichevski gave another account of his relationship to Nietzsche in his diary. There he refers to his objective of attaining an authentic selfhood within and not beyond the cultural, historical, and national borders of his people:

As long as I climbed on the steps of Jewish Romanticism, Historicism and Ahad Ha'am . . . I was not my own self and was dragged along by others. Now, I began to think my own thoughts. . . . My general-human viewpoint strengthened my attitude toward Jewish issues, but it never was their origin, as some wrongly claimed it to be. I did not emerge from Nietzsche's doctrine, but approached and met it on the way, in the course of reevaluation of values when I was getting away from Judaism and experiencing the damage that this kind of morality caused Jewish people as people. A proof of the independence of my attitude on the Jewish issues was the fact that even after the complete change in my philosophical worldview. . . . I did not abandon my Jewish position on the secular resurrection. . . . If Zionism will fall, the Jews in the Diaspora will approach their complete annihilation.[25]

To defend himself against the charge that he was merely an imitation of Nietzsche, Berdichevski used the argument that despite his inclination to this philosopher, whom he "met on the way," he remained a secular Zionist, namely within his own people's frame of reference, aspirations, and history. Nonetheless, this minimization of Nietzsche's relevance to his thought was not barren of results, because to meet somebody in the middle of one's life journey means that both are walking on common ground, and though they may depart from each other at a certain stage, the interaction between them can prove to be quite vital to the younger and less experienced man.

And indeed it was, as Berdichevski's letters to his friends during his stay in Bern (October 1894–July 1895) attest. In that period, away from his various opponents, Berdichevski wrote his Ph.D. dissertation in philosophy. At that time, he was less reluctant to define himself without any hesitations as a "Nietzschean." In a letter from that period he confesses: "Perhaps you have already figured out that *I am a Nietzschean*; a man who is skeptical about most of the world's minds, and according to whom only a heroic act and power are the real driving forces."[26]

His first discovery of Nietzsche, however, took place in Berlin, in the summer of 1893: "This summer I read a lot of Friedrich Nietzchi [*sic*, in broken Hebrew it means "my Nietzsche"]. This is the man who shatters worlds all over Europe. Perhaps you can obtain his book *On the Genealogy of Morals*. Since I first arrived at the age of reason, no other book left such an everlasting impression on me as this one—he is now in a madhouse."[27] Like Herzl, Berdichevski was not deterred by the fact that, at the time of his first encounter with Nietzsche, the philosopher was already insane. But by no means was it solely a fleeting love affair. Berdichevski continued to read Nietzsche throughout the rest of the 1890s.[28] His correspondence frequently expresses his deepest attachment to Nietzsche, to the extent that it sometimes seems he wants to become the philosopher's alter ego at the expense of his own identity.[29]

PRE-DISSERTATION ESSAYS

The first time Berdichevski mentions Nietzsche is in an essay from 1894, "To Be or Not to Be."[30] From this first public reference to Nietzsche we can gain insight into one of the main functions that the philosopher fulfilled in Berdichevski's life, namely, the reduction of the tension he felt between his longing for the "Old Ghetto" heritage of his father and his attraction to the universal European values of the Enlightenment:

> Everybody whose feelings have not been blunted can sense the vigorous new stirring in European life, the end of which nobody can figure out. Friedrich Nietzsche was in his books the means of expressing this overwhelming stirring which is depicted in his philosophy and his aphorisms in all its vigor and might. Nietzsche's writings, with all their estrangement from the prevailing spirit of Western Europe, will find their way to people's hearts. This new, ever expanding spirit that emerged from Nietzsche's school and his followers will shatter the fundaments of culture. It strives to create for man new conceptions and wishes to make him into a creature that carries itself without requiring assistance and help from any tricks and artificial feelings.[31] (p. 148)

The universal Enlightenment was threatening to swallow up the intellectual Eastern European Jews with its demands that members of "the chosen people will kneel before [the European] teachers since they have the key for life and culture" (p. 147). Nordau, as we have seen, initially worshiped this ethos of the Enlightenment, and for that reason attacked Nietzsche, whom he conceived as the archenemy of that worldview. Berdichevski, however, who had escaped from the "Old Ghetto" and had also fallen under the spell of the West, wanted to extract himself from its hold since it deepened to an unbearable measure the rent in his heart. To alleviate this tension he required Nietzsche's radical stance against the prevailing "decadent" European culture. On the other hand, he also used Nietzsche to reduce his longing for the antiquarian Jewish consciousness that suffered from overspiritualization, fossilization, and excessive emphasis on the holy Book. From both these directions, Nietzsche inspired Berdichevski to reduce the existential dissonance in his heart.

Berdichevski's criticism of enlightened Western Europe in his essay echoes several Nietzschean ideas. In particular it echoes the Nietzschean ideal of personal authenticity and his key thesis in the essay "On the Uses and Disadvantages of History for Life," which undoubtedly was before Berdichevski's eyes when he wrote this piece in 1894. Nietzsche claimed there that the criteria for an authentic

> *plastic power* of a man, a people, a culture is [their] capacity to develop out of oneself in one's own way, to transform and incorporate into oneself what is past and foreign, to heal wounds, to replace what has been lost, to recreate broken moulds. . . . The stronger the innermost roots of man's nature, the more readily will he be able to assimilate and appropriate the things of the past; the most powerful and tremendous nature would be characterized by the fact that it would know no boundary at all at which the historical sense began to overwhelm it; it would draw to itself and incorporate into itself all the past, its own and that most foreign to it, and as it were transform it into blood. (*HL*, pp. 62–63)

Berdichevski adopts these criteria and uses them to test the authenticity of his people as well as his own sentiments that were fluctuating between "West" (the European enlightenment) and "East" (his "Old Ghetto," and, more widely, the cradle and origin of his own people). Thus he asserts: "Any people and folk that possesses a genuine selfhood finds it hard to delineate borders between its own soul and the spiritual culture of the West. . . . But for us, the Hebrews, the question of establishing the borders and differentiating the realms is of specially urgent concern since our religious and national nature is the very flesh and blood of our life and the fundament of our being, as a people who live for themselves" ("To Be or Not to Be," pp. 148–49). Even for a nation settled on its own land whose destiny "lies in its own hands," natural progress will halt and its spirit will be "endangered" once it "will change its modes of life and will accept from a foreign culture its influence and stance" (p. 149). It is true, Berdichevski continues, that Jews incorporated into their own frame of references the spirit and culture of ancient peoples, such as the Egyptians and the Greeks, as well as modern science in the Renaissance, but all these external influences "could not destroy Israel's selfhood and weaken its internal power since they did not penetrate into its internal veins and nerves and did not interfere with its daily life."[32] Nowadays, however, the danger looms that the spirit of the West, namely the Enlightenment, which makes each one of us "to kneel before its idols," will cause our obliteration from the "face of the earth" (ibid.). Clearly, Berdichevski does not refer here solely to the future of the Jewish people in general, but also to his own predicament. This is corroborated by the fact that at the end of this essay, he uses a confessional tone and admits that he too "was strongly attracted towards this mighty movement to the point that my entire world was drastically changed and all my views and feelings were abolished and my heart was emptied of all its spiritual treasures" (p. 150). This "intoxication" with the Enlightenment provoked him to fight an internal "war which drained all my power" (ibid.). Evidently, Berdichevski prefers a torn heart engaged in internal struggle to an "empty heart" devoid of any roots and sense of belonging to his own people. He thus mentions his father's strong longings "for the East and for Jerusalem, the holy city" while he is preoccupied with the "West" (ibid.).

He is confronted now with an urgent existential dilemma: either "to disperse among the nations" or to remain a Hebrew, even if the cost he has to pay for that will be his torn heart. Nietzsche, by means of his devastating attack on European contemporary culture, helps Berdichevski to retain his own self, with deep roots in the heritage of his own people, despite several misgivings. Through Nietzschean eyes, Berdichevski perceives that the prevailing culture of the West causes people to "deviate from nature's ways into distorted and corrupted tastes and lives . . . estranging them from their own selfhood" (p. 147), and removes them from their authentic modes of living. This authenticity is unique to each individual according to one's own nature and capacities, and the history and destiny of one's own people. Berdichevski delineates an illegitimate parallelism between the genuine essence of a whole people and the personal authenticity of its individual members.[33] He claims that just as the perfection of a nation is attained according to its own historical circumstances, so it is with each individual.

The internal strife in Berdichevski's heart between the West and the East continues, and he attempts to reduce his attraction to the values of the Enlightenment by stating that "perfection, knowledge, beauty, the spirit of the West" are but empty names since they are adopted by only a few individuals, whereas the European masses are still mostly dedicated to their pre-Enlightenment traditions. The antiquarian consciousness also prevails in European culture, where thousands of interpretations of interpretations are written and most of scholarship has nothing to do "with nature or with life" (p. 145).

Berdichevski realizes that he cannot return to his father's "Old Ghetto" and that neither can he entirely assimilate into the Western Enlightenment by breaking off all ties with his heritage. The only way out of this syndrome of a torn heart is to accept it in *amor fati* fashion, prescribed by Nietzsche for all "free spirits" who cannot overcome certain pervasive and inevitable features of their destiny and character.

This solution, already implied in "To Be or Not to Be," is proclaimed even more clearly in an essay written later in the same year under the title "Not to Be and to Be." In this existentialist essay, Berdichevski announces that all metaphysical questions are irrelevant to his life and that the only question that bothers him deeply is "What am I? What are the roots of my power?"[34] He virtually employs Nietzschean maxims for authentic life, namely, that one becomes what one is by ceasing to be what one is not— neither the citizen of Western culture nor the Orthodox Jew of the old ghetto. Thus he decides to live in the permanent tension of the genuine "free spirit" who accepts himself as a torn individual and who cannot but remain torn within his innermost self. It is highly probable that the main reason that moved Berdichevski toward this existential solution was not necessarily the famous saying of Rabbi Nahman of Braslav that "Nothing is more complete than a broken heart," but his sober realization that even Nietzsche could not assist him in freeing himself entirely from the rent in his heart. On the contrary, he even widens that rent. When he uses Nietzsche's critique against the spirit of the Enlightenment in order to reduce the intensity of his attraction toward the West, he actually uses one of the most influential representatives of the contemporary Western culture. The more he tries to free himself from his existential dilemma with Nietzsche's help, the more deeply he entangles himself within its embraces. Thus the only solution out of this existential cul-de-sac is the acceptance of his inevitable "rent."

At this point we should ask whether Berdichevski's criticism of the Enlightenment was first elicited by Nietzsche's writings, and whether he really needed Nietzsche in order to feel unable to go on living within the walls of the "Old Ghetto."

A hint at the answer to this last question is given in "To Be or not to Be," where, referring to his days in the yeshiva in Volozhin, he asserts: "I was then quite discontented. The other spirit that possessed me took me away from the tents of Shem. It transferred me from my tiny narrow world and brought me to a wider and larger world with my heart full of new thoughts" (p. 140). If we also recall the young Berdichevski's reading of "external" literature, namely secular books that had little to do with Talmudic lore,

and losing wife and home as a result, then it is clear that several years before his readings of Nietzsche, he went astray from his father's tradition
like many other young, inquisitive Jewish intellectuals who could not remain within what they saw as the oppressive confinement of that tradition.

Moreover, it stands to reason that Berdichevski's critical attitude toward
the contemporary culture of the West, where he tried to relocate and redefine his new identity, was not initially inspired by Nietzsche. In 1891, he
wrote a confessional piece, "Light and Shadows."[35] In these "sporadic
memories" (the subtitle of the essay), he repents for moving over to the
"West" and for being enchanted by the dubious charms and artificial
"light" of the European Enlightenment. He confesses that "the land in the
West was in my eyes heaven, the salt of the earth; it was for me my God, my
spirit, my soul. . . . My father was dejected and wretched and longed for the
land in the East, for Jerusalem, whereas my heart was incessantly preoccupied with the West. A tremendous gap spanned between us" (p. 19). Unlike certain Central European marginal Jews who were born in the West
and contributed significantly to its cultural life while seeking to realize the
Nietzschean vision of "a new, united Europe," Berdichevski longed to become an equal citizen in contemporary European life and tried to savor its
universal values. He could perhaps have withstood the rent between himself and his father if those values had indeed been satisfying and precious,
and if the light of the Enlightenment had not become blurred by its "shadows." However, Berdichevski quickly realized that the "life in the West
glow[s] and shine[s] with beauty, but from below—a shoal of decadence
was building up" (p. 20). In almost the same terms as Nordau, he describes
the petty materialism, the unrestrained egotism, and the wild hedonism
that morally corrupt people. Genuine "romanticism" can be found solely
in literature but not between living human beings. Like Rousseau, who after arriving in Paris criticized its ennui, decadence, and follies, so too
Berdichevski condemned fin de siècle European "enlightened" culture,
where there was no place for any authentic and "natural moral laws"
(p. 21). The West "becomes too old" and nihilistic, and thus Berdichevski
longs for the genuine Enlightenment of the seventeenth and eighteenth
centuries, the days of "hopes and dreams" (ibid.). Observing the "shadows" of the contemporary West, he rediscovers the "light" of his own heritage and the genuine values of his people "where there is nothing but
spirit" (p. 23). Now, however, it is too late to return home; hence Berdichevski embraces the *amor fati* attitude and the inner contradictions within
his heart.

He makes these contradictions into a blessing, stating in a Nietzschean

vein: "Anything that includes many contradictions becomes more powerful and heroic" (p. 23). He goes on to claim, alongside Nietzsche's dictum
that "what does not destroy me—makes me stronger," that "so many contradictions and obstacles were greatly beneficial for my edification and improvement" (ibid.).

Nietzsche had already emphasized in many passages the constructive
power of contradiction. Witness, for example, his sayings: "Only out of
chaos a star is born" and "the ability to contradict . . . constituted what is
really great, new, and amazing in our culture; this is the step of steps of the
liberated spirit" (*GS* 297). Berdichevski echoes these sentiments in his diaries from 1905–7: "Nothing sustains the human spirit more than contradiction."[36] He expresses his admiration for Nietzsche's contradictions in a
witty aphorism: "The greatness of Nietzsche lies in the fact that he always
contradicts himself; mostly with good reason."[37] Berdichevski accepts at
this stage in an *amor fati* fashion not solely the contradictions inherent in
his heart but also his sufferings resulting from his insatiate longings, and
more precisely his existential sufferings that had their origin in his feelings
of deep estrangement from both "the East" and "the West."

More significant evidence for Nietzsche's presence in Berdichevski's
mind before 1894 are found in his first serious polemical essay, dating
from 1892, where several Nietzschean motives are presented. This the-
matically rich composition, written in an impressionistic, personal, Nietzschean style, did not aim at a systematic exposition. Its name suggests the
burning issue with which the young Berdichevski was preoccupied while
studying philosophy in Breslau: "Reshut hayahid be'ad harabim" ("The
Authority of the One for the Sake of the Many").[38] The German title,
which appears alongside the Hebrew one on the first page of this pamphlet
is *Die Ansichten eines Einzelnen über das Allgemeine*.[39] However, the Hebrew
title suggests also the authority of the individual vis-à-vis the community,
and reminds us of Nordau's essay of 1900, "Individualismus, Solidarismus." In opposition to Nordau, who emphasized the supremacy of the collective solidarity and attempted to incorporate Nietzsche's individualism
into the framework of a society (Zionist or otherwise), Berdichevski puts
"(the many [*harabim*])" in parentheses in the pamphlet edition, while in
all the other editions, "the many" is written in much smaller letters than
"the one." This is not a sheer caprice but a graphic way to emphasize the
main theme of the essay, the primacy of the concerns of the individual Jew
over the interests of the collective, namely of the Jewish people.

With Nietzschean moralistic pathos he introduces his own reevaluation
of values and argues against the importance of "charity," which stood at the

basis of various Zionist activities. According to Berdichevski in a letter to a friend, Nietzsche's *Genealogy of Morals* impressed him profoundly and he held it in high esteem.[40] Thus it is not surprising that he implicitly presents in this essay the Nietzschean dichotomy between the "morality of the slaves" and the "morality of the herd." He claims, like Nietzsche in regard to pity [*Mitleid*], that "charity is morally detrimental . . . bringing the recipient to the loathsome state of a slave, to a contemptible kneeling on one's knees" (p. 51), to a passive situation whereby the giver has mastery over the receiver. Berdichevski praises the inner freedom and the pride of "the superior man who stands on his own feet" (p. 52) and shuns any charity, which is "the origin of every sin and a poison for heart and spirit" (ibid.). Following this "beyond good and evil" argument against the shameful consequences of charity and pity, Berdichevski proclaims the right of the individual to his "own private world, which is in our eyes rich and plentiful and we do not wish to see it dilapidated" (p. 52). Many kinds of Zionist movements before Herzl, like *Hibbat Zion*, and most of the social fabric of the shtetls, were centered around various philanthropic activities, and this young rebel cry against the demoralizing effects of such activities was a radical and quite courageous act. Berdichevski understood this well and expressed his fear of being swept away by the storm he had unleashed. Nonetheless, his moral zeal and pride brought him to voice in public, "the opinions of the individual for the sake of other individuals" and for the sake of the whole Jewish people, whose "salvation will not be achieved by charity" (p. 53). Neither will the Jews be saved by emigration to America, which will solely secure them a negative freedom, freedom from persecutions and economical misery, but will not grant them the positive freedom of cultivating their own selves alongside their own history, culture, and literature. Once they tear themselves from this rich cultural-historical fabric they will lose their own "selfhood" (p. 55). Berdichevski's radicalism here is confined by his more conservative insight about the "spiritual danger" looming over a "freedom which comes suddenly on a person and is not the consequence of a progressive cultivation and of slow transformation, and which will bring in its wake only a terrible void" (p. 55). Nietzsche, who warned Paneth against the dangers that free spirits might bring on themselves and on their surroundings, could not have agreed more. In any case, Berdichevski turns now to present his views on current Hebrew literature and tries to reintegrate himself within the antiquarian tradition of "the many," of his Jewish ancestors and colleagues.

The despised status of Jews in Europe brought them "close to the literature of Israel" (p. 55). However, the poor standards of this secular Hebrew literature, the fact that it was written by "boys" and was scattered among rival journals and publishers, made it utterly irrelevant to the current life of its few potential readers. Lacking the support of any cohesive public opinion, it was unable to provide a decent living for its "idealistic writers' (p. 78). Hence it became heavily dependent upon charity and philanthropy. All this brought the rather gloomy result that "we have no literature and no writers but only different books and persons who are writing in Hebrew mainly for themselves alone" (p. 79). At this point Berdichevski refers to an incident in which one of "our famous writers met Georg Brandes and presented himself as a Hebrew writer. 'Are you kidding me?' asked Brandes. 'How can you be a Hebrew writer if there is no Hebrew literature?'" (pp. 77–78).

Foreseeing his future dispute with Ahad Ha'am, Berdichevski claims that contemporary Hebrew literature is irrelevant to the present miserable existential conditions of young acculturated Jewish intellectuals. It completely ignores the rent in the hearts of these young, bright students who, coming to the West from Eastern European shtetls, are enchanted by its culture. Current Hebrew literature does not face up to the existential rift within Berdichevski and his young friends in Berlin.

Berdichevski then claims that what lies at bottom of the present gloomy situation of Hebrew life and letters is lack of genuine educators and exemplary figures who can rise above the sordid conditions and guide the masses toward spiritual cultivation of their own selves. Like Nietzsche in his essay "Schopenhauer as Educator," he examines the influential leaders and intellectuals of contemporary Jewry in Europe and finds that they are but a "false prophets," "hypocrites," and "charlatans" (pp. 69, 72, 68).[41] He is looking for inspiring and influential moral leaders like Tolstoy (p. 61), but he is looking in vain within his own milieu for genuine leaders who "are persons of great hearts possessing great spiritual powers" (p. 69). "We need and urgently require," he asserts, "only books that will set us on fire, and will instill our vitality" (p. 85). Not being able to find such books among his own people, he turns to Nietzsche, who will help him enjoy "life within nature, vital and moving life that will not be shaded by our prayer shawls" (ibid.).

The tension that Berdichevski felt within his own heart, between the collective predicament of the Jews and the yearning to express his own individuality as a writer, manifests itself here in his call to Hebrew writers to "write for the people, for the masses, for the mob, so as to revive their spirit and revitalize their lives" (p. 88). Clearly, this attitude is a far cry from Nietzsche's aloof, aristocratic, and radical individualism, epitomized by the subtitle of *Thus Spoke Zarathustra*: "A Book for All and None." Still, Berdichevski propagates an original Hebrew literature rooted in the genuine soul of the people and in their unique history.

However, during his Berlin years and while writing his dissertation in philosophy at the University of Bern (1894–95), Berdichevski was deeply immersed in the "tents of Japhet" and enjoyed their "beauty." His Hebrew identity was somewhat suppressed by the overpowering general culture. These years were the time when his struggle for personal authenticity reached its peak and his commitment to the people of Israel and to their antiquarian sources was gravely tested. He vividly expresses the rent in his heart in occasional essays and other pieces where he vacillates between his people and Europe, between the antiquarian and the monumental historical consciousness, between "Book" and "life." But he knows only one thing: "I am human but my humanity will not be enough." He must "cross the border" since he finds himself imprisoned in existential "pincers." He cannot tell "the way and the object of his searching," but he knows only that "I am called away to another world from my selfhood, from my innermost 'I.'"[42] Employing Isaiah Berlin's well-known distinction between the fox (who knows many things) and the hedgehog (who knows only one great thing),[43] one may describe Berdichevski at this stage as the monumental hedgehog engaged in a fateful internal struggle with the antiquarian fox, deeply buried within his own consciousness. The only thing that the hedgehog knows is that a thin "line is drawn between the 'I' and the 'non-I'" and that he is "crossing that line." In other words, the only thing that Berdichevski is sure of is that he is looking to affirm his divided selfhood, and the only certain thing is the torments he experiences and the only definite thing is the quest, the search itself. Since there is no possibility for a reconciliation or a synthesis between the culture of the shtetl and the European general culture, one has to embrace this rent in the heart and to work within its contradictions.

Berdichevski, unlike Nietzsche and other existentialist thinkers, never wrote a philosophical exposition of his search for authenticity. Being first of all a writer of fiction and a faithful recorder of the life of his soul, he depicts his own innermost pathos of such a search. This accords well with the principal aim of philosophical writers on authenticity, which was to evoke in their readers the hunger for authenticity. They hoped to restore a personal mental power and sense of harmonious selfhood that modernity had diminished. Thus they used fiction to portray the sublime and heroic patterns of authentic life. They experimented with such literary styles as short stories, novels, plays, poems, aphoristic essays, fictitious diaries, biographies, and even autobiographies. This is by no means a coincidence. The variety of literary styles that can be utilized indicates that there is no one exclusive and definitive path to authenticity—to be authentic means to invent one's own way of life. Here the concept of originality does not refer so much to the idea of origin as to undogmatic openness, or, to use Nietzsche's terminology, to a "horizon of infinite perspectives" from within which the individual can survey his or her own life and mold it accordingly. Open-ended experiments with possible world-perspectives and literary styles are intended to serve as practical examples. The construction of possible worlds frees literature, especially that of the narrative variety, from strictly realistic or referential constraints. This freedom allows for experimentation with notions, such as that of authenticity, that go beyond the conventional dichotomies of true/false, sincere/insincere, honest/dishonest, and good/evil. Only literature can produce and diffuse new senses so effectively. The existential predicaments and pathos of authenticity that cannot be expressed in propositions still leave room for indirect communication: not of a "what" but of a "how." By varying styles and rhetoric we are invited to embrace authenticity, though not any particular content, for authentic expressions of self are in principle indefinite and infinite. Moreover, the writers of authenticity change their genres and styles to stress the fact that certain kinds of pathos originate within themselves. The variety of their styles is yet another expression of the revolt against the tradition of impersonal and detached objectivity, a constant reminder that we are reading their writings, the personal products of their own values and goals.[44]

Berdichevski is an illuminating Hebrew example of these features. He used different literary styles, among them novels, short stories, contemplative pieces, and philosophical essays. However, instead of presenting to his readers fictive literary heroes who were immersed in a search for personal authenticity, like Nietzsche's Zarathustra, he portrays himself as that hero, and most of his essays are predominantly autobiographical. In this way he provides us with a personal account written mostly in the first person, where his intuitions regarding his agonizing search for a harmonious self are vividly portrayed: "I am torn in my essence, am faltering in my very being. . . . I am ascending to heaven, descending to hell in order to find the substance in itself . . . and God's voice is no more there as if he has left."[45] Instead of "God's voice," there gradually appears the voice of Nietzsche, with his atheistic sentiments and the grief of an orphan who has been abandoned by his divine father. And indeed, Berdichevski does not describe, like the more militant and direct Nietzsche, "the murder of God," nor does he portray himself as God's "slayer." Instead, he provides a more passive description of his gradual secularization, so that one's impression is not that he has forsaken God but that God has forsaken him.

In any case, it is not improbable that when Berdichevski became more acquainted with Nietzsche's writings during these years and more philosophically oriented during the writing of his dissertation, he used a more philosophical language to describe the existential search for a solid, harmonious, and authentic self. Thus Nietzsche's writings, at least at this stage, provided Berdichevski with the language, idioms, and metaphors to express what Nietzsche had experienced and expressed so vividly a couple of years earlier. In another piece, written at the end of 1894 and subtitled "A Little Philosophy" (a subtitle that was removed by Berdichevski in subsequent editions), he asks himself the classical question of authenticity: "Who am I, who is the 'I' in my Self alone, without the layers and forms, qualities and dispositions that one acquires through the circumstances in which one is presently situated?"[46] He does not attempt to provide a personal answer to this existential question but instead gives us an "indirect communication" (as it was called by Kierkegaard), and produces a revised version of a story by the Yiddish romantic writer Isaac Loeb Peretz, "The Lazy Madman." This madman is an "inquisitive" person who asks himself one of the most fundamental questions regarding authenticity. This query, which has to do with the validity of introspection, is introduced by Nietzsche: "How can man know himself? He is a thing dark and veiled; and if the hare has seven skins, man can slough off seventy times seven and still not be able to say: 'this is really you, this is no longer the outer shell'" (SE, p. 129). To this problem of the defensive mechanisms of the soul that resists any knowledge of the self by the direct method of introspection, Berdichevski adds his own peculiar handicap of being a torn personality with a self deeply divided between the call of nature and vital instincts and the call of his forefathers to attend the antiquarian learning in "the corner of the *beith midrash*" (study house).[47] By the end of this piece it seems that the existential question regarding Berdichevski's own authenticity has become a rhetorical question without any definite answer. No objective and universal identity can help in answering questions about personal authenticity, as those questions evade any objectively valid answers. Language cannot help solving this question but can solely depict the circumstances which gave rise to its emergence and the agonizing existential conditions of a person who is struggling in vain to answer it. This is what Berdichevski does in this semifictional story.

It is noteworthy that once again the figure of the "madman" appears in this piece. The very fact that this figure, symbolizing the loss of sanity as a consequence of the loss of a substantial Self shaped by the belief in God, reappears so frequently in Berdichevski's most Nietzschean pieces gives some credibility to the speculation that Berdichevski was inspired here more by Nietzsche than by Peretz. In any case, the only answer that Berdichevski can provide to the question "Who am I?" at this stage is a tautological one: "I am what I am,"[48] (p. 166), meaning that I am the very entity which asks the question about its own authenticity; I am the questioning and the question; the rent in my heart and the very attempt to overcome it.

In a contemplative fragment from the end of 1894, "A Man and a Stick: A Thought," Berdichevski flatly states that "the essence of man" is to be torn between his God and his own self; it is to revolt against God and to inflict self-punishment because of such a revolt.[49] Nietzsche's ideal of authentic life includes a denial of any permanent, a priori fixed essences or definitions of human beings. We are what we are by creating ourselves and by what we are doing and thinking in our lives. This flexibility guarantees the open-ended enterprise of becoming what we are, a creative life process without any definitive end, symbolized by the very meaning of God's answer to Moses: "I am what I am." Here we find no definitive name or essence—hence the sheer dynamism of the present and the emphasis on what one is.

This indicates the biblical roots of the key moral ideal of Nietzsche's philosophy.[50] Amazingly the same line of reasoning is also introduced by Berdichevski in "A Man and a Stick," where he speaks about "the essence of man" and then refers the reader to ideas expressed in Genesis 1:26–27, concluding that God took man "to be what he is and what he becomes."[51] Thus, the very search for authenticity is seen by Berdichevski as being initiated by God himself and inspired by a divine model of ultimate, perfect, and absolute authenticity. The existential journey in search of authenticity is being conducted under the auspices of God, and hence it is legitimate and kosher. Thus, Berdichevski concurs with Nietzsche but meets him from the opposite side of the fence. If Nietzsche did indeed receive his inspiration from the same divine model so sublimely portrayed in the "Book of Books," then Nietzsche and Berdichevski are both similarly rooted in the same ideological-theistic ground of the Bible. In any case, Nietzsche's proximity to the Bible greatly facilitated Berdichevski's attraction to him and assisted Berdichevski in overcoming his hesitations about drawing his inspiration from this gentile and atheistic source.

It may even be that actually Nietzsche helped Berdichevski in looking at the holy writings through an existential prism; that is, that under Nietzsche's inspiration Berdichevski was encouraged to look in his own literary tradition, notably the Bible, for several existential motifs that were highly relevant to his own existential quest.

This is hinted at in his theoretical essay of 1894–95, "The Virtues of Our National Culture." In this programmatic essay, Berdichevski claims that in the Talmud and other holy writings there is no dichotomy between Book and life but there always has been "life" in the Book and the Book was actually written for the sake of life. The existential cardinal questions, the "riddles . . . about life and the theory of man, questions that are inspiring our life," were always there. He adds: "In the holy writings we can gain a picture of life itself, in their perfect wholeness."[52] Thus, Berdichevski projects Nietzsche's existential approach onto the holy writings, enhancing thereby our conviction that *he never was a pure Nietzschean*, but a Jewish prodigy and yeshiva boy who later underwent an intensive process of secularization. As a "new Hebrew" he was endowed with the Nietzschean sensitivities that caused him to embark upon an existential agenda of a search for meaningful life and of formation of an authentic self through the painful processes of self-overcoming and self-transfigurations.

In this short essay, Berdichevski claims that "'inscribed on the tablets' means 'dedicated to freedom'" of learning and life (ibid., p. 179). This synthesis between Nietzsche and the Bible was Berdichevski's last resort in his struggle to face and endure the rent in his heart. To accept this rent, as he must, means to stick to his heritage as well as to accommodate Nietzsche to his own version of Hebrew culture. The borderline between two cultures, between two ways of thinking and modes of experiencing, has become the natural habitat of his subsequent development. Is such a synthesis of Talmudic lore and Nietzschean existentialism viable at all? Can it succeed? Does it not require a fundamental destruction of the "old temple" in order to erect the new one? It is not in vain that in various pieces from this period, Berdichevski frequently introduces the motif of wrecking and building.[53] Can Berdichevski get some help from his studies of philosophy? Is his dissertation, written in Bern where he "was held captive by the gentiles,"[54] relevant to his existential struggles? Can we detect Nietzsche's ideas in this one and only pure philosophical work in Berdichevski's entire output?

"ON THE RELATION BETWEEN ETHICS AND AESTHETICS"

Berdichevski's dissertation is of an essentially different type of work than all his other writings. Hence we might expect that Nietzsche would be more directly present in it, especially since in these years in Bern (October 1894–February 1896), Nietzsche's impact on Berdichevski's thought (and life) reached its peak, as he confessed in an 1895 letter to a friend.[55] Surprisingly, Berdichevski refers to Nietzsche only twice in the entire treatise. Was this due to his awareness that the supervisor of his thesis, professor of philosophy and sociology Dr. Ludwig Stein (1859–1930), was ill-disposed to Nietzschean thought?

Two years before Berdichevski wrote his dissertation (1895), Stein published a book critical of Nietzsche's worldview.[56] Stein had served two years as a rabbi and, like Nordau, was an assimilated Jew from Hungary. Like Nordau, he displayed an ambivalent attitude toward Nietzsche. Like Nordau, he believed in the European Enlightenment and in Darwinian, social, and rational evolution, and hence attacked Nietzsche along the lines already set one year before in Nordau's *Degeneration*. However, being a professional and academic philosopher, unlike Nordau, he refrained from a bitter ad hominem attack on Nietzsche. Nonetheless, he too saw a great danger in Nietzsche's philosophy that he interpreted as severely undermining the achievements of the European Enlightenment. Like another marginal Jew, Georg Brandes (born Morris Kohen), he stressed Nietzsche's intellectual aristocratic elitism[57] and his individualistic approach.[58] During the period in which Berdichevski wrote his dissertation, Stein was composing his magnum opus, a sociological treatise written under the influence of Herbert Spencer.[59] There could be no greater gap between this line of thought and Berdichevski's lonely existential quest for authenticity and harmonious selfhood. Nonetheless, did Berdichevski manage to express in his scholarly dissertation something of his existential concerns and his attraction toward Nietzsche? Some scholars who have briefly dealt with the work believe that the traces of Nietzsche in it are few and insignificant.[60] Is this so?

Berdichevski's doctoral thesis is important[61] because in it he does not draw on his, and Nietzsche's, ideas to promote national or cultural ideals, and thus the resemblance of his views to Nietzsche's deepest insights is thrown into sharper relief. The dissertation clearly shows that Nietzsche had not only influenced the rhetorical and stylistic aspect of Berdichevski's work but has actually exerted a formative impact on Berdichevski's worldview. Nonetheless, Berdichevski's existential dilemmas are the hidden reason for choosing this specific theme and for dealing with it in this particular (Nietzschean) way.

The subject is quite characteristic of a young Jewish man who, despite his current estrangement from Jewish religion and the ethos of the shtetl and because of his strong attraction to the world of the gentiles and their cult of the beautiful, tries to reconcile ethics (his personal background) with aesthetics (his fascination with the world of beautiful forms and secular ways of life). By using a typical Nietzschean approach, especially the one presented in *The Birth of Tragedy,* Berdichevski attempts to formulate a viable synthesis between ethics and aesthetics. He had already revealed his underlying personal reason for attaining such a synthesis in a programmatic essay that appeared in the Chicago Hebrew journal *Ha-Pisgah*: "I am not distinguishing . . . between external and internal; Judaism and humanity . . . *we wish to become one.*"[62] A letter that Berdichevski wrote to Ahad Ha'am from Bern suggests that while he was writing his dissertation it was more the spirit of Nietzsche than that of Kant that was inspiring him: "I am inquiring now into the rift between the *Critique of Pure Reason* and the praxis of Kant's thought, or as Nietzsche called him *Der Königsberger Chinese.*"[63]

And thus, though Berdichevski refers only twice in his dissertation to Nietzsche, his references to him are by no means insignificant, and they reveal the key motifs of the entire treatise. The first is a quote from Nietzsche's *Beyond Good and Evil*: "There are no moral phenomena at all, but only a moral interpretation of phenomena" (*BGE* 108).[64] This is definitely an anti-Kantian attitude that relegates the realm of morality from the Kantian sublime world to the human, all too human world of man's interpretations and projections from his own perspective.

Berdichevski's intimate affinity with Nietzsche's philosophical, vitalist, and naturalistic outlook is explicitly acknowledged in another reference to Nietzsche and to his concept of the tragic attitude.[65] The philosophical core of the dissertation as well as its main tenets are thoroughly Nietzschean. From the first chapter onward Berdichevski places an existentialist emphasis on the subjective and individual ramifications of our knowledge and evaluations. Like Nietzsche in *The Birth of Tragedy,* Berdichevski, too, embraces a Heraclitean view of the world as becoming and as in constant flux. He exhibits a strong sense for sharp distinctions, and clearly expounds various difficult philosophical concepts, and with an air of self-assurance he dares to criticize several renowned philosophers such as Kant, Schopenhauer, and the British moral theorists like Shaftsbury and Hutcheson. Berdichevski rejects as invalid and self-contradictory the Kantian distinction between the knowledgeable world of empirical phenomena and the moral world of rational "practical reason." He claims that the human self and the human will are one, both in their cognitive judgments as well as in their moral and aesthetic evaluations. He does not propagate, however, the metaphysical blind will of Schopenhauer and explicitly rejects his speculative dualism. Like Nietzsche, he employs anthropological and existential terms of human willing, judging, and acting. Thus he refers to human "power" (*Macht*) as the unitary principle behind the whole range of human activities in all the fields of human creativity, whether moral, aesthetic, or cognitive. Upholding a monistic and immanentist worldview, he claims that "man does not belong to two worlds" (as Kant thought) and there is no will as metaphysical substance (the Schopenhauerian vision), but that "even the will belongs to the world of phenomena" and "there is only one world and this is my world, in which I exist and act in all my mental powers"(pp. 90–91). Consequently, Berdichevski rejects the Kantian distinction between the realm of aesthetic phenomena and that of morality, and claims that in a world where there are only phenomena, such a distinction does not hold water. Hence, an aesthetic manifestation of one human will has moral significance and import and vice versa. There are no transcendent entities but solely "a human will, one energy that manifests itself in multifarious phenomena," and which discloses the activity of the "human self, the I in its being and becoming" (p. 91).

I will not dwell here on the philosophical difficulties involved in speaking only in terms of "phenomena" without giving a proper account of what exactly is appearing. Rather, I will claim that Berdichevski's dissertation is actually a detailed extrapolation of Nietzsche's pivotal claim in his *Birth of Tragedy* that the whole world is but an aesthetic phenomenon and "the existence of the world is *justified* only as aesthetic phenomenon" (*BT*, p. 22). Berdichevski embraces here a typical Nietzschean psychological attitude toward our intellectual activity and claims that even our knowledge is derived from our drives, as are our moral evaluations. He uses extensively Nietzschean ideas taken from *The Birth of Tragedy*, such as the notion of Dionysian "intoxication" or, more correctly, of frenzy and ecstatic behavior, which Nietzsche called "*Rausch*" and Berdichevski calls here "*Enthusiasmus.*"[66] He speaks about the sublime art that overcomes the "principium individuationis" (p. 93; see *BT*, sec. 1), and though he does not directly employ the Nietzschean terms "Dionysian" and "Apollonian," his analyses of the aesthetic aspects of morality and of the ethical ramifications of the aesthetic echo this fundamental distinction. Thus, as Nietzsche envisaged a "healthy and productive" synthesis between the Apollonian and the Dionysian elements of human nature and culture, Berdichevski tries to provide a viable "synthesis between the beautiful and the good" (p. 93). He thinks that the "barbarian" elements of the Dionysian drives can be sublimated by the moral instincts which, like the cognitive faculties, are nothing other than the human instinct for order, logos, and self-preservation. Like Nietzsche, Berdichevski claims that humans are not solely concerned with their own survival, but aspire to a higher and more meaningful existence and justification with the aid of the beautiful forms they create. Just as Nietzsche elevates art to the level of morality, so Berdichevski raises the beautiful to the realm of the ethical and by doing so provides a corrective to the one-sided emphasis of his ancestors and his Jewish religion on the strictly moral dimensions of life. Under Nietzschean inspiration, Berdichevski actually embarks on what was to be his lifelong intellectual project: a reevaluation of Jewish values. If everything is but an interpretation of phenomena, it is legitimate to interpret the bad as beautiful just as the moral good can be beautiful or ugly. This Nietzschean reevaluation of our basic values finds its clear expression in Berdichevski.

In many of Berdichevski's first fictional stories depicting the everyday life of the shtetl, and in his first polemical essays, he used to complain about the lack of beauty and splendor in dull lives entirely dedicated to the study of "antiquarian" books, where there was no place for "sun, skies, and flowers" but only for Talmudic learning and toil. Using the Nietzschean agenda for reevaluation in this way, namely by substituting aesthetic values for ethical ones, Berdichevski urged his people to return to the time of their innocent existence in ancient Israel, where the beautiful was part and parcel of everyday praxis (p. 92).

However, beyond the more speculative discussion of the Nietzschean view of art "from the perspective of the artist," there is the ongoing inner existential dialogue of Berdichevski with his own torn heart. To overcome his unbearable inner rift he needs more than a synthesis of the conflicting tendencies and cultures of East and West; he has to attain a harmonious and authentic selfhood. To effect such a transfiguration of his divided self, Berdichevski needs "to change and recreate his own self anew," to "reevaluate his own values" (p. 105). In other words, he has to embrace Nietzsche's aesthetic model of authentic life and self according to which each of us has to be like an artist, shaping and creating his own self, transforming gross elements into a sublimated and aesthetic creation. Only when the Apollonian and Dionysian elements of one's nature are directed to foster a free and spontaneous creation of one's own self, will one be "no longer an artist, he has become a work of art" (*BT* 1). Berdichevski echoes this idea by stating that "the artist endows his own self with content and form" (p. 109).

The most plausible solution to the rent in Berdichevski's heart emerges

here, at least on the theoretical level. If one is unable to overcome this existential rent by life dynamics (and Berdichevski was the first to acknowledge his inability to do so), one should attempt to overcome it by
transforming it into an aesthetic phenomenon, by endowing it with aesthetic import, and by dealing with it on an artistic level. By making one's
divided self into a motif and subject of one's artistic creations, "the creator,
as it were, is carving his sculptures from his own body . . . and thus his soul
knows of the inner rift no more" (pp. 108–9). It is not a sheer coincidence
that Berdichevski ends this seemingly academic and technical dissertation
with an existentialist vision of one who overcomes the "split" (Nietzsche
would say *dividuum*) within his self and manifests an "inner core, one and
only one law and principle" (p. 121).

Berdichevski achieves the overcoming of the split between the aesthetics of the West and the ethics of his ancestors from the East by a viable synthesis only on the theoretical level. In real life these tensions and
conflicting sensibilities continuously plagued the young doctor of philosophy who, despite his scholarly recipe for existential turmoil, did not manage to attain in his life this peaceful state of harmonious *individuum*. The
longing for such a self continued along with the ever-growing creativity of
the torn heart. Thus, as Nietzsche said that all his writings are written "with
his blood" and are but "confessions of their thinker," so Berdichevski creates out of his irreparable inner rift. And create he must in order to transform this unbearable rift into an acceptable aesthetic phenomenon. Thus
Nietzsche functions at this stage as Berdichevski's great healer who assists
this first modern Hebrew writer to *creatively* overcome the rift in his heart.

POST-DISSERTATION WRITINGS

Just as Berdichevski's dissertation was an elaborated account of various intuitions of Nietzsche in *The Birth of Tragedy*, so his first significant polemical essay, written in 1899 after his turn to Zionism, was mainly derived from
Nietzsche's essay "On the Uses and Disadvantages of History for Life."

"The Old and Youth Age" was prefaced by Nietzsche's slogan of which
Berdichevski was so enamored that he repeated it many times: "If a temple is to be erected, *a temple must be destroyed.*"[67] Under this motto,
Berdichevski put the initials "F.N.," clearly believing that Nietzsche's full
name had already become quite familiar to the few readers of modern Hebrew journals. In any event, this abbreviation was not intended to hide
Berdichevski's main source of influence, because in his later editions of all

his writings he did not change or erase it. The revolutionary beginning and the break with the antiquarian heritage of Jewish culture was concisely epitomized by this saying, which also gives us a direct clue to the main source of inspiration that informed Berdichevski's radical attempt at reevaluating the prevalent Jewish values.

Nietzsche's attitude toward the antiquarian historical consciousness is presented in his essay on history and, indeed, Berdichevski draws heavily from it. At the beginning of his article, Berdichevski presents another aphorism, from Nietzsche's *Genealogy of Morals* that gives us an enlightening glimpse into the nature and depth of his relation to Nietzsche. He delineates two ways by means of which one can be influenced by great thinkers: one can "be directly or indirectly inspired by them; by a short or by a long way." Either their truths enter "our hearts entirely, so that we rely on them absolutely and merely propagate their certainties, doing no more than simply complete their contours, add our special flavor; or we can utterly reject their truism, a rejection that stimulates us to create for ourselves a different set of presuppositions" (p. 109). Then comes an illuminating analogy from Nietzsche's attitude to opinions of his friend Paul Rée. In effect Berdichevski uses this Nietzschean prism to describe his own relation to Ahad Ha'am. Unlike the dialectically negative and sometimes ambivalent relation that Berdichevski nurtured toward Ahad Ha'am, his relationship to his great "external" mentor and source of inspiration, Nietzsche, was more straightforward and positive.

Whereas Nietzsche was but a temporary means for Berdichevski's transfiguration of his self, Ahad Ha'am, who continued to effect a strong influence on cultural Zionism and on many of its leading ideologues and activists, was the powerful rival and adversary of Berdichevski with whom he had to struggle continuously; a struggle, however, in which Nietzsche's name was frequently mentioned by both sides. That controversy will be discussed in the next chapter. It is sufficient to state here that Ahad Ha'am and Nietzsche served Berdichevski as two polar foci of influence. Nietzsche showed Berdichevski the way to radicalism, authenticity, and personal liberation, whereas Ahad Ha'am redirected the revolutionary pathos of this enthusiastic thinker to the crucial issues of his own people. Ahad Ha'am inspired Berdichevski to become "one among his people."[68] Berdichevski's existential marginality weakened, and his sense of belonging to his people was considerably heightened. His intensively active involvement with the cultural affairs of his people became his distinguishing mark until the end of his life.

Nonetheless, while rejecting the "slavery" to the dominant antiquarian learning prevalent among the majority of the Eastern European "Old Ghettos" and yeshivas, Berdichevski deliberately uses Nietzsche's critique of such historical consciousness, the motto of which is "let the dead bury the living" (*HL*, p. 72). He follows Nietzsche's thesis in his essay on history that in order to become a "man of deeds and power" (ibid., p. 67), one should learn to refrain from remembering too much. Thus Berdichevski claims that in order to cultivate a vital, healthy, and authentic Jewish "new man," one has "to forget a lot and to begin everything anew" ("The Old and New Age," p. 112). His Zionism becomes a personal one and he defines it as "both the revival of the people and of human beings," a movement that aims at bringing forth "the freedom of man and the national freedom." His version of Zionism is directed at transforming "abstract Jews into Hebrew Jews" who will "live fully and to the utmost extent of their powers" and will belong to no one but to "themselves alone," "free from internal slavery" to their own buried past (pp. 112–13). Clearly, Berdichevski finds himself in complete accord with Nietzsche's tenet that slavery to one's own past suffocates the present and kills the future. In sharp contrast with the view of national or socialist Zionism, for Berdichevski Zionism was first and foremost needed to cultivate the authentic mode of life of the individual Zionist. It was also the main factor that enabled Berdichevski to attain a modus vivendi with his torn heart. His heart had been temporarily mended through his struggle for reevaluation of Jewish values and strengthened by his endeavor to attain a harmonious self through his involvement with Zionist cultural praxis.

As part of his struggle to shape a modern Hebrew culture, Berdichevski, like Buber, fights the overspiritualization of the everyday lives of the Jews because it leads to fossilization. He exclaims: "Woe to the man and the nation that became fossilized in their past, in their memories from ancient times that fill all their space and essence" (p. 119). At this point he quotes from Nietzsche's essay on history, which actually becomes the leitmotif of this entire programmatic essay: "*There is a degree of sleeplessness, of rumination, of the historical sense, which is harmful and ultimately fatal to the living thing, whether this living thing be a man or a people or a culture*"(p. 119; *HL*, p. 62— emphasis in the original) Along the line of Nietzsche's thought that mere preservation of life leads to its stagnation, Berdichevski urged a revitalization of life. This move necessitated a radical transformation of the Jewish attitude toward nature, which must enter as a legitimate theme into modern Hebrew literature. The Jewish people also ought to become more open to external pluralistic influences, as had been in Hellenistic times.

At this point in his argument, while rejecting the denaturalization of

Jewish ethics and religion and in order to strengthen his position, Berdichevski presents an amalgam of Nietzsche's scattered statements on the people of Israel taken from different books. These statements entail the gist of Nietzsche's main critique of the Jews in the context of his attacks on Christianity and its ascetic religion. Nietzsche accuses the Jews of initiating "slave morality" and transforming healthy "good-bad" values into "good-evil" ones, namely, in giving rise to Christianity. In sharp contrast to the allegations of the religious anti-Semite, that the Jews killed the God-Messiah Jesus, Nietzsche accuses them of the opposite: of actually producing Jesus and helping him spread his faith. Berdichevski claims to quote Nietzsche on the Jews:

> Indeed how much truth there is in Nietzsche's saying that "the most wonderful thing in the history of the world was the stance of the People of Israel when they had to answer the question: To be or not to be? They preferred to prevail at any cost that was required of them; that cost was the basic falsification of nature, naturalness, all the reality of the inner and external world. Moreover, under the worst conditions, which would prevent any nation, any language, from surviving, they created out of their innermost essence the counterelements to their natural circumstances by constantly changing the values of the world and of life, of history and of the soul." (pp. 114–15)

In fact, this passage is a mixture of different quotations from Nietzsche's various writings, and Berdichevski's ability to weave them into a seemingly unbroken whole shows his great mastery of Nietzsche's oeuvre. His mastery is asserted even more forcefully in another of his publications from the same year, where he quotes a lengthy passage from *The Antichrist*.[69]

What is especially significant, however, is less Berdichevski's mastery of Nietzschean texts than the fact that for his polemic against the antiquarian religious ethos of the Orthodox Jewish establishment, Berdichevski sees fit to mobilize Nietzsche's critique of the same phenomenon. Furthermore, against these negative ramifications of Jewish life in the Diaspora, Berdichevski employs Nietzsche's remedy of returning to more natural and monumental relations toward nature and life in general. Nietzsche's critique of the Jewish people as well as his admiration of their monumental past both occupy a central position in Berdichevski's attitude toward his own people and their troubled history.

Berdichevski's reevaluation of all Jewish (i.e., Diasporic) values was intended to turn the Jewish people back to their glorious past. He tried to reinstate the ancient Hebrew concept of God as the direct expression of the affirmation of life, and as a projection of a healthy, spontaneous, naïve, and harmonious relation to nature before this relation became "denaturalized" by Jewish-Christian theology that moralized it by introducing into it the "moral world order." The natural religion of the ancient Hebrew, described by Nietzsche and approved by Berdichevski, was a direct "expression" and affirmation of life struggling with nature, enjoying its victories and accepting in *amor fati* fashion its failures and disasters. Berdichevski stressed that whereas the ancient Hebrew religion was an expression of plenitude of power and thirst for life, the Jewish religion in the Diaspora became a tool in the hands of the rabbis who zealously guarded their monopoly on the "sacred lore" and who were afraid of their own instincts, and of the nature within them and in front of them.

But most relevant to Berdichevski's concerns was the relation that Nietzsche perhaps revealed to him, between the faith of the ancient Hebrews and the concept of an authentic life, a relation that Berdichevski was trying to relive in his personal life and to prescribe as well to Jewish nation as whole, seeing in its revival one of the main objectives of cultural Zionism.

In Nietzsche's (and Berdichevski's) eyes, the main positive function of the ancient Hebrews' faith was rooted in the fact that their projected image of God strengthened their positive powers by crystallizing and sanctifying their vitality and affirmation of life and by making these values into explicit and stimulating ideals. Their personal God, by showing them what he was, urged them to become what they were, and hence his other function was to call them to embrace what Nietzsche most cherished, the ideal of authentic life. Nietzsche believed that only a solid ground of secularity and complete immanency can guarantee the cultivation of authenticity. Berdichevski agrees with this view and applies it to his individualistic Zionism. Like Nietzsche, he believes that the religious, antiquarian attitude leads not only to fossilization of one's life but also to an inauthentic relationship to nature and to one's own self. Without the secular national framework that will become the unifying focus of one's identity, the present dominance of the sacred lore comes at the cost of life's vitality: "with the worsening of our national and political conditions, we have lost our human image and the essence of our souls. We are living only according to what has been said and written. The 'writing' is almighty" (p. 117).

Nietzsche also uncovered the natural connection between our faith in the Almighty and our modern need for creating our own selves. He claimed that in the case of the ancient Hebrews, their faith in the tribal and personal Yahweh and their intimate and natural relations to him rather than to some "abstract" ontological deity based on theological rationalizations and justifications did not obstruct their ability to create their own selves. This was another reason that Nietzsche admired their religion and preferred it to the Christian-theological version. His ideal of authentic life includes a denial of any kind of permanent, a priori fixed essences or definitions of human beings. We are what we are by creating ourselves and by what we are doing and thinking in our life. But precisely this flexibility of our essence, which is an open-ended enterprise of becoming what we are, a creative life-process without any definitive name, is the very meaning of God's answer to Moses: "Ich werde sein, der ich sein werde." Here we find no definitive name or essence but the sheer dynamism of the present and the emphasis on what one is.

This endless self-affirmation and openness characterized the Hebrew God as well as Nietzsche's ideal of personal authenticity. The connections between them can be further cemented by the following consideration: in the Bible we read: "And God said, let us make man in our image, after our likeness. . . . So God created man in his own image" (Genesis 1:26–27). Hence, if the image of God is the indefinable "I AM THAT I AM," this should be also the image of man as created by God. The biblical roots of Nietzsche's ideal of authenticity may explain his attraction to the Bible of ancient Israel and to its people. This also became one of the reasons for Berdichevski's attraction to Nietzsche and to the ancient Hebrews, as one of his Jewish-American critic W. Zeev Schur was eager to point out to him.[70]

CONCLUSION

Nietzsche's impact on Berdichevski was short-lived but very profound. His writings served Berdichevski as an enticing "ladder," a provisional, theoretical support that he climbed toward *his* "reevaluation" of Hebrew culture and literature. Once he began contributing significantly toward this reevaluation, he no longer needed Nietzsche. He moved forward, coloring or "adding" his "own special flavor" to Nietzsche's tenets. Hence, after 1899 the presence of Nietzsche in Berdichevski's writings became gradually less prominent. As in Herzl's case, when he reached his Zionist political vocation and identity, his need for Nietzsche dramatically subsided. This was exactly the function of Nietzsche's philosophy, as Nietzsche himself saw it.

Nietzsche urged his readers to regard his philosophy as a temporary perspective; to be left behind once it had fulfilled its existential aim. Hence,

Nietzschean philosophy is a means: "a mere instrument" (*BGE* 6) to lure us to get in touch with and freely employ our healthy powers. Nietzschean philosophy is thus a kind of temporary scaffolding, a provisional hypothesis or metaphorical structure, to be abandoned once it has served its purpose. In the preliminary stages of maturation, feeble personal power still needs therapeutic and philosophical crutches. But with the full ripening of power—with the attainment of Nietzschean "self-creation"—our genuine power can shed its supports and prove its authenticity by being able to thrive without them. This was exactly Berdichevski's way of using Nietzsche—until his "torn" self ripened and matured, and was unified by the single purpose of bringing forth a radical cultural reevaluation among his own people. This was not only a reevaluation of his people's conception of life and their historical consciousness, but also an existential transformation of their very lives.

Indeed, when Berdichevski finally settled down with this new vocation and accepted his torn heart in the Nietzschean manner of *amor fati*, recognizing that the rift had functioned in his case as a vital source of creativity and identity,[71] his campaign gained new vigor. The year 1899 was one of the most productive in his entire career. Nine books and collections, dozens of essays and short stories, were the amazing products of his fierce battle against the fossilization of Hebrew culture and literature and his emotional pleas for the revitalization of their content and form.

Nonetheless, despite the fact that his references to Nietzsche became less frequent in subsequent works,[72] Nietzschean ideas continued to play an important part in Berdichevski's writings. It seems that once Berdichevski got out into the open and explicitly embraced Nietzsche's philosophical tenets, and once he assimilated Nietzsche's radical ideas and conceptions into his own frame of reference and intellectual-existential preoccupations, Nietzsche's thought became so organically woven into his spiritual worldview that he expressed Nietzschean ideas even without providing, as before, any formal acknowledgments and quotations.[73]

However, Berdichevski never rejected the spirit of his philosophical mentor. For him the reevaluation of values under Nietzsche's aegis was not just an empty slogan. He spent most of his remaining years doing precisely that, namely reevaluating "critically," according to Nietzsche's view on the advantages of the "historical critical consciousness," the sacred writings, the ancient history of Jewish people, the nature of their religion, and the exaltation in the Diaspora of "the spirit of *Yavneh*."[74] Thus the Nietzschean radical and revolutionary spirit of self-liberation and personal authenticity was still stirring in Berdichevski's life and work, and, though less explicitly than in his youth, it accompanied him until the end of his life.

In any case, the foregoing pages testify to the fact that Nietzsche's impact on Berdichevski was neither passing nor superficial, and that it did not manifest itself merely in stylistic and literary imitations. Nietzsche acted as a monumental catalyst, an inspiring and encouraging force, which greatly assisted Berdichevski in his existential project of self-transfiguration. Berdichevski's original aspirations for authenticity and revitalization of the life of his people, which he did not dare to express outside a few short fictional pieces, came to full force under the impact of Nietzsche's enticing writings. He assisted Berdichevski in materializing his innermost leanings and longings. He incited him to overcome various impediments on his way to authentic selfhood and spontaneous expression of his considerable creative powers.

We should bear in mind, however, that Nietzsche did not construct Berdichevski's ideals and ideas for him, and did not bestow on him his talent and the problematic of his life (especially his torn heart).[75] Nevertheless, he did assist him in manifesting and actualizing all these things without the constraints that a Jewish refugee from the "Old Ghetto" would naturally feel while living in the midst of a foreign culture and trying to accommodate Nietzsche into his own worldview.

Berdichevski was not a Hebrew imitator or plagiarist of Nietzsche (as some of his ill-disposed critics accused him of being). He was a Nietzsche-inspired Hebrew-Zionist who never abandoned his own people or deserted the ideological battlefield where the struggle for a new and authentic Hebrew literature and culture was being fought. Hence he did not try to solve through Zionism the existential problems of his own marginality (as did Herzl and Nordau) because he had never felt marginal *in the midst of his own people.* By the force of Nietzschean inspiration and transmuted Nietzschean messages and motifs, Berdichevski became what he wanted to be: a modern Hebrew writer who reshaped his own self and his unique culture according to the feelings and views that he had nurtured from the very beginning of his literary career. Nietzsche's transmuted and accommodated legacy found its true manifestation in Berdichevski.

Berdichevski was the first Zionist who genuinely assimilated Nietzsche's spirit, though he did not always consistently embrace its existential conclusions, for example, its radical atheistic stance.[76] In contrast to Nordau, who, at least on the surface, vehemently rejected Nietzsche, and to Herzl who read him quite sporadically, Berdichevski dealt in depth with Nietzschean issues and was the first Hebrew writer with the proper philosophical education and natural gifts to cope with Nietzsche's thought and to utilize it creatively for his and his people's concerns. Hence he clearly deserves the title of the first "Hebrew Nietzschean." Nietzsche's plea to overcome one's incapacitating existential predicaments and mental agonies and crises found in Berdichevski a sensitive and attentive listener.

Berdichevski transmitted and significantly shaped Nietzsche's legacy to the second generation of modern Hebrew writers and poets. From the perspective of our present topic, he stood "At the Crossroads," and in this he was opposed by Ahad Ha'am, the renowned author of the essay of that name. Ahad Ha'am's dispute with Berdichevski over the direction of Hebrew culture and literature, in the course of which Nietzsche's name popped up quite frequently, will be the topic of the next chapter.

CHAPTER 4

Ahad Ha'am versus Berdichevski (and Nietzsche?)

Four possible alternatives lay before the secular Jewish intelligentsia in Europe for overcoming the morbid syndrome of marginal identity. (1) One could assimilate into the majority culture, either by actual conversion to Christianity (an option Herzl entertained at the beginning of his career and which Gustav Mahler, for example, embraced as a last resort), or by intensive engagement in promoting European culture (the solution of "good Europeans" and cosmopolitans like Stephan Zweig and the majority of the creative German *Grenzjuden*). (2) One could attempt to undermine the validity of the dominant European culture that delineated the margin. This was the tactic of Nordau, with his incisive Nietzschean critique of "decadent" or "degenerate" Europe. (3) One could accept one's existential marginality as an inherent factor of Jewish existence in the Diaspora, and struggle in a Nietzschean manner to sublimate marginality's negative consequences through creative work and the nostalgic yearnings for the monumental periods of Jewish history that are conspicuous in Berdichevski's writings. (4) One could adopt the Zionist solution, namely to make one's own self into the majority, either by creating an independent Jewish state (the political Zionism of Herzl and Nordau), or by emphasizing the uniqueness, spiritual cohesiveness, and historical continuity of the "Chosen People" to which one belonged. Chosen, that is, not to rule the world or Europe but to become "*am segula*" (unique people), i.e., a people of moral genius whose life was guided by moral principles. This solution reasserted the particularity of one's secular Jewishness while absorbing and accommodating to the richness of the dominant European culture. This was the way taken by Ahad Ha'am, who used Darwinian (and Hegelian) terminology[1] to replace the Jewish God by what he called the "national instinct of survival" and "the moral and cultural *Geist*." It was Ahad Ha'am who was the most brilliant advocate of this solution, which he advanced as an alternative to the "inner slavery" and spiritual degradation of the first solution to the problem of Jewish marginality, namely assimilationist tendencies of European Jewry. Was Ahad Ha'am's solution a viable one? What could be Nietzsche's role, if any, in this scheme of things?

Asher Zvi Ginzberg, better known by his Hebrew pen name Ahad Ha'am, enjoys even today a reputation in Hebrew literary and intellectual circles similar to that of Ralph Waldo Emerson in the United States. Unlike Emerson, however, Ahad Ha'am's essays are deeply steeped in the literature of his heritage—Judaism. Nonetheless, his style and mode of thinking surely earn him the title of a Cartesian Zionist. He deserves this label because of the lucidity and clarity of his writings, his search for the one "objective" truth, and his critical mind and rational approach that seek in a deductive manner to explicate "evident," rational and general principles and apply them to the Jewish people. All this makes him into a Cartesian thinker, in contrast to the more intuitive, romantic, and eruptive Berdichevski.

The differences in style of thinking between these leaders of cultural Zionism had already found their distinctive expressions in their early childhood. Berdichevski was fascinated by Hasidism and its ecstatic manner of worship, and wrote many fictional and semiautobiographical Hassidic stories. Ahad Ha'am turned against Hasidism in his boyhood and, to the sorrow of his father, became a *mitnaged* ("opponent," that is, an anti-Hasid) who relied solely on reasoning and on the Talmudic (that is, rationalist) lore and mode of thinking.[2] In opposition to his friend and opponent who tended to pathos, emotions and feelings, Ahad Ha'am faithfully adhered to the "Supremacy of Reason."[3] Nonetheless, like Descartes' metaphysics which suffers from several inner contradictions, Ahad Ha'am's thought too is plagued by various basic tensions and incongruities.[4]

Ahad Ha'am's ideology stressed the positive rather than the negative dimensions of Zionism. Unlike Herzl and Nordau, he did not envisage the Zionist solution as the only viable response to the plight of the Jews and the problem of anti-Semitism in Europe, which he claimed would be solved by immigration to the United States or Argentina. Rather, he saw in Zionism a means of spiritual and cultural renaissance for the entire Jewish people, and for the consolidation of their unique identity. Consequently he developed his version of cultural Zionism in order to establish a pristine

Hebraic society and to infuse the political Zionism with cultural and moralistic dimensions.[5] His self-assumed mission vis-à-vis the Zionist establishment was that of a cultural-spiritual ideologue and sternly moralizing Socratic gadfly.

Unlike Berdichevski, Ahad Ha'am did not experienced the acute existential state of a torn heart. He never left the Jewish people or played with the idea of becoming a German or European writer, so that his relationship to Nietzsche lacked the highly emotional quality that was present in the cases of Berdichevski and Nordau. His approach was that of an even-handed rationalist and a cultural historian who attempted an objective evaluation of this unsettling focus of influence that had such a great impact on his young adversary. His philosophical attitude, however, manifested a deep rent in his mind which may account for some basic contradictions in his intellectual world-outlook. There was a conspicuous tension between his positivist tenets (adopted from August Comte and Herbert Spencer) and the metaphysical abstractions of Hegel, which culminated in his conception of "the spirit of the nation," *ha-ruah ha-leumit.* He borrowed this term from Nachman Krochmal, the early nineteenth-century Hegelian Jewish thinker, who described the Jewish nation as an evolving "spiritual organism" whose history consisted of the unfolding of an ethical ideal. Consequently, there was also a contradiction between the immanent view of Darwinian evolution and the teleological dimensions of the Hegelian system. Ahad Ha'am's underlying Hegelianism (and his Herderism with its emphasis on the value of the *Volk* as an organic manifestations of the collective spiritual morality and heritage) clashed squarely with Berdichevski's Nietzscheanism. The confusions in Ahad Ha'am's mind could be seen as reflecting an inadvertent displacement of the rent in his heart, which he suppressed in order to embrace a more systematic, though highly eclectic, rationalist attitude. Thus his case too manifests another variation of the existential basic split which Berdichevski tried so hard to overcome and finally to accept.

Some of the few existing intellectual biographies of Ahad Ha'am have tried to perpetuate the myth of a self-made man whose knowledge was self-acquired—whose world-outlook evolved solely and immanently from within the Jewish frame of reference and heritage. Hence he has frequently been portrayed in the scholarly literature as a kind of self-sufficient sage whose worldview and intellectual preoccupations sprang full-blown from his mind, as Pallas Athene was said to have leaped fully armed from the brow of Zeus. This image, to which he willingly contributed,[6] along with other reasons, drove him to try and encapsulate his younger and stormier adversary and friend, Berdichevski, within the domain of Jewish heritage alone—though he himself, coming from a traditionalist upbringing, taught himself Russian, German, English, and French, and read voraciously the scholarly literature of these nations. Thus, it is small wonder that Ahad Ha'am's immanence thesis suffered from a paradox that had to do also with his essayistic method. He very often begins his essays by stating some commonly accepted general premise, either a scientific concept prevalent in his times, or some principle of philosophy, psychology or history. After a short discussion of this thesis, he turns from the general to the particular and tries to explicate some connections of the principle invoked to the specific questions of Jewish destiny and the proper direction of Hebrew culture. A striking example is his attempts to argue for Jewish historical and cultural autonomy and inherent evolution by using Darwinian, Spencerian, and Herderian ideas that originated in the West. Naturally, he hardly had a choice. Jewish antiquarian lore did not equip him with any philosophical notions or with a sufficient arsenal of concepts to analyze adequately the existential and cultural predicaments of educated secular Jews.

Justifiably, some of his more serious biographers have tried to fathom the basic sources of his *Weltanschauung* outside the frame of Jewish intellectual history and the biblical tradition.[7] Still, in the relatively few intellectual biographies and studies of Ahad Ha'am we can barely find any significant references to Nietzsche. Needless to say, in-depth, independent research about his relations with Nietzsche is still lacking.[8]

Yet, some of Nietzsche's writings, and the first European publications about his philosophy were quite familiar to Ahad Ha'am, if only through the stormy mediation of Berdichevski. The latter enthusiastically wrote about him in his frequent personal letters to his mentor and adversary,[9] and his name was repeatedly mentioned in their heated controversy, animated debates and personal conversations. It may even be that Ahad Ha'am became initially attracted to Nietzsche through his opponent's admiration for the German philosopher. The fact is that he, too, referred to Nietzsche several times in their personal correspondence,[10] and actually was the first to have recourse to Nietzsche in their discussions. Moreover, it stands to reason that if Nietzsche is Berdichevski's "rabbi," as he wrote to Ahad Ha'am, it was only natural for the latter to find out who this "rabbi" was that threatened to weaken his own authority and what he stood for. As he wrote to Berdichevski in 1898: "I will not keep it secret from you that you stimulate my desire to read some of the books of your 'New Testament,' namely Nietzsche's books."[11]

Steven Zipperstein aptly uses the term "the politics of sublimation" in connection with Ahad Ha'am, describing him as an aristocrat of the spirit, an elitist lacking in sensitivity for the masses and their problems.[12] The term "politics of sublimation" denotes what Nietzsche's called the "great politics" of *Macht* which assists in cultivating human greatness and cultural grandeur; and the term "radical aristocrat" was coined by Brandes in 1888, in the first scholarly essay on Nietzsche where he portrays him as hostile to democracy and socialism and as having a radical elitist cultural viewpoint.[13] Zipperstein rightly raises the crucial question whether these are accidental similarities, and claims that Ahad Ha'am saw Nietzsche's thinking as "antithetical to Judaism." Nonetheless, he is not completely blind to the key role Nietzsche played in the dispute between Berdichevski and "other Nietzschean 'youth'" and Ahad Ha'am. His basic thesis on this issue is that whereas Ahad Ha'am "sought to secularize and sustain normative Judaism," his younger opponents' "anticlericalism was much fiercer than" his own.[14]

Be that as it may, can we find and further explicate any substantial impact of Nietzsche upon Ahad Ha'am's world outlook? I will raise this question at the end of this chapter after analyzing the dispute between Berdichevski and Ahad Ha'am over the direction of modern Hebrew culture and literature. This polemic had far-reaching resonance for the history of Zionism and its echoes can still be heard in the Israel of today.

THE DISPUTE BETWEEN AHAD HA'AM AND BERDICHEVSKI

In August 1896 Berdichevski accepted Ahad Ha'am's invitation to assist him in editing the newly founded Hebrew periodical *Ha-Shilo'ah* (1896–1926). He not only became the secretary of the editorial stuff of that journal but found in it a proper organ for publicizing his views. After two years of working together, a bitter controversy arose between Berdichevski and Ahad Ha'am. Berdichevski left *Ha-Shilo'ah* and became the leader of the *Tzeirim* group, which sought to introduce revolutionary changes in Hebrew literature. Nonetheless, he and Ahad Ha'am managed to maintain their mutually respectful relations.

Before entering into details of the debate between Ahad Ha'am and Berdichevski, it might be helpful to summarize the three principal views of the meaning of Hebrew culture current among the East European Zionists by the end of the nineteenth century. The religiously Orthodox Zionists and rabbis claimed (and are still claiming in the state of Israel) that the *only* culture of the Jews, which ought to be theirs also in Zion, was the antiquarian culture of the Torah. Consequently, they did not see any urgency in reforming or reevaluating the content and scope of this culture. Anything outside the "holy book" and its vast exegetical literature was foreign and artificial and could not become in any way a foundation of Zionism.

In stark opposition, the younger generation of sophisticated, secular Jews who had been educated in Western European universities, including Berdichevski, claimed that "Hebrew culture" was an empty name for a nonexistent entity. Since the dispersal of the Jewish people from their land, the Jews had not created any original Hebrew culture, but had only built the edifice of rabbinical literature that had barely any relevance to their daily common lives and concerns.

Between these extremes were the moderate and liberal *maskilim* ("educated ones"). Though mostly secular, they did not wish to break radically from the Orthodox culture. They maintained that the Hebrew culture or "national culture" encompassed the entirety of the people's spiritual assets that had developed throughout the generations from the prophets onward, including the fruits of the Jewish spirit in *Galut* (exile), among them the secular Hebrew literature of the *Haskalah*. The most influential exponent of this view was Ahad Ha'am, who attempted to develop a doctrine of cultural Zionism that would be acceptable to both religious and secular Jews.

Underlying the dispute between Ahad Ha'am and Berdichevski were their diametrically opposite views concerning the meaning of the exile for the history of the Jewish people. For Ahad Ha'am this was but a necessary dialectical development—a temporary period in which the people, thanks to their instinct for survival, cunningly managed to employ "the spirit of *Yavneh*" in order to preserve and secure their nationality through religious autonomy and concentration on the "holy writings," despite the loss of their political and territorial power. Now, however, this identity was in jeopardy because of the assimilation and progressive secularization of the young Jews in the Diaspora. Hence they should return to *Eretz Israel* where a cultural center based on ethical Judaism would be developed, and would function as the focus of identity for all Jews who remained in exile.

In contrast to Ahad Ha'am, Berdichevski held the view that it was not the exile that had caused the degeneration of Judaism, but the antiquarian rabbinical tradition that originated with Yohanan ben Zakkai who obtained from the Romans the right for religious autonomy at the price of Jewish political-territorial sovereignty. As a result, the people of the Book became victims of two thousand years of clinging to that book which had brought them excessive spiritualization. This attitude echoed Nietzsche's view about the "Jewish priests" who by the end of the Second Temple were responsible for the decline of the "healthy and vital pagan powers" of ancient Israel and effected the gradual process of spiritualization and "decadence" of the early Christians who were motivated by sheer instincts of survival and vengefulness. Thus along the lines delineated by Nietzsche, Berdichevski juxtaposed two symbols that stood for the contradictory trends in the history of the Jewish people. "Jerusalem" represented the period before the "tyranny of the written word," and adhered to secular values, natural beauty, spontaneity, bravery, vitality, sensuality, and intimacy with nature; and *Yavneh* symbolized the supremacy of reason and antiquarian historical consciousness, excessive spiritualization, passivity, suppression of vitality, escape from life into the "book," and enslavement to legalism. This was, as Berdichevski named it in a nutshell, the "culture of the book" ("*sefer*") and its dominance over the "culture of the sword" ("*sayif*"). In his eyes, the problem of the Jews in the Diaspora was rooted in the fact that exile intensified these characteristics of "negative power" (to use my term for this pivotal part of Nietzschean teaching) in each individual, making them the most salient expression of the individual's entire life.

Ahad Ha'am distinguished between "the problem of Jewry" and the "Jewish problem." The second had to do with the fate of the Jewish people as a historical entity rather than with the fate of each individual Jew. It could be solved within the parameters of the exile by such measures as emigration, emancipation, and education. "The problem of Jewry," however, could be resolved *only* by Zionist revival of the entire Jewish culture. This would be achieved only by an intellectual and spiritual elite in one unifying place, namely in the land of Israel which would become the cohesive force and focus of identification for all Jews. Individuals should sacrifice their personal aspirations for the sake of their people, by helping to reinstate the Jewish "national spirit." This collectivist approach stood in opposition to Berdichevski's emphasis on the individual Jew who was struggling to keep intact his human as well as his Jewish personal identity.

Despite these essential differences, both Ahad Ha'am and Berdichevski shared several common premises. The main one echoed Nietzsche's assertion that belief in God had ceased to be the vital force in people's life and identity. Furthermore, they agreed with Nietzsche that the various "shadows of the dead God," such as an extreme nationalism, socialism, the European Enlightenment, and the liberal values of scientific progress and technological advancement, were hardly adequate to rejuvenate Jewish culture. Both also rejected the assimilatory tendencies of the marginal Westernized "modern Jews" and upheld the belief that a cultural revival and rejuvenation of the spiritual life and national character of the Jews must precede the material-national solution as propagated by Herzl.

Thus, at the beginning of their fierce dispute it seemed that only certain superficial differences between their respective literary outlooks were the key issues. Ahad Ha'am was reserved in regard to Berdichevski's emotional style and pathos and disliked the sporadic, fragmentary, almost Nietzschean, form of Berdichevski's essays and rhetoric which put more emphasis on the alluring force of images and metaphors than on rational argumentation. The volcanic Dionysian character of Berdichevski's style could be hardly stomached by the much more Apollonian, objective and cool attitude of Ahad Ha'am. Secondly there was the matter of the content and purpose of Hebrew literature. Berdichevski insisted that individual Jews, their inner emotional life, conflicts and aspirations, should become the main topic of the modern Hebrew literature. This literature should be capable of effecting changes in the personal lives of its readers after providing them with the necessary means and concepts for diagnosing their distressing existential predicaments.

In contrast to this existentialist approach, Ahad Ha'am aspired to affect the whole historical course of the Jewish people qua people and not qua persons. Consequently, he insisted that modern Hebrew literature should restrict itself to uniquely Jewish purposes and not squander its meager resources on universal themes and personal emotions. Thus any general European "foreign" influences and themes should be deliberately selected according to one overriding criterion: Could they be assimilated into the intrinsic "problems of contemporary Jewry"? Could they assist in diagnosing these problems and even fostering viable solutions to them?

Berdichevski rejected this "national" restriction and claimed that it shackled the spontaneous expression of the creative Jewish persona and unnecessary impeded the development of original perspectives. Such ideological censorship might result in the fossilization of Hebrew culture, and being frequently indifferent to personal concerns, it might estrange many young Hebrews from their culture and from Zion. Berdichevski wished to express also the "human, all too human" aspects of individual Jewish persons qua humans, and hence he did not hesitate to employ freely "foreign" secular literature that might help him in portraying their inner emotional handicaps and preoccupations. Ahad Ha'am, on the other hand, in his periodical and other Hebrew literary organs, wanted to provide room for "all and only" Jewish issues.[15]

However, it soon became evident to both rivals that beneath this controversy more fundamental issues were at stake. These had to do with their essentially different philosophical world-outlooks, whose application to the history of the Jewish people produced two different frames of reference, emphases, and solutions. These opposite standpoints in a nutshell were the *essentialist* mode of thinking of Ahad Ha'am, and the *existentialist* approach of Berdichevski[16] or the Hegelian perspective vis-à-vis the Nietzschean outlook.

Beyond the elements of language, literature, and history, the permanent essence of Judaism, according to Ahad Ha'am, was not faith but ethics as propagated by the ancient prophets. Their values, such as objective justice and righteousness and eternal peace, formed the ethics of the community and not of individuals. These Jewish ethical teachings possess eternal validity, and hence they will survive even after the collapse of the religious faith. They are the essence of Jewish culture, what Ahad Ha'am calls the "*Geist* (*ruah*) of the nation." Each individual can embody and manifest this "spirit" and thereby derives his or her personal identity from belonging to Jewish nation. This social morality as manifested in the history of the Jewish people is the cohesive factor in Jewish life and ensures its continuity. At this point, however, there is an essential difference between Ahad Ha'am's and the Hegelian approach, even if we can define the spirit of Judaism by the Hegelian term *Geist* and the practical morality of the Jews by the term *Sittlichkeit*. The difference is that whereas in Hegel's philosophy the universal and absolute *Geist* is strictly immanent in history and manifests itself dialectically in its various stages until its bold materialization, for Ahad Ha'am, the prophetic-moral spirit of the Jewish people is actually a historical *product* of its prophets, once fully manifested in *Eretz Israel* and only partially or relatively so in the Diaspora. Thus the historical element of Ahad Ha'am's view of the Jews clashes with the idealistic-Hegelian element. Ahad Ha'am claims that secular Jews who aspire to embrace authentic Jewish life must accept their heritage as reflected in the entire Jewish tradition, and that this tradition should be reflected also in modern Hebrew culture.

Berdichevski too knew well that the Jew cannot deny his past since he is the product of that same past and, as Nietzsche puts it in his essay "On the Uses and Disadvantages of History for Life," "the outcome of earlier generations . . . the outcome of their aberrations, passions and errors, and indeed of their crimes; it is not possible wholly to free oneself from that chain" (HL, chap. 3). Berdichevski accepted this inevitable element of one's relation to one's people's history, but rather than accepting it in the

Nietzschean spirit of *amor fati*—which he applied only to the internal "rent in his heart"—he condemned and rejected long periods of Jewish history, especially the exile. He could do so because he did not uphold, like his opponent, an essentialist view of Jewish history. For him this was not a linear and necessary continuity revolving around the exclusive and supreme paradigm of the prophetic ethics, but involved different trends and opposing manifestations, which in different times exhibited different modes of existence and ways of thinking. For him there never was such a thing as a single canonical Judaism, but each generation emphasized and lived by different aspects of Jewish faith and morality. Thus he could afford to "destroy the old temple" when he saw that it was already in decay. This was not a radical destruction of Judaism per se because there never was such a thriving entity. Consequently, Berdichevski objected solely to those contemporary aspects of Judaism which in his view were detrimental to life.

The opposite view was held by Ahad Ha'am who aspired to strengthen the old essential edifice and make it into a solid basis for a renewed structure which would endure the exigencies of modern times. Berdichevski opted for radical innovations of the Jewish spirit and values whereas Ahad Ha'am cautiously prescribed preservation and evolution and not a revolutionary abolition. His attitude fitted nicely the conservative-rightist tenor of the Hegelian standpoint that "the real is the rational," and rejected the more leftist and radical view expressed in the second part of this sentence, and embraced by the left-wing Hegelians such as Feuerbach and Marx, that "the rational is the real." Ahad Ha'am poignantly expresses this conservative celebration of Jewish tradition by saying: "The Jews have not so much observed the Sabbath as been preserved by it."[17]

Nonetheless, Ahad Ha'am was not blind to the fact that the present Jewish conditions and European progress and enlightenment might require some changes in the beliefs and attitudes of modern Jews. Hence he opted for a Hegelian dialectical process of *Aufhebung*: certain elements of Jewish religion and lore should be abolished, others preserved, and still others elevated to a higher plane of discourse and conduct, i.e., that of the sublime ethics of the ancient prophets. At this point it seems that Ahad Ha'am commits a kind of naturalistic fallacy, namely that he tries to derive the "ought" from the "has been" without providing us with any rational criterion for his quite subjective preference for the prophets' ethics. The Bible itself speaks of "false prophets," and the main way to distinguish between the false and the truly genuine prophets and sages was, as Kierkegaard was eager to state, their authentic religiosity and divine authority.[18] But without the authenticating means of religious faith (which were not at the disposal

of Ahad Ha'am) why should one adopt for himself the ethics of his forefathers' prophets and seers? Furthermore, if the morality of the prophets
was the permanent essence of Judaism, as claimed by Ahad Ha'am, how
can one explain the philosophically unaccountable, but sociologically and
historically uncontested fact that this essential spirit of the prophets deteriorated so much, was in such a dismal decline, and had even virtually dis-
appeared from the life of European Jewry, as Ahad Ha'am himself was
quick to point out, wishing desperately to reverse this unwelcome process?

In any case, against Ahad Ha'am's emphasis on the ancient Israelis
prophets, Berdichevski, preferring the sensuality and vitality of flesh and
blood, eulogized the ancient Israelite kings. To use Nietzschean terms:
Ahad Ha'am preferred the monumentality of the Jewish prophetic morality whereas Berdichevski preferred the monuments of the ancient Israeli
heroes. In distinction to Ahad Ha'am, for whom Jewish society, its cohesiveness and uniqueness, connoted the highest values, Berdichevski saw
the well-being of the individual Hebrew as superior to any other considerations and regarded the social framework and history solely as means to attain it. Spirituality versus mundanity, social ethics versus personal ethics,
national uniqueness versus personal authenticity, were the basic parameters of their deeply philosophical disagreement. Hence comes Berdichevski's typical anti–Ahad Ha'am slogan: "the Jews must come first, before
Judaism."

From the perspective of the ideal of authenticity, we can also discern basic differences. Ahad Ha'am, because of his essentialist approach, opted
for a return to basic authentic modes of conduct and thought which he
saw as culminating in the prophetic tradition. Thus he was clearly inspired
by the biological model (which naturally also derived from his Darwinian
presuppositions). Berdichevski, on the other hand, rejected any kind of
essentialism when it came to Jewish history. Instead, he stressed the spontaneous freedom of the individual's creative powers, and, following Nietzsche, embraced the aesthetic model for shaping one's own, unique self.
Indeed, there are in modern Western thought two contradictory models
of authenticity. The first derives its inspiration from the biological
metaphor of a plant actualizing the potential of the seed, and the second
employs the metaphor of art and artistic creation. The search for authenticity is seen as the wish to reflect one's own indeterminacy by spontaneous
choice of one out of many possible ways of life. The individual is a kind of
artist who freely shapes his self as a work of art.

Ahad Ha'am could not accept the application of this second model for
the unique essence of Judaism. There was only one authentic manifestation

of the Jewish spirit, the ethics of the ancient prophets, which had deteriorated owing to the rapid assimilation of Jews in Europe. Once the Jews returned to their original ground or (to put it in biological terms) to the right field where the optimal conditions for their growth prevailed, this ethics could once again flourish in the new form, by forming the basis of a genuine Hebrew culture. Berdichevski too pleaded for a return to the monumental patterns of the ancient Hebrews in their ancient land—not to return to certain essential ethical patterns, but in order to be rejuvenated in a soil where "new Hebrews" could once again exercise their creative powers in shaping their unique individual selves. In place of Ahad Ha'am's prescription to the Jews to return to their ancient "national self" and to its essential values as people and pupils of their prophets, Berdichevski urged his fellow Jews to return to the vital sources of their individual selves in order to shape them according to their own wishes, aspirations and values.[19] Hence for Ahad Ha'am, Hebrew culture and literature was the didactic means to assist in *recovering* the lost or damaged essence and "national self" of the Jews, whereas Berdichevski saw in culture and literature a powerful tool to entice individuals to "their own courage" (to use a Nietzschean slogan), in order to *uncover* their own sources of creative power. And if Nietzsche could assist Berdichevski in this process of enticing his readers for self-overcoming and self-creation, so much the better.

But does this means that Ahad Ha'am could not find any use for Nietzsche in his polemics with Berdichevski or, to that matter, in the formation of his general cultural Zionism? On the surface it seems that, nurturing such an anti-existentialist world-outlook, he could hardly find any significant place for Nietzsche. This issue, as we will see, is much more complicated than it seems at first sight, and there is far from a single clear-cut answer.

A TIMELY EXCURSUS

Before embarking upon a more detailed analyses of some of Ahad Ha'am's texts where he engages in a debate with Berdichevski's "Nietzscheanism," one general remark is called for. Can Ahad Ha'am's replacement of the Jewish faith by Jewish ethics secure the Hebrew " unique national character"? Is not the prophetic tradition also the cornerstone of the entire Judeo-Christian culture? In what way exactly can attachment to the so-called prophetic values of justice, peace, equality, and freedom distinguish the modern Hebrew from his gentile partners in Europe, educated as they were by the European Enlightenment which also upheld these very values?[20] Does not Ahad Ha'am's shift from faith to ethics endanger the Jewish identity of a Jewish student of, for example, Kantian moral philosophy? Spiritual values are more universalistic and abstract and cannot, by their nature, be limited to one people, to one territory, to one language and community. On the other hand, the more mundane and emotional aspects of a single personality are more susceptible to genuinely individualistic expressions of personal pathos and particular modes of existence. Consequently, is it not the case that precisely because Ahad Ha'am's views had the upper hand in Israeli secular society and its intellectual circles that the modern Israeli faces once again the excruciating dilemma of what it means to be a Jewish-Hebrew? What positive values can one embrace in the Israel of today if one still wishes to define oneself as a Jewish (in opposition to an Arab or a Christian) Israeli? I will postpone the discussion of these crucial issues to a future volume, where I will also deal with the question whether certain versions of the Nietzschean approach can help to answer these questions. They will become more urgent, I believe, when the negative identity of the present Israeli will not suffice anymore and when the one of the main values of the biblical prophetic tradition will reign supreme in this stormy region. When peace will finally dawn over the Mediterranean shores of the modern state of Israel, the battle for a positive Israeli identity will arise again and the Ahad Ha'am–Berdichevski controversy will be reinvigorated and will become even fiercer than it originally was, and than it is now.

AHAD HA'AM'S 1896 MANIFESTO AND ITS ENEMY

The debate erupted after Berdichevski's read Ahad Ha'am's literary and cultural manifesto announcing his editorial policy for the benefit of future contributors to *Ha-Shilo'ah*. In the manifesto, Ahad Ha'am stipulated that he planned to renew Hebrew literature, not to destroy it. The sole theme of this literature, he wrote, would have to be everything that belonged to "*our internal world*," namely to the development of the Jewish people during all generations, and to the "manifestation of its spirit in all walks of life"; the general culture on the other hand, was easily available to those who wished to pursue it, "without making Hebrew literature into its procurer." Only issues relevant to "the problem of Jewry" would be included, such as the question "what is our national and historical 'essence'?" Ahad Ha'am specifies that as far as belles-lettres and fiction were concerned, he would include only "good stories from the life of our people in the past and the present which will extend our national knowledge." But fiction that was merely "beautiful" and was read only for pleasure would not be included, since "our poor literature cannot dissipate its limited amount of talent on such things . . . therefore poetry will find only a meager place in this publication."[21] It goes without saying that any contribution dealing, say, with Nietzsche's philosophy in itself, merely out of intellectual curiosity and for sheer enlightenment, would be rejected by this strict editorial policy. Such intended censorship met with a bitter reaction from Berdichevski in an "Open Letter to Ahad Ha'am" published in the next issue of *Ha-Shilo'ah*.[22]

Against Ahad Ha'am's demand to deepen and extend the antiquarian, scientific nature of the new periodical, which in his eyes conveyed the true essence of Judaism and hence also of Hebrew culture and spirit, Berdichevski demands a more monumental, dramatic, and aesthetic approach. The arbitrary restriction of the journal to national Jewish matters will dangerously deepen the rift in young Jewish hearts between "Judaism" and "humanity," between "the beauty of Jephet and the tents of Shem" (p. 19). Echoing Nietzsche's opposition to the psychologically destructive process of repression of one's instincts and vitality, Berdichevski reminds Ahad Ha'am that "besides our national and social universe, we are still living creatures, with spiritual and personal needs which demand fulfillment" (p. 19). Repressing the expression of those "human, all too human" needs will lead to a widespread estrangement of young and capable talents from a Hebrew culture that is restricted in this way, and they would depart to find "their food in strange fields." Against Ahad Ha'am's insistence on the "supremacy of Reason," Berdichevski opts for the primacy of pathos and feelings which are the innermost part of every Hebrew writer and artist qua creator. Poetry works more vividly and effectively on people's spirit and impresses them more than "speculative abstract contemplation" (pp. 21–22). Against the spiritual elitism of Ahad Ha'am, Berdichevski reminds him that the majority of people read more "things arising from life" than works of "Comte and Spencer." "All read Shakespeare and Goethe but few read '*The Guide of the Perplexed*'" (p. 24—the philosophical-theological treatise of Moses Maimonides). It is true that the creativity of the Jewish people is but a part of humanistic culture in general, and that the Jewish people have their own distinctive way of expressing general human ideas, which other nations have also expressed each in its own distinctive way. However, there is no such thing as universal and essential ideas for all times and for all generations. New and innovative conceptions and ways of thinking that have recently appeared in Europe are strongly influencing the Jewish educated public, which is not living on a remote island. "The past predominance of religious philosophy in the world around us necessitated that we too were obliged to think and to philosophize about religion and knowledge, but now belles-lettres fill the hearts of enlightened people, and this is the case with us too. . . . each generation and its needs, each generation and its course" (p. 23). "We wish," Berdichevski exclaims, to be "Human Hebrews at once and in toto" (p. 21). Using Nietzsche's formula for personal authenticity, he declares: "we wish to become what each of us is according to his own spiritual resources and his relation to the entire world, as is practiced by other nations, which do not choke the innermost roots of the private soul" (pp. 20–21).

Berdichevski too wants to attain a viable synthesis between the nation's past and its present, between the individual and the collective, but echoing Nietzsche's main idea in his essay on history, he asserts his strong disapproval of Ahad Ha'am's attitude: "we appreciate that most of our power and essence lie in our long history and in *our past*, but every past that does not entail within its horizons the present is doomed to sever its vital chain" (p. 25, emphasis in original). He summarizes his objection to Ahad Ha'am policy by pronouncing his determination to be "two which is one" (p. 26). He does not wish to suppress and reject one of the conflicting elements of his individual personality: he wants, to use Nietzschean notions, to accept and live the rift in his heart between the Dionysian (emotional, vital), and the Apollonian (traditional, rational, moral, and social) aspects of his being. Like Nietzsche at the end of his *Birth of Tragedy* where he extols the ideal image of "Socrates playing music," i.e. the synthesis of the Apollonian with the Dionysian, Berdichevski aspires to become a poetic Hebrew writer within Jewish history and society who deals freely with every pressing human aspect of his existence. Ahad Ha'am, who tries to suppress or displace the Dionysian elements of the young Hebrews and who, has driven the poets out of his *Republic*, sends the Hebrew poets to create in foreign languages and literature. Thus, in Berdichevski's view he is an obstacle to attaining the spontaneous expression of his and others' personal authenticity within the parameters of their own nation. This issue stood at core of the heated dispute between the two.

WHITHER?

Ahad Ha'am responded sharply to these accusations. He did so initially in an article that was overtly directed against the more or less identical credo of one of Berdichevski's sympathizers, associates, and friends—Marcus Ehrenpreis (1869–1951). Like Berdichevski, Ehrenpreis protested against Ahad Ha'am's tendency to suppress the "new stream of life," namely the general European culture. Following in Berdichevski's footsteps, he claimed that this tendency was hostile to the new culture, which wanted to revolutionize rather than continue the old cultural tradition. The "spiritual revolution" must completely destroy the "old world" and cannot be satisfied with a gradual evolution from within its suffocating and old-fashioned walls. The young generation of Hebrew writers (like Berdichevski and himself) "aspire to create full harmony between the general development and our national essence. We wish to incorporate the cultural assets of the new Europe within the borders of our national spirit." This should be effected not by "a mechanical and external mix of these two components, like in the Hebrew periodical *Mi-Mizrah u-mi-Ma'rav* (From East and from West) which puts on one page something of Nietzsche and on the opposite page something Jewish," but by an "internal, spiritual synthesis . . . which will become one unity." He ends in a typical Nietzschean-Berdichevskian spirit: "We have to destroy a lot in order to build a completely new world."[23] But what will be the specific content of this "new world"? How can it become a harmonious whole, consisting as it will do of such divergent and frequently opposing elements?

Ahad Ha'am dealt with these questions in his retort to Ehrenpreis and Berdichevski. Ahad Ha'am acknowledged the "genuine need which arises on the 'borderline' between Judaism and the general culture where the struggle between them erupts." Then "we experience the basic painful rift in our hearts which can only be healed by rejecting one at the expense of the other or by arriving at a synthesis of both components into a single complete whole."[24] He draws a parallel between the "private individual" and the "whole nation." In individual cases, people incorporate organically any "thoughts, feelings, aspirations, and digest them into one flesh, whereas everything which is hard to digest is rejected." This is also the case with "the national self which assimilates into its own form everything alien and external to itself" (p. 132). These processes of natural assimilation take place only in normal nations that are autonomous in their own territories. At this point in his argument, Ahad Ha'am seems to employ Nietzsche's formula for estimating a people's "power:" that "the *plastic power* of a man, a people, a culture . . . is determined by the capacity to develop out of oneself in one's way, to transform and incorporate into oneself what is past and foreign. . . . The stronger the innermost roots of a man's nature, the more readily he will be able to assimilate and appropriate the things of the past" (HL, p. 62).

Ahad Ha'am uses this criterion and adds to it Herder's notion of the 'national self,' as well as Hegelian dialectics. He asserts that a "powerful national self" is capable of assimilating into its own "mold" and fruitfully digest any external cultural influences and modes of thinking and "adopts out of foreign material everything that can be useful to it and can be incorporated as an integral part of itself; everything else is discarded" (p. 132). However, since the Jews in the Diaspora do not as yet possess such a "powerful" national self, they cannot afford to assimilate foreign influences which might obliterate their own, still shaky, particularity.

The ramifications of this attitude are quite striking. Ahad Ha'am rejects the attempts of Berdichevski and his "Young" friends to introduce Nietzsche's influence and teaching into the dawning Hebrew culture—by using a Nietzschean reasoning! It also follows, though this conclusion is rather more speculative, that he would not object to Nietzsche's presence in the state of Israel once the Jewish people there finally succeeded in forging their own solid identity and particularity as Jewish Israelis. Thus, the measure that Nietzsche is studied and employed by contemporary Israeli culture is a measure of its self-confidence and maturity!

In any event, Ahad Ha'am stresses once again his admonition that "our national self should subdue for itself not *any* content of life and of general culture but only those that could accept the imprint of the individual forms of our people" (p. 133). He reprimands those who demand that Hebrew literature incorporate the spiritual assets of new Europe, saying that they did not provide any detailed explanation of "how to incorporate, how to subjugate" these foreign elements. "In a normal and healthy nation these processes occur spontaneously and naturally, almost semiconsciously. Even thoughts that are the most distant from a particular national spirit, when translated into its national language become ipso facto close to its very spirit." But in the case of the Jewish people, the narrowness and current poverty of their national language cannot by itself yield any positive and creative results. Hebrew translations of European material, remote from Judaism, will not secure its creative and original absorption.[25] The mere fact that a work is now written from right to left does not mean that it has been satisfactorily and adequately absorbed into Hebrew culture. "The Hebrew translation is like foreign food in a Hebrew dish: we are emptying the dish and swallowing the food alone as it is in itself . . . and those who wish to introduce 'little Nietzsche' and to create through him some internal and chemical synthesis" are mistaken, since it is not enough to "insert the foreign material but to introduce it in its already subjugated form, i.e. after it had already been integrated into our national spirit. . . .

Thus we see, for example, that the deep and general thoughts of Friedrich Nietzsche are attracting the hearts of many of our young folks, are impeding their Judaism and bringing about a 'rift' in their souls" (ibid., p. 134).

How can one heal this rift? Ahad Ha'am suggests a procedure whereby Nietzsche might be incorporated without producing these undesirable results for "young souls" and for the whole dawning Hebrew culture. It follows that Ahad Ha'am did not totally reject Nietzsche and did not react against his impact on Jewish-Hebrew culture, like Max Nordau. The latter began with an overtly aggressive-negative attitude toward Nietzsche and ended with an ambivalent synthesis, whereas Ahad Ha'am began, as we will see in a moment, with an ambivalent synthesis or *Aufhebung,* and ended with a quite positive image of Nietzsche. Thus from the start he did not wish to repress Nietzsche's influence entirely, since he shrewdly and realistically observed that such an influence already existed. It was too late to expel 'the beauty of Jephet from the tents of Shem', to use Berdichevski's beloved idiom. Ahad Ha'am wanted instead to check this influence, to divert it into channels more productive for the future of the Hebrew culture, and to have effective and full control over its impact in order to avert the danger that it might overwhelm the new Hebrew culture and sweep it away from its Jewish origins and ethos. The Dionysian-Nietzschean "frenzy" that stirred in the hearts of some of the most talented Hebrew writers and intellectuals must be controlled and sublimated (in the sense of the Hegelian process of *Aufhebung*) by Apollonian-rational forms and by the Jewish heritage. Thus Ahad Ha'am proposes that we take Nietzsche's thought and analyze it into those components that "attract the heart" and those that reject Judaism. The first component, he finds, "is human and can be established within any decent mold of spiritual life, hence it also attracts the Hebrew heart, whereas the second belongs to the 'Aryan' part of the thinker and sticks with the first because both incidentally happen to occur in a thinker who happens to be also a German." Upon completing this analysis we will free the "human" aspects of Nietzsche's thoughts from the Aryan elements and will apply them to our own selves. Thus we will introduce "into our literature *new* thoughts but not *foreign* ones" (p. 134).

"NEW BUT NOT FOREIGN"

A quite stimulating plan is offered by Ahad Ha'am's suggestion. Can we distinguish in Nietzsche's corpus between those components that are of a general, universal nature, and in other words have a humanistic import per se, and those which directly offend against Judaism as Ahad Ha'am conceived it? Is such a thought experiment possible at all? If we take Nietzsche's atheism and his world outlook of complete immanence, does it or does it not contradict directly Ahad Ha'am Judaism?

Clearly, the answer must be no, since Ahad Ha'am too is a secular thinker who regards the prophetic ethos (but not religious belief) as belonging to the historical-spiritual essence of Judaism. To put in a nutshell his view on this point versus that of Berdichevski: Ahad Ha'am wanted Judaism without the yarmulke, Berdichevski wanted the Jew without the yarmulke. But Nietzsche rejected the essentialist attitude, which reminded him too much of Hegel. Hence, though his atheism clearly belonged to those elements of his thought which were general and had nothing "Aryan" about them, Ahad Ha'am could not adopt it as part of his outlook. Could he do so, however, with Nietzsche's ideal of personal authenticity? Again, it seems that since this ideal had a wide humanistic scope and a universal significance, it might be applicable to the Hebrew scene (at least, as it was applied in Berdichevski's works), and hence that there would be no problems with incorporating it into a Hebrew culture that was so preoccupied with fostering the image of the "new Hebrew." But does this ideal makes any sense as a part of Ahad Ha'am's doctrine, which stresses "national self and national spirit"? Perhaps it might be modified to do so. In any case, Ahad Ha'am could and did incorporate some other elements of Nietzsche's thought into his doctrine. Among these were, for example, Nietzsche's ideas concerning the function of different types of historical consciousness in life, and the future cultural mission of the Jewish people in Europe which Herzl and Nordau had already tried to apply in their political Zionism.

However, there is some inner inconsistency between Ahad Ha'am's suggestion how to employ Nietzsche and his claim that a still weak, evolving, and un-self-confident culture is not ripe enough to incorporate into itself foreign elements that might smother its individuality. If this really is the current situation in the spiritual domain of the new Hebrew culture, any attempt to introduce into it something that originated outside its original history and its peculiar predicament and heritage might severely and irrevocable damage it. On the other hand, since Ahad Ha'am did introduce into his thinking on Judaism and cultural Zionism certain Nietzschean motifs, is this not a sign that, at least in his case, he was not afraid of becoming merely an *imitator* of Nietzsche (and other European thinkers)? Was he only afraid that this might happen to his less resolute, more emotional and vacillating young friend and corroborator Berdichevski, for whom Nietzsche could become a real threat, taking him away from Judaism and from the Jewish people?[26]

Another short piece by Ahad Ha'am from the period of his dispute with Berdichevski, in which he shares with his readers his understanding of what it means to accept foreign influences—and the case of Berdichevski's Nietzscheanism was surely before his eyes—shows clearly that Ahad Ha'am saw in his own accommodation of Nietzsche to the Hebrew scene a valid maneuver. The piece in question was a review in *Ha-Shilo'ah* of a work by one of Berdichevski's opponents, Dr. Bernfeld, *Jews and Judaism in the Nineteenth Century*, a kind of a popular summary of the main cultural contributions emerging from the spiritual life of German Jews. Ahad Ha'am, realizing the potential of such popular presentations for the promotion of his cultural Zionism and Hebrew culture, suggests that such compendiums should also be published in Hebrew and should encompass summaries of all the cultural developments and works on the history of Jews and Judaism in the nineteenth century. Then comes his crucial remark: "such a project will not be a genuine imitation but only a *utilization* of an European idea as a kind of stimulus for the Jewish enterprise."[27] It follows that Ahad Ha'am did not consider his "utilization" of Nietzschean motifs (and those of Spencer, Hegel, Darwin, and others) to be imitations, but rather original adaptations of Nietzsche and others to specifically Hebrew-Jewish issues and concerns. But was this not exactly Berdichevski's usage of Nietzsche? In what way, in Ahad Ha'am's eyes, did Berdichevski stray from limited and "kosher" "utilization" into an actual misuse of Nietzsche? In order to answer this question we have to turn now to the most important article of Ahad Ha'am on this whole issue.

AHAD HA'AM'S "REEVALUATION" OF HEBREW NIETZSCHEANISM

This article was the most sustained attempt of Ahad Ha'am to deal with the general problematic of 'Hebrew Nietzscheanism', exemplified most strikingly by Berdichevski, though the latter is never explicitly named.[28] Ahad Ha'am thought that his essay had more than local, that is, Hebrew, ramifications; as he put it, and wished it "for various reasons to be translated" into German.[29] Quite significantly, the German translation, authorized by Ahad Ha'am, was entitled *Nietzscheanismus und Judentum*.[30] This indicates that, Ahad Ha'am intended to deal with the general issue of the place of

Nietzsche within the entire scope of modern Judaism, and regarded Berdichevski's use of Nietzsche in their dispute as simply a case in point. It is also noteworthy and quite symbolic that Berdichevski proudly donated the original *Hebrew* version of the article to Nietzsche's Archives in Weimar, apparently with Ahad Ha'am's full cooperation and endorsement.[31]

In this essay, Ahad Ha'am presents Nietzsche as a "philosopher-poet . . . a man of thought and vision" who managed to attract European "youth" by propagating a "new moral theory" based on *"Umwertung aller Werte"* (Reevaluation of all values).[32] Slightly distorting Berdichevski's position, Ahad Ha'am attributes to him the view that *"all* Jewish history from the prophets till today" suffered from "a lingering mistake"(p. 154, my emphasis), namely, from excessive "spiritualization"—or to use Nietzsche's term, not employed here, from *Vergeistigung* (*GM* II-16). Berdichevski, however, held the view that this damaging process of a turn from "sword" to "book" had started from the time of *Yavneh* with the destruction of the Second Temple. Ahad Ha'am, referring to him as to the "one voice who loudly and angrily 'rants some news'" (p. 154), also distorts another view of Berdichevski, claiming that he preaches the "enhancement of force" in order to attain national and personal objectives "by sheer force of arms" (ibid.). There appears a certain inconsistency in attributing to Berdichevski such a purely physical view of power, since he admits that Berdichevski wishes to intensify this power in order "to remove the bonds from the soul that seeks life." Thus Berdichevski's objective was not a sheer manifestation of physical force (*Kraft*) for its own sake, but a personal and spiritual liberation and an increase of vitality and creativity (*Macht*). This distortion of Berdichevski's Nietzscheanism reflects, and perhaps echoes, Nordau's interpretive distortion of Nietzsche's theory of *Macht*, though Ahad Ha'am refrains from Nordau's ad hominem approach to Nietzsche and Berdichevski, and from his vulgar slanders against both of them. Ahad Ha'am feels less animosity towards this "man of thought and vision" than Nordau, not only because he did not believe (like Nordau) in the European Enlightenment and was less dependent for his own identity on the general European heritage, but mainly because he, like Berdichevski, felt an attraction to certain of Nietzsche's ideas which he sought to "utilize" in his cultural Zionist program. Hence he could afford to be less emotional about Nietzsche and to express his judgments more coolly. Despite his admirable efforts to remain an objective analyst of Nietzsche, however, some of his own intellectual prejudices and preconceptions got in the way of his interpretation of Nietzsche's thought. Thus, he explains Nietzsche's idea of cultivation of the perfect human type in Darwinian terms of a natural

"struggle for existence" and the survival of the "stronger types at the ex-
panse of the weaker ones" (p. 154).

This was quite a common misunderstanding of Nietzsche's theory of the
Übermensch. As I show elsewhere, Nietzsche's teaching is a far cry from the
crude Darwinian naturalistic and mechanistic attitude,[33] but Ahad Ha'am,
not being philosophically trained, could hardly realize this. He also ignored Nietzsche's fundamental distinction between the positive power
morality of the "masters" (*Herrenmoralität*) and the negative power morality of the "slaves," which involves the mental and qualitative differences between persons and the "lower" or "higher" sense and affirmations of their
selfhood. Thus Ahad Ha'am interprets Nietzsche's *Herrenmoralität* as a mixture of *Kraft* and *Macht,* and sees the emergence of a few "higher types" as
a result of their overpowering "the many weak types" who are brutally sac-
rificed and oppressed by the powerful ones. This quite one-sided interpretation of Nietzsche presents his teaching as squarely opposing "Jewish
morality"(p. 154). It is especially antagonistic to the ethos prevalent in the
Eastern European Jewish shtetls where the *gvir* (the rich and influential
pillar of the Jewish community) donated part of his fortune to cover the
expenses of various educational and social Jewish institutions. Ahad Ha'am
disregarded Nietzsche's argument that it was precisely the "most powerful
individuals" who were inclined to give unconditionally because they were
not afraid that by giving something of themselves, or what belonged to
them, they might impoverish their confident selves. He did not perceive
that Nietzsche's "healthy egoist" was the kind of person who does not refrain from performing altruistic deeds, since only the one who loves oneself is capable of loving also others. Hence Ahad Ha'am thinks that the
person endowed with a strong "will to power" will clash with persons who
are able to "grant many gracious favors" (ibid.) as was customary in the
shtetls. Ahad Ha'am judges Nietzsche's morality from the perspective of
the common Eastern European Jewish ethos and does not object to him
because of his anti-Enlightenment and antidemocratic sentiments. Ahad
Ha'am too was a spiritual elitist and thus this ramifications of Nietzsche's
teaching did not endanger his worldview.

Moreover, Ahad Ha'am speaks of the victory of "Jewish morality" over
the "Greek and Roman culture" which, in his rendering of Nietzsche, manifested the morality of the *Übermensch* and his masterful "*Wille zur Macht*"
(p. 154; German in the original). Ahad Ha'am ignores here all Nietzschean passages where the philosopher highly praises the old Hebrew religion and the "Old Testament" with its powerful and excellent morality.
He does not heed Nietzsche's depiction of the decline of the ancient Israel

as originating with the weakest and most deteriorated elements among the ancient Hebrews who were not endowed with genuine positive powers. Thus the dispute between Ahad Ha'am and Berdichevski not only revolved around their different world-outlooks and opinions concerning modern Hebrew culture and literature, but actually it also involved their different interpretations of Nietzsche's main ideas: the morality of power, the nature of the *Übermensch,* his views on the Jewish people, and first and foremost how to "utilize" his thought for the advancement of their differing Zionist ideals and cultural aspirations.

It is highly illuminating, though, that despite Ahad Ha'am's various distortions of Nietzsche's thought, he still wanted to "utilize" him for his own agenda. To be able to do so, he brought Nietzsche closer to the Jewish ethos of solidarity by speaking about the "duty" of the *Übermensch,* at the expense and "sacrifice of his private happiness," to assist in advancing the "human type" (p. 154). He even quotes from Zarathustra: "What matters happiness? I have long ceased to be concerned with happiness? Says the Overman [Zarathustra]—I am concerned with my work" (ibid.; Z IV-2).[34] This domestication of Nietzsche's thought on the *Overman* clashed strongly with Nietzsche's basic intuitions concerning this very ideal. Nietzsche portrays the figure of the *Übermensch* as acting beyond "good and evil," namely beyond the prevalent sphere of morality of duty, which Nietzsche, under the title of *Schuld,* namely also "debt," attacks quite vehemently in his *Genealogy of Morals.* Thus the ideal type of personal authenticity, the fictive personification of the image of the Overman, namely Zarathustra, acts spontaneously on the margins of society and does not feel any duty to act on its behalf. If by sheer chance his actions are beneficial to society's well-being and elevate its cultural or spiritual level, they do not aim at fulfilling certain duties towards it but are solely spontaneous expressions of the overflowing richness and unhampered natural generosity of this perfect *Übermensch.* The same can be said about the notion of duty to later generations or toward future humanity that, perhaps, Ahad Ha'am had in mind. Nietzsche's stress on sheer spontaneity and the picture of strict immanence within which the Overman is developed and acts, prevents me from accepting the much humanized and Judaized picture of Nietzsche's ideal that Ahad Ha'am presents here in order to form a viable synthesis between Nietzsche and modern Hebrew culture. At least this should be said about Ahad Ha'am: he strove quite hard and, it seems also sincerely, to incorporate Nietzsche within the dawning modern Hebrew literature, and genuinely tried to harness him to the benefit of the cultural Zionist movement. What is less certain, however, is whether this attempt originated in his realization of Nietzsche's intrinsic importance for the Jewish people, or whether it was a merely tactical move to prevent the estrangement of young Jewish intellectuals and writers, notably Berdichevski, from the Zionist camp and its future missions. In other words, was Ahad Ha'am's "utilization" of Nietzsche a sophisticated tactic to curb the widespread tendency of acculturated Jewish young people to assimilate entirely to European gentile culture?

Ahad Ha'am and Georg Simmel

Ahad Ha'am's remarks on Nietzsche in his essay cannot by themselves provide us with a clear-cut answer to this question. For example, in his first footnote he refers readers to an article on Nietzsche by that "acute philosopher Georg Simmel," who managed to extract from the "thick cloud" of Nietzsche's "extravagances" a "single coherent system" (p. 155n). It appears that Ahad Ha'am's systematic and logical mind had considerable difficulty in perceiving the underlying leitmotifs of Nietzsche's thought, scattered as they were among a multitude of aphorisms. Despite this difficulty, to which he admits, and despite Nietzsche's many "contradictions in points of detail,"[35] Ahad Ha'am honestly tried to understand the "fundamental idea of the doctrine of the 'reevaluation of values' in its original German version" (ibid.). He invested his acute mind in this because he felt, in accordance with Simmel's interpretation of Nietzsche, that he was not only a great poet and that his "effusive metaphors" hid some "deep meaning" (ibid.)—or at least they were meaningful enough for Berdichevski to prompt him to adopt Nietzsche as his uncontested "rabbi." Thus, Ahad Ha'am sincerely hoped to "utilize" for his own thought the more universal and humanistic ideas of Nietzsche.

The ground for this hope was provided by Simmel's article, which presented a quite favorable picture of Nietzsche. Simmel claimed that Nietzsche had been utterly rejected by the "professional scholars" who could not decipher in his sporadic writings and among his vast array of metaphorical and poetic idioms his underlying and quite consistent and systematic moral theory—one that, though highly original, was barely practical. However, Simmel grants Nietzsche's philosophy a respected place in the "historical development of philosophy," and puts him on the same par as Plato, Rousseau, Kant and Schopenhauer. He claims that Nietzsche's "ethical personalism is absolutely not egoistic or eudaemonic."[36] This favorable presentation of Nietzsche's moral philosophy legitimized his views and paved the way for his ever-growing recognition and reputation. Through Simmel, many young Hebrew writers and intellectuals, especially in Russia, came to know Nietzsche.[37]

Three important aspects of Simmel's commentaries on Nietzsche[38] influenced Ahad Ha'am and helped him to "utilize" Nietzsche's philosophy for the Hebrew scene. The first aspect has to do with Simmel's emphasis on Nietzsche's psychological teaching which, according to him, was the "foundation" ("Friedrich Nietzsche," p. 205) of Nietzsche's "systematic conceptions of values." In this context Simmel mentions Nietzschean notions such as his idea of "self-overcoming," his dynamic theory of drives and consciousness, and his concept of sublimation. Secondly, Simmel separates Nietzsche's ethics (what Ahad Ha'am later calls the "formal universal-humanist aspects" of Nietzsche's philosophy) from the more idiosyncratic personal elements of his own individual life and fate (p. 212), which Ahad Ha'am referred as to "the Aryan" individualistic elements of his thought. Thirdly, Ahad Ha'am adopts Simmel's view that since Nietzsche provides us with new and original standards for evaluation of our values we cannot reject his views from the immanent point of view but can only raise our objections and provide different meaning and content to his moral ideal from a standpoint external to his views. And this exactly is what Ahad Ha'am intends to do in his essay on Nietzsche.

The very fact that in his dispute with Berdichevski, Ahad Ha'am refers to and *correctly* quotes several commentaries on Nietzsche's thought by professional German philosophers is revealing.[39] It is also quite revealing that Berdichevski, who won his Ph.D. degree in philosophy, never mentions in his writings any Nietzsche scholar—even not Brandes, though he refers to him in his letters to Ahad Ha'am on another occasion and was surely aware of his research on Nietzsche. These facts indicate that Berdichevski's reception of Nietzsche was enacted on a more emotional and personal level, and that he straightforwardly reacted to Nietzsche's writings without needing to use any professional commentators. In contrast, Ahad Ha'am, who perhaps reached Nietzsche through Berdichevski's mediation, encountered the philosopher's writings in a much more balanced, methodical, and scholarly way. Thus one may safely claim that whereas Nietzsche reached Ahad Ha'am's critical objective mind, he invaded Berdichevski's heart and feelings. The usage of Nietzsche scholars by Ahad Ha'am also manifests his lack of confidence in his ability to understand Nietzsche's texts without help, and perhaps also his feelings of inferiority (from which according to his biographers he indeed suffered) vis-à-vis Berdichevski, the doctor of philosophy. The later monopolized his "rabbi" Nietzsche in his dispute with Ahad Ha'am, and against such opinionated monopolization of Nietzsche, Ahad Ha'am needed the authority and intellectual backing of famous German scholars. Nonetheless, though Ahad Ha'am acquired significant elements of Nietzsche's thought and understanding of its meaning from this secondary literature, he also read some of Nietzsche's books, as is quite evident from some of the quotations in his articles, especially in the one under discussion here. Being an autodidactic thinker and regarding Nietzsche as relevant to the Jewish people, he could not afford to ignore completely his main writings. This was specially so because he "sees no harm in using Nietzsche's notion of 'reevaluation' for Jewish doctrine ... which can only enrich Judaism in new conceptions and fruitful thoughts" (p. 155). Nietzsche as an external revitalizing stimulus is fine with him but, he warns Berdichevski, one has to completely master this stimulus, and incorporate it into the Jewish "national spirit only after a throughout dissection, analysis, and productive synthesis" (ibid.).

AHAD HA'AM'S JUDAIZATION OF NIETZSCHE

The question should be raised, however, whether this tactic is at all viable. The vitality, the attractive power and impetus of such a "stimulus" will surely evaporate following its cool manipulation. Berdichevski, with his emotional reception of Nietzsche, will find it quite difficult to be still attracted by Ahad Ha'am's Nietzsche in its domesticated and Judaized guise. And, perhaps, this was exactly what Ahad Ha'am intended to achieve. This suspicion is further corroborated by Ahad Ha'am's contention that "Friedrich Nietzsche's thoughts captured the hearts of many young Israelites and were hampering their Jewishness by provoking a rift in their souls" (p. 155). Hence he is eager to mediate these "ideas" and, after dissecting and adapting them, to adopt into the modern Hebrew culture only those congenial to what he takes to be the features of Judaism components. Ahad Ha'am seems at this point to put the cart before the horse. As we saw in the previous chapter, Berdichevski and other impressionable acculturated young Jewish intellectuals in Eastern Europe who tasted the fruits of Western culture had already suffered from torn hearts *before* their first encounters with Nietzsche's thought. Nietzsche by himself was not the reason for this rift, though surely he deepened and widened it. *Nietzsche's influence on Zionists was merely the magnified symptom of a more widespread historical and sociological-cultural phenomenon.* He put into a sharper relief this very rift, and hence, being a definable symptom with a particular name and specific doctrine, he became the most tangible and easily reached target in the cultural war waged at the fin de siècle among the different Jewish and Zionist camps and fractions. The struggle over Nietzsche, though highly illuminating and instructive, was only a particular case of a deeper struggle within acculturated European Jews between two intense polar foci of identity: Judaism and modern European culture. I am pretty sure that Nietzsche will also become the focus of the present cultural war in contemporary Israel.

Let us return, however, to Ahad Ha'am's "Judaization" of Nietzsche. Following Simmel, Ahad Ha'am clearly perceived that Nietzsche intended to evoke new standards for evaluation, that his reevaluation of values had actually been an attempt to provide a new meta-ethics where the old-fashioned measures of "good" and "evil" are turned into "good" and "bad." He conceives this new ethical criterion to be formal in nature and refers to it as the general "human" aspect of Nietzsche's morality which is not solely or specifically "Aryan" and hence does not endanger "Judaism." On the contrary, he claims, it can actually revitalize Judaism quite significantly. This ethical criterion is in his eyes the "advancement of the human type by the highest human specimen" (p. 155), who becomes the telos of humanity in general and is above its common level. Here Ahad Ha'am clearly accepts Nietzsche's elitism and his spiritual-radical aristocracy, and his own antidemocratic, anti-egalitarian tendencies are vividly expressed.

In any event, under the influence of Simmel's reading of Nietzsche, Ahad Ha'am holds that since this ethical axiom is formal and lacks any external criterion, the content and nature of this higher-type are open to different subjective choices and tastes. Nietzsche's "Aryan" content, stemming from his own subjective "aesthetic taste and moral inclinations" (p. 155) tends to stress the "primacy of physical force, of external beauty, and longs for the blond beast, the forceful and beautiful creature which masters all and possesses all according to its will" (ibid.). However, this "picture of the Overman does not necessarily follow from the fundamental premise" and it can be easily replaced by another image. Kosher candidates for *Übermensch status,* in Ahad Ha'am eyes, are the ancient Israelite prophets or the tzaddiks of the Diaspora.[40]

Ahad Ha'am, following Simmel, hangs on Nietzsche's theory of perspectivism and on his emphasis on the subjective power of one's choices and, one might add, also on the aesthetic model of authenticity, and thus sees in Nietzsche's image of the Overman the idiosyncratic expression of his creative power, which might be differently channeled. It is quite obvious that Ahad Ha'am, by resorting to the notorious picture of the *"blonde*

Bestie," with its Nazi-Aryan distorted connotations, and by replacing *Macht* with *Kraft,* distorts Nietzsche's teaching like Nordau before him. In any case, Ahad Ha'am claims that this "blond" picture of Nietzsche's *Übermensch* carries definite "Aryan' (namely not generally human), connotations and subjective prejudices. If Nietzsche had "had Hebraic taste" he clearly would have opted for "expansion of moral power, the subjugation of the bestial instincts, striving after truth and justice; he would have waged war against lies and evil, in short, would have preferred the moral ideal that Judaism instilled into our hearts" (pp. 155–56)—that is, the ethics of the prophets!

Surprisingly, there is a grain of truth in this speculation. Nietzsche, in his moral doctrine, was indeed interested in the *quality* of personal expressions of spiritual powers, and not in the qualitative manifestations and "expansion" of *Kraft*. He opted for a creative sublimation of instincts, though not for the repression or "subjugation of the bestial instincts." He wished to reverse the nihilistic (in his eyes) process—the excessive spiritualization of Dionysus by Apollo—by luring us into that full sensual life as represented by the metaphor of "the splendid blond beast" (*GM* I-11). Nietzsche believed that the way leading back from repression to sublimation must inevitably pass through the rejection of the former. Thus, we must first restore to humankind the reservoir of repressed drives, harshly repressed by culture and the ascetic Christian ethos. The choice is not simply between culture *and* raw barbarian nature. *The Birth of Tragedy* already opposed the "Dionysian barbarian," who is no less nihilistic than excessive Apollonian spiritualization. The dilemma facing Nietzsche is not culture versus nature, but culture versus civilization. Nietzsche prefers less civilization (less repression and spiritualization) in favor of more culture (more sublimation and creation). He cannot endorse the prospect of the chaotic turbulence and uncontrolled prowling of the "blond beast" of prey, for this would necessarily lead again to fear, which, according to his *Genealogy of Morals,* tends to produce the same internalization of drives and ascetic life patterns that Nietzsche wants to eradicate. The "blond beast," then, which is represented by the "lion" of the second metamorphosis in *Zarathustra,* is the inevitable intermediate stage but not the final and ultimate goal of his thought.[41]

Moreover, Nietzsche strove to attain a genuine "justice," though he defined it somewhat differently than Ahad Ha'am and though in his view it could only prevail in a society of *Übermenschen.* Nietzsche's affirmation of society as the necessary condition for the manifestation of genuine *power* slightly attenuates the radical stance of his extreme individualism. And since Nietzsche indeed affirms "a community" (*GM* II-9), and does not seek to destroy it, he attempts to explain how the morality of the *Übermensch* (or in my terms, of positive power) is at all possible within a social context. He does so by analyzing the nature of the interaction among society's members, claiming that genuine justice is possible only within a social fabric composed of equally powerful members (*GM* II-8). Nietzsche proposes that the powerful individual is characterized by egoism. This emphasis on the egoism of power, however, does not prevent Nietzsche from continuing to describe a moral and social network composed of powerful individuals who would willingly and freely enter the restrictive social fabric.[42] He clearly held that recognition of the value and freedom of others originates in egoism. Only individuals possessing an abundance of positive power and a firm selfhood are able to grant similar rights and freedoms to all those whom they recognize as equals. They are not afraid that this might diminish or destroy their own powers. It is exactly the self-affirmation and confidence in one's power and virtue that psychologically enables the affirmation of the "other" and its specific power. For Nietzsche, human egoism and emphasis on selfhood do not contradict the social and moral order; they actually create the ideal conditions for its proper functioning. Ahad Ha'am (following Riehl's commentary)[43] realized these crucial points. He clearly perceived that actually Nietzsche was expounding a project for the foundation of an ideal society of *Übermenschen* whose social interactions would manifest a genuine justice that he himself tended to endorse. Applying this teaching of Nietzsche to his own elitist prophetic ethics, he saw this as belonging to the more "general and humanistic" ramifications of Nietzsche's moral theory which seemingly were quite independent of its "Aryan" elements. However, it is plainly obvious that these latter aspects are integrally interwoven with the general teaching of the image of the Overman and vice versa. Thus Ahad Ha'am's distinction between these elements is quite questionable and artificial, and does not accurately describe Nietzsche's philosophical anthropology taken in its entirety.

Furthermore, if Ahad Ha'am had bothered to spend more time reading Nietzsche's entire corpus and employed his acute mind on a more through explication of Nietzsche's thought, he would probably have realized that Nietzsche adopted the essential features of his picture of positive power, namely much of his morality—as I have argued elsewhere—from the Old Testament.[44] In other words: contrary to the common view of Nietzsche as an unrelenting enemy of religion, Nietzsche's attitude to the Old Testament clearly shows that he did not totally repudiate religious experience, and even found some of its aspects congenial to one of the main

objectives of his philosophy, namely the reactivation of our creative powers. In Nietzsche's view, religious faith is not inherently nihilistic, and does
not invariably undermine the value of our earthly life and our spontaneous
creativity and vitality. Certain religious notions have served as conceptual
resources and as emotional stimulants for the emergence of life patterns
which Nietzsche encouraged. Nietzsche implied that he borrowed his concepts of power and of the *Übermensch*—among other things—from divinity as a model of the ideal Being. The case in point is the ancient Hebrew
image of God as portrayed in the Old Testament, and much admired by
Nietzsche who deployed it as an heuristic idea in his late thought.

In any case, it is not solely in the formal aspects of Nietzsche's ideal of
the perfectly authentic *Übermensch*, but also from the point of view of the
specific content of this ideal, that there is no essential contradiction to
Ahad Ha'am's teaching. Such a contradiction might appear only if we
make two errors in assessing both Nietzschean thought and Jewish ethics.
The first is that of incorrectly assigning Nietzsche's thought to the "Aryan,"
that is, Nazi ideology. The second error is that of identifying Judaic ethics
with the *Shulhan Aruch* of Rabbi Joseph Karo and its standard code of Jewish law as observed in Diaspora, and completely disregarding the earlier
ethical concepts of the ancient Hebrews. Ahad Ha'am is therefore right to
claim that the radical innovation of Nietzsche's meta-ethical approach can
accommodate also the "Hebraic" taste, which, as stated above, was perhaps
an important aspect of his morality. To summarize: if Ahad Ha'am had
foregone his reading of Nietzsche's "blond beast" and had regarded it as a
symbol of self-overcoming; if he had heeded the philosopher's consistent
distinction between physical *Kraft* and spiritual *Macht* and his recurrent
emphases on sublimation of our instincts and drives; and also if he had not
distinguished so sharply between Nietzsche's so-called "Aryan" characteristics and Jewish spiritual values—then he would have been able to incorporate into his thinking much of the substance of Nietzsche's morality of
positive power in addition to the formal notion of the Overman.

THE NIETZSCHEAN *ÜBERMENSCH* IS NOT
THE JEWISH TZADDIK

All this, of course, up to an essential point. The attempt to replace the
Nietzschean *Übermensch* with the prophets or the tzaddiks suffers from a
categorical mistake. The tzaddik cannot by any means be regarded as belonging to the category of Nietzschean *Übermensch* because he is not living,

acting, and thinking *beyond* the prevalent ethos of *good and evil*. On the contrary, in his figure, and those of the ancient prophets, the prevalent ethos of the good is optimally embodied and materialized in its utmost possible human actualization. The Jews in the shtetls admired and adored the tzaddik precisely because he fully expressed their own common and mostly cherished values. In contrast, Nietzsche's Overman moves in an ethically uncharted territory; he authentically prescribes new values that have not hitherto been common ones, as well as new meta-ethical standards for valuation. Thus he cannot epitomize prevalent values or standards for values. By striving so hard to accommodate Nietzsche's ideal of the *Übermensch* into the Jewish community and the prevalent ethos of the shtetls, and by claiming that "Jewish Nietzscheanism" does not need to be created anew, since it has already existed from the ancient times, Ahad Ha'am ignores the essential differences between Nietzsche and Judaism, at least as Judaism was shaped in the Diaspora. "We can excuse the German Nietzsche since he was not familiar with the spirit of Judaism and mixed it with another doctrine that descended and separated from it [Christianity], but his Jewish disciples ought to know that Judaism never made pity alone its cornerstone and has never made the Overman subordinate to the great mass" (p. 156).

Ahad Ha'am continues with his invalid "appropriation" and mentions the figures of the tzaddik and later on of the ancient prophets. He does feel that there might exist some tension between Nietzschean figure of the *Übermensch* and society, in particular the shtetl. He therefore tries to reduce this tension, this time from Nietzsche's side, rightly claiming that "after all, man is a social creature, " and hence also that the *Übermensch*, though cultivated for his own sake, "cannot completely free himself from the moral atmosphere within which it grew and developed" (ibid.). So much Nietzsche would admit: witness his saying that "we are the outcome of earlier generations" (HL, p. 76), his emphasis on the need of the *Übermenschen* to "overcome their age" and its most prevalent conceptions and values notwithstanding.

Continuing his attempt to "utilize" Nietzsche, Ahad Ha'am mentions the fact that "almost all admit that the Jewish people has a genius for morality, in this respect they are superior to all the other nations"(p. 156). Surprisingly, it was in connection with this point, and not with Ahad Ha'am's indirect slanders of him, that Berdichevski, in his first reaction to this article, reproached him: "if you were well versed in Nietzsche as I am, you could bring forward more explicit quotations from his writings about the moral genius of the People of Israel (see *Morgenröte*)" (Berdichevski refers to the famous chapter 205 in *Daybreak*, "Of the People of Israel").[45]

I shall deal with this passage in a moment, but first I would like to raise a crucial, and perhaps insoluble, question that might at this stage bother the reader. Is this a genuine attempt on behalf of Ahad Ha'am, acknowledging Nietzsche's greatness and his own attraction to him, to introduce this "rabbi" of Berdichevski into the "tents of Shem," albeit in a more "Jewish" way than that of his young colleague? Or, acknowledging the great impact of Nietzsche on Berdichevski and on his circles of acculturated *Tzeirim,* did he merely wish to join them tactically and appropriate Nietzsche in order to double-cross him on his way to Zion? In other words, is he using the tactic of the Trojan horse and entering Nietzsche's world with his own preconceptions of Judaism's essential ethics in order to explode it from within? Or, what seems to me more likely, by accommodating Nietzsche to the prophetic ethos of Judaism and by reinstating him within or pushing him back into the Judeo-Christian heritage, does he want to "declaw" Nietzsche, to make him no longer a "dynamite"(as Nietzsche used to call himself), or to change him from a "lion" (blond or of other colors) into a "camel"? One thing is quite certain: Ahad Ha'am's Nietzsche as Zionist ceased to be Nietzsche, the Antichrist—or at least, he was no longer the Nietzsche who so fascinated Berdichevski and many other fine young Jewish intellectuals.

Be that as it may, we can discern certain ambivalent feelings that Ahad Ha'am nurtured toward Nietzsche which he tried hard to overcome by splitting Nietzsche's thought into two: the humanistic, universal, formal but also positive aspect of his philosophy, and the "Aryan" and "negative" aspect which he rejected offhandedly as part of the Jewish framework. At this point we are facing a fascinating shift on Ahad Ha'am's part concerning the "positive" aspects of Nietzsche's thought about the Overman. This was the move from the *Übermensch* to the *Übervolk,* or as Ahad Ha'am puts it in his essay, to the "superior nation." Employing Herder's and Darwin's categories and his own essentialist approach and adding to it his vision of the moral superiority of the Jewish people, he proudly announces: "if we agree, then, that the Overman is the goal of all things, we must also agree that an essential condition for its attainment is the Superior Nation: that is to say, there must be a single nation that by virtue of its inherent characteristics is better adapted to moral development than other nations; orders its whole life in accordance with a moral law which stands higher than the common ordinary type. This nation will then function as a 'fruitful soil' essentially and supremely fitted to produce the desired 'Overman'" (p. 156). Just as Nietzsche picked up some of the predicates of the ancient Hebrew God and transplanted them into his ideal of the *Übermensch* with his positive and genuine power, so Ahad Ha'am moves in exactly the opposite direction: he picks up from Nietzsche the ideal of the *Übermensch* and grafts it onto the "Chosen People." He thereby completes a circle that starts and ends with the Old Testament—a circle in which Nietzsche functions as a vital intermediary!

Moreover, just as Nietzsche hoped that European Jewry would become the catalyst for elevating European culture and the harbinger of a new European Renaissance that would cultivate the *Übermensch,* so Ahad Ha'am too expounds the very same idea—with the crucial difference, however, that it would be realized not in Europe itself but in the newly established or rather reestablished cultural center of *Eretz Israel.* With this line of thought, Ahad Ha'am changes the famous saying of the prophet "From Zion will emerge Torah" into a more Nietzschean slogan "From Zion will emerge the Jewish *Übermensch,*" the new prophet or supremely moral *tzaddik* who will attain perfect righteousness which he will have absorbed from the moral supremacy of his people. Ahad Ha'am is indeed quite explicit about this: "the prophets expressed their hope that Judaism would exert a beneficial influence on the moral conditions of other nations, but . . . this result would follow naturally from the existence among the Jews of the highest patterns of morality" (pp. 156–57).

Furthermore, Nietzsche's conviction that the Jewish People are the chosen and the most powerful nation was also one of Ahad Ha'am's most cherished sentiments. It was perhaps because Berdichevski realized this similarity, that he referred his mentor to *Daybreak* with Nietzsche's famous vision of the "People of Israel" being once more "called the inventors and signposts of the nations of Europe" and producing "great men and great works." The chapter ends as follows: "when the Jews can exhibit as their work such jewels and golden vessels . . . as the European nations of a briefer and less profound experience could not and cannot produce, when Israel will have transformed its eternal vengeance into an eternal blessing for Europe: then there will again arrive that seventh day on which the ancient Jewish God may rejoice in himself, his creation and his chosen people— and let us all, all of us, rejoice with him!" (*D* 205)

This passage conveys the same ideal as Ahad Ha'am expressed in his essay on the "National Morality" of the Jewish people. In this essay, written during his dispute with Berdichevski,[46] Ahad Ha'am declares his firm belief that it is in the field of morality that the Jewish people is destined in future to make its most distinctive contribution to human thought and progress. Consequently, there are, practically speaking, no major differences between Ahad Ha'am's and Berdichevski's relation to Nietzsche, other than the collectivist versus individual values and the essential versus the existential emphases. Thus, Berdichevski objected so vehemently to Ahad Ha'am's discussion of Nietzsche not so much because of its specific content but perhaps because he suspected that Ahad Ha'am's use of Nietzsche was merely a tactical maneuver or pose. Or perhaps, to think along the "human, all too human" lines of Nietzsche's mood of suspicion, Berdichevski wanted to guard his "Rabbi Nietzsche" jealously against Ahad Ha'am's manipulation of him.

It is also quite plausible that Nietzsche's atheism attracted Ahad Ha'am as well. Nietzsche expounded a philosophical model of how to keep a moral kernel, namely the morality of positive power, even within an atheistic framework. For Ahad Ha'am, who rejects the almighty creator but wants to adhere to the moral code of the prophets, which were supposed to have been inspired by Him, such a Nietzscheanism could function as an inspiring, even monumental model. In his view it might perhaps help solve the crucial problem of how to ground or validate the prophets' ethics without their God. And indeed, Ahad Ha'am emphasizes in this essay the idea that moral cultivation of the highest type can be validly attained also within the immanent framework of Nietzsche's atheism.

Significantly, Ahad Ha'am does not resort here to the Hegelian concept of teleological progress, which is far from being an elitist one. On the contrary: it subjects the *individual* for the benefit of the many. Ahad Ha'am does not mention Hegel despite his view of the primacy of spirit, which in Ahad Ha'am changes into the primacy of prophetic ethics. Because of the predominant presence of Nietzsche in this essay, Hegel cannot find any place here. Herder, however, does find a place. Though Ahad Ha'am portrays the figure of the highest type in clearly Nietzschean terms, as wholly autonomous and "responsible for his own self"—a person who does not seek to make his values into a universal prescription because his duty is solely his—he also adopts Herder's view of the people as an organism. Speaking about the People of Israel, the *am segula* (excelling in moral values), he evaluates them as if they constitute one entity, as if they possess a single essence. At this point, Ahad Ha'am strives through his cultural Zionism to bridge the gap between this very sentiment of *am segula* which stirs as a dormant potential within his people, and the actual contemporary circumstances which prevent them from attaining this sublime ideal of moral excellence. As we have seen, Nietzsche also believed in such a potential for moral supremacy in "the People of Israel" and tried to reactivate it for the benefit of Europe. From this point of view one can even argue that Ahad Ha'am as a cultural Zionist could be thankful to Nietzsche for legitimizing this ideal within the gentile world, though of course, Ahad Ha'am did not need Nietzsche in order to arrive at the ideal.

In any event, Ahad Ha'am employs a quite sophisticated strategy in his dispute with Berdichevski. Thus, he uses what he regards as Nietzsche's "formal" morality of the *Übermensch* for grounding his own views. In this way he fully "utilizes" Nietzsche: with the authority of Nietzsche's name he objects to Berdichevski's attitude toward the modern Hebrew culture and also confirms his own cultural Zionism. In Ahad Ha'am's objections to Berdichevski's Nietzscheanism of the "sword" and the "blond beast," his essentialist approach comes to the fore. By using frequently in his essay on Nietzsche the Hegelian-Herderian notion of the "spirit of the nation" and " '*völkisch*' language" (p. 158), he appears to reject Nietzsche's anti-essentialist attitude. Thus, in his adopting the image of the *Übermensch,* he ignores the fact that according to Nietzsche, the *Übermensch* is a perfect and singular *individual,* and not just a specimen of a *type* that embodies the essence of Judaism, namely its prophetic ethics. For Ahad Ha'am "prophet" and "tzaddik" are essential categories, whereas in Nietzsche's eyes they can only be the titles or specific ways of life of certain exceptional individual persons. Ahad Ha'am does not see any problem here, and goes even further toward Nietzsche in what more and more appears to be a sincere project of adopting and adapting him not just for mere tactical purposes. Thus he significantly reduces the "Aryan" elements of Nietzsche's thought, introduces a Kantian element into it and claims quite revealingly that

> Nietzsche himself, with all his abundant fondness for the force of arms and for the might of the physical life, regards justice as the highest perfection attainable on earth, so much so that he even finds it hard to believe that it is within the power of man, even of the Overman, to overcome the feeling of hatred and revenge and to relate to his friends and enemies alike with absolute justice. Hence he finds it very advantageous that justice is embodied in fixed abstract laws that enable one to test the justice of his actions by objective laws. (p. 157)

He also comes halfway toward Nietzsche (and Berdichevski) and asserts the primacy of moral power over the "book" which in his eyes is solely the result of this power. In this way he reiterates Nietzsche's pivotal claim that the power of the ancient Hebrews was reflected in their God, their tribal and personal Jehovah, and in their "powerful book" which was only the consequence of their intrinsic spiritual powers. Moreover, Ahad Ha'am too, like his young friend and opponent and like Nietzsche, is against the

antiquarian stagnation of the people of the book who "fossilized themselves within this book without initiating any significant innovations and
developments" (p. 158). Moreover, like Nietzsche, he explains the deterioration of Israel's moral powers and excellence by the negative effects of
life in the Diaspora. Thus it seems that an eternal peace should prevail
among Nietzsche, Berdichevski, and Ahad Ha'am, and that all of them
should jointly contribute to the advancement of a new and thriving modern Hebrew culture.

SOME RESERVATIONS

Some reservations concerning Ahad Ha'am's way of reconciling the
"good" and formal element of Nietzsche's teaching with the prophetic
ideals of Judaism should be stated. According to Nietzsche, what characterizes the *Übermensch* is his capacity for heroic self-overcoming, rejecting
the "human, all too human" aspects of his personality in order to freely
shape a harmonious, creative, and authentic self—to attain a viable synthesis or working unity of the "Apollonian" with the "Dionysian." The main
weakness in Ahad Ha'am's synthesis of the Apollonian-Nietzschean with
Jewish-ethical elements lies precisely in that he artificially separates what
according to Nietzsche cannot be separated: the Apollonian form (the
ideal-ethical type of the *Übermensch*) from the Dionysian content (the human instincts and drives—*Triebe*). Nietzsche's notions of sublimation and
self-overcoming of the Dionysian barbarian are part and parcel of his idea
of the *Übermensch*, who needs raw instincts in order to creatively overcome
them by means of sublimation. But these notions hinder Ahad Ha'am's attempt to use Nietzsche within modern Hebrew culture solely for its own
sake. Thus Ahad Ha'am's dispute over Nietzsche with Berdichevski seems
to focus on how much of the Dionysian and how much of the Apollonian
could and should be used in various forms of life and cultural creations.
Nietzsche, with his notion of sublimation of instincts, and his image of
"Socrates playing music" makes instinct a sine qua non for any creative and
vibrant culture. Ahad Ha'am, like Nietzsche's Socrates, aspires to emascu-
late or reject the Dionysian elements whereas Berdichevski tries to stress
them and to put the "sword" over and above the "book." However, perhaps
due to his moderate and reconciliatory temperament and his genuine attempts not to estrange Berdichevski and other young Jewish intellectuals,
Ahad Ha'am comes quite close to Nietzsche's original view but he cannot
coherently uphold it if he insists upon his essentialist prophetic ethics and

upon his view that a priori grants primacy to society over the individual, to Jewish solidarity over personal Jewish agonies and "torn hearts."

"These Are the Sayings of Rabbi Nietzsche"

At the very end of his Jewish-Nietzschean *manifesto,* Ahad Ha'am quotes from Nietzsche's *Beyond Good and Evil:*

> The way in which reverence for the *Bible* has on the whole been maintained so far in Europe is perhaps the best bit of discipline and refinement of manners. . . . such books of profundity and ultimate significance require some external tyranny of authority for their protection in order to gain those millennia of *persistence* which are necessary to exhaust them and figure them out.
>
> Much is gained once the feeling has finally been cultivated in the masses . . . that they are not to touch everything; that there are holy experiences before which they have to take off their shoes and keep away their unclean hands. . . . Conversely, perhaps there is nothing about so-called educated people and believers in 'modern ideas' that is as nauseous as their lack of modesty and the . . . insolence of their eyes and hands with which they touch, lick, and finger everything . . . [47]

Ahad Ha'am concludes ironically: "these are the sayings of the Rabbi, and when we then listen to the words of his Hebrew disciples we cannot resist this thought: it is better for our children to wander in "foreign fields" and draw bad water from the original fountainhead than to drink it from the secondhand Hebrew vessel of the literature of the rift' which promises to make 'peace' between Judaism and humanity" (p. 158). Admittedly, Ahad Ha'am is quite unfair to Berdichevski, first because Ahad Ha'an, too, drew his knowledge of Nietzsche mainly from "secondhand vessels," and secondly because Berdichevski did not aspire to make peace between "Judaism and humanity" but solely between some Jews (including first and foremost himself) and Nietzsche.

In any event, the personal insults he inflicts on Berdichevski here, with their arrogant overtones of a master who understands Nietzsche better than his "Dionysian" opponent, were a hard blow that angered this proud and insecure young writer. Did his anger lead him to ignore the more positive side of Ahad Ha'am's attitude toward Nietzsche? This question has to remain open to the subjective interpretations of readers. The emotions

that Nietzsche aroused, and is still arousing, in Zion are a formidable obstacle to reaching a cooler and relatively objective judgment on these crucial issues.

REPERCUSSIONS

In any case, Ahad Ha'am's essay had repercussions. An article published
in *Ha-Shilo'ah* several years later used the perspective of political Zionism
in an attempt to correct Ahad Ha'am's synthesis of Nietzsche and Judaism.[48] Its author claims that Judaism, too, saw in physical force and external beauty important aspects of human existence. Hence, in contrast to
Ahad Ha'am's rejection of these "Aryan" components of Nietzsche's ideal
of the *Übermensch,* Rabinovitch reckons that they can find a proper place
within modern Hebrew culture. Berdichevski, of course, would accept this
correction as well applauding the partial rehabilitation of his version of
Nietzsche, and he would wholeheartedly agree with Rabinovitch's remark
about the "heroic monumentality" found in *aggadah* (the proverbial sections of rabbinic literature). Thus Rabinovitch turns to the beloved idiom
of Berdichevski and concludes that Nietzsche's "beauty of Jephet" ("which
is new but not foreign") can and should be introduced into the "tents of
Shem." We ought to do so since solely by virtue of our "moral excellence
we cannot preserve ourselves" in the future. In other words, Rabinovitch
claims that for political Zionism to succeed, *Kraft* is necessary and hence
we should adopt from "our gentile neighbors" the tendency to "enhance
physical force (or prowess)." However, Rabinovitch criticizes Berdichevski
as well as asserting that we need not "destroy" the spiritual aspects of "the
book" and glorify the "sword." It is enough if we "show" that "we are as all
the gentiles" and that our "aspirations are like those of the other nations."
  It is noteworthy, that this slogan of political Zionism, that "we are as all
the gentiles," found its most formidable opponent in Ahad Ha'am's vision
of the uniqueness of the People of Israel. Because of this vision he forcefully opposed Herzl's and Nordau's tendencies to import into Zion western liberal values, institutions, and most of the European Enlightenment.
Thus, in a scathing critique of Herzl's *Altneuland* in 1903, Ahad Ha'am
makes mock of Herzl's visionary opera building in Haifa, so elegant that
one "should first equip himself with white gloves before trying to enter
it."[49] The rivalry between Ahad Ha'am's cultural Zionism and Herzl's and
Nordau's political Zionism is well known, as also is the bad blood that often arose between these exemplary persons. In the present context it is suf-

ficient to note that this explains why Ahad Ha'am did not use Nordau's savage critique of Nietzsche (or at least of the "Aryan" part of his thought) though he undoubtedly read it. Paradoxically or not, he actually sided with Nietzsche against Nordau in the philosopher's critique of European culture and most of its "enlightened" values. Perhaps he realized that his real ally in his attempts to foster a unique Hebrew culture was Nietzsche rather than his own Zionist brothers. In any case, Herzl asked Nordau to respond to Ahad Ha'am's critique. Nordau unsheathed his pen, and wrote typically aggressive retort against Ahad Ha'am. He argued, in his usual way, that a Jewish culture that did not incorporate European values was doomed to degenerate and to become "Asiatic, wild, and hostile," and that that was what Ahad Ha'am wanted with his pronounced spirit of "intolerance" and dogmatism stemming from the old ghetto.[50] Given Nordau's and Ahad Ha'am's differing relationships to Nietzsche, surely the more tolerant attitude toward this epitome of intellectual tolerance was manifested by the later.

To return to Rabinovitch's article, in his response Ahad Ha'am argues against the proposed synthesis. He mentions Kant in defense of his essentialist approach and resorts to his thesis about the autonomy of morality.[51] Then he depicts Nietzsche's *Übermensch* in Kantian categories as a person who excels in overcoming his natural inclinations and his instinct for "self-interest," and claims in Kantian vein that "the *Übermensch* will struggle for justice for its own sake." Thus it appears once again that Ahad Ha'am desperately attempts to domesticate and Judaize Nietzsche, either according to what he perceives to be "Jewish essentialist ethics" or by using Kantian essentialist and rational morality. The use of Kantian concepts manifests Ahad Ha'am's incapacity to accept (or to understand) and to sympathize with Nietzsche's anti-essentialist, a-rational, individualistic, and aesthetic (that is, not biological and Darwinian) approach. In regard to cultural Zionism, Ahad Ha'am argues that only the "absolute need to evoke moral power within ourselves can assist us in overcoming the fossilization that prevails in our life." The "innovation" of our youth which demands that "we live naturally as other nations" is actually not an innovation but is inherent in the ethics of the "elders." He concludes that there is no real contradiction between the "people of the book" and the sword, and hence there is no need to reject the "general laws of history" that are so radically rejected by the young writers and by their "defenders." One gains the impression that Ahad Ha'am suspects that Berdichevski's adoption of the "Aryan" aspects of Nietzsche's thought makes him into an associate of the leader of national-political Zionism, namely of Herzl who in his play

The New Ghetto, analyzed in chapter 1, sent his Jewish protagonist into a duel with swords.[52]

NIETZSCHE AT THE "CROSSROADS"

As we have seen, however, underlying this whole polemic was the general and more severe accusation of Ahad Ha'am that Berdichevski's radical "re-evaluation of values" was entirely rooted in "strangers' vineyards, namely Nietzsche's books," and that Berdichevski's radical position regarding the future direction and content of Hebrew culture and literature did not stem immanently from Jewish history and its unique predicaments, but was imported from external sources. Rejecting this charge (and the other one, namely that he strove "with one leap to create a new moral theory") the accused wrote: "these war tactics are phony. We all are persons of our times and our generation. We do not learn solely from Nietzsche's and Spencer's mouths; they are only the final consequences of our own thoughts. We are Hebrews as we are human beings and we do not distinguish, as you frequently do, between the external and the internal. Judaism and humanity, all these are united in us, we wish to become one."[53]

This passage reveals vividly Berdichevski's suspicion that Ahad Ha'am's use of Nietzsche was mainly for tactical reasons and that he was not sincere in his attempts to incorporate Nietzsche into the Hebrew culture. One could indeed ask, using Berdichevski's terms, whether Ahad Ha'am too had "learned" something from Nietzsche, and not just from Social Darwinism and French positivism when he shaped his general worldview. If the answer is in the affirmative, it appears that his attachment to Nietzsche had deeper significance than that of a tactical maneuver, and that even in the case of Nietzsche's influence he could not stick consistently to his quite artificial distinction between "external" and "internal." Nietzsche cast too long a shadow upon Ahad Ha'am himself, for him to be able to restrict the philosopher to the "external" world of European culture of the fin de siècle and the beginning of the twentieth century.

An essay by the psychoanalyst Jacob Arlow showed striking similarities between Ahad Ha'am's psychological views and Freudian psychoanalysis.[54] He states that though these two great men of the Jewish people were born in the same year (1856) there is no evidence to suggest that they ever knew each other's works. This does not prevent him from describing several psychological concepts that they shared. Among these are the picture of our mental life as the interplay of "intrapsychic conflict"; a dynamic view of mental function as the interplay of forces in the mind; the pleasure principle; the notion of the unconscious working of the mind; and the notion of the "superego." Arlow ascribes these concepts in Ahad Ha'am's thought to the influence of French psychologists, especially Taine and Paulhan. The last is explicitly mentioned in a 1894 essay where Ahad Ha'am describes "certain primal forces" of our mind that operate on the unconscious mental level.[55] However, one can also validly claim that these motifs of depth psychology were part and parcel of Nietzsche's psychological theory, which had a profound impact on Freud's psychoanalysis. Thus one might be tempted to ascribe to Nietzsche a significant influence on Ahad Ha'am's psychological insights. This is particularly striking in Ahad Ha'am's descriptions of our mental life as driven "unconsciously" by our will to power and by "the desire for life and well-being."[56] Likewise, Ahad Ha'am's description of the "external ego" saying "such and such shall be your opinions; such and such your actions; the individual obeys, unconsciously"[57]) is almost the same as Nietzsche's description of the "Higher Self": "many live in awe of and abasement before their ideal and would like to deny it: they are afraid of their higher self because when it speaks, it speaks imperiously."[58] In view of these and other striking similarities between Ahad Ha'am's and Nietzsche's psychological theses, one cannot help wondering how much of these insights were borrowed by Ahad Ha'am directly from Nietzsche, or indirectly by way of Simmel, who emphasized the dynamic aspects of Nietzsche's psychological doctrine. However, this line of reasoning is not conclusive, given that most of Ahad Ha'am's essays expressing views on psychological themes were already written before his documented first encounter with Nietzsche's universe, and some of them were also influenced by the French psychologists.

In order to reach definite conclusions, however, it will be wise to turn to Ahad Ha'am's very Nietzschean essay of 1904, "Moses." Here Ahad Ha'am opts for the monumental historical consciousness which he names "real history," whose "concern is only with the living hero, whose image is graven in the hearts of men, which has become a force in human life," and rejects the consciousness of the "antiquarians" under the very Nietzschean slogan, "not every archeological truth is also a historical truth."[59] This obviously includes "biographical" truth as well. In the long run, therefore, it is quite irrelevant whether Ahad Ha'am's positive attitude toward Nietzsche was a tactical maneuver or a genuine state of mind. What really counts is the effect of his "Jewish Nietzscheanism" as it was disseminated to the next generation of Zionist spiritual leaders, philosophers, and writers.

To conclude this discussion of Berdichevski's and Ahad Ha'am's relations to Nietzsche, one may safely claim that, though one can criticize on strictly philosophical grounds Ahad Ha'am's "utilization" of Nietzsche, in the wider context that we are concerned with here, namely from the perspective of "Nietzsche and Zion," it is fair to claim that Ahad Ha'am played a more significant role than Berdichevski in adopting, and adapting Nietzsche into Zion. We shall find out that following his example, many influential figures in the mainstream of Zionism, in its socialist movements, and later on in the Hebrew-Israeli scene came to Nietzsche's philosophy. However, under Berdichevski's spell the more romantic and individualistic (one is tempted to say the more "Dionysian") fraction of the multifarious Zionist movement (today they are called the "Israeli Right") was attracted to the towering figure of Nietzsche, and to his existentialist philosophy of authenticity and self-transfiguration.

In any case, the real "Crossroads," which was the title Ahad Ha'am gave to his anthology of polemical essays, in respect to Nietzsche's presence in Zion was populated by these two great friends and rivals: there was the Judaized-"Apollonian" Nietzsche of Ahad Ha'am and the "Dionysian" Nietzsche of Berdichevski. What kind of Nietzsche did the seventeen-year-old Martin Buber turn to when he decided to translate into Polish Nietzsche's *Thus Spoke Zarathustra?*

PART III

NIETZSCHE AND
SPIRITUAL/RELIGIOUS ZIONISM

Martin Buber sought to turn the Jewish people to Judaism. By "Judaism" he did not mean the antiquarian lore, nor, like Ahad Ha'am, Jewish ethics. What made him the most prominent representative of "spiritual Zionism" were his efforts to shape a personal and humanistic religious Hebraism and to encourage a renaissance of Jewish creativity. Hence, what attracted the young Buber to Nietzsche was his vision of the individual's outpouring of creative vitality, which he had read about in *The Birth of Tragedy*. Buber, like Ahad Ha'am, protested the political nature of the Zionist movement under the auspices of Herzl and Nordau, convinced that genuine Jewish culture and authentic Jews were needed more urgently than a Jewish state. Selfhood must come before statehood, he argued. That is why, according to the testimony of some of his more attentive listeners, Buber (like Nietzsche) aspired to change his audience's basic attitudes toward life and put less emphasis in his lectures and writings on the delivery of information.[1] In any case, it was largely through Buber that Nietzsche was partly assimilated into German Zionism.

But beyond the future of the Zionist movement, the pressing issue of Buber's personal predicament was no less relevant. Due to his peculiar kind of marginality, he had a greater need for Nietzsche than other Zionist thinkers. Nietzsche's teaching on authenticity made him, in the first phase of his versatile career, its most prominent Jewish disciple. As the result of Buber's relatively early exposure to the European culture of his time, he became temporarily estranged from his Jewish roots. Hence the motif that frequently recurs in his writings is his longing for a return. In

Hebrew this notion is known as *teshuvah,* literally, an answer. This term, however, also contains the root *shuv,* which means coming back after taking leave. In Buber's case it means a return to his Jewish roots. But his was not a regressive return to what one once was—his return did not entail a faithful adoption of the antiquarian heritage accumulated for thousands of years by the Jewish people. He attempted, instead, to recreate his heritage for productive use in the present. He sought to introduce new, more personal meaning to Judaism by emphasizing different trends in its rich past. Following his own retreat to secularism and his perception of the nihilistic atmosphere that permeated fin-de-siècle culture, especially in Vienna, Buber sought to overcome the catastrophic consequences—for his people and for Europe as a whole—of what he called the *Eclipse of God*[2] (rather than His death, as Nietzsche proclaimed it). This shift from death to eclipse symbolically expresses the fundamental difference between both philosophers.

The eclipse of God is a temporary event; its passing enables one to return to Him and to His renewed glory. However, the way toward God presents itself to Buber less as the renewal of the entire Jewish tradition and more as one's personal, creative own way. Buber's own way was to instill into the biological model of authenticity an aesthetic component that would combine "authenticity and essence" into one united Being. The German notion of *Wesen* that Buber employed, commonly translated as "essence," refers also to "Being," to one's own individual existence. Hence Buber reminds us in his most philosophical composition, *I and Thou,* that "basic words are spoken with one's being [*Wesen*]."[3] Such basic notions as personal authenticity, unity and harmony, truthfulness of life, and identity are the elements of which our meaningful lives are made. These ideals, fully implemented in one's individual life as well as in the life of one's people, may overcome what Buber calls in *I and Thou* the "sickness of our age" (p. 104). Nietzsche, too, was trying to fight such sickness or decadence by calling on us to embrace the immanent atheistic world of the "tragic truth": to make ourselves so spiritually powerful that we will be able to "dance even near abysses."

Still, the four leading figures of the Zionist movement and Hebrew culture discussed so far were atheists. The first two—Herzl and Nordau—were born into Western-Jewish acculturated families and therefore manifested from the very beginning the syndromes of existential marginality that, among other things, led to a suppression or even a complete obliteration of any traces of Jewish religiousness. Their Eastern counterparts—Berdichevski and Ahad Ha'am—though raised in Jewish Orthodox surroundings, disregarded religious lore relatively early in their lives. Thus it is hardly surprising that all four of them were quite attracted to the German "slayer" of all gods and idols. The picture becomes more complicated, however, when we come to deal with Jewish-Zionist admirers of Nietzsche who nurtured deep religious sentiments and even made these sentiments into the main objectives of their thought (Buber) and life (Zeitlin). How one can explain their strong attraction to the herald of the atheistic Zarathustra? Was their clinging to Nietzsche only a passing whim in a period when they wanted to overthrow their religious upbringing and become "free spirits"? How can one fathom the reasons for Nietzsche's "invasion" into the life and thought of Martin Buber, who tried, according to his own account, to "liberate" himself from what he called this "sublime intoxication"? Was this liberation successful? Can we discern certain aspects of Nietzsche's thought and mode of thinking in the late Buber, after this so-called liberation? What happened to Hillel Zeitlin's initial infatuation with Nietzsche? Were his pious sentiments really anti-Nietzschean ones?

These and other questions will be discussed in the following two chapters.

CHAPTER 5

Martin Buber's "Liberation" from Nietzsche's "Invasion"

In his "Autobiographical Fragments," Buber recounts his encounter, at the age of seventeen in 1895, with Nietzsche and *Thus Spoke Zarathustra*: "The philosopher not only stirred me up but transported me into a sublime intoxication. Only after a long time was I able to escape this intoxication completely ... This book ... worked on me not in the manner of a gift but in the manner of an invasion (*Überfall*) which deprived me of my freedom, and it was a long time until I could liberate myself from it." Then, after mentioning Nietzsche's conception of the "eternal return of the same" and calling it a "negative seduction" (*negative Verführung*, the same term that Nietzsche used to refer to the effects, negative in his eyes, of the Pauline Christians), he reports that he was so much "taken" by *Thus Spoke Zarathustra* that he decided to translate it into Polish and "even translated the first part." After learning that an established Polish author had translated several sections of the book, he preferred to renounce this project "in his favor."[1]

The terms Buber used in this moment of revealing candor are highly significant. Firstly, "invasion" implies that Buber's intoxication with Nietzsche was not of his own making. It suggests that this influence worked as a kind of force majeure, an irresistible compulsion that he could not fight. Nobody can accuse him of falling under the spell of the charismatic philosopher of his own accord at such a young age; indeed, one has to sympathize with his efforts to regain his intellectual freedom and to "escape completely" this "invasion." Second, the invasion "transported" Buber's very being, and transformed him into another person. Nietzsche's impact upon him was not confined solely to his mind but touched the very core of his being and considerably changed it. Naturally, a question arises: can one liberate oneself completely from such a profound impact? And indeed, one of my main theses in this chapter is that Buber's "liberation" from Nietzsche was not as complete as he thought it was.

All in all, this chapter shows that Buber appeared most Nietzschean on his way to Zionism. When he became a Zionist, though he introduced certain Nietzschean motifs into his program of cultural Zionism, he moved away from Nietzsche (with the help of Kierkegaard) and returned to Judaism—or, to put it more precisely, to his new-old version of Judaism. We will see, however, that his humanist-existentialist version of religion also contained certain Nietzschean elements.

Another central claim of this chapter is that Buber's initial passionate endorsement of Nietzsche had its roots in his peculiar form of multimarginality, which he occasionally revealed.[2] His friend Ernst Simon aptly called Buber "an East-Western or West-Eastern Jew,"[3] meaning that Buber (born in Vienna in 1878) personified a kind of a peculiar synthesis between those two Jewish types: his religious upbringing in the house of his grandfather, a well-known Talmudic scholar in Lemberg (Polish Lwów) was that of an Eastern Jew, while his university studies and doctorate in Vienna made him a marginal Western Jew.[4]

To illustrate the threefold division (Jewish, Polish and Austrian-German) that characterized Buber's existential profile, it is sufficient to quote his ironic description: "My school was called 'Franz Joseph's Gymnasium.' The language of instruction and of social intercourse was Polish, but the atmosphere . . . which prevailed among the peoples of the Austro-Hungarian empire: was of mutual tolerance without mutual understanding . . . The pupils were for the most part Poles, in addition to which there was a small Jewish minority . . . but the two groups as such knew almost nothing about each other."[5]

For Buber, the primary means to mend this threefold rift in the heart and mind was his version of spiritual Zionism. As he admits: "Zionism provided the first impetus for my release. I can only suggest here what it meant to me: revival of *coherence*, equilibrium and replacement in the community. No one needs the salvation of a racial bond so much as the youth gripped in *spiritual search*."[6] However, the real "first impetus" to mending his existential schism and embarking upon a search for authenticity, coherence, and inner harmony, for which he longed even more desperately than Berdichevski, was Nietzsche; Hassidism was the second impetus, and then came Zionism. In reference to the latter he admits: "national confession alone does not change the Jew."[7] (p. 517). It cannot shape him into an authentic Jew if he lacks understanding of the deeper, spiritual meaning of Judaism. Such meaning Buber found in Hasidism, and hence his attempts to create a "personal humanist religion" without theology, and without the antiquarian lore of the old ghetto to which, like the other figures discussed in this book, he could not return.[8] This was Buber's solution to the problem of attaining "coherence" within his triple identity. Such an individualistic religion, unmediated by any religious establishment and theological corpus, be it Jewish or Christian, together with a spiritual Zionism which grounded this religion in a definite community, was a perfect means to mend his inner schism and to overcome it creatively. This explains Buber's existential religious stance of the unmediated relation between the lonely individual and the Absolute, or, to use Buber's terms from the last religious section of his *I and Thou*, between "I" and "the eternal You."[9] As a religious thinker, Buber hardly needed the rabbinate and was quite satisfied with the Hasidic rabbis.

Nonetheless, Buber attained an inner harmony and coherence of being when he officially embraced the Zionist cultural project and delivered his famous *Three Addresses on Judaism* (1911).[10] But when he and Franz Rosenzweig began translating the Hebrew Bible into German and after publishing a collection of Hasidic tales,[11] he decided to "liberate" himself from Nietzsche's invasion. This trajectory of Nietzsche's reception appeared also in other Zionist-Jewish figures. We have seen above that when Nietzsche's heuristic call for personal authenticity bore fruit and his existential influence succeeded, he was summarily discarded from the life and thoughts of the people in question since he was no longer useful, and was even detrimental, to their subsequent Zionist activity.

At this point, one can raise an opposite line of argument. Does not the very fact that, after Buber adopted Zionism, he decided to liberate himself from Nietzsche's "invasion" mean (and this is a crucial question for this entire book) that he saw Jewish Nietzscheanism and Zionism as conflicting options for the European marginal Jew? A preliminary answer to this is a flat "No." The fact that Buber introduced many elements of Nietzsche's thought into his own version of Zionism supports this answer.

Though Buber's religious philosophy was also influenced by Kierkegaardian insights, he was much more critical of the Danish philosopher than of Nietzsche.[12] The reason was that he strove to reactivate and mobilize the spiritual creative powers of Jewish individuals—what Nietzsche summarized with his notion of *Macht*. Hence, in what follows I will mainly analyze Buber's Zionist polemical essays and try to clarify his highly complicated relationship to Nietzsche.

This relationship best exemplifies the strong affinities between the syndrome of Jewish marginality, Nietzsche's call for personal authenticity, the philosopher's function as a temporary means of solving personal existential problems, and Zionist ideology which embodied this call on a collective level. This is especially true of the Zionist trend that Buber tried to promote, where the cultural and spiritual needs of modern Jews and the first modern Hebrews were addressed seriously, where individual Jews were not swallowed by a socialist or nationalist program, and where their cultural heritage was accommodated to the urgent task of creating a new image of a Hebrew. This objective was one of the most pronounced Nietzschean elements that informed Buber's Zionist thinking—apart from Berdichevski but in amazing concurrence with him. Hence one can understand Buber's affiliation to the first modern Hebrew writer. The alliance between them was forged under Nietzschean auspices of rebirth, reevaluation of all values, longings for personal authenticity, self-overcoming, creation of new or renewed selves, Dionysian vitality, life affirmation, and an aesthetic orientation toward life.

All these hypotheses will be tested by reading those of Buber's texts that show the most conspicuous presence of Nietzsche, starting at the beginning of Nietzsche's great "invasion," and ending with Buber's no less great but more limited "liberation."

Nietzsche's "Invasion"

Though Nietzsche entered Buber's life in 1893, when he was fourteen,[13] Buber's primer for a proper understanding of Nietzsche's teachings and unpublished essay "Zarathustra," written around 1900,[14] provides the first opportunity to catch intimate sight of what initially attracted Buber to Nietzsche and the role the philosopher played in the young man's development.

Early in his essay, Buber calls Zarathustra "a good European,"[15] using the very name by which Nietzsche liked to call himself. The status of "European" was also one that many acculturated marginal Jews sought to attain by trying to shape their cultural identities beyond narrow national European borders and the walls of their fathers' ghettos. Buber then mentions Nietzsche's "Schopenhauer as Educator," the work in which Nietzsche for the first time presents his teaching on personal authenticity and delineates the way in which one can attain it.[16] Buber followed this way: he "learned from this book that one must find for himself an educator if one wants above all to . . . reach one's Self" (p. 3). A fascinating analogy clearly emerges: just as Nietzsche used the model of Schopenhauer to shape his own authentic self, so Buber turns to Nietzsche and to his heuristic-fictive image of the authentic hero Zarathustra. Thus the recollection of one of Buber's former classmates at the Polish gymnasium in Lwów sounds quite credible: "I remember your being enthusiastic about *Zarathustra*—how you always brought that book to school."[17] Thus, Buber was far from exaggerating when he noted in his "Autobiographical Fragments" that this book of Nietzsche "transported" his very being.

However, despite the great "invasion," the young Buber made several critical observations on Nietzsche's teaching that plague his serious commentators even today. For example, he asks Nietzsche why he regards his "master morality" (*Herrenmoral*) as true when he knows that all truth is but an illusion of the herd. He adds ironically: "But perhaps you wanted yourself be the shepherd?" (p. 4) Here, of course, Buber is wondering about the cognitive status of the positive aspects of Nietzsche's teaching, especially about his moral valuations against the background of his relativistic approach: if everything is simply an interpretation or projection of power and there are no solid or objective facts, this thesis itself is but one out of an infinite number of possible interpretations. Why do we have to accept it? This actually is one of the gravest problems of Nietzsche's philosophy: what exactly is the relationship between the negative aspects of his doctrine (his perspectivism, his criticism of all values and truth) and the positive aspects (his theory of the Overman, the eternal return, the notion of positive and creative power)?[18] Buber does not attempt to solve this cardinal problem. But surely he conceived some parts of Nietzsche's doctrine to be positive, and did not embrace the view, quite common at that time, especially among Jewish anti-Nietzscheans, that Nietzsche is a negative thinker who only destroys but does not provide us with something genuinely positive.

In the key sentence of this primer, Buber dramatically confesses: "*Das war meine Krankheit: nicht glaubte ich an dich, ich glaubte dir*" (*That was my sickness: I did not believe in you, I believed you*) (p. 4; emphasis in the original). The next sentence explains the nature of this "sickness": Buber confesses that at the time of the "first" invasion, when he was only fourteen, Nietzsche's true "character" and figure had not as yet appeared as such before him. "Only recently did I recover from my sickness and this I did by following your recipe" (ibid.). In other words, as a young boy, Buber naively followed Nietzsche's positive doctrines (what he calls in this essay his "system") and believed in his philosophical teachings (what Nietzsche calls *Wahrheit*), completely ignoring the philosopher's quality of personal truthfulness (*Wahrhaftigkeit*). He did not follow what was, at that time, Nietzsche's procedure (delineated in his "Schopenhauer as Educator": "to see through the book and to imagine the living man" (SE, p. 136).[19] And, indeed, when Buber detected Nietzsche's personality behind his teachings, then a second invasion started and the "sick" first infatuation with his writings gave way to more mature insights. Surely, at this stage Buber's identification with Nietzsche was so intense that he actually performed a reversal of roles: it was not Nietzsche who was gravely sick at the time Buber wrote this work, but rather Buber, because he did not fully grasp Nietzsche's spirit and truthfulness as Nietzsche would have liked him to do.

After several pages of lengthy direct quotations from Nietzsche's books, Buber suddenly bursts out: "I love you, Friedrich Nietzsche, for your free, fresh, and cheerful, all too human poetry, for your appearing to be like an old master builder . . . I love the artist in you and the psychologist . . . and moralist" (p. 108). Nowhere else do we find among the Jewish Nietzscheans such an intense, emotional attraction toward the German philosopher. Obviously, Buber's self-consciousness—and self-consciousness was one of the most positive qualities that Buber ascribes to Nietzsche in this essay (p. 109 et passim)[20]—concerning the vital function that Nietzsche played in his thought and existential stance motivated such adoration for someone he had never met in person.

Above everything else, Nietzsche encouraged Buber to become what he was, to dare to be his own self, to create freely this self as an artist creates his own sublime creations. Hence the concrete doctrine was not crucial for Buber, nor "the Overman dream," but the why and the how. In Buber's eyes this was Nietzsche's "true" and greatest insight, which is forever irrefutable because one cannot refute life itself, only (if at all) its intellectual products and dogmas. The fact that young Buber discovered this insight through and in Nietzsche—the very insight that assisted him to shape his "coherence" and harmony, to overcome his shaky triple identity—was in my view the main pole of attraction that so irresistibly invaded his soul and his whole being. In any case, Nietzsche's impact penetrated Buber so deeply that he concludes: "One must desert Nietzsche in order to be able to *grow fond* of him" (p. 22)[21] This was the initial ground for Buber's attempts to "liberate" himself from his spell.

One might think that Buber's strong attachment toward Nietzsche, uninhibitedly expressed in "Zarathustra," was solely limited to the intimate level of a text that he did not intend to publish. That this was not the case can be easily seen from Buber's first published German article, "A Word about Nietzsche and Life Values,"[22] a eulogy of Nietzsche which appeared in December 1900, four months after the philosopher's death. In its warm and direct tone of sheer admiration, and its deep understanding of Nietzsche's positive philosophy, it is perhaps the most perceptive essay on Nietzsche written that year and surely it far surpassed Nordau's ambivalent piece, published in October in Herzl's *Neue Freie Presse*. Significant, however, is the fact that this first of Buber's public pronouncements on Nietzsche endorsed his ideal of aesthetic authenticity.[23]

Buber emphasizes here not the formal ideal of Nietzsche's aesthetic authenticity but the substantial content of the authentic hero, a content that he tried to introduce also into his Zionist agenda. Thus, he stresses that Nietzsche taught new values of life, and that, out of the endemic sickness of his age, which he unwillingly shared, he affirmed and wished to promote the life of instincts, vitality, and cheerfulness. What he proclaimed was not his "own being but a longing for a true [i.e., authentic] being." By the force of this longing he performed a radical reevaluation of life, opting for shared happiness (*Mitfreude*) instead of negative compassion (*Mitleid*); preferring healthy egoism to barren altruism; wishing for the nurturing of "great persons" over the "happiness of the many."[24]

All in all, Buber embraces here without any reservation the positive teaching of Nietzsche's morality, which I have subsumed elsewhere under the overall notion of "positive power." These "positive" predicaments of one's genuine power are conducive to self-creation, to the daring and difficult existential project of creating one's own self, rather than passively letting it be a sheer copy or an a priori essence of some transcendental entity. Buber accepts the God-like role of Nietzsche's authentic hero and concludes his eulogy with an observation that Nietzsche brought against the "Creator of the World"—his "great adversary: the God in the making (*werdende Gott*) in whose development we may share."

Forty years later, in a Hebrew article written in Palestine at the beginning of the Holocaust, after Buber returned to the God of Genesis, he once again described the Nietzschean ideal of authenticity, the *Übermensch*, as the "*werdende Gott*," and rejected it. Thus Buber later changed his admiring posture toward Nietzsche to a more critical attitude by a shift from Zarathustra, "the God in the making," to God as maker—the God of Abraham, Isaac, and Jacob.

BUBER'S "NIETZIONISM"

However, the young and (at that time) still secular Zionist did not wait for God to reawaken his brothers from their inertia, but in an essay of 1901 he called on them to reenter the history of the "general culture of beauty" by turning their "positive energy" into aesthetic creations. He wished thereby to awake the inert Jews for a "Jewish Renaissance."[25]

The idea of "Jewish Renaissance" had a seminal effect on Zionist discourse in the twentieth century. It also remains highly relevant to the contemporary cultural war in the state of Israel. Moreover, it shows that Buber's growing commitment to Zionism was not in any way the reason for his wish to "liberate" himself from Nietzsche's spell. On the contrary, his affinity for this German slayer of all modern "idols," including nationalism, helped him to delineate his early Zionist program, where Nietzschean motifs are visible to such a degree that one may coin for this program the neologism "Nietzionism."

Buber argued in his essay that the two thousand years in the Diaspora had forced the Jews to transform their physical energy into a purely spiritual one. Buber called upon modern Jews to liberate themselves from their "fettered spirituality" (*"unfreie Geistigkeit,"* col. 9). Going beyond their "senseless tradition" and "expanding the feelings of life" (ibid.), will lead to "resurrection from semilife to life" (p. 31) and to a "unified personality" (col. 10). This call for a despiritualization of Jewish life echoed Nietzsche's psychological explanation of the impoverished "spirit." For Nietzsche, that spirit, due to inner repression (caused by the ascetic teachings of Christianity) and to oppressive pressures of the "mighty" ones, internalizes all its instincts and directs them against itself. This in turn brings about the appearance of the meek *dividuum* which utterly destroys the *individuum*. This spiritual asceticism is a result of repression of instincts and of an excessive spiritualization (*GM* II-16). To reverse these destructive tendencies, Nietzsche advocates a return to sensual life that promotes aesthetic creation.

Marginal, acculturated Jews, acutely aware of their anomalous existence and longing for a healthy and natural life outside the ghetto's walls, responded to this directive enthusiastically. Rejecting the repressive patterns of traditional life, they virtually exploded with astonishing creative drive, markedly enriching the Weimar Republic, Vienna, and general European culture. Buber, however, did not have in mind these assimilatory tendencies but envisaged a new category of Jews: acculturated European Jews who would contribute to "European treasures," but would do so as Jews within a Zionist movement that would defend their "innermost essence." These "heralds of a new renaissance" (among them, Buber himself) would work toward "the evolving formulation of a new human life." Buber used this expression in his 1900 eulogy to describe Nietzsche's main contribution to mankind; thus on this point he implicitly identifies himself with Nietzsche. Buber went on in "Jewish Renaissance," claiming that these harbingers of Jewish Renaissance "suffer as once did the prophets" and hence "we must trust their prophecy." These modern "prophets" had envisioned a Zionist movement that, unlike Herzl's thrust to secure political, legal, and economic rights for the return to Zion, intended to effect a radical reevaluation and reaffirmation of the Zionists' souls and individualities. We should recall that Berdichevski, too, emphasized such an internal transfiguration which, in both his and Buber's eyes, must precede political freedom and the reclaiming of the new-old land.

Not surprisingly, this shift from political to spiritual Zionism is achieved under the Nietzschean banner. After evoking (in a Nietzschean manner) the ancient Hebrews "who were filled with a strong, expansive sense of life that often overflowed" (p. 33), Buber ends his programmatic Zionist credo with the prophecy that "the movement will eliminate the dichotomy between deed and thought, the inconsistency between enthusiasm and energy . . . and will again restore the unified personality that produces out of a burning will power" (ibid.). Consequently, the "rebirth of the Jewish people . . . is only a branch of the stream of the new renaissance" (p. 34) that Nietzsche heralded for Europe.

Buber is not dealing solely with Jewish resurrection as a nation, but defines as the ultimate and the most essential objective of Zionism a radical transfiguration of the whole personality, a complete transvaluation of personal values and patterns of life. He has in mind, like many other Nietzschean Zionists, an existentialist revolution more difficult to attain than the cultivation of new and devastated lands: the cultivation of a new type of Jew. In subsequent essays, these Nietzschean existential motifs were forcefully expressed: "the Jewish Renaissance is . . . a rebirth of the whole man . . . *A new type of Jew is gradually emerging.*"[26]

Though it is true that Buber's conversion to Zionism was his means to "take root anew in the [Jewish] community,"[27] his call for "Jewish Renaissance" intended to get rid of those elements in *Galut* (exile) that manifested unhealthy degeneration and were the real impediments for cultivation of the "new type of Jew," endowed with positive power and with most of the features that characterize the autonomous, noble, powerful, and creative authentic individual. This version of "Nietzionism" is clearly expressed in Buber's definition of Zionist politics: "a transvaluation (*Umwertung*) of all aspects of . . . the life of the people to its depths and very foundations. It must touch the soul. . . . We must unlock the vital powers of the nation and let loose its fettered instincts."[28] Buber wished to pave the way for such a Nietzschean transvaluation, mainly by promoting Jewish art and educating Jews to perceive life aesthetically, thereby empowering them to live fully and creatively. To this end he organized an exhibition of contemporary Jewish art in conjunction with the Fifth Zionist Congress in Basel in December 1901 under the motto, "Only full human beings can be full Jews, who are capable of and worthy of achieving for themselves a homeland."[29] Buber's aesthetic program for the Jewish Renaissance is informed by his reading of Nietzsche's *Birth of Tragedy,* where Nietzsche launched his cultural project for European "Dionysian" revolution and rebirth of the Greek ancient heritage. Nietzsche also emphasizes artistic creation as the epitome of the creative processes of sublimation that assist one to overcome the dread of the tragic elements of life, so that the artist himself becomes "a work of art" (*BT* 1). But can sheer aestheticism solve the inner tension that Buber gradually came to feel was tearing apart his "Nietzionism"?

What are the genuine Jewish elements of Buber's so-called "Jewish Renaissance"? What viable connection could he imagined to exist between the Jewish "innermost essence," its unfettered creative instincts and powers, and the general European Renaissance, which swept across national borders and religious denominations? In chapter 2 this problem was defined in relation to Nordau by the question of how to secure the humanist and universalistic ramifications of the Zionist revolution within its tribal and national aspects. Here this same question reappears, but this time on the cultural-spiritual level. Nietzsche's stress on creativity, his embrace of aesthetic values, his support of vitalism over legalism and pure rationalism, his plea to enhance our will to life, his stress on the authenticity of one's life, all denote formal principles. True, Buber attempted to infuse his Zionist vision with a Nietzschean antidote to "pure spirituality" by expanding the vital forces and "life-feeling" of the instincts. But what specifically Jewish content can we grant these "life-feelings," which by their very nature, as naturalistic-biological inclinations of human beings as such, do not possess any specific cultural, religious, or tribal characteristics? Berdichevski struggled with almost the same issue, spending the last years of his life on antiquarian researches into ancient Israelite history. What was Buber's solution? As he already deeply believed at this stage of his existential metamorphoses, "it is not enough to have solely a national experience or a national culture which does not call for a national service of the supranational."[30] Clearly, Buber was not satisfied with Nietzschean formalism. Despite his intensive activity in promoting Jewish art and artists in accordance with his Nietzschean early views of the primacy of aesthetic creation over the ethical and scientific ethos, he struggled to fill this formal principle of creativity with a specific and unique Jewish content. He already attempted this in his 1902 article that bore a definite stamp of Ahad Ha'am: "A Spiritual Center."[31]

"A Spiritual Center"

In this article, besides using Ahad Ha'am's Hegelian-Herderian terms like "national identity" (*Volksart*), "national spirit" (*Volksgeist*), and "national soul" (*Volksseele*), Buber strongly supports Ahad Ha'am's view that "salvation begins in one's heart"—namely, that before embarking on Herzl's vision of political salvation and economic Jewish liberation, one must take an initial, necessary step already in exile: a Jewish reeducation and "cultural elevation of the people" that will bring about their personal transfiguration. In the course of his argument he refers to the Nietzschean formula of "the transvaluation of values," and to Ahad Ha'am's Nietzschean essay bearing this very name. He rhetorically exclaims: "I do not believe that we should consider loading a people onto ships like dead freight, send them across to the land, and then expect the soil to perform a miracle—the restoration of the sickest of all people to true life . . . Rather we must work on transvaluating the Jewish mentality" (p. 123). Together with Chaim Weizmann, later the first president of Israel, he proposed to establish a "Jewish college" (p. 128) that would resurrect the "Hebrew language" (pp. 124–25), because in his view a "complete transformation" of the Jewish mentality would work "best with young and open minds." The only tangible result of this project was the first Hebrew university on Mount Scopus in Jerusalem (established in 1925).

In any case, Buber seems to be uneasy at his inability to invest his "Jewish culture" with a specific Jewish content. This clearly emerges from his statement that "we do not have to bother with definitions" (p. 125). Nonetheless, besides the arts, which he promoted eagerly, he introduces to his description of Jewish culture the main elements of folklore: "We must emphasize that every psychological expression of national identity belongs to a people's culture. A folk song, a dance, a wedding custom, a metaphor, a legend . . . a menorah, tefillin" (p. 125). Most of these religious folk characteristics require "our own land" ibid.) where the Jews will be able to nurture a culture that will be "rich, healthy, well-rounded, and fully developed" (ibid.). However, according to Buber's definition, a secular Israeli who eats falafel, dances the hora, and serves in the Israel Defense Forces is no less contributing to Jewish culture than a *bachur* (young man, p. 119) in a *heder* who studies Talmud and wears *tefillin*. But could both of them communicate and cooperate in order to contribute together to the future development of a renewed culture in this new-old land?

This question remains unanswered, though heatedly debated, in Israel today, but surely this local "volkish" dimension of "national Jewish culture" stands in apparent tension with the "supranational" dimension about which Buber wrote elsewhere.

In any case, Nietzsche claimed in his essay on history that "since we are the outcome of earlier generations, we are also the outcome of their aberrations, passions and errors, and indeed of their crimes; it is not possible wholly to free oneself from this chain" (HL, p. 76). Buber realized that by the same token we are what we are also because of what we once were. He expressed this insight in manifestly Nietzschean language. Summarizing one of his later addresses, "On Judaism," he exclaimed: "Let us recognize ourselves: we are the keepers of the roots. How can we become what we are?"[32] And since the young Buber wished to shape his own authentic identity, he had to examine the Hasidic "legends," tales, and folklore of his ancestors' past. This explains why, before coming to his "homeland" in "Eretz Israel" (p. 122), Buber spent a lot of his time, energy, and considerable talent in collecting and circulating the Hasidic tales and legends in the German-speaking countries.

Though it lies beyond the scope of this chapter to deal with Buber's significant contributions to the study of Hasidism, one point should be made concerning his explorations of Hasidism, namely that they, too, were inspired by Nietzsche's attitude toward religion and myth. His introduction to *The Legend of the Baal-Shem* echoes Nietzsche's *Birth of Tragedy* with its distinction between what I have called positive and negative religions: "All *positive religion* rests on an enormous simplification of the manifold and wildly engulfing forces that invade us: it is the *subduing* of the fullness of existence. All myth, in contrast, is *the expression of the fullness of existence*, its image, its sign; it drinks incessantly from the gushing fountains of life."[33] What Buber calls here "positive religion," being ascetic and repressive of other human instincts, was regarded by Nietzsche as a negative manifestation of human power (*Macht*). In contrast, what Buber here calls "myth" (meaning, beyond anything else, Hasidism, which is in his eyes "the latest form of the Jewish myth,"[34] was in Nietzsche's eyes an expression of positive power. The "fullness of existence" was, according to Nietzsche, expressed in the Dionysian rituals and "tragedy" of pre-Socratic ancient Greece, but also in the ancient Hebrew religious cult.

Nietzsche claimed that the ancient Hebrew religion was an expression of the plenitude of power and positive resources of the people who created it. Its heroes had "strong instincts" and behaved spontaneously and impulsively. They manifested Dionysian ecstatic vitality and affirmation of life. Not surprisingly, Buber considered the Hasidic rabbis and their ideal of the just man (the tzaddik) in almost the same terms. Such "affirmation of life" and of the here and now is found in Buber's collection of Hasidic tales, *Gog und Magog*.[35] When Rabbi Nachman of Braslav was asked, "What is the most important thing on earth?" He answered, "The thing that you are doing now."

Furthermore, Nietzsche claimed that the ancient Hebrew concept of God was a direct expression of life's affirmation, and a projection of a healthy, spontaneous, and harmonious relation to nature before it became denaturalized by Jewish-Christian theology by introducing into it the "moral world order." Whereas the ancient Hebrew religion was an expression of plenitude of power and life, the Jewish-Christian religion became a "tool in the hands of priestly agitators" who were afraid of life, of their instincts, and of the nature within them and before them; it became an instrument for overcoming their negative and feeble powers and a means for the subjugation of others by the manipulative introduction of devious concepts like "guilt" and "sin." Buber seemed to embrace such a view since he, like Nietzsche (and Kierkegaard), shunned any theology and any religious lore based on the sophisticated, antiquarian, and exclusively rational exegeses of the holy writings that only the most educated could study and use in the ghettos. Buber embraced the warm, intuitive morality and wisdom of the Hasidic populist rabbis, described in so many of his collected tales and legends. This was his solution to various problems he had faced at this period of his development. The most important of these was a personal problem that his formalistic "Nietzionism" could not solve, namely, providing himself with a concrete identity and positive content.

According to Nietzsche, the main positive function of the ancient Hebrews' faith was rooted in the fact that their projected image of a personal God strengthened their positive powers by crystallizing and sanctifying their vitality and affirmation of life, and by making these values into explicit and stimulating ideals. But this was also the function of the exemplary Hasidic figures who, because of the intensive personal relations they had with their followers, could elevate them to their own sublime level of righteousness. The personal God of the ancient Hebrews, by showing them what he was, urged them to become what they were, and hence his other function was to call them to embrace what Nietzsche cherished most—the ideal of the authentic life. This was also, according to Buber, the sublime function of the Hasidic leaders and rabbis. Just as the Nietzschean authentic artist in *The Birth of Tragedy* becomes himself a "work of art," so Hasidism holds that "man's final objective is . . . to become, himself, a law, a Torah."[36] Most important, however, Hasidism performed these two existential functions without falling back on the antiquarian, Talmudic tradition that bred the excessive spiritualization of the Jewish people in the "Old Ghetto."

For all these reasons (as well as his Nietzschean views), Buber was so enthusiastic about Hasidism that he endorsed somewhat mystical expressions of Judaism and even tried to appear and sometimes to act as a rabbi. Nevertheless, we should not forget the most basic difference between Hasidism and Nietzsche that perhaps later estranged Buber from the philosopher's teachings. Nietzsche's authentic hero was living in a solitude beyond "good and evil," whereas the Hasidic rabbi was deeply rooted in his community and exemplified its ethos of good and bad. Buber, who above all wished to find roots in the Jewish community and society and worked intensively for common Zionist objectives, could not estrange himself from his people. Thus, as we will see, one of the criticisms that he most often directed against Nietzsche was that the latter neglected the social sphere that was so crucial to Hasidism and to Buber's own life and activity. Still, when we examine Buber's main philosophical work, *I and Thou,* we will see that the personal relationship between the individual and the personal God exist mainly on the one-to-one subjective level. Hence, the so-called "asociality" of Nietzsche did not bother Buber on the purely philosophical-existential level of discourse, but solely on the level of his personal experience and praxis.

In any case, one who was so pervasively and emotionally inspired by Nietzsche could not "liberate" himself entirely from his spell. Even Buber's desperate struggle to do that had something very Nietzschean about it. As Nietzsche put it himself, "if one stares too long at the monster—the monster will look back at him." Nietzsche, however, had never been and would never become in Buber's eyes such a monster.

But was it really Nietzsche's atheism that somehow estranged Buber from him? In my view, the main reason for Buber's wish to liberate himself from Nietzsche was the latter's radical and, according to Brandes, "aristocratic" individualism, and what Buber later called the "asociality" of his approach, which obviously was not conducive to the future of Judaism in Zion as Buber envisaged it. Clearly, this aspect of Nietzsche's philosophy, more even than his atheism, was the main factor in the growing estrangement of Buber (and other Zionists as well) from his philosophy.

A convincing proof for this contention is the puzzling fact that this estrangement was not expressed in Buber's main philosophical work, first published in 1923, *I and Thou*. On the contrary, even this deeply religious essay contains many Nietzschean insights as well as a kind of apology for Nietzsche's atheism.

I AND THOU

Buber is indebted to Nietzsche's philosophical anthropology in his basic distinction between the I-Thou and the I-It relationship, which echoes the Nietzschean distinctions between positive and the negative patterns of power and between authentic and inauthentic relations. Following Buber's warning [37], it is important to stress that these relations do not connote any ontological framework. Buber's distinction is purely anthropological: each individual, according to him, consists of the "basic human duality of his I" (p. 115). Just as Nietzsche portrays each of us as manifesting, in varying degrees, the fluctuating patterns of positive versus negative power vectors, so Buber declares: "No human being is pure person, and none is pure ego; none is entirely actual, none entirely lacking in actuality. Each lives in a twofold I" (p. 114). Moreover, Nietzschean predicates that describe the patterns of positive power versus those of negative power, [38] are astonishingly similar to Buber's descriptions of the relations that prevail between the I-Thou and I-It.

In the realm of I-It relations, the I manifests patterns of negative power, because it lacks the positive mental resources of a firm selfhood and personal power. In order to enhance its feeble sense of selfhood it formulates the "project of conquering the world" (p. 91); it objectifies the other person and makes him into an object of his uses, manipulations, and, what Nietzsche would call *Gewalt* (violence). In these sadomasochistic relations, the other becomes an object for exploitation and "scientific" investigation (pp. 80–81), and loses his or her intrinsic value as a significant individual whose liberties and values stand in their own right. In contrast to this "functional one-dimensionality" and "conditionality" (pp. 80, 81) of the I-It relations, the I-Thou intercourse is unconditional and manifests "reciprocity" between fully harmonious, autonomous, and authentic personalities who both possess positive power patterns and communicate with each other "with one's whole being" (pp. 81, 54) while recognizing each other's rights of other persons to their own authenticity and even assisting each other in attaining it.[39] Here the relations are one of complete "reciprocity" (pp. 58, 67) and mutuality and not of one-sided, pragmatic exploitation. In the realm of I-Thou, relation "is the cradle of actual life" (p. 60), and Buber means here authentic and genuine life and interrelations whereby one commits oneself to others with all one's being. Within this sphere of an authentic interrelation, the "soul's creative powers" (ibid.) manifest themselves optimally in building and sustaining such relations.

Furthermore, Buber stresses the fact that the I-It and I-Thou types of relations (like Nietzsche's positive and negative powers) are historical phenomena, and as such they require what Nietzsche used to call a "genealogy," beginning in "primal history," that repeats itself on the ontogenetic level of "the prenatal life of the child" (pp. 75, 76). And thus like Nietzsche (and Freud), who occasionally make parallels between phylogenesis and ontogenesis, between the development of cultural patterns and their evolution in individual members of that culture,[40] Buber draws parallels between the "natural" emergence of I-Thou versus I-It relations in the child (p. 76) and also in "the history of the race" (p. 82).

Most of the second part of *I and Thou*, in fact, deals with the social and historical ramifications of the I-It and the I-Thou relations (in Nietzsche's language in *The Genealogy of Morals*, with the patterns of relations that prevail within the sphere of slave morality versus those that prevail within the realm of the master morality). In this context Buber, unlike Nordau and Herzl, categorically rejects "technical achievements" (p. 88) because they significantly contribute to "the progressive increase of the It-world" (ibid.), that is, "the preservation, alleviation, and equipment of human life" which include "the acquisition of information" and "utilization" (ibid.).

I cannot elaborate here the criticism that Buber directs against his times (and Kierkegaard's *Present Age* immediately springs to mind) and I have to limit myself to the more striking similarities between Buber's and Nietzsche's anthropology—for example, the epistemological difficulties that both encounter. The first similarity has to do with the problem of the possibility of attaining objective recognition and judgment of whether one is really dealing in any particular case with an I-Thou or an I-It relation. Both Buber and Nietzsche have no objective criterion for distinguishing between authentic I-Thou relations and inauthentic I-It relations. Buber admits this explicitly when he flatly states that in the case of the I-Thou, "truth of the relation . . . surpasses understanding" (p. 91) and embraces what is beyond "conceptual knowledge" (p. 90). Nietzsche had struggled with the same problem of recognizing and judging the personal authenticity of other persons.

Moreover, as with Nietzsche's notion of *Wahrhaftigkeit* (truthfulness), so Buber's notion of existential engagement with and commitment to each other is not relevant to the cognitive, conceptual, and epistemological notion of *Wahrheit*. Buber's notion of "human truth," which one may manifest authentically in social relations but cannot express in clear conceptual terms, must necessarily lead him to the religious domain of faith and to the adoption of the Kierkegaardian attitude that "truth is subjectivity." Surely, the religious sentiment and the I-God relationship was for Buber the ultimate perspective from which he surveyed human relations.

This brings us to another philosophical problem facing Buber's distinction between I-Thou and I-It relations. Buber definitely values the first, more genuine and authentic encounter. Nietzsche too spoke significantly more highly of his ideal manifestation of authenticity, of the *Übermensch*. But could both thinkers demonstrate the validity of their preferences? Surely not. So why try to be authentic or to painfully sustain the sometimes stormy I-Thou relations? Like Nietzsche's Zarathustra, Buber could not provide a rational answer to this question. He could only repeat, in Nietzschean fashion, the "terrifying Either/Or: 'Either abolish your reverences or—*yourselves!*'" The dissolution of our selves, however, "would be nihilism" (*GS* 346), and Nietzsche encourages us to will and create our authentic selfhood simply because it would be spiritual suicide to do otherwise. Buber is using almost the same "enticing" tactic when he warns us: "Every relationship in which one is not at all present to the other, but each uses the other only for self-enjoyment—what would remain?" (p. 95).

However, the basic question facing Buber's teaching on the authentic relations between I and Thou, which is a direct reflection of a similar problem in Nietzsche, is: Why does the authentic *Übermensch* need a society, and how (if at all) can authenticity be cultivated and preserved within the social context? The cry for authenticity mainly appeared at the twilight of the rational ethic—at the "Twilight of the Idols," or, in Buber's language, in "a sick age" (p. 102). It is an explicit expression of revolt against the spirit of objectivity, scientism, and "common causality" (ibid.). Thus it is inconceivable to have a fully authentic individual living in society, which by its intrinsic nature is founded upon a set of objective norms and a common ethos. Buber asks himself the most pertinent and crucial question: "Isn't the communal life of modern man bound to be submerged in the It-world?" (p. 96). He speaks in this context about "politics" and "economy and the state" (ibid.), which makes clear why he objected to Herzl's political Zionism and to Nordau's school, never subscribing to Zionism in its narrow nationalist meaning.

Man is a social animal and as such has no choice but to immerse himself also in an I-It relationship. But by means of the spirit (the cultural world of ideas and works of art), by one's creativity and that of others, "one can nevertheless be transfigured to the point where 'the It' confronts us and represents the You" (p. 99). Today, however, "the spirituality that represents the spirit . . . is so scattered, weakened, degenerate . . . that it could not possibly do this until it had first *returned* to the *essence* of the spirit: being able to say You" (p. 100; my emphasis). The motif of the "return" (which in Hebrew, *teshuvah,* also connotes returning to faith in God) appears here and elsewhere (e.g., pp. 104–5) together with the notion of "grace" (p. 102). Thus we face here the typical Buberian and anti-Nietzschean solution to the paradoxes entailed in the wish to sustain the ideal authentic relation in an anti-authentic society. Nietzsche's deus ex machina is not (as in Buber's case) *deus.* It is personified by the atheistic Zarathustra, the *Übermensch,* who aspires to attain more moderate aims.

In regard to Buber's existentialist-biographical predicaments which underlay his religious stance here, one may add the observation that when a person has been utterly uprooted from his early childhood to the extent of losing one's mother's love, no roots that do not originate in the solid eternity of the Absolute can suffice. Such a person is doomed by his own fate (which is also of his own making) to be an unceasing and weary wanderer. Not at home in Polish Lwów, not at home in German Vienna and Berlin, not at home in Jerusalem, a person finds his shelter and roots in one's belief in the one God. Such a belief provides one with long-sought unity and peaceful harmony. God is one's mother's womb, is the earth of one's homeland, is the silent, religious language that is the most universally meaningful.

And indeed, alongside the personal and highly individual ramifications of his religiosity that resemble those of Kierkegaard, Buber also stressed the universalistic dimensions of the authentic faith with which all kinds of believers in one absolute God could identify, be they Christians, Moslems, or Jews. An authentic faith does not distinguish between races, languages of prayer, the theological content of different creeds, and so on. Just as Kierkegaard in his *Fear and Trembling* could use Abraham's attempt at sacrificing his son Isaac to exemplify the "knight of faith," so Buber could use the example of Jesus for the same purpose.[41]

Authentic faith has no borders and no creed limitations because it is essentially an inward experience and a subjectively intentional relation. Buber, who at that time he wrote *I and Thou* had neither homeland, concrete social affiliations, nor solid identity, was the perfect listener ("son") for such a Kierkegaardian faith. Like Nietzsche, Kierkegaard put his main emphasis on the personal experience and the authentic pattern of lives, but he did this under the auspices of God and within His embrace. Thus many marginal Jews (including Buber), terrified by their marginality, could thank Kierkegaard for providing them with a less radical (than Nietzsche's) solution of their identity problem—one that enabled them to keep their new identity intact. This was an identity of believing Jews, who strayed from their forefathers' tradition and were not able, or willing, to follow in letter and in spirit the rabbinical Jewish Orthodoxy that insisted on observing all the *mitzvoth* (religious commandments). Kierkegaard was significantly less radical than Nietzsche in matters of faith, though he was no less radical in matters of religion: both rejected the religious-institutional framework. This was Kierkegaard's main charm for Zionist thinkers like Gershom Scholem and Buber, and for religious Zionists in contemporary Israel, who reject attempts to mobilize the Jewish religion for the cause of nationalist fanatics.[42]

Consequently, the profile of Buber's relations to Nietzsche and to Kierkegaard was characteristic of the relations that Jewish intellectuals nurtured toward both thinkers. When marginal Jews overcame the mental schism between European culture and their attraction to Zion, where they hoped to return to the genuine Jewish faith, and when they completed the existential as well as geographical move expressed so poignantly by the title of Scholem's memoirs, *Von Berlin nach Jerusalem,* they ceased to grapple with Nietzsche and became more attentive to and preoccupied with Kierkegaard. The latter presented them with a "kosher" model of authentic faith: Abraham, the "Knight of Faith" with whom they were already familiar from their childhood.[43]

Buber, however, could not shake off the profound influence of Nietzsche on his life and thought just as he could not shake off his religious roots. Though he embraced Zionist ideology, he could not subscribe to its radical secularization of Judaism. Hence he looked for some kind of a privately created sense of Jewish faith that would distance him from the old Orthodox religiosity and emphasize a subjective attitude toward Judaism. In this attempt Buber was encouraged by Kierkegaard's attitude. The Danish philosopher inspired him to forge his personal Jewish faith which, on the one hand, does not clash with Zionist ideology, and, on the other, does not fall too far from Orthodox Judaism. Thus as Kierkegaard, according to his own testimony, spent all his life trying to "become a Christian," so Buber was trying to become a Jew, namely, to shape for himself his own Jewish religious identity.

In any case, in *I and Thou*, Buber tries to vindicate Nietzsche in two ways. The first involves excusing himself for his infatuation with Nietzsche: "Whoever abhors the name and fancies that he is godless—when he addresses with his whole devoted being the You of his life that cannot be restricted by any other, he addresses God" (p. 124). Thus Nietzsche, who was addressing his sublime ideal of the *Übermensch,* was actually addressing his God. For Buber, if the living God is not only a God who reveals Himself but also One who conceals Himself—then he is the One who conceals Himself from Nietzsche. Consequently Nietzsche's atheism is not an atheism without God. Moreover, whereas for Nietzsche personal authenticity is grounded in the atheistic rejection of the Absolute and in the heroic attempt of the *Übermensch* to create himself in an immanent world, from Buber's theistic perspective this very *Übermensch* is endowed by Nietzsche with a God-like role; hence this ideal for Buber is like God.[44] But Buber does not believe in a *Mensch* who can be God: such an ideal is too lofty and vague, whereas one's faith in God is the most tangible feeling that ensures the concrete authenticity of one's self.

Buber's second way of vindicating Nietzsche's alleged atheism addresses his basic philosophical stance affirming the complete immanency of our world (for example, in sections 108–11 of *The Gay Science*). Buber, paradoxically, provides a theological argument for such a view by stating that to deny any importance to the world here and now amounts to saying that God has created it for mere whim or appearance. And thus in his pronouncedly Nietzschean and existentialist essay "The Question to the Single One,"[45] Buber, while engaged in a sharp polemic against Kierkegaard, utters this semi-Nietzschean statement: "Creation is not a hurdle on the road to God, it is the road itself."[46]

"What Is Man?"

The final part of Buber's inaugural lectures as professor of social philosophy at the Hebrew University of Jerusalem in 1938, *What is Man?*, deals with "Feuerbach and Nietzsche."[47] The grouping together of the two greatest atheists of the nineteenth century suggests that Buber is trying to fight the destructive import of these two approaches that reduce religious faith to various anthropological phenomena.

In regard to Nietzsche's thought, Buber is not concerned at all here with his atheism but with the anthropological arguments presented by Nietzsche in his *Genealogy of Morals*. In that work, Nietzsche speculates about the reasons for the defeat of the positive-power morality (the authentic "good and evil" of the masters), and explains the psychological circumstances that led to the emergence of morality in general of a "man who can promise," and the arousal of the patterns of negative power, of "bad conscience" and "guilt" (*Schuld*, F&N, pp. 149ff.).

Buber stresses the correctness and timeliness of Nietzsche's questions concerning the nature of man, but rejects his answers. He is especially critical of Nietzsche's genealogy of guilt feelings, which according to Nietzsche was rooted in the ancient relations between "creditor and debtor" (p. 150). At this point, Buber shows an impressive philosophical acumen which leads him, rightly in my view, to criticize this part of Nietzsche's genealogy by stressing its circularity.

In the second essay of *The Genealogy of Morals*, dealing with the genesis of "Guilt, Bad Conscience and the Like," Nietzsche refers to the double meaning of the German word *Schuld* in an attempt to discover the origin of "conscience," "responsibility," and "guilt." *Schuld* is both guilt and a debt in the nonfigurative sense, indicating that "the feeling of guilt, of personal obligation, had its origin . . . in the oldest and most primitive personal relationship, that between buyer and seller, creditor and debtor" (*GM* II-8). This explanation is circular, since the commercial interrelationship and the consciousness of responsibility and "obligation" assumes the preexistence of a certain organized social context (namely of morality and personal conscience), without which the terms "debt" and "responsibility" have no meaning.

Logical circularity and psychological absurdity threaten also the complementary explanation in the second essay, which purports to give the "genealogy" of "bad conscience" and guilt feelings. Nietzsche maintains that their true origin is to be sought in the phenomenon of "internalization" (*GM* II-16), whereby most of "man's" instincts were turned "inward" against "man himself" to protect "the political organization." But who is responsible for the constitution of the "State," this "oppressive and remorseless machine"? Nietzsche answers that it is the "powerful" men— "Some pack of blond beasts of prey, a conqueror and master race with the ability to organize. . . . It is not in them that the "bad conscience" developed . . . but it would not have developed without them" (*GM* II-17). By projecting their creative, organizing powers onto the inferior masses they evoked among the latter the feeling of *ressentiment* which characterizes the first stage of the "slave revolt." This feeling then becomes "bad conscience" in the second stage, when the *"instinct for freedom* [was] pushed back and repressed . . . [and was] finally able to discharge and vent itself only on it-self " (ibid., emphasis in the original). The powerful ones, however, these "born organizers" and "artists"—"do not know what guilt, responsibility or consideration are." In this essay, Nietzsche seems to believe that a soci-ety of masters once existed. They lacked moral conscience (the Freudian superego) and became an organized team imposing rules and "forms" upon the psychologically inferior "slaves." However, the powerful must have already been operating within a specific social context, even if it were only "some pack"; thus, they were already living within the circles of duty and responsibility, the necessary basic conditions of any social framework. Moreover, by creating and living within any type of society, the powerful individuals would have necessarily internalized and repressed some of their own instincts, so that individuals with positive power could not have been the sole reason for the development of "bad conscience" and guilt feelings among the powerless agents. Nietzsche's genealogical search for the primary origins of prevalent morality thus involves him once again in a circular explanation.

This was grasped by Buber, who argues against Nietzsche's genealogy: "The concept of guilt is found most powerfully developed even in the most primitive communal forms which we know, where the relation between creditor and debtor is almost non-existent." Against Nietzsche's genealogy of *Schuld* he claims: "Just because the man has learned to promise . . . it is possible for the contract-relation in private economy to develop between the debtor who promises and the creditor who is promised" (p. 150).

Buber also has problems with what he calls the "ambiguity" of Nietz-sche's central principle of "the will to power" (ibid.). He has some obvious difficulties in finding an inner consistency between Nietzsche's quantita-tive definition of the will to power as the "will to acquire ever more and more power" and his other definition, "the insatiable desire to display power or to practice power" (ibid.). The first definition clearly character-izes persons endowed with feeble or negative power who aspire to acquire the sense or, as Nietzsche puts it, the "feeling of power" by external means of manipulation and conquest, including violence and unrestrained use of *Kraft*. By the second definition, Nietzsche refers to the anthropological and psychological phenomena of persons manifesting positive power who are therefore not preoccupied with acquiring "more power" but are sponta-neously expressing their intrinsic resources of power. On this reading, there is no contradiction in Nietzsche's explications of power patterns because each refers to a distinctly different, even opposed, phenomenon. Buber is close to realizing this when he defines "greatness" or "genius" in terms of Nietzsche's features of positive power, saying that "greatness by nature includes a power, but not a will to power . . . [It] has an inner powerfulness [and hence] strives neither to 'increase' or 'display' power." This statement fits very well Nietzsche's explication of the person who possesses positive power and hence is expressing it spontaneously without having any ulterior motives of bragging, intimidating, or threatening others by its sheer manifestation. Buber even seems to accept Nietzsche's distinction between "slaves" (possessing negative powers) and "masters" (possessing positive powers) when he speaks about "slaves for power" who are "being by nature without power" (p. 151).

Despite Buber's critical remarks about certain aspects of Nietzsche's philosophical anthropology, in the realm of politics he adopts Nietzsche's distinction between *Macht* and *Kraft* ("force" and "power"), which is based on the assumption that power is sublimated force (*HH* II 1–220). (We should remember that this lecture was delivered in Jerusalem in 1938 after Buber had to flee from Nazi Germany.) The distinction is evident from Buber's discussion of the "connexion between power and culture" (p. 151). Endorsing Nietzsche's distinctions between *Macht, Kraft,* and *Gewalt,* and between *Kulturmacht* and the nationalistic state, Buber agrees with Nietzsche's claim that although the qualitative power of an individual or society is no guarantee of material success and victory, it nonetheless ensures a spiritual and cultural superiority. For this reason, Nietzsche and Buber distinguish between the history of power (spiritual and intellectual progress) and the history of force (physical and material domination). It is precisely those who have been in the weaker position relative to the history of force who are responsible for cultural advances relative to power. Buber says explicitly: "National power in itself . . . will only weaken and paralyze the national culture" (p. 152). Thus one feels that his theoretical discussion of the most fundamental Nietzschean notions was largely motivated by his wish to facilitate Nietzsche's reception in Palestine and to foster "great, genuine, spontaneous cultural productivity" (ibid.). Like Nietzsche, Buber saw in a genuine philosopher the creator of values for a rejuvenated society.

This attitude, which concurs with Nietzsche's basic views, was, I believe, the main reason that Buber, who wanted above anything else to propagate cultural Zionism in Palestine, adopted in due course an extreme (if such a term applies at all in matters of peace and justice) pacifist view regarding the strife between Arab Palestinian and Jewish Palestinian over the one land. Consequently, we can find in this lecture also a devastating criticism directed against the nationalistic and militaristic state, "the New Idol" in Nietzsche's language,[48] that sees in its political might the highest value and objective. The "political leadership," which seeks to "increase the power of the nation" for its own self, namely "power which betrays the spirit," "corrupts the history of the world" (pp. 151, 153).

Thus it is small wonder that in the rest of his lecture, Buber portrays Nietzsche in a quite favorable light. He calls him, for example, the "mystic of Enlightenment" who "is deeply conscious of the specifically human questionableness." Its roots Nietzsche grounds naturalistically in the fact that man is "a sick animal" because of his "aberration from his instincts" (p. 154). Buber stresses these Nietzschean ideas and notions because of his Zionist concern for a "Jewish Renaissance." From Nietzsche's perspective, the Jews of Europe suffered not only from the general "sickness" of mankind but also from their even heavier load of "aberration" and suppression of instincts. They were the specimens par excellence of the sickness of mankind. Buber's cry for Jewish Renaissance, in fact, was his plea to overcome this particularly Jewish sickness.

Nonetheless, Buber's positive affinity for Nietzsche does not prevent him from drawing a quite balanced and critical attitude, revealing some of Nietzsche's main weaknesses. Buber emphasizes the naturalistic overtones of Nietzsche's anthropology. From this perspective man is either a "herd animal" currently in decline and approaching decadence because of his "growing morality," or he is a powerful creature that overcomes the merely natural and opts for the creative and affirmative will to power that climaxes in the "conscious breeding of a widespread" type of the authentic *Übermensch* (p. 155). At this point Buber points out the crucial problem of the second option: how, out of the "animal man" and "herd animal," the *Übermensch* will emerge. How will the call and the thirst for the "real [i.e. authentic] man" arise amid the inauthentic herd? This was indeed the main problem that faced all European thinkers (from Rousseau onward) who make the implementation of the ideal of personal authenticity in society their cherished objective. Each of them attempts to provide his own solution.[49]

Buber definitely is not concerned in this lecture only to criticize Nietzsche and does not dwell on "inner contradictions in Nietzsche's thought" (p. 155). But he underlies what he felt was Nietzsche's essential problem, that of explaining humans by solely naturalistic categories. Buber asks, in essence, "But how has man emerged from nature to be able to promise"? This was also the main explicit question of *The Genealogy of Morals*. For founding morality one needs also reflexive consciousness and self-critical faculties, but all these are barely explicable solely in naturalistic terms. Buber therefore claims that the human feat of "knowing that one knows" cannot be "comprehended" solely by "concepts of nature" (p. 155), and accuses Nietzsche of upholding a too narrow and too exclusive naturalism. He objects to such a crude naturalism[50] also because of his keen and enduring interest in "community" (p. 156). Nietzsche failed to explain the reasons for man's "community" and wanted to go beyond its legitimate "power" (ibid.). Hence it becomes clear that Buber's "will to community," more than Nietzsche's atheism or "will to power," was the underlying reason for Buber's subsequent relative neglect of Nietzsche.

That this was the case is also evident from "Nietzsche's Teaching about Man," a condensed version of his lecture, that Buber published in a Tel Aviv Hebrew literary magazine.[51] This version, by its sheer conciseness, highlights several motifs that were directly relevant to Buber's communal preoccupation. Let us also recall that the article appeared at a time when the still very young and vulnerable Zionist entity stood greatly in need of communal cohesiveness. This was additionally important for Buber because of his existential multimarginality.

Despite his reservations concerning Nietzsche's anthropology, Buber stresses its main theses here, and dwells on the manifestations of negative power patterns in history. He does so because he wishes to separate Nietzsche from the ongoing (at that time) criminal misappropriation of his teaching by the Nazis, and to show that Hitler's thirst for mere physical *Kraft* actually manifested a mentality of the "slave," an insight of which the small, isolated, and powerless Jewish community in Palestine was in great need.

However, Buber could not endorse what now appeared to him to be Nietzsche's indifference toward the central role of community in one's life and one's I-Thou relations. The question naturally arises why Buber in the period of his greatest infatuation with Nietzsche's philosophy had taken so long to realize these shortcomings. Apparently, what Buber perceived while staying in interwar Palestine he had ignored or not been aware of while in Europe. When it comes to Zionist thought, geography sometimes makes a cardinal difference.

In any case, Buber emphasizes at the beginning of the Hebrew version the open, nonessentialist image of man and the aesthetic model for creating one's personal authenticity. Such an emphasis in the article, which was also directed at the founders of the state in the making, was very relevant for the transformation of a Jew into an Israeli. Buber stresses Nietzsche's view about complete immanency, since most of his Hebrew readers were secular or, at least, non-Orthodox Jews. He also stresses the need for cultivating a new type of man, the Hebrew *halutz* (pioneer). The Zionist version of Nietzsche's claim that " a man is a bridge to the Overman," to a new type and image of man, is that "a Zionist Jew in Europe is the bridge to the new Israeli Hebrew," to the secular *halutz* who reclaims the desert for his people.

Buber also became acutely aware that if man, as Nietzsche would wish it, does not have an a priori nature and essence, he is not ipso facto the Aristotelian "social animal." Thus he may be estranged from or live in constant dissonance with the community. Nonetheless, Buber stresses the idea that since Nietzsche did not subscribe to an essentialist approach to man, he could demand of man to create his own authentic image. This creation of one's self out of "one's own resources"—or the vast resources of one's people—fits well with Buber's spiritual and religious Zionism. However, he is afraid that without the obligation to and the directives of a "community," especially among the newly established settlements, the creation of such selves might result in total anarchy. Thus Buber puts into sharp relief the inherent paradox with which this work is concerned, of Nietzsche among the Zionists. Either one opts for Nietzsche's authentic creation of one's self and of the new image of a Hebrew, facing thereby the danger of social anarchy and the disturbingly unsolved problem of the viability of authenticity within a community; or one starts, like Buber at this stage, from the primacy of the "social animal" and the I-Thou relation and from the essential approach to mankind, thereby hindering the authentic cultivation of the Zionist as a self-forming and self-creating new Hebrew. Buber, as the end of this article implies, prefers the second option, ending his exposition of Nietzsche's anthropology with the accusation that Nietzsche ignored the "social sphere." Significantly, Buber deliberately expressed this in an Aramaic phrase (*shphirat ha-hevrutah*) that originally means that a human being is not really human and is not a perfect person before the creation of a society.

What is really amazing, though, is the fact that throughout this exposition of Nietzsche's anthropological philosophy—its objectives, scope, and problems—Buber hardly mentions Nietzsche's pivotal ideal of the optimally authentic *Übermensch*. Did this omission occur due to the Nazis' misappropriation of this ideal, which in their eyes referred to the Aryan superman? And more generally, can we ascribe Buber's loud silence about Nietzsche during subsequent years to the Nazis' criminal abuse of Nietzsche's philosophy?

BUBER ON NIETZSCHE AND THE NAZIS

Not at all! Actually the contrary is true: as early as 1933, in his essay "The Question to the Single One,"[52] Buber attacked the Nazis' misappropriation of Nietzsche, as promoted, for example, by Oswald Spengler.

Picking the much abused image of Nietzsche's "beast of prey" (which, together with the "blond beast," was the main starting point for the Nazi misappropriation of Nietzsche, Buber perceptively asserts that "beasts of prey have no history" (p. 73) and, one may add, no "genealogy." History and genealogy clearly belong to man's "anthropological content" (p. 72), and to his creation and manifestation of cultural meanings. As such, they cannot be reduced to the narrow and deterministic sphere of "biological terms" (ibid.). The Nazi ideal of the Nordic-Aryan race was purely a biological and eugenic ideal whose implementation purported to make the Third Reich into the starting point of a new era of history. But the Nietzschean image of the "beast of prey," as Buber rightly perceived, had definite historical roots that might be uncovered by a genealogy that concentrated solely on the psychological and historical grounds for its emergence. In other words, the method of genealogical inquiry presupposes beginnings in the past and continuation in the present, whereas the Nazi biological misappropriation of Nietzsche presupposes a new and fresh "pure" biological start.

In 1962 Buber said of Hitler: "His idea of the higher race was not biological, it stemmed from Nietzsche. Hitler considered himself to belong to the lower race, but by constructing his own definition of what the higher race should be, he could count himself as belonging to it."[53] Though today we know that Hitler barely read Nietzsche,[54] Buber's perceptive remarks are consistent with his view of Nietzsche's notion of *Macht* and "higher race," as expressed in his youth in his unpublished essay on Zarathustra and in his Polish essays,[55] where he speaks about the "abundant, overflowing life" that characterizes the "new race of superior men." Clearly this characteristic has nothing to do with any biological or eugenic aspects of these "superior men." Moreover, as his remarks indicate, Buber perceived that it was precisely Nietzsche's anthropology that allows one to explain such phenomena as Hitler's *ressentiment*," his "*self-hatred*," and the whole Nazi movement, in terms of the successful "revolt of the slaves."[56]

It is also highly significant that, despite the approach of the Holocaust, Buber felt it imperative to defend Nietzsche against misappropriation by the Nazis in "People and Leader," an essay first published in February 1940: "Nietzsche, who was not one of the great thinkers nor one of the great poets but a genius in writing aphorisms, never dreamed that his idea of the God in the making would be exploited not by the type of man whom he called the noble man but, in fact, by the subhuman man (*Untermensch*)."[57] From the context and from Buber's references to Nietzsche's idea of the *Übermensch* (pp. 143–44), as well as from his ironical remark about Hitler's identification with the figure of this *Übermensch*, it clearly follows that by the idiom "God in the making" Buber means the Overman. He quite rightly attributes the Nazis' misappropriation of this notion to Nietzsche's sister, "who warmly welcomed Hitler's saying that 'I am the *Übermensch*' and who saw in him the embodiment of her brother's dream of the Overman" (pp. 143–44). Buber sarcastically adds: "Our period is marked by the phony realization of great dreams. What the blissful dreamers have dreamt materializes before our very eyes as a caricature" (p. 144). Alluding to Nietzsche's distinction between physical *Kraft* and spiritual *Macht*, he warns his readers: "To aspire to attain power for the sake of power and dominance means to aspire for nothingness. . . . the will to force for its own sake leads . . . to the nation's suicide" (p. 142). *Kraft* without *Macht* is an impoverishing factor.

It follows that Buber rejects out of hand Hitler's misappropriation of Nietzsche's notions of the *Übermensch* and of *Macht* for his own murderous racial ideology. However, he also rejects these notions of Nietzsche with arguments he already presented in "Nietzsche's Teaching about Man." Here he emphasizes his critique of Nietzsche's conception that man may function and behave like God. He objects to Nietzsche's ideal of a person who is able to create his own life, that "a man is becoming God" (p. 144), in a sense creating for himself his own image without being at all dependent on being created "in God's image." What is noteworthy, however, is the fact that Buber's rejection of this ideal of ultimate authenticity stems not from the association of this ideal with the Nazis, but from his religious belief that, like the Kierkegaardian faith, puts an infinite distance between the individual and the Absolute. We can never close this essential distance between divinity and ourselves, so that Nietzsche's key idea—that after the "Death" of our belief in "God" one may adopt for oneself the God-like role of being the originator of truth and of one's own self—is a sheer myth. For Buber (even during the Holocaust atrocities) God is alive, and hence he rejects Nietzsche's claim that in the absence of a "preestablished harmony" between our cognition and reality we may and should shift our emphasis to the creation of our own genuine selves. Buber's prophetic ending of this essay impressively discloses his credo: "Israel means the belief in one truth, that no one can attain, but is allowed to serve. Hitler cannot exist if the human world has a real relation to this one truth" (p. 145). In a Kierkegaardian vein he summarizes: "The one truth cannot be proven except by the actual service we render it. Nation alone is not enough, language alone is not enough, land alone is not enough. It is not enough to have a merely national experience or a merely national culture which does not carry out a national service to the supranational, to the one truth. . . . Hitler has the power to annihilate numerous Jews, but not Israel and not Zion, *if they exist in truth*" (p. 145, emphasis in the original).

EPILOGUE

In the state of Israel, before and after independence, Buber and especially his political views did not attract the wide attention they had won in the Diaspora. His pacifist and conciliatory attitude and his plea for a just peace between the Palestinians and the Zionists did not gain the desired impact. He always insisted that the historical *Eretz Israel* should be given to both these nations. If history had complied with this attitude, a lot of senseless bloodshed could have been avoided in the Middle East. This is not the place to elaborate these points,[58] but it is quite clear that the contemporary liberal "Peace Now" movement in Israel had a very worthy predecessor in the figure of the Zionist humanist Mordechai Martin Buber.

His involvement as an active member of the pacifist Jewish fraction Brith Shalom (Covenant of Peace)[59] strayed far from the more military and activist consensus. Even after 1948, the year of Israeli independence, his version of spiritual Zionism never gained a wide hearing. He really believed (as did Ahad Ha'am), that Zionism should establish the Jewish State as a means for realizing the prophetic vision of a community of justice and everlasting peace. One wonders, however, whether Ahad Ha'am had better chances of realizing his vision of Zionism. Because of the latter's perfect mastery of Hebrew (a language in which Buber gained fluency, but not to the level of his German), he seemed to exert a wider impact than Buber. But both failed to influence the mainstream of Israeli public, not necessarily due solely to the Arabs' adamant refusal to accept the state of Israel and their continual aggressions against it. The politics of violence always reigns supreme when it clashes with spiritual powers.[60] Just as the Nietzschean ideal of spiritual *Macht* succumbed in history to the aggressive politics of *Kraft*, so, regrettably, the same happened to Buber's spiritual Zionism.

Here, however, we should raise the obvious question: How can one reconcile Buber's pacifist tendencies, pronounced almost from the beginning of his career, with the somewhat warlike attitudes that Nietzsche expressed in his writings? In other words, how could Buber become so attracted to the warrior-like figure of Zarathustra? Why did this tension not cause Buber from the beginning to fight Nietzsche's "invasion" of his thought and life?

Perhaps one answer lies in the fact that Buber greatly sympathized with Nietzsche's criticism of nationalistic sentiment and with his rejection of the state of Bismarck's making as the most "cold monster," a monster that tends to swallow the individual. Thus Buber, like Nietzsche, longed for the creation of smaller communities where an authentic and genuine relationship would prevail among their members. Hence Buber could stomach the allegedly warlike Nietzschean stance by regarding it as mainly a metaphor and a rhetorical means for attaining objectives that both of them shared. True, Nietzsche wrote "not contentedness but more power; not peace but war."[61] But he meant here and in other places spiritual wars between ideas and states of mind and soul, especially the fluctuations within one's self between the positive and negative manifestations of spiritual powers, thoughts, and patterns of behavior. By these metaphors of "war" and "warrior" he also referred to the perpetual self-overcoming of one's self to attain personal authenticity that prevents one from being content with one's present state and mental predicaments. Such internal wars were familiar to Buber, who during his life was immersed in a struggle to overcome his multimarginality and to attain solid personal identity, "unity," sense of "belonging," and authenticity.

From the preceding discussion it becomes clear that Buber's "liberation" from Nietzsche's spell was far from a radical one. The impact of Nietzsche's "invasion" of Buber's life and thought became more subtle, the tone less personal and emotional, more sober and critical. But a complete liberation? Hardly. Nietzsche was quite alive in Buber's universe till the last moments of this first and foremost Hebrew humanist[62] philosopher.

CHAPTER 6

Hillel Zeitlin

FROM NIETZSCHEAN *ÜBERMENSCH* TO JEWISH ALMIGHTY GOD

Hillel Zeitlin was the most religious, and the most tragic figure of all those presented here. In 1942, wrapped in *tallith* and *tefillin* and carrying a volume of the *Zohar*,[1] he proudly walked from the Warsaw Ghetto to his death in Treblinka. Significantly, he was born in 1871, the year Bismarck unified Germany into a nationalistic state that eventually exterminated most of European Jewry. Zeitlin was the only Nietzschean figure discussed in this book who was a victim of the Holocaust, despite his premonitions about the impending doom. This last Eastern European Jewish Nietzschean was also the first author to write a book-length monograph in Hebrew on Nietzsche.

Zeitlin's encounter with Nietzsche will help us answer the question that we have raised concerning the religious Nietzscheans: How could they be so attracted to this staunch atheist? This question may be answered on two levels. First, Zeitlin's (and Buber's) needs for personal authenticity and for the liberating aspects of Nietzschean philosophy were so great that they outweighed their religious leanings. Second, Zeitlin, like Buber, underrated Nietzschean atheism and provided several rationalizations for perceiving him as a basically religious thinker.

While Buber was one of the most prominent spiritual leaders of German Jewry, Zeitlin fulfilled the same function among Polish Jews. Buber managed to escape the Nazis by fleeing to Palestine in 1938. Zeitlin, on the other hand, could hardly be called a Zionist in the narrow sense of wishing to gather the Jewish people in Zion: he preferred an ingathering of exiles away from Palestine. For this reason he was called a "territorialist," who perceived the threat to Eastern European Jews and wished to resettle them in Uganda (an option rejected by the Sixth Zionist Congress in 1903), or in any other peaceful territory, such as Argentina. To be sure, his preference stemmed from Zionist considerations: to find a secure land for European Jews, who were on a collision course with catastrophe. In his eyes Zion carried the overpowering burden of tradition, whereas Uganda (or for that matter any other history-free territory) symbolized the Nietzschean philosophy of life.[2]

As early as 1900–1901, at the beginning of his Nietzschean period, Zeitlin wrote a provocative manifesto to show young Hebrews the right direction.[3] Though he approvingly quotes Nietzsche's slogan to "overcome man" (p. 35), one can feel his reservations about this idea. To overcome one's self on one's road to personal authenticity is fine, but to suppress and go beyond one's Jewish identity and ignore the present distressful predicament is an altogether different and disastrous matter. As we shall see, at precisely this point, Zeitlin leaves Nietzsche and returns to his people. Evidently, Zeitlin could not live like Zarathustra's "eagle," soaring alone high in the sky. His communal feelings of deepest empathy and his compassionate nature take him far away from Zarathustra's lonely "cave." You can overcome most of your self most of the time, but you cannot overcome all of yourself all of the time. This is especially true of those parts of your self that were not formed by yourself—parts that echo the Jewish heritage, and are deeply and unconsciously imprinted in your self.[4] Thus you cannot become a "free spirit *par excellence,*" as Nietzsche demanded from his faithful followers, but only someone who believes in relative spiritual autonomy and freedom. One should recall that Nietzsche himself did not believe in the viability of his own ideal of the "free spirit," especially where the Jewish people were concerned. He warned his Jewish friend, Joseph Paneth, that to "live detached from any heritage and community might become very dangerous to that person and to his surroundings."[5]

In his manifesto, Zeitlin refers to the stormy debate between Ahad Ha'am and Berdichevski and sides with neither of them. He rejects Ahad Ha'am's "romanticism" and "lofty idealism" that propagated the "kingdom of the prophets" (pp. 43ff.) because he could not suggest a viable solution to the disastrous situation of Eastern European Jewry. In contradistinction to Ahad Ha'am, he denigrates the history of the Jews, sharing Nietzsche's contempt for antiquarian learning and enthusiasm for an ahistorical existential attitude.

On the other hand, Zeitlin also rejects Berdichevski's charge that the Jews *alone* are to be blamed for their low vitality and creativity: "*We* are not to be blamed—but they!" (p. 53). He writes that Berdichevski, as a scholar, was too easily attracted to "Nietzsche's shallow sayings" (ibid.), and goes so far as to accuse Berdichevski of inauthenticity and even self-hatred. Berdichevski, as a poet, "had *to be what he is* and ought to remove from his heart all those foreign thoughts that others instilled in him" (p. 54; emphasis added). Thus Zeitlin is using Nietzsche's formula for personal authenticity in order to fight what he regards as Berdichevski's inauthenticity—instilled in his heart by none other than Nietzsche! This paradox best illustrates the paradox of Nietzsche's influence on Zionists and his role in intensifying the processes of modernization and secularization among them.

Whereas Ahad Ha'am emphasizes the ethical qualities and mission of his people, and Berdichevski stresses their aesthetic qualities (or more precisely the lack of them), Zeitlin claims that formulas about "new values" and "new life" are irrelevant when people have to secure their physical lives. What Berdichevski lacks is not unity (he really does not suffer from a rent in his heart) but duality—the ability to criticize and keep in check his own aspirations, and to maintain a sober judgment about what preoccupies him. He lacks "the pathos of distance" (another of Nietzsche's expressions), the ability to distinguish between ideality and reality, between the inner and the external world: "Zarathustra is a poet, and like every poet he might lie" (p. 64). Zeitlin later directs this same argument as a last resort against the ideal of the *Übermensch* in order to overcome Nietzsche's spell. Here he employs Nietzsche's ideal of authenticity to attack one of his staunchest supporters, Berdichevski. He argues that this modern Hebrew writer lacks the sublime authenticity to deeply feel what he is, what he wants to be, and what he cannot become. He lacks a critical approach toward himself and thus cannot create his authentic self.

Zeitlin ends his Nietzschean critique of Berdichevski's Nietzschean views by defending the ancient prophets against Berdichevski's tendency to make them appear just as present-day rabbis. He employs Nietzsche's distinction (in *Human, All Too Human*) between the ordinary metaphysical view according to which human beings are endowed with an eternal, immutable essence and the scientific-historical attitude that speaks of the relative and variable nature of man. The ancient prophets belonged to the ahistorical, metaphysical essence of Judaism, whereas the present antiquarian and scholarly rabbis belong to an era that is not typical of Judaism (pp. 72–73). Thus Zeitlin's manifesto highlights the genuine problematic of the present volume. Most of those inside and outside the Zionist camp who polemicized about the direction and content of the reawakening Hebrew culture could hardly have awakened to the issues involved without Nietzsche, but by the same token they could not sustain their devotion to him or live with his ideas and his ideals.

In any case, it is highly appropriate to conclude this book with Zeitlin, Nietzsche's intense admirer who symbolized the tragic end of Jewish Nietzscheanism among Eastern European Jewry. However, beyond this emotional symbolism, Zeitlin is important for the present study for three reasons.

First, his considerable influence became a vital link between Nietzschean Eastern European Jews and their Nietzsche-inspired brothers in Palestine. This link manifested itself in the Baum Circle in Homel, also called the Nietzschean Circle, where several Jewish intellectuals and Hebrew writers used to meet frequently to discuss Nietzsche's writings. They were profoundly influenced by the Nietzschean theme of the death of God. Besides Uri Nisan Gnessin[6] and Zeitlin, the group's mentor, notable among them was Zeitlin's brilliant student and dear friend Joseph Hayyim Brenner, the pioneering modern Hebrew writer of the early Zionist movement in Palestine, who was murdered in Jaffa during the Arab riots of 1921.[7]

Second, Zeitlin's case provides us with an opportunity to witness the fate of an Eastern European Jewish "free spirit," a genuine Nietzschean character. Such "free spirits" could not remain Nietzschean for their entire lives. Zeitlin exemplified this by his "return" from Nietzschean thinking to his Jewish heritage. This return to an austerely Orthodox pattern of life was unique, both in its intensity and depth, among the Jewish Nietzscheans of this period. And indeed, one cannot be original without recourse to one's origins, just as one "cannot destroy without building" (as Ahad Ha'am and Buber emphasized). Being a European Jew, one could not create in a complete vacuum, disregarding the Jewish communities during their intense rejuvenation and painful search for new meanings, values, and directions. This raises a question: Does the failure of the Eastern European Nietzscheans attest to the failure of the basic themes of Nietzsche's philosophy in their confrontation with and transmutation by the Jewish people?

The Jewish transfiguration of Nietzsche's secular ideal of the *Übermensch* into the holy tzaddik within the wider context of Jewish culture, urged upon the "Hebrew Nietzscheans" by Ahad Ha'am and inspiring Buber's activities in his Hasidic period, was warmly endorsed by Hillel Zeitlin. Was it doomed to failure? Was the shift from the *Übermensch* to the Jewish Almighty God the end of Nietzsche's career among the Zionists? Did it signify the final judgment of the Zionists on the practical and/or existential impossibility of appropriating his philosophy?

Based on the extensive evidence of Nietzsche's vibrant presence in

Zion,[8] one may safely claim that he remains alive and well in the state of Israel. His images, sensibilities, ideals, and presence among Israeli writers, men of letters, and political-social leaders were (and still are) continuing inspirations for the Israeli cultural scene. To be sure, this rebirth of Nietzsche in Zion was preceded by his "death" among his Jewish followers in Europe, together with their own doom. Zeitlin was the last Eastern European Jewish Nietzschean. How this tragic role was concretely expressed in his writings will be the subject of this chapter.

Third, Zeitlin's Nietzscheanism was also unique from another point of view. He exemplified the remarkable blend of Jewish Hasidism with the version of Nietzscheanism propagated at the end of the nineteenth century by the Russian intelligentsia. His attitude toward Nietzsche and his spiritual evolution partly resembled that of some of the Russian interpreters of Nietzsche, notably the Russian mystic of Jewish origin Lev Isaakovich Schwarzman (alias Shestov), whom Zeitlin admired and about whom he wrote several articles.[9] This unique combination with the Russian Nietzscheans will provide us with the opportunity to define more precisely the specific phenomenon of Jewish Nietzscheanism. To be sure, unlike many other Russian Jewish intellectuals who came to know Nietzsche through secondary works, such as Russian translations of Georg Brandes and Georg Simmel,[10] Zeitlin read Nietzsche in the original.

This extraordinary mixture in one person of Russian culture, Nietzschean influence, and Jewish lore is vividly portrayed in the following description of Zeitlin: "This tall, red-bearded, mystic-eyed White Russian Jew, who was no less acquainted with Nietzsche and Dostoevsky than with the *Zohar* and the *Likkutei Torah,* was the heir to the long-past courtyards of the Polish Rebbes."[11] Thus the rift in Zeitlin's heart was the deepest one may experience. It was an unbridgeable existential rift between two diametrically opposed universes: between the secular, free-thinking intelligentsia epitomized by his adherence to Nietzsche, and religious, Hasidic, kabbalistic, and mystical piety. The deeper the rift, the deeper was his devotion to Nietzsche and the more difficult was his break from him, as Zeitlin's second and final essay on Nietzsche (1919) clearly testifies.

A Chronicle of Life's Overcoming

Because of the Holocaust, there are very few biographical sources that offer us a full, unbiased picture of Zeitlin's life. The most available biographies were written by his admiring friends, like Brenner,[12] or by his two sons, literary figures in their own right.[13] Thus, we have to look at Zeitlin's own highly subjective self-portrait written in 1928, when he had already adopted a religious point of view.[14]

In his "Synopsis of My Life,"[15] Zeitlin begins with his birth in Korma, a small, pious shtetl in the Mohilever, a province of White Russia. He describes how, at the age of eleven, he came to be known as a Talmudic *illuy* (prodigy), and how, despite a subsequent "severe internal war," his "natural religiosity did not let [him] fall." He learned several languages as well as science, and his "thought was preoccupied with philosophy." He immersed himself in the study of Jewish philosophy, but also in the "books of Spinoza, Kant, Fichte, Spencer, and the other Positivists." A "deep rift opened" in his soul when he encountered criticism of the Bible, though his soul yearned for "faith and nothing but a faith." In Homel (between 1894 and 1901, when he was twenty-three years old), he acquired the friendship of Shalom Sander Baum and with him "learned in depth Schopenhauer, Hartmann, and Friedrich Nietzsche." These "so-called absolute heretics brought me closer to my own inner selfhood. . . . Beyond the outward extreme heresy of Friedrich Nietzsche I became acquainted with the seeker of God on earth unto madness."

This bizarre confession is highly significant. Though apologetic for his attraction to Nietzsche, in a way that reminds one of Buber's similar statement about Nietzsche's supposedly religious sentiments, Zeitlin describes his atheistic period in terms of Nietzsche's well-known picture (*GS* 125) of the "madman" who paradoxically is looking for the "dead God" in the marketplace. However, from the perspective of the believer, Zeitlin did not entrap himself in any paradoxical situation. In order to find your God you first have to lose him by undergoing a genuine atheistic period in your life.[16] And though it seems retrospectively as if Zeitlin's short period of atheism was a kind of Nietzschean *Versuch* (existential test), Zeitlin's heresy, and eventually his regained faith, echoed Nietzsche's statement regarding the nature of the philosopher's thinking, which may apply also to believing: "their thinking [or believing] is, in fact, far less a discovery than a recognition, a remembering, a return, and a homecoming to a remote, *primordial,* and inclusive *household of the soul*" (*BGE,* 20; emphasis added). Every stage in Zeitlin's life was a lived experience that reflected Nietzsche's attitude: in order to attain full personal authenticity, you must overcome in yourself what is not you. To be sure, Zeitlin's loss of belief in God was also triggered by his exposure to Western philosophy and science. Nonetheless, such an exposure happens only to one who has already begun to lose his faith.

But it would be wrong to assume that Nietzsche's "invasion" of Zeitlin's "soul" (to use Buber's term) was a passive occurrence as Buber, apologetically, wished us to believe in his own case. Zeitlin intentionally sought Nietzsche in order to kill what was, until then, his unwavering belief in the Jewish God. He attempted to reach the ultimate "abyss" from which he could climb so as to become what he wanted to be: an authentic firm believer. To paraphrase Nietzsche: what does not utterly destroy my belief makes it even firmer. And thus Zeitlin, in the synopsis of his life and elsewhere, describes his constant self-overcomings, his inner struggle with the "foreign God," and his intellectual inquisitiveness as a wanderer in "foreign fields."[17] Upon reading the details of Zeitlin's biography one gains the impression that his spiritual fluctuations and his constant inner struggles reflected Nietzsche's prescribed way to attain authenticity. Zeitlin's search (or "The Thirst," as one of his poetic semiautobiographical essays is called)[18] for God also led him to the existential attempt to go astray from the path of faith—only to find again its object and rekindle his faith. And indeed, during his "Nietzschean period," Zeitlin was known to leave the strict observance of the Jewish commandments.

For Zeitlin, unlike for Ahad Ha'am, the new was foreign because the new threatened the old faith, which was an ever-present force that permeated and informed his whole life. Such a force, in its original, "primordial" manifestations, was surely missing from Ahad Ha'am's more rationalist and secular attitude and was less prominent in Buber's more philosophical and theological thought.

Furthermore, in his autobiography, Zeitlin remarks that besides Nietzsche he is also very "grateful to the most original Jew [he] met in his life— Lev Shestov," who taught him that "particularly out of the most intense mental tragedy, one comes to really know God." Consequently he immersed himself once again in Kabbalah and in Hasidism, attempting to attain "a synthesis between deep pessimism and profound faith." Zeitlin ends this highly tendentious short autobiography with a kind of religious Zionist wish, namely that with "God's blessing" he might be granted to spend his "remaining years in the Holy Land." The Nazis, whom Nietzsche would have despised so vehemently, saw to it that this wish remained tragically unfulfilled.

Be that as it may, this autobiographical synopsis illuminates Zeitlin's restless nature, his existential wandering, his severe internal struggles, the painful overcoming of his own inclinations, and the revival of a religious serenity that was never a fait accompli for him. Most significantly, it provides us with a first-hand account of how Nietzsche's "invasion" of a basically religious, sensitive Jewish soul could wreak havoc in the life of such a soul.

At this point one may use once again the three existential Nietzschean life metamorphoses to present an approximate portrait of Zeitlin's existential journey. The "Camel" was the stage of Zeitlin's adolescence when faith reigned supreme and brought him to several periods of religious ecstasy. Then came the stage of the "Lion": the heroic revolt against his faith and lifestyle; and finally the stage of the "Newborn Child," the return to faith and its original innocence. A person's life, however, cannot be accurately described by a series of neatly delineated phases. Though Zeitlin's religious phase began in 1907 and extended beyond 1919, we find in 1919 an article by Zeitlin that still refers to Nietzsche (who was the main catalyst for his "Lion" stage). The fact that fourteen years passed between Zeitlin's first and his last articles on Nietzsche is testimony to the pervasive and steady presence of this heretic in Zeitlin's spiritual world. Moreover, of all the Nietzschean figures discussed so far, Zeitlin came from the most deeply religious background, and hence his turn from Nietzsche and his return to Orthodoxy seemed inevitable. But by the same token, his turn to Nietzsche was perhaps the most dramatic and revealing.

Before turning to Zeitlin's oeuvre it might be helpful to identify three distinctive stages of Zeitlin's complex relations to Nietzsche. In his first essay that mentions Nietzsche ("Good and Evil," written in 1899), he manifests a real admiration for this philosopher's genuine nature; nonetheless, by the end of it Zeitlin's religious sentiments have gained the upper hand and he pleads for transcendentalism. His first essay specifically dealing with Nietzsche (1905) shows his adoption of atheism and immanency (though not before he has played with the divine immanency of Spinoza). The last stage of his relationship with Nietzsche (expressed in his last essay dedicated to him, in 1919) is dominated by a return to the religious "household of his soul." At this final stage, Nietzsche is portrayed through a dominant Jewish perspective. Following the reconstructed Nietzschean dictum "not to destroy a temple but to add to it an additional edifice," the Hasidic tzaddik becomes the Overman and the will to power finds its most perfect version in the "Chosen People" and their monumental history.

ZEITLIN'S NIETZSCHEAN-ATHEISTIC PERIOD

By the end of the nineteenth century Nietzsche's fame was so widespread in Eastern European Jewish communities that Ber Borochov, the leader of

Poalei Zion (Workers of Zion) (a socialist Zionist party), reported that one could make a steady income by delivering popular lectures on his philosophy.[19] Not surprisingly, then, Nietzsche first appeared in Zeitlin's writings in the course of a popular theological-philosophical essay.[20] "The Good and the Evil," was virtually a concise encyclopedia of philosophy without precedent in the modern Hebrew literature. Its overwhelming breadth revealed the scope of Zeitlin's autodidactic erudition: from the biblical, Indian, and ancient Greek traditions to very contemporary thinkers such as Schopenhauer and Nietzsche.

Speaking precisely, the real topic of this essay is not good or evil as such, but our responses to their presence in our world. These responses entail two basic attitudes: the optimistic and the pessimistic. Thus this essay is basically not a theological or a philosophical treatise but an anthropological survey that centers on the typology of human existential attitudes. This typology resembles Nietzsche's *The Birth of Tragedy*, which is quoted in the penultimate section dealing with Nietzsche.

Nietzsche distinguishes in *The Birth of Tragedy* between the "shallow optimism" of the rationalist Socrates and his literary counterpart Euripides, and the genuinely tragic and powerful pessimism prevalent in the pre-Socratic period and expressed by the early dramatists. Those thinkers and writers did not explain away the existence of evil. They adopted the tragic Dionysian vision that did not succumb to the evil around us by any kind of escapism or nihilism, and were trying to create "within the evil and the tragic." Consequently, after arriving at his notion of power, Nietzsche distinguished between two types of pessimism: the positive one that urges people to face and combat evil creatively and squarely by sublimating it; and the negative pessimism that led people to resignation, nihilism, asceticism, self-abnegation, and even suicide. This latter type has its genealogy in the negative power patterns of the weak and cowardly. This distinction runs throughout Zeitlin's essay, and is referred to in the conclusion under Nietzsche's name. It culminates in Hillel's claim that negative pessimism is actually an escape from the evil in this world by means of shallow ideals that promise one a permanent "shelter" against it. These yearnings for shelter signify the inherent weakness of persons who cannot courageously face life in this world.

In an autobiographical vein, Zeitlin remarks that Hasidism, with its notion that this very world is but a "narrow bridge" to another, truer, and better world, and the mystical Kabbalah "do not soothe the hearts of these who see, know and feel the real troubles in life and whose views on the world are not theological at all" (6:502).[21] Thus we may conclude that

Zeitlin conducted his scholarly survey from an atheistic standpoint that appreciated the heroic stance of the "positive pessimist" and rejected both "shallow scientific optimism"—and here Zeitlin sarcastically criticizes Nordau's attitude that subscribed to progress and European enlightenment)—[22] and the negative, ascetic, and pessimistic attitude of Buddhism and Schopenhauer. Zeitlin uses Nietzsche in this essay to consolidate his own attitude of "powerful and positive pessimism" and of affirmation of life and the world without having to resort to the transcendental views of Judaism, or more specifically to Hasidism and Kabbalah. With Nietzsche's help, he tries to overcome his pessimistic personal feelings as well as Schopenhauer's negative and destructive pessimism that deeply attracted his friend in Homel, Sender Baum, and pervaded their whole circle.[23]

The five pages Zeitlin dedicates to Nietzsche (8:201–5) are highly revealing. For one thing, they show his mastery of the whole Nietzschean corpus. Zeitlin distinguishes between the first period of Nietzsche's philosophy, which centered on the Dionysian "metaphysics of aesthetic"; the second, which focused on Socratic scientific positivism;[24] and the third, positive period when the notion of power and the ideal of the Overman appeared. Zeitlin also quotes directly from *The Birth of Tragedy, Schopenhauer as Educator, The Gay Science,* and *Thus Spoke Zarathustra.*

The discussion of Nietzsche also throws light on Zeitlin's own attitude to the German philosopher. He starts with an expression of personal admiration and affection for this "great and enlightened thinker who deals with the question of good and evil, as with the question of life itself, in his own unique way and, as in everything else, seeks here too the transfiguration of values" (8:201). This personal tone is quite uncharacteristic of his previous discussions of thinkers and writers (other than perhaps Spinoza). Despite the eulogistic tone of empathy and approval, Zeitlin is not a blind follower but occasionally provides us with critical assessments of Nietzsche's shortcomings, such as his "typical excesses" (8:203) and the radical alternations and contradictions between the three stages of his thought.

Zeitlin claims that in contrast to Schopenhauer's theory, Nietzsche aspired to realize what he preached without any compromises, and hence he had to leave Schopenhauer's metaphysical and Buddhist speculations about the negation of life. Zeitlin adopts Nietzsche's criterion for evaluating the authenticity of the philosopher's personality by checking whether he has ever really lived according to his philosophy and whether his philosophy is conducive to life. As a result of this test, Zeitlin clearly prefers Nietzschean existential *Wahrhaftigkeit,* integrity, and authenticity over Schopenhauer's speculative metaphysics.

Trying to live what Nietzsche preached, namely to attain an authentic self after periods of his life dominated by restlessness and uncompromising self-overcoming, Zeitlin, like Berdichevski almost in the same year, highlights the Nietzschean dictum that "every creation is also a destruction" (8:202).[25] He describes Nietzsche's positive ideal of personal perfection in such a manner that he has no difficulties appropriating it for his own frame of thought and life. For Zeitlin, the ideal of the Overman has an exclusively spiritual content. He ignores the atheistic import of the Nietzschean *Übermensch*, Nietzsche's endorsement of an attitude of a complete immanence, and emphasizes instead Nietzsche's unsatisfied drive for excellence and self-transcendence. He quotes approvingly Nietzsche's recurring motto from *Thus Spoke Zarathustra* and other writings, that "man is a thing that must overcome himself" (6:203), claiming that this is the chief characteristic of the ideal of the Overman. Thus Zeitlin emphasizes the will to authenticity that in this ideal figure comes to perfection. With this spiritualization of the *Übermensch*, Zeitlin also spiritualizes Nietzsche's basic anthropological principle of the "will to power," indicating his awareness of the distinction Nietzsche made between spiritual *Macht* and physical *Kraft*.[26]

Consequently, Zeitlin claims that this "will to power" (his Hebrew translation is literally the "will to govern and to control") is the essence of life and its existential truth. It is far from being the brutal physical "strength" that "*shallow Nietzsche commentators love to stress*" (8:204; emphasis added). This ideal connotes the will to perfection that "glorifies and beautifies every individual and every species" (ibid.). However, it is incorrect to regard this principle as a Darwinian tendency to attain perfection through physical violence and the sheer struggle for survival. If that were all that was to it, Nietzsche could be satisfied with presenting the Darwinian doctrine directly and approvingly without having to resort to a highly poetic, visionary, and prescriptive language. If Nietzsche were a Darwinist he would not have ridiculed Bismarck but, on the contrary, would have presented him as the Overman and set him up as an example for all to follow (8:204). In other words, Zeitlin rightly claims that with his two positive ideals (the Overman and the will to power) Nietzsche does not describe the Darwinian struggle for sheer survival and pleasure but entices us to try to attain self-perfection and a meaningful, authentic life.

What is quite exciting, however, at least for the present author, is the fact that this last Eastern European Jewish Nietzschean gives us the most balanced and accurate survey of Nietzsche's philosophy to be met with in Hebrew literature at this time. It was tragic that this sage, who was exterminated by the

Nazis, should have argued, thirty-three years *before* the Nazi rise to power, against the criminal misappropriation of his philosophy. And thus, when the Nazis were disseminating the idea that Nietzsche's *Übermensch* was the prototype of the superior Aryan *Führer,* Zeitlin portrayed a sublime and spiritually heroic picture of this ideal. Though Zeitlin did not possess in his conceptual repertoire the notion of aesthetic authenticity according to which one creates one's own self and life like an artist creating an original work, his picture of the Nietzschean Overman approaches this description quite closely.

Furthermore, though Zeitlin approvingly quotes Nietzsche's key idea in *The Birth of Tragedy,* that "the existence of the world is *justified* only as an aesthetic phenomenon" (*BT* Preface, 5), and claims that this idea was the culmination of Nietzsche's first stage of thinking, he later realizes that genuinely powerful persons do not seek any justification for their lives, both because there is no valid justification, and because they no longer feel any need to justify their lives, but solely to affirm these endlessly and accept them with all their "woe and joy." Thus Zeitlin claims that in the figure of the *Übermensch,* Nietzsche provides the solution to the problem of good and evil, because, according to him, personal distress and suffering are the necessary conditions for the emergence of this highest type of humanity, the "sublime fruit of creation" (8:205). Zeitlin here alludes to Nietzsche's thesis about the dialectics of suffering, sickness, and health as expressed in the aphorism that "What does not kill me—makes me stronger."

Zeitlin ends his section on Nietzsche with a clearly autobiographical confession that gives us a clue to the reasons for his later disappointment with Nietzsche's ideal: "We may bring the objection: 'man is a bridge to the Overman' but the Overman in itself for what he has come [*sic*]? . . . We cannot be satisfied with narrow and limited life, full of tears, conflicts and contradictions; we should aspire to live a more sublime lives, to pave the way for the *Übermensch*" (8:205) In the conclusion of this work, Nietzschean motifs are predominant. Zeitlin stresses the fact that Nietzsche was the first to point to the deep pessimism of Greek tragedy and culture, that he was "the exceptional, sublime genius to feel that tragedy in all its gloomy manifestations" (8:207). Zeitlin then states that the *Übermensch* "*is what he is* in all its glory and freedom" (ibid.; emphasis added), thereby stressing the formula of personal authenticity.

By the very end of the essay, Zeitlin expresses his transcendental yearning. This longing is not logically derived from his discussion so far, but it is Zeitlin's "leap" (to use Kierkegaard's notion) from Nietzschean immanence toward heavenly transcendence. His religiosity, at least here, still has the final word: "And there is no path and refuge for you, man, from all the vanity and pettiness, from all the sorrow and the suffering but only in the high ideal of love. If you will gaze to the earth and find anguish and darkness, weariness and travail—another path is facing humans: turn upward" (8:211) Did Zeitlin now turn to Spinoza to quench this transcendental longing and to overcome his growing attraction to Nietzsche?

BETWEEN TRANSCENDENTALISM AND SHEER IMMANENCY

In 1900, the year after his brief exposition of Nietzsche, Zeitlin published a two-volume work on the life and philosophy of Spinoza.[27] Zeitlin's interest in Spinoza as well as Nietzsche was no coincidence. Spinoza, like Nietzsche, legitimizes Jewish atheism and sheer immanence devoid of transcendental and divine intervention. However, by his basic tenet *Deus sive Natura* (God is Nature), Spinoza still equates ontology with theology, and it was only Nietzsche who made the full turn from pantheism to existentialism. For the latter there is no other world, no domain different from, or superior to, our own—be it immanent God or immanent nature. This outlook was the relevant philosophical message that Zeitlin, in the midst of his process of secularization, urgently needed. Nietzsche's call to embrace the idea of complete immanence and to do away with all gods had a strong appeal, especially to once-religious Jews who desperately needed support in their journeys away from their ancient tradition. The impotence of metaphysics, religion, and all the other "abstract ideologies" felt so keenly by Zeitlin at the turn of the century, attracted him to Nietzsche, who posited the antithesis of salvation from the hardship of life: salvation from transcendental doctrines of and personal needs for salvation.

But in 1900 Zeitlin still fluctuated between transcendentalism and sheer immanency. As his intellectual pendulum began its swing, it was easier for him to identify with Spinoza, the most prominent early Jewish heretic, who had emerged out of the tradition from which Zeitlin now felt estranged. Thus it is highly significant that by the end of his monograph on Spinoza, Zeitlin stresses Spinoza's pantheistic view of God as sheer immanence and objects to any attempt to equate him with the teachings of the great Hasidic rabbis (pp. 135–36).

Furthermore, by means of Spinoza's metaphysics, Zeitlin freed himself from the spell that Schopenhauer's outlook had over him, and over his other friends in the Homel Nietzschean circle.[28] From this intellectual perspective, one may claim that Spinoza's philosophy paved the way toward Zeitlin's encounter with Nietzsche's thought and actually eased its temporary assimilation into Zeitlin's worldview. In any case, the sequence of Zeitlin's work on Spinoza and then, five years later, on Nietzsche, as well as their contents, testify to the progressive process of secularization that Zeitlin underwent, intellectually as well as existentially, in this period of his life. Thus we can document this personal journey from Hasidic to semi-heretical Jew (like Spinoza) and then to fully fledged heretic (such as Nietzsche). Here, I will highlight only those motifs that his attitudes to Spinoza and to Nietzsche share, and which virtually echo Nietzsche's attitude to philosophy and to philosophers in general.

Just as Nietzsche wanted to "see through the book [of Schopenhauer] and to imagine the living man" (SE 2, p. 136), Zeitlin wishes to provide a vivid picture of Spinoza's personality by anchoring his philosophy (dealt with in the second volume of his book) in the concrete historical-social predicaments and biography of the thinker (discussed in the first volume). Consequently, he follows Spinoza's philosophy by examining his life. There is nothing monumental in Spinoza's life, he claims, but the genuine ethical ideal. Spinoza's thought is his true life. Hence Zeitlin judges Spinoza's life by Nietzsche's ideal of the "true philosopher"—his *Wahrhaftigkeit* (personal truthfulness or authenticity). Zeitlin does not, however, concentrate on the "human, all too human" aspects of Spinoza's life, and reprimands those critics for being "so eager and happy to find flaws in the lives of the great men of spirit so that they see the spots on the sun and fail to enjoy its light" (p. 4). This does not mean that Zeitlin entirely omits the psychological attitude. In his exposition of Spinoza's thought he highlights its psychological teaching, in sharp contrast to "all the other commentators who were mostly preoccupied with Spinoza's outlook on God and nature, mentioning his psychological and ethical views only in passing" (p. 5).

However, the most pervasive Nietzschean motif that informs this monograph is its Nietzschean way of using other philosophers (such as Schopenhauer) to reveal a person's "innermost history, [his] becoming."[29] This motif comes to the fore through Zeitlin's personal identification with several of Spinoza's tenets. The first sentence of the preface already indicates Zeitlin's profound empathy with Spinoza and his approval of his intellectual and existential posture. At times, though he describes Spinoza's life and thought through his own existential prism, with a Nietzschean perspective lurking behind it. For example, he says of Spinoza: "One who bears in his heart a very strong religious feeling suffers from a very fierce inner struggle when he subjects the whole tradition of his forefathers and teachers to incisive criticism; when he casts doubt on everything that in his time is considered sacred; when he wrecks the old edifice in order to erect on its ground a new building" (p. 24). Then come a eulogy of Spinoza and a reference to Nietzsche:

> Spinoza was one of the heroes and luminaries in the world of the spirit who wished to wreck everything and rebuild everything from the ground up. . . . Spiritual heroes destroy without compassion anything they regard as opposing their selfhood. . . . The new opposes the old and strives to replace it. This results in a tremendous struggle . . . which impoverishes one's vitality and leads to one's collapse and untimely death. . . . "The one that knows himself," Nietzsche says, "is his own hangman."[30] (Ibid.)

His preference for Spinoza over Nietzsche at this period of his life is quite evident when he defends Spinoza against "the arrows of Nietzsche" (p. 114 n.), stating that actually "Nietzsche could learn a lot from Spinoza about the 'morality of the slaves' and 'morality of free men'" (ibid.) who act according to reason and are not slaves to their passions. Thus it seems that at this period of his development, in order to overcome his Romantic tendencies, he opts for the primacy of reason over the individual will. Moreover, he rejects Nietzsche's elitism by emphasizing that the prophets sought "the welfare of the many [of all the Hebrew people] over the welfare of individuals" (pp. 114–15). Here we may already sense the seeds of Zeitlin's later disagreement with Nietzsche and his future rejection of the spiritual aristocracy of the Nietzschean *Übermensch*. He expresses his anti-elitist attitude by claiming that the mob is sometimes more capable of accepting some truth than educated people (p. 121). Zeitlin's affection for his people, his empathy with their helplessness, lead him to embark upon a penetrating discussion of Spinoza's view on pity and compassion. Like Nietzsche, he rejected this view, but he modifies this rejection by stating that Spinoza replaced capricious and unstable pity by "love and union with the All . . . for the sake of Society" (pp. 128–29). He claims that Spinoza has no philosophy of Judaism but that his objectives were Jewish in their "genuine meaning" because he propagated eternal Jewish ideals: "absolute justice, absolute peace, and absolute love" (p. 132).

THE FIRST HEBREW MONOGRAPH ON NIETZSCHE

After writing on Spinoza, Zeitlin realized that it was already too late to turn to metaphysics, one of the "dead God's shadows." Nietzsche, who went radically beyond "metaphysical crutches" and tried to inspire modern humanity to live creatively in a completely immanent world, increasingly appealed to Zeitlin and decisively won the ideological battle with Spinoza, at least in Zeitlin's heart (as in the heart of Herzl). Nietzsche's worldview allowed liberation from the constraints of various doctrines of metaphysical salvation and was therefore more relevant to Zeitlin's and Herzl's existential concerns than Spinoza's traditional model of salvation, which was powerless to sustain them.

Moreover, Zeitlin's growing secularism gave him the feeling that he was closer to Nietzsche than to Spinoza. Zeitlin, like Nietzsche and unlike Spinoza,—the "God-drunken sage," as Heine called him—believed in free will, whereas Spinoza did not stress enough the significant and task-oriented activity that Zeitlin, like Herzl, sought so as to attain the existential transfiguration of his self and his people. Consequently and unsurprisingly, in the same year as he published his book on Spinoza, he also wrote an aphoristic essay where Nietzsche's spirit reigns free and where there are frequent references to his writings and notions.[31]

Five years later, in 1905, Zeitlin published the longest essay on Nietzsche written by a Jewish-Hebrew thinker up to that time. Already the subtitle of this work gives a clue to his main point: instead of Spinoza's "Life, Writings and His Philosophical Method," Zeitlin writes about Nietzsche's "Life, *Poetry,* and Philosophy."[32] At the outset he asserts that Nietzsche did not have "a 'doctrine' in the usual sense, but a soul encompassing the entire world" (p. 125). His empathetic identification with Nietzsche the man is evident from his phraseology: "the tormented genius . . . and his sublime messages" (ibid.); "the closest and dearest philosopher," "the great man" (p. 127); "a hermit and a saint" (p. 134). Clearly, Nietzsche was—at this stage of Zeitlin's life—his alter ego, his foremost focus of identity.

Zeitlin's personal projections in presenting Nietzsche's personality, thought, and poetry had a far-reaching effect on his approach to the philosopher. The emotional tone is dominant, and he stresses the artist and the poet in Nietzsche's character and thought. He emphasizes the tension in Nietzsche between the poet and the scholar, perceiving that whereas the poet seeks the unattainable and tries to create his life out of his existential predicaments, the scholar investigates what has already been achieved and is relatively indifferent to his own being, aspirations, and ideals. Hence, Zeitlin delineates the internal tension in the young Nietzsche between his search for scientific and cognitive *Wahrheit,* manifested in his untiring search for the Absolute, and his determination to shape for himself a life endowed with authentic meaning (*Wahrhaftigkeit;* pt. 2:428).

The same tension between mind and heart that Zeitlin inherited from his scholarly father and his romantic mother is now projected onto Nietzsche. Clearly, whereas Spinoza attracted his mind, Nietzsche attracted his heart.

Zeitlin is well aware of the highly subjective perspective from which he treats Nietzsche, and he stresses it explicitly: "I am presenting the reader with a full description of Nietzsche's life and his tragedy as *I* understand them . . . and I have looked at certain issues according to my heart's inclinations" (p. 127; emphasis in the original). He adopts Nietzsche's attitude that philosophy is a "confession" of its creator, and applies it also to interpretations of that philosophy, the interpreter actually confessing his own existential predicaments in the act of interpreting the philosophy that is relevant to his life.

This attitude comes to the fore already in the introductory section, which opens with a distinction between the many populist, shallow, and pseudo-Nietzscheans, who are eager to "flirt" with Nietzsche in their saloon talks for their sheer "amusement" (p. 125) and the few, like himself, who "comprehend and who are able to feel, out of their spiritual kinship with him and deep compassion to his pains and sorrows, what lay at the bottom of his heart" (p. 126). It is not clear from this passage whether Zeitlin discredits here the previous theoretical treatments of Nietzsche in Hebrew literature, but one is reminded of Nietzsche's similar distinction (*GS* 125) between the pseudo-atheist who toys with the idea that "God is Dead," ridiculing him who is still searching for God, and the serious atheist who, after losing his God, is painfully and even "madly" aware of this momentous loss. This common existential loss that occurred in Nietzsche's and Zeitlin's lives and their respective struggles to face it courageously initially attracted the latter to the German harbinger of the modern "madman."

In any event, Zeitlin sought in his study of Nietzsche to provide a remedy to the outrageous popularization of Nietzsche by "the educated mob" (p. 126) whom Nietzsche so despised. Against the "faked love and hatred of Nietzsche," he feels himself "forced to speak a little out of a sheer and genuine love" about the "creator of Zarathustra." Hence he presents Nietzsche's "spiritual picture in all its glory and splendor" (p. 126). He does so merely by following his own path and refraining from walking on already trodden ones. This does not prevent him from enumerating all the primary and secondary sources of his study. Acknowledging that in the final account the best sources "are Friedrich Nietzsche's books themselves" (p. 127), he lists almost all of Nietzsche's works, including even the recently published (1895) "Will to Power." Furthermore, his impressive command of the secondary literature on Nietzsche is evident from the fact that he mentions (and occasionally quotes) fairly recent studies, for example, those written by Lou Andreas-Salomé[33] and by Elisabeth Förster-Nietzsche, who published her second volume of her biography of her brother the year before Zeitlin's essay appeared.[34] Besides these sources, which Zeitlin did not take at face value, he mentions (like Ahad Ha'am) Alois Riehl,[35] Berdichevski's dissertation supervisor Ludwig Stein,[36] and many others.

What is, however, highly interesting is Zeitlin's attitude toward Russian interpreters of Nietzsche: the bizarre Marxist-Nietzschean Lunacharsky,[37] and above all Lev Shestov. Shestov tried to unite Nietzsche, Tolstoy, and Dostoevsky into a triad of religious seekers. Consequently, it was only natural that Zeitlin should declare that the closest view to his own interpretation of Nietzsche was that of Shestov. However, he expressed his reservations concerning Shestov's view already at the end of the introduction to his study: "Shestov understands well Nietzsche's tormented feelings of destructiveness, but does not comprehend Nietzsche the lover, the dreamer, the visionary, the poet, the saint, the recluse" (p. 127). This is quite incorrect, if only because Shestov, in his essay of 1900, "The Good in the Teaching of Tolstoy and Nietzsche: Philosophy and Preaching,"[38] made it a fundamental point to assert that Tolstoy's declaration that "God is the good" is actually equivalent in meaning to Nietzsche's proclamation that "God is dead."[39] However, Zeitlin was attracted to Shestov's interpretations because this critic expressed a pronounced religious sentiment that Zeitlin shared,[40] and because this Russian-Jewish thinker provided him with a legitimization of his own feeling of affinity with the atheistic German philosopher. Shestov's insistence that Nietzsche was a passionate and devout seeker after God[41] (himself playing the role of his "madman")[42] removed the main obstacle to Zeitlin's deep identification with "the extreme heresy of Friedrich Nietzsche" (as he put it in his "Synopsis of My Life"). Shestov's description of Nietzsche was very well suited to Zeitlin's continuing existential predicaments, and this went far to obscure any essential points of difference between these two God-seekers. This is directly expressed by Zeitlin's confession at the end of the introduction to his study of Nietzsche: "I do not comprehend the fundamental difference between Nietzsche's holiness and common religious holiness."[43] Nonetheless, in his view Shestov's strong emphasis on the negative and critical aspects of Nietzsche's thought (which in Shestov's eyes were largely symptoms of his maladies); his insistence that the Nietzschean notions of the "will to power" and the *Übermensch* denoted cruelty, violence, and destruction;[44] and his ignorance of Nietzsche's idea of authenticity, were all flaws in Shestov's picture of Nietzsche, which Zeitlin must improve.

Consequently, Zeitlin stressed that Nietzsche's notion of self-overcoming also contains the idea of maturity and spiritual growth, and that in the later stages of his development Nietzsche had to vanquish whatever elements threatened the attainment of authentic creativity and freedom. Thus Zeitlin held (in contrast to Shestov) that in this respect, Nietzsche's idea of the will to power is similar to the will to selfhood—namely, to becoming an autonomous person capable of devising and effectuating positive (in his or her eyes) values.

That this was Zeitlin's interpretation of Nietzsche is attested also by the fact that in his study of Nietzsche he divided the philosopher's life into the same three stages that we earlier applied to Zeitlin's own life: those of the "Camel," the "Lion," and the "Newborn Child." Perhaps Zeitlin was following Shestov's example here, too,[45] but surely his own experience of this existential process was the most decisive factor in adapting Nietzsche's teaching on authenticity to the master himself (pp. 130–31). In this case, as in many others, it was the thoughts and feelings he experienced and shared with Nietzsche that were of utmost importance to him and to his life, not Nietzsche's abstract constructions. The image of Nietzsche as "free spirit" (p. 131) that Zeitlin extols in these pages was his most cherished personal ideal at this stage of his own existential development.

Zeitlin's own aspirations and intellectual development become visible to him when he portrays for his readers, in this highly selective biography, the innermost features of Nietzsche's life. Thus, Zeitlin mentions Nietzsche's "passion for creation and innovation" (p. 426); his "spiritual nobility" (p. 427); tension in his thought between existential *Wahrhaftigkeit* and cognitive *Wahrheit* (p. 428); his constant hidden "inner truth," despite many contradictions in his thought (p. 399); and, above all, what Zeitlin sees as the main ingredient of Nietzsche's soul, "religious enthusiasm and religious poetry" (p. 428). Thus Zeitlin uncovers those elements of Nietzsche's life and thought that he wished to adopt and manifest in his own life.

Still, despite his admiration of Nietzsche, and his insistence that actually Nietzsche as "innovator and reformer" resembles his fictive *Übermensch* (p. 120), he does not blindly idolize Nietzsche. Occasionally he exposes Nietzsche's human, all too human traits, such as his boastfulness upon receiving his professorship in Basle (p. 115). What is particularly striking, however, is the fact that Zeitlin does not refer at all to Nietzsche's views on the Jewish people and Judaism, and does not dwell on his anti-anti-Semitism. From such an ardent Jewish patriot as Zeitlin, this seems quite curious, especially when he deals with Nietzsche's convoluted relationship with

Wagner. Despite a laconic remark that Nietzsche did not approve of Wagner's anti-Semitism because this signified in his eyes "narrow-mindedness" (p. 123), nothing more is said on this emotionally laden and, for Zeitlin, quite ominous theme. This should not surprise us, however, since Zeitlin was attracted to Nietzsche on a very personal and intimate level and not because of the philosopher's general views on the Jews or any other nation. The ideological ramifications of Nietzsche's philo-Semitism were more important to figures like Berdichevski or Ahad Ha'am, who were mainly interested in shaping and creating their respective national-cultural ideologies and policies. But Zeitlin stood above these "Zionist" considerations when he approached Nietzsche as a companion on a personal journey of self-overcoming and self-creation.

All in all, when Zeitlin provides the reader with more or less faithful surveys and succinct summaries of Nietzsche's main writings (*BT*; *UM*; *HH* and *D*), one gains the impression that he strives to maintain the Nietzschean pathos by endowing it with ancient Hebrew styles and meanings (as when he remarks that the god Dionysus was called by the "ancient people also Thammuz") (p. 5, n. 1). Evidently he tries hard to instill Nietzsche and his rhetoric into the ancient heritage of his people. Thus, it may have been he who encouraged his friend David Frischmann to translate *Thus Spoke Zarathustra* into biblical Hebrew.

Like other Jewish Nietzscheans, notably Berdichevski, Zeitlin too dwells at length on Nietzsche's essay on history, and like the others he stresses Nietzsche's preference for monumental events and heroes, for the vitality of the here and now at the expense of antiquarian consciousness and learning (pp. 410–13). Zeitlin identifies himself with the Nietzschean figure of the artist-creator who gives shape to his life by sublimating the overflow and abundance of his instincts, drives, and vitality (p. 412). His adoption of the aesthetic model for creating one's authenticity is clearly evident in his discussion of Nietzsche's "Schopenhauer as Educator," where he calls Nietzsche the philosopher of "the enhancement or elevation of life and its truthfulness" (p. 417), emphasizing the central motive of Nietzsche's anthropology: cultivation and perfection of the self. In this context he also stresses the psychological attitude behind Nietzsche's approach to the human, all too human elements in people.

What is also noteworthy, however, is Zeitlin's departure from Nietzsche when the latter denigrates central Jewish values. For example, he notes (pp. 133–41) that Nietzsche's moral views at times sharply contradict Jewish ethics, as in Nietzsche's rejection of compassion, which was a fundamental virtue in the shtetl. Thus, when Nietzsche squarely endangers the most cherished Jewish values, Zeitlin manages to sustain his Jewishness.

THE STAGE OF THE RETURN (*TESHUVAH*)

Some years ago, when I still had not found the gate to *my* world, I went astray and was lost in other worlds, in foreign worlds. I was caught and mesmerized by the inner world of the *Übermensch*—Friedrich Nietzsche. I have already abandoned these worlds . . . and closed their gates. I live the life of my soul in the world, where there is no place for all these poisonous questions that torment the souls of those who seek ways solely to the world, to nature, to creation, or to their "self" and not to God.[46]

This confessional passage opens Zeitlin's next (and last) specific discussion of Nietzsche written in 1919, twelve years after his *teshuvah* or return to the practice of Judaism. Nietzsche distinguishes between two models of creating one's self: the Nietzschean-aesthetic model of shaping one's destiny and life in a completely immanent world, and the divine model that accepts the self whose essence is created by a divinity that is prior to its particular existence.

In his Nietzschean period, Zeitlin sought to follow the Nietzschean paradigm and create his secular self in a completely immanent and natural world. He failed, since his underlying deep religiosity which he could not shed, and his deep commitment to the destiny of his people, forced him to "return" to their God. This return was not enforced externally. He was raised as a pious believer in the God of Israel. After the existential failure of his Nietzschean experiment (*Versuch*, which also means to try and live novel modes of life), he returned to the God of his ancestors. Thus, if for Buber *teshuvah* was more or less a theoretical notion, Zeitlin painfully experienced it in his life.

After the *teshuvah*, when one is convinced that one is created in God's image, the issue of creating one's self seems to lie far beyond the relevant existential frames of reference. But does it really? When one is so preoccupied (as Zeitlin was) with the "inner meaning" and with the authenticity of one's self, one quite legitimate solution, as Kierkegaard incisively pointed out, leads toward the ultimate, genuine, and "highest" Creator. If one is unable to become an *Übermensch* or a "free spirit par excellence," one has to return to the almighty Creator of one's self—especially as the belief in such a Creator lies dormant in what Nietzsche calls the "atavistic household of one's soul." Heidegger's aphorism is amazingly relevant in Zeitlin's case: "Our past meets us in our future," and we can even see to it that we reactivate it in our present, thereby becoming finally what we were and always wanted to be, faithful believers in the God of Israel, or, more precisely in Zeitlin's case, passionate seekers of that God.

Consequently, from his renewed religious perspective, Zeitlin reinterprets his intimate relationship with Nietzsche and tries to rationalize it, among other things by closing the almost unbridgeable gap between Nietzsche's atheistic ideal of the *Übermensch* and a Jewish religious stance. Thus, Zeitlin claims that though the *Übermensch's* "spirit soars to the sky" (p. 49), he becomes sublime and possesses any genuine value only insofar as he admits his imperfection vis-à-vis God. Nietzsche's *Übermensch* sees in his own self the Alpha and Omega of everything else. "But man in itself—what is he?" (ibid.). Zeitlin now "*loves*" the ideal of the *Übermensch* insofar as he perceives man only as a "bridge" to God: "But I see that also the *Übermensch* is a bridge to the *Übergott* (*El Elyon*). One has to cross over from the *Übermensch* to the *Übergott*" (ibid.).

Evidently, Zeitlin has become aware that his individual search for his personal authentic self has brought him once again to face his God. It becomes even clearer that Nietzsche has functioned for Zeitlin as a temporary "bridge" (on which he can no longer linger) between two periods of his religiosity. Thus one may claim that whereas for Ahad Ha'am the Nietzschean ideal of the *Übermensch* was "new but not foreign," for Zeitlin it was foreign but not new. But Ahad Ha'am's religious commitment to the Jewish God was far less intense because in his worldview Jewish culture and heritage replaced this God.

Zeitlin's authentic faith was finally attained after he lost his God and overcame Nietzsche's anti-Godly, immanent worldview. Would Nietzsche have had any problems with this outcome of Zeitlin's journey? I do not think so, since the journey was bona fide, including the genuine attraction of Zeitlin to Nietzsche's teachings and ideals. Let us recall that Zarathustra encouraged his followers to leave him and go their own ways. Not the "what" but the "how" is what really matters for Nietzsche in the quest for personal authenticity. And if this "what" concurs with the old one, so much the better. Admitting that one becomes what one is by not being anymore what one is not, the question arises as to how one can know what one is not. Simply by trying to live and experience it, as Zeitlin did. From this point of view, this last Eastern European Jewish Nietzschean was the most authentic Nietzschean of all the European Jewish intellectuals and Zionists.

Zeitlin feels close affinity with what he calls Nietzsche's last and "negating" period of thinking (from *Zarathustra* onward) because in that period Nietzsche tried to transcend humanity. Since Nietzsche did not wish "to yield before the creator of his soul, he invented his *Übermensch*" (p. 49). It is highly probable that at this point, Zeitlin projects onto Nietzsche his own existential predicaments and thinks that Nietzsche's inability to make the "leap of faith" resulted in his construction of the image of the *Übermensch*. But Zeitlin did not have to "leap," but only to uncover and reactivate his dormant religious feelings. Thus it might be said that Nietzsche's "enticing" tactic succeeded entirely with one of his most faithful (to a point) readers: the reactivation of positive power patterns and firm selfhood.

It might also be said that Zeitlin's whole new study of Nietzsche is testimony to two significant motifs that stand in tension with one another: Zeitlin's wish to apologize for his former attraction to this "foreign" source of inspiration, and the pervasive presence of Nietzsche in Zeitlin's world, long after his *teshuvah* (in 1907). These two elements were present as well in the thinkers and writers presented in earlier chapters, but in Zeitlin's case their intensity reached an amazing culmination. This first, apologetic aspect gradually disappears among Zionists and literary figures actually in Zion. Perhaps the openness of Israelis to Western literature and modes of life and thought, and their ongoing secularization, made this aspect almost irrelevant. On the other hand, the second aspect becomes strikingly present and influential.

Be that as it may, since Zeitlin left his first long exposition of Nietzsche (from 1905) uncompleted, breaking off with a concise presentation of *Daybreak,* here he deals with Nietzsche's subsequent works: *Beyond Good and Evil, Thus Spoke Zarathustra,* and *The Gay Science.* Even as a deeply convinced believer, he still finds it necessary to complete his exposition of Nietzsche's writings. Thus we have to take Zeitlin's statement that he left the "foreign" Nietzsche with a grain of salt. How can Nietzsche be so "foreign" for Zeitlin if he is so attracted to him even now, and if in many of his other essays and national projects, Nietzsche hovers over his pages?[47]

We cannot provide an answer using the rather vague notion of ambivalence, since clearly even in his "religious phase" Zeitlin continues to identify with Nietzsche and to project his own life and thought onto Nietzsche's writings. Moreover, he continues to extol Nietzsche and raises hardly any essential objections against his philosophy. For example, Zeitlin asserts that in Nietzsche's rage against metaphysics and romanticism, "one may feel a strong longing and a soul stirring" (p. 50). Previously, Nietzsche waged his philosophical war and wielded his "hammers" to destroy everything that was above humanity, in order to erect in its place the "temple" of humanity. Now, however, Nietzsche's anger arises from the longing for things that are above humanity, and here Zeitlin quotes Nietzsche's words on wrecking the old temple to build a new one (p. 51). Nietzsche destroys not to build a new temple but to pave the way for replacing man himself with a higher ideal. Thus Zeitlin destroys his Nietzschean belief in secular aesthetic authenticity in order to re-create in its place a transcendental identity. And thus Zeitlin seems to narrow the gap between Nietzsche's secular anthropology and the Jewish theological one. Such a narrowing, of course, cannot succeed on a strictly theoretical level, but it works, at least for Zeitlin, on a personal level. The fact is that here, too, Zeitlin continues to extol Nietzsche's personality and finds in him "a religious and honest soul, that understands that man has to demand from himself more than he demands from others" (p. 53). The expression "Nietzsche's special religious feeling" (ibid.) is repeated frequently in this essay, so that one might wonder whether this is actually a projection of Zeitlin's own feelings and a way to narrow the gap between himself and Nietzsche. Or, perhaps more probably, he conceives Nietzsche's search for personal authenticity, honesty, and integrity as embodying religious values.

When Zeitlin comes to summarize Nietzsche's later writings and life, he adopts Shestov's attitude in stressing the formative influence of Nietzsche's sickness on his philosophy and applies commonsense psychology to understand his thought. The recurrent motif here is taken from Nietzsche, that "the sick have no right to become pessimists" (pp. 52, 53). He also employs Nietzsche's idea of the dialectic of health and sickness, stating that "precisely when Nietzsche overcame sickness, the 'healthy' books were written" (p. 56). Several times, however, Zeitlin relapses into Nietzsche's teaching on aesthetic authenticity, which he endows with religious significance. Speaking of the inner art of "creation," for instance (p. 56), he asserts that "to overcome one's self, to surpass one's self—that is the spiritual heroism" of this "sick genius" who by "creating his own self" and by "overcoming his sickness" "fulfilled his peculiar religious duty" (ibid.). Thus authenticity and religiosity become one and the same thing, and Nietzsche's *Übermensch* becomes the Almighty. The dissonance between Zeitlin's admiration of and attraction to Nietzsche and his present religiosity is explained or rationalized away. Moreover, Zeitlin's stress on Nietzsche's sickness and his resulting solitude enables him also to explain away Nietzsche's asocial attitude. Nietzsche's sickness made him stay away from society and publicity (p. 59). This was a crucial point for Zeitlin the publicist, the critic among his people and for his people. By this argument he provides Nietzsche with another alibi (besides the semireligious one) for those elements in his thought that squarely collide with Zeitlin's public and national preoccupations.

Zeitlin ends this essay by reiterating his conception of Nietzsche's *Übermensch*, who is "only a human, all too human . . . an echo of man's aspirations to go beyond one's narrow horizons and distresses" (p. 68). But Zeitlin made it a point here to express his Jewish religious reservation: "We will not put our faith and hopes in the *Übermensch*, a fictive image created by *a poet in his own image*, but place our hopes in the highest *God, who created man in his own image*" (p. 68; emphasis added). By the end of his stormy existential journey, Zeitlin prefers the God who has created him (and hence also his self) over Nietzsche who creates his own ideal in his own earthly image. Thus the search for personal truthfulness rests and even ends in the bosom of the most perfect Creator. Zeitlin's self is secured and sealed by the Jewish Almighty God.

However, his continuous dialogue with Nietzsche does not end here. In his 1923 essay "Lev Shestov's Search for God," Zeitlin once again refers admiringly to Nietzsche. He contrasts Kantian philosophers, who erected philosophy on the foundations of pure morality, to Nietzsche, who dared to shatter these very foundations, "criticizing and analyzing the basic ethical terms in a very exceptional, poignant, and penetrating way."[48] Zeitlin quotes Nietzsche's slogan about the old and the new temples, though, consistent with his 1919 essay, he does not accept here Nietzsche's "new temple," which in his eyes is the ideal of the *Übermensch*. He makes a revealing remark attesting to the fact that his relationship to Nietzsche was not solely on a personal and emotional level but actually changed certain axioms of his intellectual outlook: "Even if the reader agrees with Nietzsche's views or does not agree, or agrees only partly with some of them and objects to others, in any case he can no longer build the whole world on ethical foundations alone" (p. 84); in other words, faith also is required. Thus, it is plausible to assume that due to Nietzsche's impact, Zeitlin's youthful religious zest changed into mature convictions and moral choice. This is a fascinating outcome to this emotional and personal encounter of an Eastern European Jew with the German slayer of all gods. But both these figures were unique given the backgrounds of their heritages, histories, and peoples.

This chapter has sought to portray a Jewish Nietzschean who did not like this term. Initially, Zeitlin turned to Nietzsche not as a Zionist but as an individual who had lost his faith and was looking for new foci of personal identity and authenticity. He tried to become a free spirit in Nietzschean mode, but his failure to do so only attested to the correctness of Nietzsche's perceptive observation that free spirits need a firm ground, an anchor in a particular heritage and tradition; otherwise, in a cultural vacuum, so to speak, they would become dangerous to themselves and to their surroundings. Zeitlin recognized this: when he regained his Jewish religious roots and faith he turned away from Nietzsche, though not entirely. In other words, the foregoing exposition portrays the shortcomings of Nietzsche's crutches and their inability to sustain an individual who believes in free thinking but cannot live it. The pathos of freedom, combined with the fetters of his Jewish faith and antiquarian past, could not make Zeitlin into a genuine free spirit as much as he wanted. Not everybody can become a genuine Zarathustra, let alone a Jewish one.

This is especially true of a person who manifests such non-Nietzschean feelings as compassion for his people. But despite Zeitlin's awareness that Nietzsche rejected pity and wanted his *Übermensch* to go beyond and overcome the views of "the herd," an attitude that was anathema to Zeitlin's Jewish beliefs, he still admired Nietzsche. And what functioned as the real stimulus for his attraction toward Nietzsche were his subjective inclinations and the feelings of his heart. But his mind was definitely against any sort of Jewish Nietzscheanism, be it that of the Berdichevski or Ahad Ha'am variety. Zeitlin turned to Nietzsche as an individual. As a free individual he groped for his own authentic way. He left Nietzsche when his preoccupation with the destiny of his people finally gained the upper hand over the by now irrelevant Jewish Nietzscheanism. When one has a strong foreboding about an ominous end, let alone when one faces the Nazi death camp, Nietzsche becomes a remote and utterly irrelevant companion. When one faces his own extermination as *a Jew*, one has to expunge from his own being any "foreign" elements that seem irrelevant to one's tragic fate. Evidently, the book of the Jewish mystical Kabbalah—*Sefer Ha-Zohar*—proved to be much more sustaining than *Thus Spoke Zarathustra*.

Conclusion

Our discussion of the strong affinity that many of the most prominent Zionist leaders and writers felt with Nietzsche raised a number of questions. How did they use him? How did they interpret him? What period of his philosophy did they stress? And, the most fundamental question of all: To which of his ideas and/or ideals were they most attracted? Clearly it was not his antipolitical stance (discussed in the introduction to this book), which especially impressed those Zionist sages and writers. Rather, it was Nietzsche's teaching on authenticity that attracted most of the persons discussed here.

This brings us to the crucial problem that underlies the basic tension any Zionist (political or cultural, and especially the religiously oriented) might have felt toward the elitist, almost asocial, tendencies inherent in Nietzsche's attitude, which made individuals and their personal authenticity the primary motif of his existentialist philosophy.

Still, the gap between the Nietzschean ideal of personal authenticity, and the social aspect necessarily inherent in the Zionist idea and praxis, seems not to be as essential as, for example, Buber imagined it. By narrowing the gap between authenticity and Zionism, one is able to demonstrate the validity of Nietzsche's presence among the Zionists, a presence that becomes more "kosher" when significant efforts are made to bridge this gap.

Nietzsche's ideal of authenticity calls for an ongoing life of significant actions. It is actions that shape our authenticity. He definitely preferred action, rather than reflection and knowledge, which in his view "kill action."

But surely meaningful activity is only possible in the wider context of intersubjective interactions, namely, within the framework of a society.

Nietzsche's account of authenticity is modeled on the aesthetic ideal: spontaneous creation of one's self and life. Yet no creativity is possible without the social and cultural context that provides the raw material one uses—the conventions, ideas, and institutions against which one must occasionally struggle to fashion one's authentic self. Society provides the ethical norms and potential sources of self-identity that must be freely overcome, changed, or assimilated into one's life if one is to become what one wants to be.

Authenticity is best forged and revealed in *Grenzsituationen*[1]—boundary or extreme existential situations, such as Zarathustra's solitude. The existential circumstances of Western European Jews' marginality or Eastern European Jews' "rift in their hearts" were precisely such situations. Yet surely such circumstances presuppose a social context. On a remote island one is measured solely according to physical criteria of survival; it would be pointless to speak of authenticity in such a situation. Authenticity does not refer to sheer factual life but to the life worth living. All the Zionist thinkers and writers discussed in this book passionately searched for exactly such meaningful lives.

Nietzsche consistently argued that one knows what one is—only after realizing what one is not. It is essential for the individual to encounter and experiment with the various lifestyles, patterns, and belief systems that arise in human society, history, and ethics. Hence, not only is there no theoretical incompatibility between the notions of authenticity and society, but the social context is an indispensable condition of authenticity.

Nonetheless, Nietzsche himself was well aware of the tension that might ensue between his lofty ideal of personal authenticity and the social context within which it must necessarily operate. Hence his *Genealogy of Morals* attempted, among other things, to examine the most important question concerning authenticity, namely, whether the *Übermensch* can in principle develop and live in society as such. Given his emphasis upon the immanency, autarchy, and extreme individuality of authentic power, is it compatible with morality? Since Nietzsche affirms "community" (see, e.g., *GM* II-9) and does not seek to destroy it, he must explain how the morality of authenticity is at all possible within the social context, and analyze the nature of the interaction among its members. This is what he does in his genealogical inquiry, where he maintains that genuine justice is possible only within a social fabric composed of equally powerful members (ibid., II-8). He declares that recognition of the value and freedom of others originates in egoism (*BGE* 264). Only an individual who possesses an abundance of positive power and firm authentic selfhood is able to grant similar rights and freedoms to all those whom he recognizes as his equals. He is not afraid that this might diminish his own authentic power. It is the self-affirmation of one's power and virtues that psychologically enables (but, of course, does not necessitate) the affirmation of others and their authenticity. Human egoism and emphasis on authenticity do not contradict the moral order; indeed, Nietzsche thinks, they create the conditions for its proper and genuine functioning.

Moreover, if we are not convinced by this argument, Nietzsche's genealogical account also attempts to show that the moral patterns of positive *Macht* were occasionally manifested within a particular social and historical context. Witness his remarks about "an ancient Greek polis, or Venice" and his references to Rome and the Renaissance (*BGE* 262; *GM* I-16). And clearly, it would in principle be possible to add to these historical examples the future Zionist society. This was precisely what most of the Zionist ideologues and writers envisioned (witness Herzl's *Altneuland* and Ahad Ha'am's publicistic writings).

At this point a crucial question arises: do powerful and authentic *Übermenschen* need a society at all? Is it not the case that the need for others indicates a feebleness and insufficiency of positive power or authenticity? Nietzsche might have answered by pointing out that the powerful and authentic person is not identical with an omnipotent and absolutely perfect God. There is no upper limit to power and there is no optimum for authenticity. Moreover, cultural enterprises necessarily require the association and collaboration of various creative powers, each contributing its distinct capacities to the common enterprise—such as the Zionist movement, which was comprised of creative Jews and entailed multifarious schools of thought and approaches. To make a personal and social manifestation possible, any creation, even the most individual and idiosyncratic, requires the linguistic and social fabric as a necessary condition. There is no power without creation, as there is no authenticity without some kind of determined action. Hence there is no power and no authenticity without society, and their essential manifestations are impossible apart from any social context.

Further, since absolute authentic power never actually exists, and since there is no creation ex nihilo, powerful and authentic individuals need each other, and need society and culture as the vital framework within which they create themselves and their objects. This point was poignantly demonstrated by the famous Talmudic dictum: "kol Israel arevim ze le-ze"

("All Israel is responsible for one another"). Its more recent derivative was the Alliance Society's[2] slogan which was also adopted by various political and cultural groups within the Zionist movement: "Bney Israel Arevim ze le-ze" ("Children of Israel, stand for each other"). In any case, society obviously requires morality to organize and consolidate it. Nietzsche, then, is not a negating nihilist: he does not wish to overthrow society and go beyond its limits. The "Antichrist" within him does not make him into an anarchist. This point was perceived by the Hebrew Nietzscheans in Palestine and in Israel.

Another possible source of tension between Nietzsche and Zionism is the fact that most of the figures discussed here toyed with the values of progress and enlightenment. But what about Nietzsche's notorious opposition to the idea of progress, and his attacks upon the values of the European Enlightenment which most of the Zionist leaders seemed to uphold?

The belief in progress and in the values of enlightened human society (the famous trinity of *liberté, égalité, fraternité*) seemed not only to be the sine qua non of the thriving Zionist settlements in Palestine and the main goal of the Zionist programs, but they also seemed to grant marginal Jews, before they joined the Zionist movement, the firm identity they sought and equal participation in the affairs and culture of "enlightened" Europe. This was especially notable in the case of Max Nordau. So why did those very figures become so attracted to Nietzsche?

Indeed, these humanist ideals of progress and enlightenment seemed at the beginning to procure equal rights for the marginal Western Jews and a passport to becoming a recognized and integral part of the universal brotherhood. Equal rights were indeed granted, but recognition and brotherhood? Never. After they renounced the traditional and *heimish* identity of the "Old Ghetto," they found themselves estranged in the "New Ghetto," living on the margins of two universes and two traditions, feeling themselves at home in neither. Thus when the figures discussed above became deeply disappointed with their hard-won place in the "New Ghetto," when they became disillusioned with the so-called European Enlightenment, Nietzsche's appeal to them became even stronger. Consequently, they joined in his devastating critique of these very values.

But can we say with a clear conscience that Nietzsche stood absolutely against progress and enlightenment? The answer depends, of course, on what we mean by these terms and how Nietzsche understood them.

Between *Human, All Too Human* and *The Gay Science*, that is, between 1878 and 1882, Nietzsche tended to support enlightenment, progress, and liberalism. And he never opposed one of the most important themes of the European Enlightenment: the striving of the individual to attain perfection and moral-personal advancement.[3] Consequently, his political ideas in this period were essentially different from those he announced at other times.[4] In addition, despite Nietzsche's elitism and his dislike of socialism, in the first twenty years following his collapse there were actually leftists (including those who belonged to the Zionist labor movements) who were attracted to his thought and propagated it in original and revised versions.[5]

But the most important point in this context is that if we liberate the notion of progress from its excessive historical dependence on the ideology of the Enlightenment and on European socialist movements, and if we grant it a personal meaning in the sense of moral improvement of individuals and the elevation of their culture to new achievements, it is undeniable that Nietzsche believed in progress and in human cultural development. Thus if we take for granted the historical fact, documented above, that most modern Hebrew writers and Zionist ideologues believed in progress mainly, but not exclusively, in the sense of the advancement of Hebrew-Zionist culture that would assist in the cultivation and perfection of Jewish-Hebrew individuals within its sustaining framework, the gap between Nietzsche's philosophical worldview and the attitudes embraced by figures discussed here will be significantly narrowed. This becomes even more evident if we consider the fact that Nietzsche was not such a staunch enemy of enlightenment and progress; his philosophy was actually a legitimate derivative of these movements.[6]

Moreover, the so-called gap between Nietzsche's views and the tendencies of the Zionist thinkers and writers will narrow further if we recall several enlightened motifs that frequently recur in Nietzsche's writings. Thus, for example, when supporting the ideal of the Enlightenment and the view of evolutionary progress against "Rousseau's passionate follies and half-lies that called forth the optimistic spirit of the revolution," Nietzsche exclaims: "It is this spirit that has for a long time banished the spirit of the Enlightenment and of progressive evolution: let us see—each of us within himself—whether it is possible to call it back!" (*HH* I–463; emphasis in the original).[7] With this unequivocal statement one should not be surprised to find Nietzschean aphorisms that even support democratic regimes as the most efficient shield of sublime culture (*HH* II–275).

All the same, it is important to stress that Nietzsche did not believe in the ideal of progress as posited by enlightened rationalism, according to which (especially in Hegel) progress is defined as the evolutionary materialization of reason in history. Nietzsche rejects this idea by stating that "progress is merely a modern idea, that is, a false idea" (*A* 4). But this rejection of the idea of progress as it appeared within the framework of the European Enlightenment does not prevent him from speaking about progress in another sense: not historical-global and rational progress, but the moral-personal edification embodied by the "higher type" or the Overman. Such a development does not take place in a linear manner across rational history, but occurs in the shape of "fortunate accidents of great success" that "have always been possible and will perhaps always be possible. And even whole families, tribes, or peoples may occasionally represent such a bull's eye" (ibid.).

Nietzsche does not reject out of hand the possibility of the emergence of a society of *Übermenschen*. In such an emerging society, this ideal acquires ethical connotations because of the required interaction between the Overman and the society that cultivates him or her. The Nietzschean Overman is a person neither ultimately self-sufficient, nor absolutely autarkic like the God of the philosophers. Nor does the ideal connote solipsism or social autism. Since Nietzsche rejects the view that Hegelian historical and rational dialectics will necessarily bring the materialization of reason in humanity, he seeks to mobilize human goodness, free will, and the society that cultivates and promotes "higher types," namely, Overmen, who will be qualitatively more advanced than average persons. The advent of such types will initiate significant moral-cultural progress; Nietzsche claimed that such progress had already taken place in the ancient Greek polis.

From this point of view one may claim that in Nietzsche's eyes the Zionist enterprise was perfectly legitimate and even a welcome undertaking if it would succeed in creating and cultivating in Palestine a kind of *Überjude*. But for this purpose one must create a new image of a Jew capable of transfiguring itself to the level of the Jewish Overman. For the sake of cultivating such an image, the reclaimed or rejuvenated Land of Israel becomes vital. Hence Zionism, which realized its ideals and created a new or renewed society, culture, and literature, did not necessarily contradict Nietzsche's aristocratic ideal of the Overman. Was this process undertaken during and after the period of the Zionist *halutzim* (pioneers) in Palestine under the auspices of Nietzsche's philosophy?

What should be clear by now, however, is that we should distinguish between Nietzsche's general philosophy (which has never been unanimously interpreted); his relations to Jews, Judaism, and Zionism (which also suffers from multifarious understandings); and what Zionist leaders and writers read into his writings and used for their existential and ideological agendas. And as a summary of the legitimate controversy concerning the questions "What exactly is Nietzsche's political theory?" and "To what extent did it influence Zionist writers and leaders?" one must assert that his political-social doctrine is complicated and, lacking a systematic treatment, open to various readings. Thus any unequivocal statement to the effect that "Nietzsche is against statehood (and hence against political Zionism)," or "Nietzsche is against progress and enlightenment," or "He is against [or for] Zionism" necessitates many reservations and stipulations. Such statements can only be defended based on comprehensive research that will deal with these issues from more than one perspective, apart from one's philosophical and cultural prejudices. This book has expressed my perspective on all these questions without pretending to be exhaustive. But if it encourages refutations, qualifications, and further research, I may claim to have achieved my chief objective.

One last word about Nietzsche's thriving career in Palestine and the state of Israel. As we have seen, Berdichevski's ideological slogan sounds both ominous and valid: "either the last Jew" (that is, essence, antiquarian consciousness, community) or "the first Hebrew." But the crucial question of how to become a Jewish Hebrew (a secular Israeli Jew), or how to synthesize authenticity and individual aspirations with Judaism and/or communal-collective Zionism, remains unsettled in this book. Perhaps a more productive resolution of this problem will be found in a future volume, one which is set against conditions where the primacy of the community is relatively assured, politically and historically, or taken for granted. We will see that there will emerge an opposite trend that is still quite prevalent in contemporary Israel: the ever-increasing move from community to individuality, from the collective kibbutz to personal authenticity. This is in opposition to the earlier move from individuality and personal problems of identity and existential marginality to the national-cultural community. One may already surmise that Nietzsche's heuristic role in shaping the personal authenticity of the *halutzim,* whose individuality was almost dissolved in pursuing pressing collective-national purposes, will be more prominent.

Beyond any doubt, however, is the centrality of Nietzsche's ideal of personal authenticity. It was and still is predominant in both movements: from the Diaspora to Israel and socialist collectives in Zion, and from the Zionist state and kibbutz to individual Hebrews. We will find in literature, social polemics, and public discussions in contemporary Israel that the authentic Hebrew is a person who strives *to be himself* beyond the stern demands of the state and the extreme military-political exigencies that have

frequently delayed this struggle for one's personal authenticity. Not unsurprisingly, we will see how the Israeli Hebrew Nietzscheans strove to become uniquely Hebrew individuals beyond Israel, as the Jewish Zionist
wanted to remain oneself beyond Zion. For both groups, Nietzsche's call
"to become what you are" by overcoming "what you are not" was an inspiring call that informed and even illuminated their whole being. Finally,
we will see concretely how in some Israelis' lives and writings, these existential "herald's cries" "called the bravest to their courage."[8]

NOTES

INTRODUCTION

1. This is already evident from a cursory glance at the hundreds of bibliographical items I compiled for the collection of essays *Nietzsche in Hebrew Culture*, ed. Jacob Golomb (Jerusalem, 2002), pp. 383–406 (in Hebrew). This first-of-its-kind bibliography contains virtually all the Hebrew books and articles on Nietzsche, all the Hebrew translations of his works, and many personal letters written by the most prominent Zionist leaders and modern Hebrew writers, that copiously refer to Nietzsche, from 1892 on.

2. This phrase is adopted from Kierkegaard's description of the objectives of his philosophy—to "continually . . . provide the existential corrective by poetically presenting the ideals and inciting people," *Søren Kierkegaard's Journals and Papers*, ed. and trans. H. V. Hong and E. H. Hong, vol. 1 (Bloomington, Ind., 1967), p. 331. Just as Kierkegaard introduced the existentialist revolution to overcome the theoretical preoccupation of his "Present Age" with its lofty Hegelian speculations and its universal absolute *Geist* that had "swallowed" the existential concerns of individuals, so this book stresses the individual Zionists' personal conflicts and objectives. The fact that Hegel was also the most influential theoretician of the modern state further strengthens this analogy. For Kierkegaard see my *In Search of Authenticity: From Kierkegaard to Camus* (London, 1995).

3. See, among many others, Benny Morris: *The Birth of the Palestinian Problem 1947–1949* (Cambridge, 1987); idem, *1948 and after: Israel and the Palestinians* (Oxford, 1990); Tom Segev, *1949: The First Israelis* (New York, 1986); idem, *The New Zionists* (Jerusalem, 2001); Ilan Pappe, *Aristocracy of the Land: The Husayni Family—Political Biography* (Jerusalem, 2002).

4. Cf. Daniel Boyarin, *Unheroic Conduct: The Rise of Heterosexuality and the Invention of the Jewish Man* (Berkeley, Calif., 1967) and in Israel: Rina Peled, *"The New Man" of the Zionist Revolution* (Tel Aviv, 2002) and see especially her article "Zionism—A Reflected Image of Anti-Semitism," in *German Antisemitism* (in Hebrew) ed. Jacob Borut and Oded Heilbronner (Tel Aviv, 2000), pp. 133–56. The critique of the "new Jew" ideal will be addressed in a future publication, *Nietzsche in Zion*, since all the "new histories" were written long after Jews won their own state.

5. See his highly critical polemic against them: *Fabricating Israeli History: The "New Historians"* (London, 1997).

6. It is no coincidence that many of the first works of the "New Historians" were published in the *Journal of Palestine Studies*.

7. Azar (Rabinovitz), "Hirhurim" (Meditations), *Ha-Adamah* (The Earth) (Tel Aviv, 1920); my emphasis. This issue appeared when Joseph Hayyim Brenner was still its editor, which explains the almost Nietzschean tenor of many of the articles. On Brenner's Nietzscheanism see the first chapter of the second volume.

8. See Frederic V. Grunfeld, *Prophets without Honour* (London, 1979), p. 17; and Solomon Liptzin, *Germany's Stepchildren* (Philadelphia, 1944), p. 195.

9. *The Maurizius Case* (London, 1930), p. 297.

10. Gershom Scholem, "Jews and Germans," *Commentary* (November 1966): p. 35.

11. Arthur Schnitzler, *Jugend in Wien*, ed. Therese Nickl and Heinrich Schnitzler (Vienna, 1968), p. 328 Because of this realization, as we will see in chapter 1, Herzl relinquished his dream of becoming an influential Austrian politician.

12. On another fascinating group of Jewish Nietzscheans—those, like the notable "free spirit" Stefan Zweig, who remained in a state of suspended identity in spite of existential pressure, neither opting for socialism nor Zionism, nor embracing some form of Catholicism like Alfred Döblin, see my "Nietzsche and the Marginal Jews," in *Nietzsche and Jewish Culture*, ed. Jacob Golomb (London, 1997), pp. 158–92. On Stefan Zweig see my "Stefan Zweig: The Jewish Tragedy of a Nietzschean 'Free Spirit,'" in *Nietzsche and the Austrian Mind*, ed. Jacob Golomb (Vienna, in press).

13. On the Nietzschean aesthetic model of authentic selves see my "Nietzsche on Authenticity," *Philosophy Today* 34 (1990): 243–58, and *In Search of Authenticity*, chap. 4.

14. On the enticing function of Nietzsche's philosophy see my *Nietzsche's Enticing Psychology of Power* (Ames, Iowa, 1989; Jerusalem, 1987).

15. "Jüdische Renaissance," *Ost und West* 1 (Berlin, 1901), pp. 7–10.

16. As Arthur Schnitzler put it: "The problem of religion occupied me more . . . than ever before. . . . it had to flow together with the basic questions of philosophy. . . . It is nonsense to say 'As God wills.' We will, God has to." *My Youth in Vienna*, trans. Catherine Hutter (New York, 1970), pp. 77–78. See also Jacob Wassermann's *My Life as German and Jew*, trans. S. N. Breinin (New York, 1933), where he confesses that for him, "The Jewish God was a mere shadow" (p. 19).

17. The Spinozistic model of salvation, which offered a metaphysical and rationalistic *amor dei intellectualis*, was a worthy, though anachronistic, rival of the Nietzschean *amor fati*. See the chapter on "Spinoza and Nietzsche" in volume 2 of Yirmiyahu Yovel's *Spinoza and Other Heretics* (Princeton, N.J., 1989); Joan Stambaugh, "*Amor dei* and *Amor fati*: Spinoza and Nietzsche," in *Studies in Nietzsche and the Judaeo-Christian Tradition*, ed. James C. O'Flaherty, Timothy F. Sellner, and Robert M. Helm (Chapel Hill, N.C., 1985), pp. 130–41. Indeed both names appear frequently in the writings and memoirs of marginal Jews and modern Hebrew writers. One notable example is Hillel Zeitlin, but the coupling of Spinoza and Nietzsche can be found also in Herzl's diaries.

18. See H. Nunberg and E. Federn, eds., *Minutes of the Vienna Psychoanalytic Society* (New York, 1967) and Ernst Jones, *Sigmund Freud: Life and Work*, vol. 2 (London, 1955).

19. Theodor Lessing, *Schopenhauer, Wagner, Nietzsche: Einführung in moderne deutsche Philosophie* (Munich, 1908), and his announcement of this work in *Die Zukunft* (Berlin), no. 15 (12 January 1907): 75; idem, *Nietzsche* (1925; Munich, 1985) with an epilogue, "Ein Doppel-Portrait," by Rita Bischof. See also the Nietzsche-inspired work written by Lessing during the First World War, *Geschichte als Sinngebung des Sinnlosen oder die Geburt der Geschichte aus dem Mythos* (Hamburg, 1962), in which Nietzsche is frequently quoted.

20. Theodor Lessing, *Der jüdische Selbsthass* (1930; reprint, introd. Boris Groys, Munich. 1984). In a lecture he delivered three months before being murdered in August 1933 by a Nazi agent in Marienbad, Lessing appeals to these Jews to assert their "*Machtwille*" and return to "*Natur und Erde*." *Deutschland und seine Juden* (Prague, 1933), p. 14.

21. See my *Nietzsche's Enticing Psychology of Power*, chaps. 4, 5, and 6.

22. For example, Richard Maximilian Cahen (writing under the name Richard Maximilian Lonsbach), published *Friedrich Nietzsche und die Juden: Ein Versuch* (1939; reprint, ed. Heinz Robert Schlette, Bonn, 1985), explaining why Nietzsche regarded the rising tide of anti-Semitism as a new revolt of the slave-man and fought it bitterly. Anti-Semitism was for Nietzsche the viewpoint not of a people or a class but of vile and worthless individuals who had been defeated in the struggle for existence. Nietzsche coined a new word to designate these: *die Schlechtweggekommenen*. Anti-Semitism was the revolt of those who were poor in spiritual values, and it indicated an envious and cowardly personality against which Nietzsche's philosophy of power was directed.

23. Notably, Menachem Brinker and Yirmijahu Yovel. See their essays in Golomb, *Nietzsche, Zionism and Hebrew Culture*.

24. The letters of Paneth were first published in a biography of Nietzsche by his sister Elisabeth Förster-Nietzsche, *Das Leben Friedrich Nietzsches*, vol. 2 (Leipzig, 1904), pp. 474–75, 479–93; see pp. 486ff. See also Richard Frank Krummel, "Joseph Paneth über seine Begegnung mit Nietzsche in der Zarathustra-Zeit," *Nietzsche Studien* 17 (1988): 478–95.

25. Thus he emphatically claims: "For since we are the outcome of earlier generations, we are also the outcome of their aberrations, passions and errors. . . . It is not possible wholly to free oneself from these chains" (*HL* p. 76).

26. See *HL* chap. 3, and chap. 3 in my *Nietzsche's Enticing Psychology of Power.*

27. The exact quotation is: "If a temple is to be erected *a temple must be destroyed*" (*GM* II—24, emphasis in original).

28. See, among many others, the following works: Daniel W. Conway, *Nietzsche and the Political* (London, 1997); idem, *Nietzsche's Dangerous Game* (Cambridge, 1997); Keith Ansell-Pearson, *An Introduction to Nietzsche as Political Thinker* (Cambridge, 1994); Tracy B. Strong, "Nietzsche's Political Aesthetics," in *Nietzsche's New Seas: Explorations in Philosophy, Aesthetics, and Politics*, ed. Michael Allen Gillespie and Tracy B. Strong (Chicago, 1988), 153–74; Geoff Waite, *Nietzsche's Corps/e* (Durham, N.C., 1996); Peter Berkowitz, *Nietzsche: The Ethics of an Immoralist* (Cambridge, Mass., 1995). Berkowitz writes: "It is tempting to conclude that Nietzsche does not practice or contribute to political philosophy. . . . Yet Nietzsche moves within the domain of moral and political philosophy . . . [since] the question of human perfection lies at the heart of Nietzsche's inquiries" (ibid., pp. 1–2). See also Richard Rorty, *Contingency, Irony, and Solidarity* (Cambridge, 1989), where Nietzsche is portrayed as an "ironic liberal" who functions as a heuristic means to promote Rorty's postmodern liberalism.

29. Nietzsche, "Der griechische Staat" (1872), *KSA* 1:764–77. See also part 8 of the first volume of *Menschliches, Allzumenschliches* entitled "Ein Blick auf den Staat" ("A Glance at the State," in Hollingdale's translation).

30. *Thus Spoke Zarathustra*, pt. 1: "On the New Idol," trans. Walter Kaufman, in *The Portable Nietzsche*, p. 160.

CHAPTER 1. "THUS SPOKE HERZL"

1. *The Complete Diaries of Theodor Herzl*, ed. Raphael Patai, trans. Harry Zohn, vol. 1 (New York, 1960), p. 191. This edition does not include Herzl's diaries from 1882–87, which are found in *Theodor Herzl: Briefe und Tagebücher*, ed. Alex Bain, et al., vol. 1 (Berlin, 1983) (hereafter *HBT*) 585–648. When necessary, I have translated from this edition.

2. See, e.g., Herzl's letter to Georg Brandes of 13 January 1897, in which he exclaims: "ich bin kein Socialist"; quoted in Klaus Bohnen, "Ein Dialog als Provokation: Unveröffentlichter Briefwechsel zwischen Theodor Herzl und Georg Brandes," in *Emuna: Israel Forum*, no. 4 (1977): 1–8. See also in *HBT* 4:178.

3. See Jacob L. Talmon's perceptive observation: "Herzl's Jewish nationalism derives from liberal and individualistic categories of thought." "Types of Jewish Self-Awareness: Herzl's 'Jewish State' after Seventy Years (1896–1966)" in idem, *Israel among the Nations* (London, 1970), pp. 88–127. See also Ernst Ludwig Ehrlich, "Liberalismus und Zionismus," in *Theodor Herzl Symposion* (Vienna, 1996), pp. 35–43. Robert Weltsch also claimed that "Zionism is a personal task imposed upon every individual. . . . the whole life of the young Jew undergoes a transformation." Robert Weltsch, "Theodor Herzl and We," in *The Young Jew Series* 2 (1929): 23, 24. Recently, these rather neglected ramifications of the Zionist revolution have attracted new attention. For example, Eyal Chowers rightly asserts that "Zionism meant more than political independence in Palestine. It promised both material and spiritual transformation," "Time in Zionism: The Life and Afterlife of a Temporal Revolution," *Political Theory* 26, no. 5 (October 1998): 652–85. On Herzl's vision of a Jewish state based on his admiration for the English aristocracy see Ian Buruma, *Voltaire's Coconuts: or Anglomania in Europe* (London, 1999).

4. See the Introduction above, and Jacob Golomb, "Nietzsche and the Marginal Jews," in *Nietzsche and Jewish Culture*, ed. Jacob Golomb (London, 1997), pp. 158–92.

5. Herzl's letter to Hugo Wittmann, dated 30 March 1893. *HBT* vol. 1.

6. See the editors' note on this passage in *HBT* (2:803 n. 22), which stresses that Nietzsche was at that time "in geistiger Umnachtung," that is, mentally deranged.

7. Max Nordau, *Entartung*, vol. 2, 2nd ed. (Berlin, 1893), p. 363. This volume can be found in Herzl's library in the Herzl Museum, Jerusalem. For details see the next chapter.

8. Among the philosophical items to be found are a French edition of Francis Bacon; a four-volume edition of Herder; Kant's *Kritik der reinen Vernunft*; five volumes by Lessing; volumes by Rousseau; and a twelve-volume edition of Schopenhauer's oeuvre.

9. Herzl's private library contains the following editions of Nietzsche's works: *Jenseits von Gut und Böse* (Leipzig, 1886); *Zur Genealogie der Moral* (Leipzig, 1887); *Morgenröte* (Leipzig, 1887); *Also sprach Zarathustra* (Leipzig, 1886); *Die fröhliche Wissenschaft* (Leipzig, 1887); *Die Geburt der Tragödie* (Leipzig, 1886); *Der Fall Wagner* (Leipzig, 1888); *Menschliches, Allzumenschliches* (Leipzig, 1886); *Unzeitgemässe Betrachtungen* (Leipzig, 1886); *Götzen-Dämmerung* (Leipzig, 1889).

10. Letter written in Vienna, 22 April 1891, *HBT* 1:438. Some speculate that this was actually a letter to the theater critic of the *Wiener Presse*.

11. Nordau's manuscript arrived only after the issue had gone to print. Letter written in Vienna, 14 September 1900, *HBT* 6:38.

12. Max Nordau, "Individualismus?, Solidarismus?" *NFP*, 3 October 1900, pp. 1–3.

13. *NFP*, 31 December 1891.

14. Significantly also in Zionist periodicals and those aimed at wider Jewish intellectual circles. It is worth mentioning the German-Jewish journal *Ost und West: Illustrierte Monatsschrift für Modernes Judentum* (Berlin). Its editors, Hermann Cohen, Ludwig Geiger, Otto Warburg, Martin Buber, Max Nordau, and Jacob Wassermann, belonged to the Jewish intellectual elite. It was not a coincidence that the first issue

included a manifesto that shaped Western European Zionism and that was heavily colored by Nietzschean motifs: Martin Buber, "Jüdische Renaissance," *Ost und West* 1 (1901): 7–10. For analysis of this essay, see the chapter on Buber below.

15. This contrasted with the Pan-German *Leseverein der deutschen Studenten,* founded in 1872, which became the famous *Albia* that was disbanded by the authorities following anti-Semitic riots. Details of this affair are provided by Ernst Pawel, *The Labyrinth of Exile: A Life of Theodor Herzl* (New York, 1980), pp. 46–48, 66, 70. In spring 1881, Herzl joined this dueling fraternity but the following year he distanced himself from the *Albia's* social life and stopped contributing to its official publication. However, it is quite probable that he had attended Josef Paneth's lecture delivered before this society that dealt with Nietzsche's second *Untimely Meditation.* See Richard Frank Krummel, "Josef Paneth über seine Begegnung mit Nietzsche in der Zarathustra-Zeit," *Nietzsche-Studien* 17 (1988): 478–95.

16. Cf. William J. McGrath, "Student Radicalism in Vienna," *Journal of Contemporary History* 2 (1967): 183–201; idem, "Mahler and the Vienna Nietzsche Society," in Golomb, ed. *Nietzsche and Jewish Culture,* pp. 218–32.

17. *Kritische Gesamtausgabe, Nietzsche Briefwechsel,* ed. Giorgio Colli and Mazzino Montinari (Berlin, 1975–93), sect. II, vol. 6, p. 314.

18. See Olga Schnitzler, *Spiegelbild der Freundschaft* (Salzburg, 1962), for a description of the close relationships Schnitzler had with Herzl, Hermann Bahr, Georg Brandes, Karl Krauss, Jacob Wassermann, and Gerhart Hauptmann—all of them known *admirers* of Nietzsche.

19. *HBT* 1:585–648.

20. *HBT* 2:492.

21. Ibid., pp. 76, 131, 143 (in which Herzl refers to Thomas More's *Utopia*), 220 (in which he quotes from Voltaire's *Candide*).

22. See, for example, some of the essays in *Nietzsche and Depth Psychology,* ed. Jacob Golomb, Weaver Santaniello, and Ron Lehrer (Albany, N.Y., 1999).

23. Under the title *Nietzsches Werke: Gesamtausgabe,* ed. Peter Gast (Leipzig, 1892ff.), and discontinued after volume 5.

24. Lou Andreas-Salomé, *Friedrich Nietzsche in seinen Werken* (Vienna, 1894).

25. Elisabeth Förster-Nietzsche, *Das Leben Friedrich Nietzsches,* 2 vols. (Leipzig, 1895–1904).

26. Both as part of the *Gesamtausgabe* (both Leipzig: Naumann, 1895).

27. Ola Hansson, "Nietzscheanismus in Skandinavien," 15 October 1889; Malvida von Meysenburg, "Erinnerungen an Friedrich Nietzsche," 16 and 17 June 1893; idem, "Aus meinem Tagebuch über Nietzsche," 14 October, 1893; Karl Federn, "R. W. Emerson und Friedrich Nietzsche," 10 July 1894; Moritz Necker, "Nietzsche's Jugend," 11 October 1895; Ludwig Stein, "Friedrich Nietzsche als 'philosophischer Klassiker,'" 3 July 1897; two articles on Nietzsche's death (by Hugo Ganz and Ludwig Stein), 26 August 1900; Karl Bulcke, "Die Trauerfeierlichkeit am Sarge Friedrich Nietzsche's," 30 August 1900; Georg Brandes, "Friedrich Nietzsche 1844–1900," 14 September 1900; Malvida von Meysenburg, "Der erste Nietzsche," five articles between 18 and 28 September 1900; Gabriele Reuter, "Eine Nietzsche-Büste," 31 October 1901. To these we must add also Nordau's article on Nietzsche (see above, note 12).

28. Cf. Harry Zohn, "The Herzl Diaries: A Self-Portrait of the Man and the Leader," *Herzl Year Book* 2 (1960): 207–15.

29. Raul Auernheimer, "Uncle Dori: Memories of a Cousin and a Literary Colleague," in *Theodor Herzl: A Memorial*, ed. Meyer W. Weisgal (New York, 1929), p. 35 (my emphasis). Cf. also a chapter of Herzl's autobiography translated by Harry Zohn as "Beard of the Prophet," in *Herzl Year Book* 6 (1964–1965): 69–76.

30. Tel Aviv, 1940.

31. See Kaufmann's translation of *The Gay Science* p. 4 and in KSA 3:343.

32. *Complete Diaries of Theodor Herzl*, 1: 7. See also Jacques Kornberg's invaluable *Theodor Herzl: From Assimilation to Zionism* (Bloomington, Ind., 1993), pp. 115, 118–21.

33. Hence I can hardly agree with Alex Bein, who is at pains to explain the profound impact that the Dreyfus trial had on Herzl and on his conversion to Zionism (*Theodor Herzl: A Biography of the Founder of Modern Zionism*, trans. Maurice Samuel [1934; reprint, New York, 1970], p. 87 n. 22).

34. My translation from Act 2, Scene 6. An abridged English translation by Heinz Norden appears in *Theodor Herzl: A Portrait for This Age*, ed. Ludwig Lewisohn (Cleveland, 1955), pp. 152–93.

35. On the intimate relations between fiction and philosophy in the existential philosophies of authenticity see Jacob Golomb, *In Search of Authenticity* (London, 1995), chap. 2.

36. Note 34, p. 169. Nietzsche himself, after claiming that "perhaps the young stock-exchange Jew is altogether the most disgusting invention of mankind," asks his readers: "In spite of that, I should like to know how much one must forgive a people in a total accounting when they have had the most painful history of all peoples, not without the fault of all of us, and when one owes them the noblest man (Christ), the purest sage (Spinoza), the most powerful book, and the most effective moral law in the world." *HH*, I-475, trans. Walter Kaufman in *The Portable Nietzsche* (New York, 1954), p. 62. For this quotation I prefer Kaufman's more accurate translation.

37. See, for example, his *Gay Science*, section 137; cf. Golomb, "Nietzsche on Jews and Judaism," *Archiv für Geschichte der Philosophie* 67 (1985): 139–61; idem, "Nietzsche's Judaism of Power," *Revue des études juives* 147 (1988): 353–85.

38. Although Herzl incorporates into this play a short story about Moshe from Magenza, who functions for Jacob as an exemplary figure and who behaved as authentically and humanly as a genuine *Mensch*, Moshe's humanity originated with the ancient Hebrews and was preserved within the Jewish tradition.

39. See ZI—137–40 in the chapter entitled "On the three Metamorphoses."

40. Herzl, *The Jewish State*, trans. Sylvie D'Avigdor (London, 1936), p. 21. Herzl obliquely refers to this aphorism almost five years before Micha Josef Berdichevski adopted it as an epigraph for his Hebrew polemic. See below, chapter 3.

41. Herzl, *Philosophische Erzählungen* (Berlin, 1919), pp. 1–23. Subsequent references appear in the text.

42. See above, note 13.

43. Herzl, *The Jewish State*, p. 21 n. 39.

44. Speech before the Israeli Union, in Pollack, ed., *Ko Amar Herzl* (note 30), p. 30.

45. See below, chapter 5.

46. For details see my *Nietzsche's Enticing Psychology of Power* (Ames, Iowa, 1989), part 3.

47. Pollack, ed., *Ko Amar Herzl*, pp. 15–16.

48. Ibid., p. 21.

49. Ibid., pp. 108, 89.

50. Auerhheimer, "Uncle Dori," p. 35.

51. "Der Gedankenleser." Surprisingly, this philosophically significant story was not included in *Philosophische Erzählungen*. It appeared first in the *Wiener Allgemeine Zeitung*, 25 May 1887, and then in Theodor Herzl, *Neues von der Venus: Plaudereien und Geschichten* (Leipzig, 1987).

52. Edward Young, *The Complaint, or Night Thoughts on Life, Death and Immortality* (1742), IV, p. 629.

53. Karl Jaspers referred to *Grenzsituationen* (boundary situations), the vital importance of which in matters of authenticity is discussed by me *In Search of Authenticity*, chap. 2.

54. Herzl also reflects this aphorism in "Sarah Holzmann" (*Philosophische Erzählungen*, p. 50), in which he states that "the motives for our actions are sometimes quite odd and most of the time very gloomy." These actions are rooted mainly in the unconscious, as he indicates by quoting the term "*unbewusst*" from a poem by Friedrich Rikert, ibid., p. 52.

55. "Die Heilung vom Spleen," *Philosophische Erzählungen*, p. 205.

56. Herzl, "The Good Things of Life," in Lewisohn, *Theodor Herzl: A Portrait for this Age*, pp. 121, 129.

57. Ibid., p. 120.

58. Ibid.

59. Ibid., p. 121.

60. Ibid., p. 129.

61. Ibid., p. 129. See also a statement in which he explicitly admits that he is fed up with Schopenhauer's philosophy: "The beauty no longer attracts my heart. The world for me is no more appearance but a will." Pollack, ed., *Ko Amar Herzl*, p. 48.

62. Pollack, ed., *Ko Amar Herzl*, p. 36.

63. David Ben-Gurion's statement that Herzl "had faith in science and technology" requires serious reservation. See his preface to Lewisohn, ed., *Theodor Herzl: A Portrait for This Age*, p. 14.

64. Pollack, ed., *Ko Amar Herzl*, p. 88.

65. Ibid.

66. What Chowers perceptively calls "sundered history," meaning an interlude during which human existence in time is seen as open and devoid of any divine guidance or natural order, or any unfolding reason such as Hegel introduced to history and Nietzsche attempted to free it from (see note 3).

67. Herzl, "Der sterbende Fiaker," *NFP*, 17 April 1898.

68. This is the motif of his story "*Radfahren*," ibid., 1 November 1896.

69. Herzl, "Das Automobil," ibid., 6 August 1899

70. See the discussion in the Introduction.

71. Pollack, ed., *Ko Amar Herzl*, p. 18. Cf. Ritchie Roberston, "The Problem of 'Jewish Self-Hatred' in Herzl, Kraus, and Kafka," *Oxford German Studies* 16 (1985): 81–108.

72. Eugen Dühring, *Die Judenfrage als Racen-, Sitten- und Kulturfrage* (Karlsruhe, 1881).

73. Herzl, *HBT* 1:611.

74. Ibid., pp. 612, 615.

75. See Nietzsche's critique of Eugen Dühring in *BGE* 204; and in *GM* II –11, III–14 and 26.
76. Pollack, ed., *Ko Amar Herzl*, pp. 26, 24.
77. Ibid., pp. 33–34.
78. Franz Werfel, foreword (1944) to *Between Heaven and Earth*, trans. Maxim Newmark (London, 1947), p. viii.
79. Pollack, ed., *Ko Amar Herzl*, pp. 13, 76.
80. Ibid., pp. 83–84.
81. Ibid., pp. 16, 18.
82. Ibid., pp. 72, 106.
83. Ibid., pp. 87, 92.
84. Ibid., pp. 92, 31, 7. Herzl identified with another leader of ancient Israel, Moses, about whom he planned to write "a biblical drama" (ibid., p. 109).
85. Ibid., pp. 68, 67. On Herzl's uses of icons and symbols and on his inclination to cultivate myth, see Robert S. Wistrich, "Theodor Herzl: Zionist Icon, Myth-Maker and Social Utopian," in *The Shaping of Israeli Identity*, ed. Robert Wistrich and David Ohana (London, 1995), pp. 1–37.
86. Pollack, *Ko Amar Herzl*, p. 85.
87. Ibid., p. 90; concluding quotation, p. 97.

CHAPTER 2. MAX NORDAU VERSUS NIETZSCHE

1. Max Nordau, *Entartung*, vol. 2, 3d ed.(Berlin, 1896), p. 301 and in the English edition, *Degeneration* (Lincoln, Neb., 1993), p. 416. Subsequent references to the English edition are in the text.
2. Anna Nordau and Maxa Nordau, *Max Nordau: A Biography* (New York, 1943), p. 405.
3. Ibid., pp. 96–97.
4. See Jacob Golomb, "Freudian Uses and Misuses of Nietzsche," *American Imago* 37 (1980): 371–85, and Rudolph Binion, *Frau Lou: Nietzsche's Wayward Disciple* (Princeton, N.J., 1968), esp. pp. 335–457.
5. Nordau and Nordau, *Max Nordau: A Biography*, pp. 1, 74.
6. Ibid., p. 98.
7. Robert S. Wistrich, "Max Nordau, Degeneration, and the *Fin-de-Siècle*," in *Krisenwahrnehmungen im Fin-de-Siècle*, ed. Michael Graetz and Aram Mattioli (Zurich, 1997), pp. 83–100.
8. Cf. George L. Mosse, "Max Nordau, Liberalism and the New Jew," *Journal of Contemporary History* 27 (1992): 561–81, and *Confronting the Nation: Jewish and Western Nationalism* (Hanover, Mass., 1993), 161–75.
9. See, for example, Nordau, *Degeneration*, p. 406. Since another famous marginal Jew, Georg Brandes (born Morris Cohen), significantly contributed to Ibsen's (and also Nietzsche's) fame, Nordau does not spare him from his typically vehement and unbridled attacks (ibid., p. 356 and elsewhere).
10. Robert Wistrich perceptively discerned that at bottom of Nordau's diagnosis of the "culturally deracinated, atomised and morally dissolute European society . . . lies a similar sense of the atomised anomie, self-alienation and psychological deracination of Jewry in the West." "Max Nordau, Degeneration, and the Fin-de-Siècle," p. 96.

George Mosse too refers to a strong element of self-hatred manifested in Nordau's *Degeneration*, since when "one reads the description of his enemies, one is reminded of the stereotypes of others, whom society considered outsiders, Jews, tramps, criminals, the insane or the permanently sick" ("Max Nordau, Liberalism and the New Jew," pp. 566–67). See also Sander L. Gilman, "The Madness of the Jew," in his *Difference and Pathology: Stereotypes of Sexuality, Race and Madness* (Ithaca, 1985), pp. 150–62. It follows that by writing this book Nordau subconsciously sought to overcome his own degeneration. Another scholar has also noticed Nordau's self-hatred, claiming that Nordau "described himself with vocabulary formerly reserved for the degenerates and contrasted this with the excitement of his newly rediscovered national identity," P. M. Baldwin, "Liberalism, Nationalism, and Degeneration: The Case of Max Nordau," *Central European History* 13 (1980): 99–120, 112.

11. Compare Nietzsche's exclamation "What does a philosopher demand of himself first and last? To overcome his time in himself, to become 'timeless.'" *CW* Preface, p. 155.

12. Nietzsche, *NCW* Preface and chapter "We Antipodes."

13. Thus, for example, he was the victim of a vicious anti-Semitic assault on his person in the town of Borkum in 1893 Nordau and Nordau, *Max Nordau: A Biography*, p. 117.

14. The selective and fragmentary nature of the findings that supposedly support Nordau's views are also accentuated by the fact that, though Nordau emphasized the organic causes of degeneration, he never performed any laboratory experiments or dissections of degenerates' brains. He is content to quote selectively from several researchers who performed such experiments. But when he finds something in their conclusions that opposes his own views (or, more accurately, his prejudices), he rejects their findings, sometimes explicitly—for example, those of his friend and colleague Caesar Lombroso. Nordau, *Degeneration*, p. 17.

15. Thus, e.g., in *NCW*, after Nietzsche delineates Wagner's decadent personality and art, he returns in the Epilogue to his former basic distinction between "master" and "Christian" morality, claiming that all the "aesthetics of decadence" are nothing but derivations of the Christian ethical terms analyzed by him in his previous books as "slave morality," which is the pattern of negative power.

16. It can be found in my *Nietzsche's Enticing Psychology of Power* (Ames, Iowa, 1989), and in my article "Nietzsche on Jews and Judaism," *Archiv für Geschichte der Philosophie* 67 (1985): 139–61.

17. See, e.g., *BGE*, pp. 197, 199, 209, 232, 244, 245, 256; *GM* I-16; *TI*, chaps. 4, 37, 44, 48; *A* 46, 61.

18. *NCW* Preface and chapter "We Antipodes."

19. In Nordau's attacks on Nietzsche for his lack of systematic exposition and his "wild" and "Dionysian" style (*Degeneration*, pp. 416ff.), his difficulty in liberating himself from the naïve perceptions of the Enlightenment and of scientific positivism becomes quite apparent. Nordau also commits one of his many genetic fallacies by drawing from Nietzsche's style the diagnosis that he was mad (ibid., p. 463) and by passing too easily from his writings to his sickness (ibid., p. 458). Nordau also claims that Nietzsche's writings were full of banal and trivial insights ("Gemeinplätze," *Entartung*, 2:304). This is quite an original accusation since no serious critic of Nietzsche, however ill-disposed toward him, has ever spoken about him as "the most ordinary herd-animal"

(ibid., p. 446). Furthermore, this description clashes starkly with Nordau's characterization of Nietzsche's so-called "autism and solipsism." In any case, Nordau admits that he has read all of Nietzsche's works (ibid., p. 419), and for one who claims that *everything* Nietzsche wrote was mere commonplaces, this seems somewhat puzzling.

20. Ibid., pp. 421, 423 ff. Discussing Nietzsche's views on the revolt of Jewish "slaves" who out of resentment toward their "masters" and feelings of vengeance created Christianity, Nordau sees a dangerous potential for stirring up anti-Semitic sentiments. However he does not accuse Nietzsche of anti-Semitism since he has read his attacks on Wagner's anti-Semitism and even quotes them in his chapter on Wagner. Thus it is reasonable to assume that only his fear that Nietzsche's provocative thesis—which also sought to give credit to the Jews in order to aggravate what Nietzsche hated most—his own German nation—would cause severe damage to the Jewish people was the main reason for his objection.

21. Nordau, ignoring the Nietzschean notion of sublimation, thinks that the basic driving force in humans according to Nietzsche is "cruelty" (ibid., pp. 424, 450). Resorting to his Darwinian prejudices, Nordau seeks to subsume Nietzsche's notion of power under the Darwinian principle of "self-preservation," and claims that this concept of Nietzsche is absolutely redundant (ibid., pp. 442–43). Hence he intentionally ignores all the passages in Nietzsche's writings where the philosopher rejects the idea that the basic human instinct is a drive for self-preservation and where he states, for example, that "life is no argument" (*GS* 121).

22. Nordau also presents Nietzschean *Übermensch* as lacking any Apollonian element and sublimation, and as externalizing without any moral restraints the cruelty of the Dionysian barbarian instincts and drives by performing acts of crime and violence (Nordau, *Degeneration, p.* 431).

23. Nordau prefers to ignore the metaphorical quality of this image and chooses to take it literally as meaning savage and oppressive "blond beasts of prey," namely " the proper Aryans" who perform "selfish acts of violence" and "vengeance" (ibid., p. 427). Undoubtedly, Nietzsche should have been more careful and sensitive in the choice of his metaphors and literary formulations, which were heavily laden with dangerous connotations, especially as in his time the rise of Nazism had already begun, even within his own family. But Nordau does not claim that Nietzsche's language and literary style are dangerous (which they were) and might become a destructive means against the Jewish people (which they did). His accusation is more far-reaching: he attributes to Nietzsche ideas of racial aggression and domination. Indeed, Nordau was well aware of Nietzsche's criticism of German nationalism and of Bismarck (ibid., pp. 466ff.), and even uses the same argument against Bismarck's militarism that Nietzsche introduced in his *Twilight of the Idols,* where he states of Bismarck's policy, "*Deutschland, Deutschland über alles*—that was the end of German philosophy." Walter Kaufman, trans. and ed., *The Portable Nietzsche* (New York, 1954), p. 506. In the same vein, Nordau claims that "The Germany of William I, of Moltke and Bismarck, could not produce a Goethe or a Schiller" (*Degeneration*, p. 534).

24. Nordau ends his chapter on Nietzsche by contrasting his ideal of Enlightenment, namely "the man of richer knowledge, higher intelligence, clearer judgment and firmer self-discipline" with what he takes to be Nietzsche's ideal of the "over-man," that is that of "the ego-maniac, the criminal, the robber, the slave of his maddened instincts" (*Degeneration*, p. 472).

25. Thus providing the basis for a dubious postwar claim that "Adolf Hitler's ghastly Third Reich has confirmed and justified every word Nordau has written. His refutation of Nietzsche's theories from the anthropological, historical, philosophical, and biological points of view have not lost anything of their validity, up to this date." Richard Van Dyck, "The Jewish Influence on Journalism," in *The Hebrew Impact on Western Civilization*, ed. D. D. Runes (New York, 1951), pp. 640–43, quoted by Meir Ben-Horin in *Max Nordau: Philosopher of Human Solidarity* (London, 1956), p. 14.

26. This is the main theme of Jacob Golomb and Robert S. Wistrich, eds., *Nietzsche, The Godfather of Fascism? On the Uses and Abuses of Philosophy* (Princeton, N.J., 2002).

27. This is what Eyal Chowers calls the "sundered history." "Time in Zionism: The Life and Afterlife of a Temporal Revolution," *Political Theory* 26, 5 (October 1998): pp. 652–85. See chap. 1, note 66.

28. Max Nordau, *Max Nordau to His People*, introd. B. Netanyahu (New York, 1941), pp. 65–66.

29. Kaufmann's translation in *The Portable Nietzsche* of *HH* I-475 (my emphasis).

30. *Max Nordau to His People*, op. cit., pp. 162–63.

31. Zeev Jabotinsky, *Autobiography* (Jerusalem, 1947), p. 113.

32. The original name of Nordau's play from 1898, *Dr. Kohn*, emphasizes the Jewish motif. The play in English translation is called *A Question of Honor: A Tragedy of the Present Day*, trans. Mary J. Safford (Boston, 1907). Not incidentally two fathers of political Zionism—Herzl and Nordau—have chosen to express their views through drama. Both plays delineate dramatically the identity conflict of the assimilated Jew and the hesitations about its positive content and about the right way to solve the uncertainties of the protagonists' Jewish marginality. A play is intended for a wide public, and in these cases, especially for the gentile public. The sense of insult that they took from this audience which rejected them to the margins of society called for reaction. Their wounded honor demanded retribution from those who had hurt them. Hence we can see in the very act of putting these plays on stage a kind of intellectual-literary duel with a hostile public. These two marginal Jews sought a high-profile return to center stage and to communicate to the society that rejected them that they were leaving it on their way to Zion. For this purpose, a play before a living (but occasionally hostile) audience, could become an effective means to get even or even to win the struggle.

33. Ibid., p. 160.

34. Max Nordau, *Zionistische Schriften* (Cologne, 1909), pp. 379–81. For elaboration of this notion in Nordau and within the Zionist movement see Shmuel Almog, *Zionism and History: The Rise of a New Jewish Consciousness* (New York, 1987), esp. pp. 108–18.

35. Jabotinsky is referring to Nordau's book of 1883 that dealt with a central Nietzschean motif: *Conventional Lies of our Civilization* (Chicago, 1884, 1887).

36. Zeev Jabotinsky, "On America" (1926) in *Literature and Art* (in Hebrew) (Jerusalem, 1948), pp. 189–88.

37. Ibid., p. 189.

38. See ibid., p. 187: "What was the nature of 'decadence'? A leap beyond the routine products of the conventional psyche, a journey to uncommon spiritual experiences which so far were unexplored."

39. He testifies that when he was a fourteen-year-old schoolboy in Odessa "we were discussing Nietzsche and the question of morals." Jabotinsky, *Autobiography*, p. 21.

Jabotinsky also claims that "Gorky was only an echo of Nietzsche's teaching in Russian clothing—first glorification of men of will and action and spite toward the slaves of barren reflexive thoughts which kill any monumental and daring deeds" (ibid., p. 33). This is an echo of Nietzsche's essay (at that time famous in Russia) *HL.*

40. Ibid., p. 38; emphasis in original.

41. Cf. Israel Eldad, "Nietzsche and the Old Testament," in *Studies in Nietzsche and the Judeo-Christian Tradition,* ed. J. C. O'Flaherty, T. F. Sellner, and R. M. Helm (Chapel Hill, N.C. 1985), pp. 47–68.

42. The *Turnverein,* first founded by Friedrich Ludwig Jahn in 1811.

43. Cf. Gilman, "The Madness of the Jew," pp. 157–58.

44. Nordau, *Max Nordau to His People,* p. 188.

45. Published by Herzl in *NFP,* in 3 October 1900.

46. Ibid.

47. Nordau rejects the Hegelian attitude toward history as science and claims that " history was an art, not a science, aiming, not at truth, but beauty . . ." (*The Interpretation of History,* trans. M. A. Hamilton [London, 1910], p. 5; see also p. 40). He opposes historicism (pp. 39ff.), and attacks Hegel. Like Nietzsche, he stresses the subjective dimension in history writing: "Written history can never compass the actual event. It is not science, but literature" (pp. 10–11). Nordau, like Nietzsche, emphasizes the psychological functions of our relation to history and performs a Nietzschean genealogy of morals in claiming that "the conceptions good and evil" originated in the "weak" who have suffered and called for help" (pp. 140–41). Many other notions derived from Nietzsche are to be found in a very Nietzschean chapter, "The Psychological Premises of History," where Nordau speaks of "the superior man . . . as master" who is "impelled to command" (pp. 247ff.), and who in contrast to "the average man" is "the man of will and deeds" (p. 250). What really surprises the reader who is familiar with Nordau's doctrine of solidarity is the fact that in his last theoretical book, Nordau definitely bestows higher value on the individual than on society.

48. Nordau, *History,* p. 153.

49. Nordau and Nordau, *Max Nordau: A Biography,* p. 435.

PART II. NIETZSCHE AND CULTURAL ZIONISM

1. For details see the introduction.

2. The rise and fall of the Russian-Jewish intelligentsia is incisively discussed in Jonathan Frankel's *Prophecy and Politics: Socialism, Nationalism and the Russian Jews, 1862–1917* (Cambridge, 1981).

3. See chap. 4, note 49.

4. For example, Ahad Ha'am writes in his reminiscences: "I went to Berlin and Breslau, and to Vienna again. But each time I returned tortured and broken-hearted. These years [1882–83] were the worst years of my life. The constant state of war, internal and external . . . embittered my life, and plunged me in the depths of depression . . . I left [my father's village] disillusioned and sick at heart." "Reminiscences," in *Ahad Ha'am: Essays, Letters, Memoirs,* trans. and ed. Leon Simon (Oxford, 1946), pp. 330–32.

5. The difference between Nordau and Ahad Ha'am, in their relations to their people and their past during their formative years, can be succinctly portrayed by the

assumed names they chose for themselves. In contrast to Simha Südfeld's choice of Max Nordau, Asher Ginzberg assumed the pen name Ahad Ha'am, which in Hebrew literally means "One of the People."

6. Arthur Hertzberg, *The Zionist Idea* (Philadelphia, 1997), p. 291. Leon Simon describes this phenomenon as a "split personality . . . a cleavage in the soul." *Ahad Ha-am* (Philadelphia, 1960), p. 160.

7. Hertzberg, *The Zionist Idea,* p. 294.

8. This was in distinction to the *Haskalah,* a literary movement that from about 1750 had purported to disseminate in Hebrew the ideas of the European Enlightenment among the Jews in Russia and Poland.

Chapter 3. Micha Joseph Berdichevski

1. The epigraphs are taken from Berdichevski, "*Al parashat drachim: Michtav galui le-Ahad Ha'am*" in *Al ha-perek* (On the agenda) (Warsaw, 1899), p. 25, first published in *Ha-Shilo'ah* (Berlin) 1, no. 2 (November 1896) (emphasis in original); and Berdichevski, "Al em ha-derekh" (On the high road), *Ha-Pisgah* (The Apex) (Chicago) 5, no. 43 (1898): 3.

2. "Thus Spoke Zarathustra," First Part, First Speech, translated by Walter Kaufmann in *The Portable Nietzsche* (New York, 1954), p. 137.

3. *Orva Parah* (Far-fetched) (Warsaw, 1899)

4. David Neumark, "Friedrich Nietzsche: Mavo Le-Torat Ha-Adam Ha-Elion" ("Introduction to the teaching on the *Über-mensch*'), in *Mi-Mizrah Umi-Marav* (From East and West), vol. 1 (Vienna, 1894), pp. 115–24.

5. Nordau, *Paradoxes* (1895), trans. J. R. McIlraith (London, 1906).

6. Translated by Reuben Breinin (Piotrekov), p. ii.

7. Nordau, *Paradoxes,* pp. ii–iii.

8. "Hesbona shel Shifrutenu" (The account of our literature), *Ha-Shilo'ah* (Berlin) 3 (1898): 31–41; "Galuth Be-toh Galuth" (A Diaspora within a Diaspora), *Ha-Dor* (The generation) (Cracow) 1 (1901), nos. 11: 3–5, and 12: 2–4, and "Be-Mi Ha-Ashem?" (Who is to be blamed?), ibid., no. 29 (1904): 1–6. It is not altogether clear whether the bitter objections to Berdichevski's revolutionary visions of new Hebrew culture caused these critics to oppose Nietzsche's teaching, which they thought was the main inspiring force behind Berdichevski's standpoint, or the other way around, namely that their objections to Nietzsche's philosophy per se made them reject Berdichevski because of his so-called "Nietzscheanism." The first interpretation is more plausible considering the background of Nietzsche's reception among the Zionists. Most of these writers did not read Nietzsche's German writings and hence did not know them firsthand. They barely quoted his writings and did not address themselves directly to his thought. Cf. also Yehuda Leib Levin's (1844–1925), "Lebilbul Ha-Deoth" (On confused opinions), *Ha-Tsefirah* (The sirer) 28 (1901), nos. 151: 606–7, 152: 611, 153: 614–15, 154: p. 617.

9. "Lama Ragzu?" (Why were they agitated?), *Ha-Dor* 1 (1901): 3–4, and "Al ha-tahapuhot" (On vicissitudes), *Luah Ahiasaf* (Warsaw) 8 (1900): 183–206.

10. It might, perhaps, be of some interest to American readers that the same abuse was being inflicted on Berdichevski's "Nietzscheanism" in the United States. *Ha-Pisgah,* a Hebrew literary weekly in Chicago, published several articles by Berdichevski

in 1898 and appended to them severe and brusque responses by its editor and publisher W. (Zeev) Shur. He attacked Berdichevski for filling his brain with "Nietzsche's *Übermensch*," forgetting that "Nietzsche died in an asylum for lunatics and all his theory is the theory of a madman that has no place in life of a healthy people." "Havu li Halifot Utmurot Mamas" (Bring me real alternatives and changes), *Ha-Pisgah*, 6, nos. 2 and 3 (October and November 1898) (front cover). Berdichevski responded by emphasizing Schur's genetic fallacy: "Seemingly the matter is a simple one, you mention the mad Nietzsche and all the other mentally sick and there is no room anymore for a solid argument." "The Earlier and the Later," in *Nemoshot: Shneym asar davar* (Weaklings: Twelve subjects) (Warsaw, 1899), p. 64.

11. A good case in point is S. Z. Zecher. In his "Anaschim Ve-shfarim: Friedrich Nietzsche" (People and books), *Ha-Dor*, vol. 1 (1900), nos. 15: 9–11, 22: 11–13, 23: 8–11, 24: 10–11, 25: 11–12, 26: 8–9, 27: 9–10. He presents Nietzsche's teaching firsthand so that Hebrew readers will know it more directly rather than by means of its literary expositors such as Berdichevski. Expressing a quite enthusiastic attitude about the presence of Nietzsche among the young modern Hebrew writers, he states: "It is wonderful that in our Hebrew literature and among our people—who by their nature and spirit actually stand in opposition to Nietzsche's theory—this doctrine found its proper and extensive place, and the traces of his teachings are quite conspicuous in the intellectual fruits of many of our young ones" (issue 27, p. 10).

12. An instructive example is Joseph Hamlin "Le-Berur ha-deoth ve-hamusagim" (Toward clarification of views and notions), *Ha-Tsefirah* 28 (1901), nos. 23: 90, 24: 94, 25: 98, 26: 102, 27: 106, 28: 110, 29: 114. Realizing that Berdichevski's critics were "trying to cancel out Berdichevski by Nietzsche and his blond beast," Hamlin insists that Berdichevski opposes Nietzsche and his notion of the *Übermensch*: "Nietzsche's *Übermensch* is mankind's essence and its goal and everyone else was created solely to serve him and to become a means for his cultivation, whereas Berdichevski directs his polemical writings toward the whole nation and wants the success of the whole people, namely—he wants exactly the opposite to Nietzsche" (no. 28). Nietzsche's extreme individualism, he claims, has no place within the rising national and collective Zionist consciousness. Hamlin defends Berdichevski's attempts to introduce "beauty" into the life of the Eastern European Jews and rejects the objection that he tried to uproot Jewish ethics and replace it with the "Greek aesthetics" (no. 23). He refers, by analogy, to the dispute during the Second Temple period between the Sadducees, who were influenced by Hellenism, and the Pharisees, who tried to defend the Torah. This observation implies an interesting insight about the relation between Berdichevski and Nietzsche. Just as Nietzsche attempted to introduce Dionysian-Greek art into the prevalent scientism and historicism of the Europe of his time (under the slogan of "Socrates who practices music," *BT*, chap. 15), so Berdichevski tried to do the same with the antiquarian and anti-aesthetic attitude of the Jews buried alive in the old ghettos of Eastern Europe.

13. Thus, Yaakov Rabinowich, "Micah Joseph Berdichevski," *Ha-Tkufah*, 13 (1922): 429–45, argues that Berdichevski could not be assigned to any intellectual camp. He raises the most pertinent question: "Was Berdichevski really Nietzsche's student?" His answer: "Yes, he learned also from Nietzsche, was enthusiastic about him for a moment . . . but he was not only Nietzsche's pupil. He learned from him how to negate but he did not accept his positive ideas" (p. 431). Rabinowich concludes that Berdichevski ac-

tually "came from within, the outside world only enriched him, incited his sense for life . . . but he returned from there to uncover what was hidden in us" (p. 432). Rabinowich also stipulated that Berdichevski was a *doppelte Jude* with two faces: one was overt and traditional Judaism and the other was cryptic and secret Judaism (meaning the literature of Agadha, Kaballah, etc.). On this double nature of Berdichevski see Marcus Moseley, "Between Memory and Forgetfulness: The Janus Face of Micha Yosef Berdichevsky," in *Studies in Contemporary Jewry* (Oxford, U.K., 1996), 12:78–117.

14. Especially Joseph Hayyim Brenner. This admirer of Berdichevski, the first great modern Hebrew writer in Palestine, will be explored in future work.

15. Thus, Moshe Glikson saw in "pure Nietzschean individualism" a recipe for "absolute solitude" and "solipsism." "Al pi ha-thom" (On the edge of an abyss), *Masuot* (Torches) (Odessa) 1 (1919): 194–218. Consequently, when Glikson proclaimed Berdichevski to be "a Hebrew Nietzschean" ("Goralo" [His fate], *Ha-Po'el ha-Tza'ir* [The new worker] [Tel Aviv] 15, no. 7 [1922]: 12–13), he did not intend this as a compliment. Neither did Yehezkiel Kaufman, the first professor of biblical studies at the Hebrew University of Jerusalem, who stressed the fact that Berdichevski's notion of "reevaluation of values" was taken from Nietzsche (see the chapter entitled "Reevaluation of Values" in his book *Golah ve-Nehar* [Diaspora and estrangement], vol. 2 (Tel-Aviv, 1930), pp. 386–404.) He even accused Berdichevski of speaking "in Nietzschean style" in favor of "the sword," the "fist," "vengeance and Ressentiment" and in depreciation of "humility" (p. 389).

16. This explains why Fischel Lachower, despite his sympathy for Nietzsche and Berdichevski, could not stomach the individualism of both and focused his attacks on this element of their thought. "Mikha-Josef Berdichevski: Mamar rishon" (First essay), in his *Rishonim ve-aharonim* (The first and last ones) (Tel Aviv, 1934), pp. 226–47 (first published in 1913).

17. This is clearly demonstrable in Lachower's two articles dedicated to Nietzsche on the occasion of the thirtieth anniversary of his death, where he stressed the genius and grandeur of Nietzsche's philosophy but did not fail to declare that his "heart cannot follow the great brilliance of his thought." "Nietzsche" (in Hebrew), *Moznayim* (the literary organ of the Hebrew Writers' Association, Jerusalem–Tel Aviv) 2, no. 17 (1930,): 1–2 and "Nietzsche and the Jews" (in Hebrew), ibid., no. 18: 6–8.

18. Jehiel Halpern, *Hamahapeha ha-jehudit* (The Jewish revolution: Spiritual struggles in the modern period), vol. 2 (Tel Aviv, 1961), p. 392.

19. Avigdor Shaanan, *Ze-ramim be Sifrut Ivrit Hadashah* (The currents of the Hebrew modern literature), vol. 3 (Tel Aviv, 1962–64), p. 77.

20. I can mention here only a few of these accounts. Baruch Kurzweil, the renowned literary critic in postwar Israel, described the "significance of Nietzsche's influence on Berdichevski" in his essay, "Influence of the Philosophy of Life on the Hebrew Literature at the Beginning of the Twentieth Century" (in Hebrew), in *Sifrutenu ha-hadashah: Hemshekh o mahapekhah?* (Our modern literature: Continuation or revolution?) (Jerusalem, 1971), p. 230. The most influential modern Israeli philosopher (and my beloved teacher), Nathan Rotenstreich, perceptively called Berdichevski's version of Zionism a "vitalistic Zionism" (*Jews and German Philosophy: The Polemics of Emancipation* [New York, 1984], p. 219). Though he cautions us not to "exaggerate the impact of . . . Nietzsche" on Berdichevski (p. 214), when he presents Berdichevski's views, especially his "inclination to affirm life, including the right to self-creativity in the pre-

sent," he flatly admits that "at this point, Nietzsche's impact becomes predominant" (ibid., p. 218), and acknowledges that Berdichevski's "emphasis on the aesthetic phenomenon" is more indebted to "Nietzsche's thrust towards independent self-creativity" than to Schopenhauer's "dichotomy between appearances and the thing-in-itself" against which Berdichevski argued (especially in his dissertation, analyzed below). See also Menahem Brinker, "Nietzsche's Influence on Hebrew Writers of the Russian Empire," in *Nietzsche and Soviet Culture: Ally and Adversary*, ed. Bernice Glatzer-Rosenthal (Cambridge, 1994), pp. 393–413; idem, "Nietzsche and Hebrew Writers: An Attempt at A Synoptic View," in *Nietzsche be-Tarbut Ivrit* (Nietzsche and Hebrew culture), ed. Jacob Golomb (Jerusalem, 2002), pp. 131–59; Steven Aschheim, *The Nietzsche Legacy in Germany 1890–1990* (Berkeley, Calif., 1992), pp. 108ff.

21. Steven Aschheim, "Nietzsche and the Nietzschean Moment in Jewish Life (1890–1939)," *Leo Baeck Yearbook* 37 (1992): 212. This opinion was already expressed at the beginning of the twentieth century by Joseph Klausner, who ends his survey of Berdichevski's short stories with reference to him as "the so-called Nietzschean." Joseph Klausner, "Shipurim ha-dashim" (New stories), *Shefer ha-shana* (Book of the year) vol. 2 (Warsaw) (1901): 114–21; Joseph Klausner, "Sifrutenu ha-iafa be-snat 1901" (Our belles-lettres in the year 1901), ibid., pp. 230–77.

22. "Me-iri ha-khtana,"(Pietrekov, 1899).

23. *Kitvei Micha Josef Bin-Gurion,* 26 vols. (Leipzig, 1922–25; reprint, Tel Aviv, 1936). Twenty volumes are in Hebrew and six volumes in Yiddish.

24. See above, note 1, and next chap.

25. Berdichevski, "Pirkei Yoman" (Diary chapters), 27 July 1905, in *Archive Micha Joseph,* ed. Avner Holtzman (Tel Aviv, 1995), pp. 58–59.

26. Emphasis added; this undated letter belongs to a collection of letters called by Berdichevski *"Nehzarim"* (Returned). They are kept in the Micha Joseph Berdichevski Archives in Holon near Tel Aviv. The addressee has not been identified. This collection contains about two hundred letters written by Berdichevski in the 1890s that were returned to him by his friends at his request. (For this and other references to Berdichevski's letters, I am indebted to Prof. Avner Holtzman of Tel Aviv University.) In another letter, Berdichevski named Nietzsche among the kindred spirits that "have spoken to me as if by my own mouth, from within my own selfhood" (letter to Alter Druyanov, approximately from November–December 1895. No other words can so poignantly express the depth of Berdichevski's identification (at that particular time) with Nietzsche.

27. Letter to Yerahmiel Shakpeniuk, *Nehzarim.*

28. As many of his letters to his friends during that decade bear witness. For example, in a letter to Efraim Frisch of 26 April 1897, he informed him that he was now preoccupied with reading Nietzsche and Schopenhauer. In two other letters to this friend (28 May and 4 June 1897) he reports that he decided to name the German translation of his Hebrew book *Sefer hasidim* (Warsaw, 1900) after Nietzsche's collection of aphorisms, *Der Wanderer und sein Schatten* (The wanderer and his shadow), which forms the second part of volume 2 of Nietzsche's *Human, All Too Human.*

29. See Berdichevski's many letters from his stay in Weimar (October–November 1898). In a letter from the end of 1898 (*Nehzarim*) after expressing his moods of superiority over and estrangement from others, he compared himself to Nietzsche's

Zarathustra. Significantly, he particularly quoted his beloved "Zarathustra's Prologue," which describes how Zarathustra, after ten years of solitude in the mountains, leaves his cave and goes to the "marketplace" to share his wisdom and teachings with other humans. There he meets with hostility, derision, and contempt. Thus it seems plausible that the more Berdichevski was attacked by his opponents, the more he came to identify himself with the lonely Nietzsche and with his fictive hero of existential solitude—Zarathustra. Other instances of such deep identification with Nietzsche are provided in his letters from Weimar to his friend David Neumark. In a letter from October 1898 he writes about "the miserable philosopher who lives with his sister over there on the mountain" and in the same paragraph he expresses his sorrow that at that time when he and his muse are dedicated to "another nation," "the images of my forefathers are coming to my mind, reprimanding me." He adds: "Particularly now I am deeply saddened by the fact that I was rejected so thoroughly from our literature." At the end of this letter, Berdichevski asks Neumark to send him his essay on Nietzsche (see above, note 4), which he promises to deliver to the Nietzsche Archive in Weimar: *Ginzei Mikha Yosef* (Archive of Mikha Yosef) ed. Avner Holtzman, vol. 4 (Tel Aviv, 1990), pp. 64–65. In a letter to Neumark of 9 October 1898, he describes his pilgrimage to Nietzsche's house, saying that Nietzsche "is called here the sick one." Though he has a letter of introduction from a writer in Berlin for Nietzsche's sister, he still hesitates to visit her and his "heart is too pounding" to do so (ibid., p. 67). In another letter, he mentions his visit to Nietzsche's sister who was "greatly impressed by my story" (5 November 1898, ibid., p. 69), and then expresses his "deep Hebrew sorrow" as to the present conditions of the Hebrew literature. In a letter of 3 October 1898, to his friend Josef Melnik he describes how "Nietzsche and his sister are sitting in the corner of their house—the soul of this great man will now accompany me forever." The pendulum between Nietzsche and the Hebrews (i.e., his Jewish milieu and roots) continued to swing and grew faster, impelled by the "sick Nietzsche." Until his last days, Berdichevski was unable to free himself completely from this aspect of his "torn heart." Avner Holtzman, in his article "Berdichevski in Weimar" (*Ha'aretz*, 25 March 1994), quotes several passages from Berdichevski's letters, where he gives vent to his excitement, pity, and sense of purpose whenever he visits Nietzsche. What is of a special significance, however, is his letter to Ahad Ha'am, where he speaks about Nietzsche's "great tragedy" and describes how he sits alone in the attic "in one peace in his body and perhaps also in his mind," peaceful with his " own self" (ibid.). This picture of *amor fati* and self-affirmation is of course Berdichevski's own projection onto the paralyzed philosopher. Such a projection, however, discloses that aspect of Nietzsche's thought that touched Berdichevski's own torn heart. By identifying himself with the living, though sick, Nietzsche, who supposedly attained in the end his own authenticity, Berdichevski aspired to arrive at the same existential predicaments that were portrayed in Nietzsche's writings, and in Berdichevski's somewhat idealized picture of him.

30. "Lihyot o lahdol" (to be or not to be), *Mi-Mizrah-u-mi-Ma'arav* (From East and from West), vol. 1 (Vienna, 1894), pp. 93–104; republished in a collection of ten Berdichevski essays entitled *Arakhin* (Values) (Warsaw, 1899), pp. 7–15, and in *Micha Josef Berdychevski (Bin-Gorion): Ketavim* (Collected works), ed. Avner Holtzmann and Yitzhak Kafkafi, vol. 3 (Tel Aviv, 1998), pp. 137–51. All the references in the text are to this recent scientific edition.

31. This passage was deleted by Berdichevski from his collected works, and see *Kitvei*

Micha Josef Bin-Gurion, Masot: "Baderekh" (On the road) (Leipzig, 1922), vol. 2: "Shinui arachim," pp. 11–18.

32. Ibid., p. 150. Berdichevski ignores here the Hellenistic period of the Second Temple when many Israelites, especially the *Zdokkim* (Sadducees), were heavily influenced by Greek culture in their everyday lives.

33. As I tried to show in my *In Search of Authenticity: From Kierkegaard to Camus* (London, 1995), where I argued that personal authenticity has nothing to do with objective and general "essences" and "natures" and that actually it stands for a revolt against the essentialist approach prevalent in traditional rationalistic philosophy.

34. "Lahdol ve Lihyot," *Ha-Zevi* (The deer) (Jerusalem), 1 and 9 April 1897; republished in Holtzmann and Kafkafi, eds., *Micha Josef Berdychevski (Bin-Gorion): Collected Works*, 3:152–55 (quotation, p. 152).

35. "Or ve-Tchlalim," *Ha-Zeman* (Cracow) 2, no. 1 (1 January 1891): cols. 3–9; republished in Holtzmann and Kafkafi, *Micha Josef Berdychevski (Bin-Gorion) Collected Works*, pp. 19–24. References in the text are to this recent scientific edition.

36. Berdichevski, *Notizen (Lose Gedanken)*, p. 41; and in Micha Josef Berdichevski, *Sayings*, ed. and trans. Josef Even (Jerusalem, 1982), p. 70 (in Hebrew).

37. Berdichevski, *Notizen*, p. 70, and *Sayings*, p. 156. The editor, even informs us in the introduction to the latter collection that these aphorisms (written approximately between 1890 and 1907), were strongly inspired by several collections of aphorisms by Lichtenberg, Goethe, Novalis, Schopenhauer, and, of course, Nietzsche. Several of these collections were in Berdichevski's private library in editions that were published in those years (ibid., p. 14).

38. *Ozar ha-shifrut* (The literary treasure) (Cracow) 4 (1892): 1–40; republished in Holtzmann and Kafkafi, *Micha Josef Berdychevski (Bin-Gorion): Collected Works*, 3:48–93. References in the text are to this edition.

39. M. J. Berditschewski (Cracow, 1892).

40. See above, note 27.

41. Among these he mentions and attacks the poet Yehuda Leib Levin; thus it is small wonder that Levin reciprocated with a venomous article against Berdichevski. See note 8.

42. "Ahat ani Yodea" (One thing I know), written in Berlin in autumn 1894, published in *Ha-Zevi 11* (18 June 1897); republished in Holtzmann and Kafkafi, *Micha Josef Berdychevski (Bin-Gorion): Collected Works*, 3:156–59 (quotations, pp. 156, 157).

43. Isaiah Berlin, *The Hedgehog and the Fox* (London, 1953).

44. For an elaboration of these points see my *In Search of Authenticity*, chap. 2.

45. "Ahat ani Yodea," p. 158.

46. "Se-yodea lisol (me-at philosophia)" (One who knows how to ask [a little philosophy]), in Holtzmann and Kafkafi, *Micha Josef Berdychevski (Bin-Gorion): Collected Works*, 3:163–67 (quotation, p. 163).

47. Ibid., p. 165.

48. Ibid., p. 166.

49. "Ha-adam ve-hamakel (mahsava)," in Holtzmann and Kafkafi, *Micha Josef Berdychevski (Bin-Gorion): Collected Works*, 3:168–69.

50. For elaboration see my "Nietzsche's Positive Religion and the Old Testament," in *Nietzsche and the Divine*, ed. Jim Urpeth and John Lippitt (Manchester, 2000) pp. 30–56.

51. Ibid., p. 169.
52. "Ha-sguloth se-betarbutenu ha-leumit," in Holtzmann and Kafkafi, *Micha Josef Berdychevski (Bin-Gorion): Collected Works,* 3:177–79 (quotations, p. 177).
53. See, e.g., his piece from 1896, "Hurbano shel olam" [The destruction of the world], ibid., pp. 173–76, and a two-part article, "Stira ve-binian: Hegionot Ivri Tzair" (Wrecking and building: Meditations of a young Hebrew), *Ha-Zevi,* 26 November 1897, pp. 22–23, and 3 December 1897, p. 29.
54. "The Destruction of the World," p. 173.
55. See above, note 26.
56. Ludwig Stein, *Friedrich Nietzsche's Weltanschauung und ihre Gefahren: Ein kritischer Essay* (Friedrich Nietzsche's world outlook and its dangers: A critical essay) (Berlin, 1893).
57. Ludwig Stein, "Der Philosoph der Aristokratie," in his *Der Sinn des Daseins: Streifzüge eines Optimisten* (Tübingen, 1904), pp. 336–44. Compare Brandes's 1888 essay "Friedrich Nietzsche: Eine Abhandlung über Aristokratischen Radikalismus," in *Menschen und Werke: Essays* (Frankfurt a. M, 1895), pp. 137–213.
58. Ludwig Stein, "Individualistic Optimism (Friedrich Nietzsche)," chapter 10 in his *Evolution and Optimism* (New York, 1926), pp. 164–75. In this lecture, delivered "in several American universities," Stein's positive attitude toward Nietzsche gains the upper hand. True, he mentions that even now he is still one of Nietzsche's "pronounced opponents" (p. 168) and (disregarding Brandes's and Nordau's writings on Nietzsche) mistakenly attributes to himself "the very first book on and against Nietzsche" (p. 169). But he expresses deep admiration for the philosopher, referring to him as to "the genius of irreverence" (p. 167), as "the great poet-philosopher of the human race"; and he respects "his peculiar genius" and his "supremely personal stamp" (ibid. and p. 172). Cf. also his chapter "Die individualistische Bewegung" in his book *Philosophische Strömungen der Gegenwart* (Stuttgart, 1908), pp. 230–42. He is strongly attracted toward "the poet of the 'Overman'"—"the Titan Nietzsche, who is really consumed in his flame" (*Evolution and Optimism,* p. 174).
59. *Die Sociale Frage im Lichte der Philosophie* (Stuttgart, 1903).
60. See, for example, Alexander Barzel's introduction to his Hebrew translation of Berdichevski's dissertation: *Al hakeser bein etica le-asthetica* (Tel Aviv, 1989), pp. 29, 33.
61. That it was also considered a worthy original contribution to philosophy is shown by the fact that it was published in the University of Bern's series of philosophical monographs edited by Ludwig Stein: *Über den Zusammenhang zwischen Ethik und Aesthetik,* Berner Studien zur Philosophie und ihrer Geschichte, vol. 9 (Bern, 1897). Since the print on the copy I have has faded so as to be unreadable, I had to resort to the scholarly Hebrew edition of this dissertation in Holtzmann and Kafkafi, *Micha Josef Berdychewski (Bin-Gorion): Collected Works,* 4:85–126. References in the text are to this edition.
62. "On the high road," see above, note 1.
63. Letter of 15 November 1895, Ahad Ha'am Archives, Jewish National and University Library, Jerusalem. Nietzsche, ridiculing the fact that Kant was known never to have left his hometown of Königsberg, refers to him in *BGE* 210, as "the great Chinese of Königsberg." See also *A* 11.
64. *Al hakeser,* p. 119.
65. Ibid., 116.
66. *Über den Zusammenhang zwischen Ethik und Aesthetik* (Bern, 1897), pp. 16–17.

67. "Ziknah uvaharut," *Mi-Mizrah u mi-Ma'arav* 4 (1899): 109–24. Subsequent references are given in the text.

68. Berdichevski's return to his people found also a literary expression, as, for example, his essay, written in Yiddish in the summer of 1902, "For the People and from within the People." The essay was subsequently collected in *Yiddische Ktavim Fon Weiten Karov* (Yiddish writings from a distant relative), vol. 6 (Berlin, 1924), pp. 13–19; vol. 2 (New York, 1948), pp. 214–17.

69. "Perurim" (Crumbs), in the essay collection *Nemoshot*, pp. 33–39, Berdichevski says: "Perhaps here is the place to share with you some of Friedrich Nietzsche's sayings, in his last book before his sickness. It is very difficult to translate his words literally and thus I am bringing them roughly" (p. 36). Berdichevski then quotes quite correctly most of section 25 of *The Antichrist*. He moves on to section 26, up to the words: "In the hands of the Jewish priests the great age of the history of Israel became an age of decay; the Exile was transformed into an eternal punishment for the great age . . . they made . . . wretchedly meek and sleek prigs out of the powerful, often very bold, figures in the history of Israel" (*A*, pp. 596–97). What is even more noteworthy, however, is the fact that Berdichevski accepted Nietzsche's basic distinction between the powerful heroic period of the ancient Hebrews in the time of the Bible and the powerless, resentful, and avenging Jewish "priests," namely the early Christians as they emerged by the end of the Second Temple. Berdichevski reiterates this distinction in many of his subsequent polemical writings and even seeks to prove, through lengthy historical research, that the first period was more predominant and effective in the ancient history of the Jewish people.

70. Berdichevski seems to acknowledge this part of Schur's article when he quotes from it as follows: "In Jewish origins we find the grain of all those new systems (also those of the mad Nietzsche and Tolstoy) as well as of the necessary adaptations to the life of the people's." Berdichevski, "The earlier and the later," op cit., note 10, p. 64.

71. See, e.g., his self-referential observation that "the internal strife and the duality in the soul of the Hebrew . . . enriches his heart and his soul, his life and his humanity." *Arakhin*, note 30, p. 70.

72. Though by no means entirely missing. For example: "Thus as the 'bad animal—according to F. Nietzsche . . . when it is prevented from externalizing itself—tends to internalization,' so too this happens to the good animal." *Al em ha-derekh* (On the high road) (Warsaw, 1899], p. 46. This is an allusion to Nietzsche's idea in *GM* of *Verinnerlichung*, i.e., the process of internalization of the "slaves," which is the source of "bad conscience"; see my *Nietzsche's Enticing Psychology of Power* (Ames, Iowa, 1989), pp. 321–25. See also Berdichevski's *Arakhim* (*Values*) from the same year, pp. 88–92, where he calls Nietzsche "Rabbi" and uses his notion of the "Overman." The notion of the "Overman" returns also in *Al Ha-perek* p. 32, and is mentioned on pp. 27, 35. In *Nemoshot*, p. 36, Berdichevski once again quotes from Nietzsche's *Antichrist*, section 25, and on p. 52, he responds to Zitran's attack on his Nietzscheanism (in *Ha-Shilo'ah*), stating sardonically that he would like his critics to "prepare tables for those who follow Nietzsche and his friends and for those who first and foremost would like to know themselves." In "Shney Ktuvim" (Two writings) in *Din Udvarim: Ten Essays* (Warsaw, 1902), pp. 10–11, he enters into polemics with two of Klausner's essays from 1901 (see above, n. 21) and quotes his remark about him being the "so-called son of Nietzsche" and his conclusion that there is no need to be afraid of such "sons."

73. See, e.g., his very Nietzschean distinction between "personal truthfulness" versus cognitive truth in his *Aravim* (Breslau, 1910), p. 41. In *Al em ha-derekh* he approves forgetfulness "of most of our history," whereby one "can stand on his own feet" and regain his "inner freedom" (p. 42). In the same book (on pp. 68–69) Berdichevski urges us toward authenticity and incites us "to be what we are" since "all our life is only one unity" Following this plea he speaks of a "new morality" (p. 72) and "dreams of a new man," seeing from "distance the new man, the renewed man" (p. 73). This authentic harmonious personality he aspires to attain by means of the "Hebraic elements in us, in Hebraism in itself" (p. 68).

74. Menaham Brinker correctly reminds us that "Berdichevsky was the first Jewish thinker to condemn the spirit of Yavneh and to praise unambiguously the courage and determination of the rebels" who had fought against Rome for Jewish political sovereignty—this notwithstanding the fact that Orthodox tradition praised the first-century scholar Yohanan ben-Zakkai from Yavneh for accepting the Roman domination at the price of religious autonomy. And thus, according to a Talmudic legend, Yohanan's request "Give me Yavneh and its sages" became the symbol "of Jewish willingness to accept political slavery as long as spiritual and religious autonomy were guaranteed." "Nietzsche's Influence on Hebrew Writers of the Russian Empire," n. 17. It is beyond the scope of the present chapter to deal with Berdichevski's radical critique and exegesis of the holy writings (both Jewish and Christian) but see his posthumous *Sinai und Garizim: Über den Ursprung der israelitischen Religion — Forschungen zum Hexateuch auf Grund rabbinischer Quellen* (Berlin, 1926); Jeshurun Keshet (Kopelewitz), *M. J. Berditchewsky (Bin-Gorion): His Life and Work* (in Hebrew) (Jerusalem, 1958), pp. 281–98; Emanuel Bin-Gorion, *Reshut hayahid* [Domain of the individual]: *Life and Work of Micha Josef Berdichevski (Bin-Gorion) in His Last Twenty Years* (Tel-Aviv, 1980), pp. 212–37, and Avner Holtzmann, *Essays on Micha Josef Berdichevski (Bin-Gorion)* (in Hebrew) (Tel-Aviv, 1993), pp. 211–12.

75. This was not adequately perceived by Aliza Klausner-Eshkol in the most comprehensive comparison to date between Nietzsche and Berdichevski. In her monograph, she draws many detailed textual comparisons on a variety of issues, such as opposition to historicism, the perception of culture as a single unity, appreciation of skepticism, the emphasis on individualism and will to power, until she reaches the somewhat exaggerated conclusion that "Nietzsche had a great and decisive influence on Berdichevski's spiritual world. Bin-Gorion accepted the main Nietzschean tenets on issues of morality and culture and completely identified with Nietzsche, from the point of view of content as well as of form. He uprooted them from their German breeding ground and planted them in the Hebrew earth." *Hashpa'at Nietzsche ve-Schopenhauer al M. J. Bin-Gorion (Berdichevski)* (The influence of Nietzsche and Schopenhauer on Micha Josef Bin-Gorion [Berdichevski]) (Tel Aviv, 1954), p. 31. Berdichevski's son commented on Klausner-Eshkol that "the conclusions and their formulations are not free from the prejudice that influence and originality are in opposition to each other." Emanuel Bin-Gorion, *Kore Ha-dorot* (Reader of the generations) (Tel Aviv, 1981), p. 193. He adds that his father's "philosophical period" was but one stage of his life, limited in time and in importance. The riddle of Judaism was his father's main preoccupation and what he got from his teachers in the West were but instruments to solve it.

76. This difficulty is evident especially in his writings after 1899, when Berdichev-

ski expresses occasionally and with great emotional pathos the remnants of his Jewish faith. See, e.g., his preface to *Din Udvarim*, p. 46, where he wishes to "come closer to an inner religion, to God dwelling in the innermost parts of our heart."

CHAPTER 4. AHAD HA'AM VERSUS BERDICHEVSKI (AND NIETZSCHE?)

1. Witness, e.g., his fondness for using dialectical categories in the titles of many of his essays, such as "Positive and Negative," "Sacred and Profane," "Past and Future," "Flesh and Spirit," "Priest and Prophet." Thus Ahad Ha'am's admission at the end of his brief autobiography that "in German I was fond of books of general culture like those of Herder, but the more profound writers (Kant, Hegel, etc.) did not appeal to me, and I have not read much of them" has to be taken with a grain of salt, or as a confession that he had at least tried to read some Hegel and Kant but, lacking any formal education in philosophy, did not feel confident enough to cope with their "profoundness." "Reminiscences," in *Ahad Ha-am: Essays, Letters, Memoirs*, trans. and ed. Leon Simon (Oxford, 1946), p. 340.

2. See Ahad Ha'am, "Memories of Childhood" in *Memoirs of My People*, ed. Leo W. Schwarz (New York, 1943), pp. 248–53, or in the paperback edition (New York, 1963), pp. 248–53.

3. "Shilton ha-sehel," and see Ahad Ha'am, "The Supremacy of Reason" (1904), in *Basic Writings of Ahad Ha'am: Nationalism and the Jewish Ethic*, ed. Hans Kohn (New York, 1962), pp. 228–88. Ahad Ha'am eulogizes the memory of Maimonides seven hundred years after his death, claiming that he wishes to show that Maimonides "really based his view of human life on philosophy alone, and did not give way a single inch in order to effect a compromise between his philosophy and the religious ideas which were accepted by Jews in his time" (p. 247). On the background of such a rationalist credo it might perhaps surprise the reader to find in this essay a short comparison between "Maimonides' ethics and another doctrine which has recently gained such wide currency—the doctrine of Nietzsche" (ibid., p. 246).

4. Thus the statement of Ahad Ha'am's disciple and English translator, Leon Simon, in his biography of his mentor (*Ahad Ha-Am* [Philadelphia, 1960]), to the effect that he possessed "a coherent philosophy of Judaism and Jewish history" (p. 158) suffers from one-sided idealization. One can therefore understand Steven J. Zipperstein's determination in his comprehensive *Elusive Prophet: Ahad Ha'am and the Origins of Zionism* (Berkeley, Calif., 1993), not to use Leon Simon's translations because they are "inspired by devotion to Ahad Ha'am" and "frequently take liberties with Ahad Ha'am's texts in their effort to render his ideas attractive to Anglo-American readers" (p. 327).

5. One of his more famous followers rightly claimed that "for Ahad Ha'am, Zionism was the Jewish renaissance in a spiritual-national sense." Chaim Weizman, *Trial and Error* (New York, 1949), pp. 36–37.

6. Though his intellectual honesty led him to admit once that "what little I have done in literary and public work during these latter years would never have been done if there had not been some external stimulus." "Reminiscences," p. 330.

7. Thus, Yehiel Alfred Gottschalk, claims in his dissertation that Ahad Ha'am's "basic sources of his philosophy remained the Bible" (The Hebrew University of Jerusalem, 1965, p. 9); but in his subsequent book he describes these sources as ex-

tending far beyond the Bible, and mentions Herbert Spencer and German idealism (principally Herder): *Ahad Ha'am veharuh haleumi* (Ahad Ha'am and the national spirit) (Jerusalem, 1992). Anita Shapira claims, in contrast, that the main intellectual source was British empiricism along with the British model of political life; see her "Ahad Ha'am: The Politics of Sublimation," in *Studies in Contemporary Jewry*, vol. 11, ed. Peter Y. Medding (Oxford, 1995), pp. 205–14. Gideon Shimoni in his *The Zionist Ideology* (Hanover, Mass., 1995) concurs with her views though he also refers to Hegel in this context (pp. 270–71).

8. A comprehensive bibliography on Ahad Ha'am is provided by Zipperstein, *Elusive Prophet*, pp. 360–68. Gottschalk only refers once to Nietzsche (*Ahad Ha'am veharuh haleumi*, p. 21) and even this reference has nothing to do with Ahad Ha'am's *Weltanschauung*. The same can be said of Joseph Goldstein's Hebrew biography *Ahad Ha-am* (Jerusalem, 1992).

9. I was able to uncover in the Ahad Ha'am Archives at the Jewish National and University Library, Givat Ram, Jerusalem (file number [I] 144; 791 4°) about twelve letters and postcards of Berdichevski to Ahad Ha'am which refer to Nietzsche. The following are of particular interest: his postcard of 24 July 1893, in which he refers to Nietzsche as to his "rabbi"; a letter of December 1893 where he mentions Georg Brandes's book *Menschen und Werke* which includes his 1888 essay "Friedrich Nietzsche: Eine Abhandlung über aristokratischen Radikalismus"; a postcard of 18 December 1897 where, perhaps realizing that his close attachment to Nietzsche met with a deep disapproval from Ahad Ha'am and diverts their dialogue into a side issue, asserts that he wants to distinguish between "Nietzsche on the one hand and what we desire on the other"; a letter of 19 January 1898 from Berlin in which he mentions "Lou-Andreas Salomé (the poetess, philosopher, and Nietzsche's friend)" and also refers to Georg Brandes "who is currently in Berlin"; a postcard from Weimar of 3 October 1898 where he writes about his promise to Nietzsche's sister to deliver to Nietzsche's Archives, Ahad Ha'am's "Nietzschean article from *Ha-Shilo'ah*," to be added to Nietzsche's papers; a letter of 15 November 1898 from Weimar in which he reports the delivery of this essay "for which he received much thanks"; a letter of 18 October 1898 from Weimar, following a visit to Nietzsche, in which he describes the philosopher's present "tragic" condition; a postcard of 16 July 1898, referring Ahad Ha'am to Nietzsche's *Morgenröte* (*Daybreak*). It is reasonable to speculate that Ahad Ha'am, who was quite thorough in his autodidact education, immersed himself fairly attentively and intensely in Nietzsche's writings, especially as Berdichevski directs his attention to similarities between the German philosopher's view and his own on the "People of Israel." See also note 10.

10. See, e.g., Ahad Ha'am's letters to Berdichevski of 6 January, 16 June, and 21 July 1898, in which he defends himself against Berdichevski's rebuke (in his postcard to him of 16 July 1898) that he is not familiar with Nietzsche's saying about "the moral genius of the people of Israel." *Igrot Aahad Ha'am* (Letters of Ahad Ha'am), vol. 2 (Tel Aviv, 1956), pp. 10, 91, 113–14. See also below, note 56. See also Ahad Ha'am's letter of 14 October 1901 to Dr. Friedlaender, the German translator of what he called "my article on Nietzsche" which he wished "for various reasons to be translated." *Igrot Ahad Ha'am*, vol. 3 (Tel Aviv, 1957), p. 83.

11. Ibid., vol. 2, p. 82.

12. Ironically, despite his assumed name as "One of the People," Ahad Ha'am ac-

tually strove to dominate Hebrew culture as if he was "One above His People," like Moses bringing the Torah to his people from Mount Sinai. Not incidentally, the Mosaic self-image is evoked in Ahad Ha'am's veiled autobiographical essay "Moses" (1904), in *Selected Essays by Ahad Ha-'am*, trans. and ed. Leon Simon (Cleveland, 1962), pp. 306–29. This self-image and basic elitism were also evoked by the name and purpose of the short-lived "Bnei Moshe" (Sons of Moses) society that Ahad Ha'am helped found in Odessa in 1889, which strove to create a cultural elite for "the renaissance of our people in the land of our fathers." "Reminiscences," p. 334.

13. "Friedrich Nietzsche: Eine Abhandlung über aristokratischen Radikalismus," in *Menschen und Werke: Essays,* ed. Georg Brandes (Frankfurt a. M., 1895), pp. 137–213 (and see above, note 9). In this second edition Brandes adds in a footnote a passage from a letter from Nietzsche dated 2 December 1887, in which Nietzsche approvingly accepts the label "aristokratischer Radikalismus" (p. 137). English edition: *Friedrich Nietzsche: An Essay on Aristocratic Radicalism* (London, 1914).

14. Zipperstein, *Elusive Prophet,* pp. 123, 148.

15. For detailed discussion of the literary dispute between Ahad Ha'am and his opponents (who included, besides Berdichevski, David Frishmann, Shaul Tschernichowsky, Hayyim Brenner, among others), see Asher Rivlin, *Ahad Ha'am u-mitnagdav ve-hashkafoteihem al ha-sifrut ha-ivrit be-doram* (Ahad Ha'am and his opponents and their views on the Hebrew literature of their generation) (Tel Aviv, 1955).

16. This was already perceived by Arnold J. Band in his essay "The Ahad Ha'am and Berdichewski Polarity," in *At the Crossroads: Essays on Ahad Ha-am,* ed. Jacques Kornberg (Albany: State University of New York Press, 1983), pp. 49–59.

17. Ahad Ha'am, "Yalkut Katan" (Small miscellany), *Ha-Shilo'ah* 3 (1898): 560, quoted in Simon, *Ahad Ha'am,* p. 158.

18. See the chapter on Kierkegaard in my *In Search of Authenticity: from Kierkegaard to Camus* (London, 1995) and my article "Kierkegaard's Ironic Ladder to Authentic Faith," in *Søren Kierkegaard: Critical Assessments of Leading Philosophers,* ed. Daniel W. Conway, vol. 1 (London, 2002), pp. 97–112.

19. And cf. Berdichevski's anti–Ahad Ha'am slogan: "We cannot be saved as a nation until we become other men," in his *Al em ha-derekh* (On the high road) (Warsaw, 1900), p. 28.

20. This problematic was perceptively grasped by Ehud Luz in his superb and concise exposition of "The Controversy between Ahad Ha-am and Berdyczewski," in *Parallels Meet: Religion and Nationalism in the Early Zionist Movement,* trans. Lenn J. Schramm (Philadelphia, 1988), pp. 159–72. I concur with Luz's conclusion that "Ahad Ha-am thus left the split between the 'Jew' and the 'human being' . . . unrepaired" (p. 164).

21. "Lese-alat ha-shifrut ha-ivrit" (The question concerning Hebrew literature), in *Kol kitvei Ahad Ha'am* (The collected writings of Ahad Ha'am) (Tel Aviv, 1947), pp. 126, 127, 128.

22. Micha Josef Berdichevski, "Al parashat drakhim: *Michtav* galui le-Ahad Ha'am," *Ha-Shilo'ah* 1, no. 2 (November 1896): 154–59; republished in *Al ha-perek* (On the agenda) (Warsaw, 1899), pp. 17–26. References in the text are to this later edition.

23. Mordehai Ehrenpreis, "Lean?" (Whither?)," *Ha-Shilo'ah* 1 (1897): 489–503.

24. Ahad Ha'am, "Etza tova" (Good advice), ibid., pp. 504–8; reprinted in *Kol kitvei,* pp. 132–34. References in the text are to the later edition.

25. I have doubts about this quite dogmatic claim, especially if we recall the trans-

lation of *Thus Spoke Zarathustra* into beautiful biblical Hebrew by Berdichevski's friend, David Frischmann. This translation appeared for the first time between the years 1909 and 1911 in a Hebrew literary magazine edited by Frischmann in Warsaw, *Reshafim,* and its frequent republication 1914, 1924, 1964, and other years had an enormous effect upon the whole circle of modern Hebrew writers and poets. The prophetic biblical style makes Zarathustra's figure closer to the ancient prophets and provides the Hebrew reader with an interpretation of Nietzsche's most important work that can be utilized by impressionable young Hebrew *halutzim* (pioneers), especially in *Eretz Israel,* in a landscape where the original prophets once lived and taught. Curiously enough, Frischmann's translation of Zarathustra found its way to a young Orthodox Jew, the late Arye Weissfish, who became influenced by it all his life long. Though living in the most fanatically religious quarter of Jerusalem, he lectured widely on Nietzsche. He memorized all the existing Hebrew translations of Nietzsche's writings and preached to different, mostly secular audiences, in Israel and Germany, as well as on their national TV networks about "Nietzsche: The New Jewish Prophet." See his letter in Jacob Golomb, ed., *Nietzsche in Hebrew Culture* (Jerusalem, 2001), pp. 313–15 (in Hebrew).

26. That this might be the case follows from Berdichevski's letter to Ahad Ha'am (of 29 April 1898, in the Ahad Ha'am Archive in the Hebrew National Library in Jerusalem) where he accuses Ahad Ha'am of "explaining to me quite wrongly that the 'Loazi' [the foreign] in me suppresses and rejects the Hebrew within me . . . whereas in the last days I have completed my first story in the Hebrew language: 'Meever le-nahar' (Beyond the river) in which I presented a big fraction of our long sorrow."

27. Review of S. Bernfeld, *Juden und Judentum im neunzehnten Jahrhundert* (Berlin, 1898), in "Small Miscellany," *Ha-Shilo'ah* 3 (1898): p. 563; my emphasis.

28. In a letter to Berdichevski of 16 June 1898, Ahad Ha'am informs him that "I have already begun writing my essay against the Hebrew 'Nietzscheans,' namely against you. . . . I do not mention your name explicitly since, as you know, I do not like to fight private persons under their actual names. But informed persons will understand," *Igrot Ahad Ha'am* (Letters of Ahad Ha'am), vol. 2 (Tel Aviv, 1956), p. 91.

29. See above, note 10.

30. Translated by J. Friedlaender and published in *Ost und West: Illustrierte Monatsschrift für modernes Judentum* (Berlin), 2, nos. 3 and 4 (March and April 1902): 145–52, 241–54.

31. See above, note 9.

32. "Leseelot hayom" (On contemporary questions), *Ha-Shilo'ah* 4 (1898) 97–105, republished under the title "Shinui ha-arachin" (Reevaluation of values) in *Kol kitvei,* pp. 154–58. The quotation is from p. 154; the German phrase is in the original. References in the text are to this edition. The English translation by Leon Simon, "The Transvaluation of Values," in *Selected Essays by Ahad Ha'am,* pp. 217–41 and in a separately published pamphlet of the same title (London, 1917) is quite unreliable. Translations from this article were therefore made by me from the Hebrew original in *Kol kitvei.* It is noteworthy that the changing titles of this essay represent a progressive "Nietzscheanization."

33. See, e.g., *HL* 9, *SE* 159, *HH* II-2-198, and my *Nietzsche's Enticing Psychology of Power* (Ames, Iowa, 1989), pp. 109–10, 139–50, 295–304.

34. The After comparing Ahad Ha'am's version to the German original version and to Georg Simmel's version in an article on Nietzsche that Ahad Ha'am mentions in the next paragraph of his article, I can safely conclude that Ahad Ha'am did not read the original *Also sprach Zarathustra* but was content to confine himself mostly to the then limited secondary literature on Nietzsche. The original reads: "Was liegt am Glücke! antwortete er, ich trachte lange nicht mehr nach Glücke, ich trachte nach meinem Werke." (*KSA*, 4:295) Simmel's version, translated literally into Hebrew by Ahad Ha'am, is: "'Trachte ich denn nach Glück?' fragt Zarathustra; ich trachte nach meinem Werke." Georg Simmel, "Friedrich Nietzsche: Eine moralphilosophische Silhouette," *Zeitschrift für Philosophie und philosophische Kritik* (Leipzig) 107, no. 2 (1896):. 202–15. The fact that Ahad Ha'am did not read Nietzsche's main writings at first hand and based his knowledge of him mainly on a few secondary sources goes a long way to justify Berdichevski's exasperation in his postcard to him: "if you were versed in Nietzsche, as I am . . . ," and see below, note 45.

35. Thus Ahad Ha'am did not heed Nietzsche's famous saying that "the ability to accept contradictions is a good sign of a great mind and culture," and also did not understand that an essential part of Nietzsche's enticing strategy was deliberately to introduce glaring contradictions into his own doctrine in order to help us overcome his own thought, undertake our own intellectual therapy, and embark on our autonomous and genuine "own way." See the chapter in the third part of *Z* entitled "On the Spirit of Gravity," and my concluding chapter in *Nietzsche's Enticing Psychology of Power.*

36. Simmel, "Friedrich Nietzsche," pp. 203, 208.

37. Cf. Menahem Brinker, "Nietzsche's Influence on Hebrew Writers of the Russian Empire," in *Nietzsche and Soviet Culture: Ally and Adversary,* ed. Bernice Glatzer-Rosenthal (Cambridge, 1994), pp. 393–413.

38. Besides "Friedrich Nietzsche," see also Simmel's more comprehensive presentation of Nietzsche's philosophy which, however, was published only in 1907, so that it perhaps had lesser impact on Ahad Ha'am and on his dispute with Berdichevski; and see his *Schopenhauer and Nietzsche,* trans. Helmut Loiskandl, Deena Weinstein, and Michael Weinstein (Urbana, Ill., 1991).

39. Besides Simmel, Ahad Ha'am also refers twice (p. 156nn.) to Alois Riehl, *Friedrich Nietzsche, Der Künstler und der Denker: Ein Essay* (Stuttgart, 1897), which incidentally I was able to locate in Einstein's private library in the National and Hebrew University Library in Jerusalem. Hence it seems that not only Ahad Ha'am read this book but also another great Jewish mind found it interesting enough. As far as I know no research exists on the possible relations between these two geniuses.

40. A Hasidic rebbe, a righteous person, the ideal type of Jewish ethical teaching, a kind of spiritual leader who was often credited by superstitious followers with supernatural powers.

41. This was not grasped by Thomas Mann who, in his "Nietzsche's Philosophy in the Light of Recent History" in *Last Essays* (New York, 1959), pp. 141–77, accuses Nietzsche of "heroization of instincts." Nietzsche does not call for the massive and anarchic release of repressed instincts, but for their artistic sublimation. Thus, he does not subscribe to the "heroization of instincts," but perhaps only to the heroization of sublimation. For elaboration, see the concluding chapter of my *Nietzsche's Enticing Psychology of Power.*

42. "The noble soul accepts this fact of its egoism without any question mark . . .

under certain circumstances there are some who have rights equal to its own . . . it moves among these equals with their equal privileges, showing the same sureness of modesty and delicate reverence that characterize its relation with itself . . . every star is such an egoist . . . it honors itself in them and in the rights it cedes to them; it does not doubt that the exchange of honors and rights is of the nature of all social relations and thus also belongs to the natural condition of things" (*BGE* 264).

43. Riehl, *Friedrich Nietzsche,* p. 125. Ahad Ha'am refers correctly to this passage in Riehl, saying that "Nietzsche says in one place that under certain circumstances it would be possible that whole families, tribes and nations will attain the status of the *Übermensch*" ("Shinui ha-arachin," p. 156 n. 3).

44. See my "Nietzsche's Positive Religion and the Old Testament," in *Nietzsche and the Divine,* ed. J. Urpeth and J. Lippitt (Manchester, 2000), pp. 30–56.

45. Postcard of 16 August 1898, Ahad Ha'am Archive, Hebrew National Library, Jerusalem. Ahad Ha'am answered him immediately, with obvious irritation: "I mentioned an explicit quote from his *main* book and additionally said that also in *many* other places he admits of it,—what else do you require?" Letter of 21 July 1898, in *Igrot Aahad Ha'am,* 2:113–14. Later he angrily condemned Berdichevski for daring to react to his essay. *Ha-Pisgah* (Chicago) 5 (1898,) nos. 42:6, 43:3. He sent Berdichevski this material before it was printed in *Ha-Shilo'ah.* Reading this and other private correspondence between these luminaries of the cultural Zionist movement, one cannot fail to notice the highly emotional (and sometimes far from cultured) tone of their exchanges involving Nietzsche and the ways of "utilizing" him.

46. Ahad Ha'am, "Hamusar ha-leumi" (National morality), *Kol kitvei,* pp. 159–64.

47. Walter Kaufmann's translation of sec. 263. The text is given here in the original order, but Ahad Ha'am reversed those two paragraphs in his Hebrew essay.

48. Michael Rabinovitch, "Ha'jahadut ve'ha'adam ha'elion" ("Judaism and the *Übermensch*"), *Ha-Shilo'ah* 9 (1902): 376–83.

49. "Altneuland," in *Kol kitvei,* p. 313–23.

50. Max Nordau, "Ahad Haam über Altneuland," *Die Welt,* 13 March 1903.

51. Ahad Ha'am, "Tshuva Ke'cara" (Short answer), *Ha-Shilo'ah* 9 (1902): 382–83; republished in *Kol kitvei,* pp. 158–59. References in the text are to *Ha-Shilo'ah.*

52. In his essay on "National Morality" Ahad Ha'am severely criticizes Nordau's play *Dr. Kohn* (analyzed in chapter 2), in which the hero fights a duel on the grounds that his refusal to fight would be regarded as cowardly, and would bring dishonor on the Jewish people. Ahad Ha'am declares that from the point of view of Jewish ethics, dueling is an act of criminal folly, and suggests that it is precisely by refusing to fight that a Jew would do his people honor. "Hamusar ha-leumi." This was exactly the sentiment of Dr. Kohn's Orthodox father in the play.

53. Berdichevski, "Al em ha-derekh," *Ha-Pisgah* (Chicago) 5, no. 42 (1898): 3.

54. Jacob A. Arlow, "Ahad Ha'am, Freud and the Wellsprings of Psychoanalysis," *Hebrew University Studies in Literature and the Arts* 14 (1986): 189–204.

55. Ahad Ha'am, "Priest and Prophet," in *Selected Essays,* p. 127.

56. Ahad Ha'am, "Many Inventions" (1890), in *Selected Essays,* p. 160; cf. "Priest and Prophet," p. 128.

57. Ahad Ha'am, "Two Domains," in *Selected Essays,* p. 92.

58. HAH I-624; cf. chap. 3 of my *Nietzsche's Enticing Psychology of Power,* esp. pp. 128–31.

59. Ahad Ha'am, "Moses," in *Selected Essays*, pp. 306–29; the quotes are from pp. 307, 308.

PART III. NIETZSCHE AND SPIRITUAL/RELIGIOUS ZIONISM

1. See, for example, Walter Kaufmann in his "Buber's Failures and His Victory" in *Martin Buber: One Hundred Years of His Birth*, ed. Yohanan Bloch, Haim Gordon, and Menahem Dorman (Tel Aviv, 1981), pp. 21–35. The remark to this effect is found on p. 22.

2. See his *Eclipse of God: Studies in the Relation between Religion and Philosophy*, trans. Maurice S. Friedman and others (New York, 1952).

3. Martin Buber, *I and Thou* (hereafter *I&T*) trans. from 1923 *Ich und Du* by Walter Kaufmann (New York, 1970), p. 54. This book, highly popular in the United States, has appeared in many editions and translations.

CHAPTER 5. MARTIN BUBER'S "LIBERATION" FROM NIETZSCHE'S "INVASION"

1. Martin Buber, "Autobiographical Fragments," in Paul Schilpp, ed., *The Philosophy of Martin Buber* (La Salle, Ill., 1967), pp. 11, 12, 13 n. 4. The German original of the "Autobiographical Fragments" was published in 1960, five years before Buber's death, in *Begegnung: Autobiographische Fragmente* (Meetings) (Stuttgart, 1960). The main quotation here is on p. 18. In the revised and expanded German edition (Heidelberg, 1978) the quote is on pp. 29–30. See also his *Meetings*, ed. and introd. Maurice Friedman (La Salle, Ill., 1973), pp. 29–30.

2. For example, in the following confession: "I am a Polish Jew, and though I hail from a family of pioneers of enlightenment, I was exposed to the influence of a Chassidic atmosphere in the impressionable period of my boyhood." Quoted by Ernst Simon in his "Martin Buber and German Jewry," *Leo Baeck Institute Year Book* 3 (1958): 3, from Martin Buber, *Gog und Magog: Eine Chronik* (Frankfurt a. M., 1957), p. 234. This autobiographical epilogue appended to these Hasidic tales appears only in the German version and is missing from the original Hebrew version (Jerusalem, 1943) as well as from its English rendition: *From the Sake of Heaven*, trans. Ludwig Lewisohn (Philadelphia, 1945).

3. Simon, "Martin Buber and German Jewry," p. 4. On p. 11 Simon states that the "German-Jewish symbiosis achieved its peak in his person just before its tragic end."

4. Let us not forget that in 1896, when Buber left Galicia to begin his studies of philosophy and art history at the University of Vienna where eight years later he received his doctorate, he studied and worked in a decidedly Nietzschean ambiance that permeated fin-de-siècle Vienna. Thus it is not mere coincidence that Buber's first four publications (in Polish) dealt with such "Nietzschean" writers as Hofmannsthal, Schnitzler, Hermann Bahr, and Altenberg. Buber wished to introduce to Polish readers the most prominent authors of the "Young Vienna" movement whom he enthusiastically read during his first year in Vienna University (some of these were staunch Nietzscheans—see chapter 1), and Buber subsequently had intensive personal relations and correspondence with some of them. See Martin Buber, "On Viennese Literature" (in Polish) (1. Herman Bahr; 2. Hugo von Hofmannsthal; 3. Peter Altenberg; 4. Arthur Schnitzler), *Przeglad tygodniowy* (Weekly review) (Warsaw) 23 (June and July

1897). Already these first published essays of Buber bear a definite Nietzschean stamp. Though Nietzsche is not mentioned directly, nor the fact that Schnitzler and Altenberg were Jewish and Hugo von Hofmannsthal was one-quarter Jewish, Buber did emphasize his view that most of these men of letters poignantly expressed "the malady of our time," namely the absence of a genuine "I of one's own self," and "absence of unity and harmony . . ." Martin Buber, "On Viennese Literature," trans. Robert A. Rothstein, *German Quarterly* 47, no. 4 (November 1974): 559–66. Moreover, perceiving the significance of Nietzsche's influence on these writers, Buber deliberately introduced his ideas and idioms using the same terminology as Nietzsche in his essay on history and elsewhere. For example, in the writings of Peter Altenberg he reads "a longing for a 'new race' of superior men, whose coming we ought to hasten."

5. Buber, "Autobiographical Fragments," p. 8.

6. Martin Buber, "My Road to Hasidism," trans. Libby Benedict, in *Memoirs of My People*, ed. Leo W. Schwarz (New York, 1943), p. 517; my emphases. See M. Buber, *Die chassidischen Bücher: Gesamtausgabe* (Hellerau, 1928), pp. 659–72.

7. Buber, "My Road to Hasidism," p. 517.

8. Typical in this context is Robert Weltsch's statement that Nietzsche would create more powerful Jews than "forced return to a ritual in which we do not believe." Quoted by Steven E. Aschheim, "Nietzsche and the Nietzschean Moment," *Leo Baeck Institute Year Book* 27 (1992): 204.

9. Martin Buber, *I and Thou*, trans. Walter Kaufmann (New York, 1970), p. 123.

10. *Drei Reden über das Judentum* (Frankfurt a. M., 1911). The first three addresses were delivered to the Prague Zionist student organization Bar Kochba between 1909 and 1911. All of them were incorporated in Martin Buber, *On Judaism*, ed. Nahum N. Glatzer, trans. Eva Jospe (New York, 1972).

11. Buber, *Die chassidischen Bücher: Gesamtausgabe*. His passionate interest in Hasidism, however, dates from earlier, in 1905 when he contributed several legends of Rabbi Nachman of Braslav to the Berlin journal *Ost und West*, which subsequently appeared in *Die Geschichten des Rabbi Nachman, ihm nacherzält von M. B.* (Frankfurt a. M., 1906).

12. Cf. my "Buber's *I and Thou* vis-à-vis Nietzsche and Kierkegaard," *Existentia* 12 (2002): 413–27.

13. See Maurice Friedman, *Martin Buber's Life and Work*, vol. 1: *The Early Years 1878–1923* (New York, 1981), p. 26.

14. Paul Mendes-Flohr, *From Mysticism to Dialogue: Martin Buber's Transformation of German Social Thought* (Detroit, 1989), p. 147 n. 2.

15. "Zarathustra" in *Martin Buber Werkausgabe*, vol. 1 of *Frühe kulturkritische und philosophische Schriften 1891–1924*, ed. Paul Mendes-Flohr and Peter Schäfer (Gütersloh, 2002), pp. 103–17, quote on p. 103.

16. Cf. my "Nietzsche's Early Educational Thought," *Journal of Philosophy of Education* 19 (1985): 99–109.

17. Witold O., letter of 27 July 1962, in *The Letters of Martin Buber: A life of Dialogue*, ed. Nahum N. Glatzer and Paul Mendes-Flohr, trans. Richard Winston, Clara Winston, and Harry Zohn (New York, 1994), p. 648. The German original is found in *Martin Buber: Briefwechsel aus sieben Jahrzehnten*, vol. 3: *1938–1965*, ed. Grete Schaeder (Heidelberg, 1975), letter 487, p. 551. It is noteworthy that Buber's wife, Paula Winkler,

published a book in 1912 entitled "The Inauthentic Children of Adam": *Die unechten Kinder Adams* (Leipzig, 1912). Bringing Nietzsche's writings to the gymnasiums and even reading them under their desks while their teachers delivered "time-worn," boring lectures apparently was quite common among the Jewish enthusiasts and admirers of Nietzsche. See, e.g., Stefan Zweig, *The World of Yesterday* (New York, 1970), p. 39 and read Jabotinsky's testimony (chapter 2 above, n. 39).

18. These issues are dealt with extensively by Rüdiger H. Grimm, *Nietzsche's Theory of Knowledge*, "Monographien und Texte zur Nietzsche-Forschung," vol. 4 (Berlin, 1977); John T. Wilcox, *Truth and Value in Nietzsche* (Ann Arbor, Mich., 1974); Jean Granier, *Le problème de la vérité dans la philosophie de Nietzsche* (Paris, 1966); Alexander Nehamas, *Nietzsche: Life as Literature* (Cambridge, Mass., 1985); and my *Nietzsche's Enticing Psychology of Power*, pt. 3.

19. Buber probably never read Nietzsche's declaration that "the only thing of interest in a refuted system is the personal element. It alone is what is forever irrefutable." *Philosophy in the Tragic Age of the Greeks*, trans. Marianne Cowan (Chicago, 1962), p. 25; "Die Philosophie im tragischen Zeitalter der Griechen," *KSA* 1:803. This conviction continues to resound in later works, where Nietzsche describes "identity" and morality in terms of how our own instincts stand in relation to each other: "In the philosopher ... there is nothing whatever that is impersonal; and above all, his morality bears decided and decisive witness to *who he is*" (*BGE* 6, emphasis in the original).

20. Throughout the whole essay Buber highlights Nietzsche's psychology and his daring uncovering of our unconscious drives. Several times he calls Nietzsche "the psychologist par excellence (Zarathustra, p. 16). This aspect of Nietzsche's philosophy attracted many marginal Jews who needed help in coping with extreme identity crises. They sought consolidation of their souls and the like. They, and notably Buber among them, wished to reactivate the inner cores of their personalities which had been lost in the tug of internal war between conflicting polar foci of identity. For elaboration of this point see the introduction to this volume and my "Nietzsche and the Marginal Jews," in *Nietzsche and Jewish Culture*, ed. Jacob Golomb (London, 1997), pp. 169–71.

21. "Man muss von Nietzsche abfallen um ihn *liebgewinnen* zu können."

22. Martin Buber, "Ein Wort über Nietzsche und die Lebenswerte," *Die Kunst im Leben* 1, no. 2 (1900): 13; and *Martin Buber Werkausgabe*, pp. 149–52.

23. Largely because the twenty-two-year-old Buber's intensive preoccupation with his own identity and authenticity, he emphasizes the fact that this "apostle of life," whose "greatness was as indefinable as life itself," was a harbinger of "new human forms" (ibid., p. 13) in ways that went beyond common longings. Being neither a mere philosopher, nor a poet, nor an artist, nor a psychologist, nor the "founder of a new society," but a combination of all of these, he is the epitome of a "creator" [*Schöpfer*] "who placed before our eyes heroic human beings who created their own selves and surpassed themselves" (ibid.).

24. Ibid. We can easily discern here echoes of Nietzsche's essay on history which, as we recall, was also enthusiastically endorsed by Berdichevski.

25. "Jüdische Renaissance," *Ost und West* (Berlin) 1, no. 1 (January 1901), cols. 7–10. References in the text by column number are to this publication, in my translation. References by page number are to the English translation in *The First Buber: Youthful*

Zionist Writings of Martin Buber, ed. and trans. Gilya G. Schmidt (Syracuse, N.Y., 1999), pp. 30–34.

26. Martin Buber, "Renaissance und Bewegung" (1903), *Die jüdische Bewegung: Gesammelte Aufsätze und Ansprachen 1900–1915* (Berlin, 1916), p. 99, trans. Paul Mendes-Flohr in his "Zarathustra's Apostle: Martin Buber and the Jewish Renaissance," in *Nietzsche and Jewish Culture* (London, 1997), p. 237. My emphasis.

27. Friedman, *Martin Buber's Life and Work,* 1:36.

28. "Zionistische Politik" (1903), in *Die jüdische Bewegung,* pp. 113 ff.; quoted by Mendes-Flohr, "Zarathustra's Apostle," p. 241. Mendes-Flohr also quotes from Hans Kohn, *Martin Buber: Sein Werk und Seine Zeit,* 2d ed. (Cologne, 1961), p. 36, where Buber indicates that Nietzsche was the *Wegbereiter* (the forerunner) who by creating "new life values and a new feel for existence" facilitated the Jewish Renaissance ("Zarathustra's Apostle," pp. 238–39).

29. "Von jüdischer Kunst," in *Die jüdische Bewegung,* p. 64 f.; quoted in Mendes-Flohr, "Zarathustra's Apostle," p. 237.

30. "People and Leader" (in Hebrew), *Moznayim* (Scales) (Tel Aviv) 14 (1952): 145.

31. *Ost und West* 2 (1902): cols. 663–72; trans. Gilya G. Schmidt, *The First Buber,* pp. 118–28. References in the text are to this translation.

32. In Buber, *On Judaism,* p. 201.

33. Quoted by Maurice Friedman in his *Martin Buber's Life and Work,* 1:111; my emphasis. See also *The Legend of the Baal-Schem,* trans. Maurice Friedman (New York, 1955). The original German edition is *Die Legende des Baal Schem* (Frankfurt a. M., 1916).

34. Friedman, *Martin Buber's Life and Work,* 1:111.

35. See above note 2.

36. Buber, *On Judaism,* p. 48.

37. Buber, *I and Thou,* p. 65.

38. See the detailed table of these patterns in my "Nietzsche on Jews and Judaism," *Archiv für Geschichte der Philosophie* 67 (1985): 143.

39. Nietzsche, however, unlike Buber, emphasizes the "healthy egoism" of such relations that leads to mutual authenticity: "The noble soul . . . moves among these equals with their equal privileges, showing the same sureness of modesty and delicate reverence that characterize its relation with itself . . . every star is such an egoist . . . it honors itself in them and in the rights it cedes to them; it does not doubt that the exchange of honors and rights is of the nature of all social relations and thus also belongs to the natural condition of things" (*BGE* 264). One may formulate Nietzsche's attitude in Buber's language as claiming that I-Thou relations and the mutual recognition of the value and freedom of others originate between individuals possessing an abundance of positive power and a firm selfhood, who are thereby able to grant similar rights and freedoms to all those whom they recognize as equals. They are not afraid that this might diminish or destroy their own power. This is a self-affirmation and a confidence in one's power and virtues that enable the affirmation of the "other" and their right to freely create their own authentic selfhood. However, Buber's Hasidic religious sentiments and his wish to become a part of the Zionist community and movement prevented him from adopting this Nietzschean approval of healthy egoism. Actually he claims the opposite and in *I and Thou* he relegates the ego to the inferior domain of I-It relations: "Egos (in distinctions to persons) appear by setting themselves apart from other egos" (p. 112).

40. For elaboration see my *Nietzsche's Enticing Psychology of Power,* pp. 278–89.

41. "How powerful, even overpowering, is Jesus' I-saying, and how legitimate. . . . For it is the I of the unconditional relation in which man calls his You 'Father' in such a way that he himself becomes nothing but a son" (*I and Thou,* p. 116). On Kierkegaard's "Abraham" see chap. 3 of my *In Search of Authenticity.*

42. This was the case with the late Y. Leibowitz, one of the most influential Jewish thinkers in modern Israel, some aspects of whose thought remind one of Kierkegaard. Cf. Avi Sagi (Schweitzer), "The 'Akeda'—A Comparative Study of Kierkegaard and Leibowitz," *Daat: A Journal of Jewish Philosophy and Kabbalah,* no. 23 (1989): 121–34 (in Hebrew).

43. For elaboration see my "Kierkegaard in Zion," *Kierkegaardiana* 19 (1998): 130–37.

44. And read to this effect Buber's admission that by his "superman," Nietzsche "establishes so to speak a relative absolute." "What is Man," in *Between Man and Man,* trans. Ronald Gregor Smith (London, 1947), p. 183, n. 80. In this essay, which is discussed below, Buber is perceptive of and sympathetic enough to Nietzsche's main tenets, holding that Nietzsche's core anthropological principle, the "will to power," "makes" one "into real man," that is, that the optimal positive power in people enables them spontaneously to express their authenticity. See ibid., p. 195. This is the central thesis of my *Nietzsche's Enticing Psychology of Power* and of my *In Search of Authenticity from Kierkegaard to Camus* (London, 1995), chap. 4.

45. *Die Fragen an den Einzelnen* (Berlin, 1936).

46. "The Question to the Single One," in *Between Man and Man,* p. 52.

47. *Between Man and Man,* pp. 145–56. Subsequent references are given in the text.

48. See the chapter in the first part of *Thus Spoke Zarathustra,* entitled "On the New Idol."

49. For details see my *In Search of Authenticity,* and "Authenticity in Rousseau," *Iyyun* 42 (April 1993): 249–73 (in Hebrew).

50. Which, in my view, Nietzsche did not uphold, and see the section in my *Nietzsche's Enticing Psychology of Power,* entitled "Beyond Psychologism and Crude Naturalism," pp. 295–304.

51. Martin Buber, "Letorath ha-adam shel Nietzsche" (Nietzsche's teaching about man), *Gilyonot* 7, no. 4 (1938): 279–85.

52. See above, note. 45. Subsequent references are in the text.

53. Werner Kraft, *Gespräche mit Martin Buber* (Munich, 1966), p. 111: "Über Hitler. Seine Idee der höheren rasse sei nicht biologisch, sie stamme von Nietzsche. Er habe sich selbst für niedrige Rasse gehalten, aber durch die Selbstbestimmung, was höhere Rasse sei, sollte er dazugehören."

54. Actually, Hitler's own connection with Nietzsche remains uncertain. There is no reference to Nietzsche in *Mein Kampf* (though there is to Schopenhauer), and in *Hitler's Table Talk,* he refers only once indirectly to Nietzsche, saying: "In our part of the world, the Jews would have immediately eliminated Schopenhauer, Nietzsche, and Kant. If the Bolsheviks had dominion over us for two hundred years, what works of our past would be handed on to posterity? Our great men would fall into oblivion, or else they'd be presented to future generations as criminals and bandits." Norman Cameron and R. H. Stevens, trans., *Hitler's Table Talk,* 2d ed. (London, 1973), p. 89, and cf. the Jacob Golomb and Robert S. Wistrich, introduction to *Nietzsche:*

The Godfather of Fascism? On the Uses and Abuses of Philosophy (Princeton, N.J., 2002). pp. 1–16.

55. See above, notes 4, 15.

56. It is noteworthy that Buber's friend, the historian Max Picard, in his book on Hitler uses almost the same explanation of the Nazis phenomenon that Buber, inspired by Nietzsche, used in reference to the emergence of Hitler. See his *Hitler in uns Selbst* (Zurich, 1946).

57. "Am Ve-manhig: Leberur mahuto shel haphasism" (People and leader: Toward the examination of the essence of fascism)," republished in *Moznayim* 14 (1942): 137–45 References in the text are to this version. This passage appears in the concise German version, "Volk und Führer" in Buber, *Hinweise: Gesammelte Essays* (Zurich, 1953), p. 311. An abridged English version, "People and Leader," is in *Pointing the Way: Collected Essays*, trans and ed. Maurice Friedman (New York, 1957), pp. 148–60.

58. See "Politics, Community, and Peace," pt. 3 of *The First Buber*, pp. 109–239; *A Land of Two Peoples: Martin Buber on Jews and Arabs*, ed. Paul Mendes-Flohr (New York, 1983); *Israel and The World: Essays in a Time of Crisis* (New York, 1948), esp. pt. 5: "Nationalism and Zion," pp. 197–251.

59. See "Brith Shalom," in *A Land of Two Peoples*, pp. 72–75.

60. Buber expressed his personal and painful awareness of this in describing his reaction to the Nazis' forbidding him to speak publicly following his address "The Power of the Spirit" (1934): "I became conscious of the fact that though the power of the spirit is the hidden kernel of history—its visible husk remains the spirit's lack of power." Preface to *A Land of Two Peoples*, p. 6.

61. *A* 2, and cf. his other statement: "You shall love peace as a means to new wars, and the short peace more than the long," *Z*, pt. 4: "Conversation with the Kings" 2, p. 359) and "The secret for harvesting from existence the greatest fruitfulness and the greatest enjoyment is—to live dangerously!" (*GS*, 283)

62. See also Buber's essay "Hebrew Humanism" in *Israel and The World*, pp. 240–52. In addition to its instructive content, Grete Schaeder's extensive intellectual biography of Buber has an aptly chosen title: *The Hebrew Humanism of Martin Buber*, trans. Noah J. Jacobs (Detroit, 1973).

CHAPTER 6. HILLEL ZEITLIN

1. *Sefer Ha-Zohar* (Book of splendor), a theosophical book, written in Aramaic by Moses de León in the last quarter of the thirteenth century in Spain. It became over the centuries the key text of Jewish esoteric mysticism (the Kabbalah). Cf. Zeitlin's exegesis of the *Zohar* in his collected essays, *Bepardes ha-hasiduth ve-ha-kabbaleh* (In the field of Hassidism and Kabbalah) (Tel Aviv, 1965), pp. 55–279. An extensive bibliography of Zeitlin's Hebrew and Yiddish publications up to 1947, including many articles about him, was compiled by A. R. Malachi, *Ha-Tekufah* (The era) (New York) 32/33 (1947): 848–76.

2. Cf. Ehud Luz, "Zion and *Judenstaat*: The Significance of the Uganda Controversy," in *Essays in Modern Jewish History: A Tribute to Ben Halpern*, ed. F. Malino and P. Albert (Madison, N.J., 1982), pp. 217–39. Cf. also Zeitlin's polemic against Herzl, Ahad Ha'am, and Berdichevski in his "She-eloth" (Questions), *Reshafim* (Sparks) 1 (1910), nos. 3: 15–25, and 5:18–26.

3. "Mikitveyi Ahad Hazeirim" (From the writings of the young ones), *Ha-Dor* 1 (1900–1901), nos. 32, 33, 37, 48. Reprinted in his *Ketavim Nivharim* (Selected writings), vol. 2, pt. 1: *Mahsava ve-shira* (Thought and poetry) (Warsaw, 1911), pp. 29–82. Page references in the text are to the latter publication.

4. Many Israelis who decide to break all their connections with Israel and make a good living in the United States can attest to this. When the nation stood on the brink of obliteration (in the years 1967 and 1973), those *Yordim* were the first to run back to Israel to volunteer in their combat units to defend the state they had seemingly abandoned. It really did not matter how long they had been abroad. Another pertinent phenomenon in modern Israel is the tendency of its many rebellious youth actively (sometimes even satirically) to demythologize the "founding fathers of the *Yishuv*" (the first Zionist pioneers) or the "heroic" generation of the *Palmach* fighters in 1948. These shadows were too heavy upon young Israelis who wished to go on and create their own lives. Nonetheless, in times of crisis, they joined the besieged Israeli community and performed no worse than their fathers.

5. See the introduction, above, p. 14 and note 24.

6. Gnessin (1879–1913) regarded as one of the first modernists in Hebrew literature, helped Brenner to edit the Hebrew literary organ *Ha-Me'orer* (The alert) in London in 1907. Through Zeitlin he became involved with the *Tzeirim*, defining himself as a critical member of that faction of new Hebrew culture.

7. Another link between Zeitlin, the Eastern European Nietzschean, and Palestine was embodied by Yitzhak Sadeh, a student and admirer of Zeitlin and a leader of labor Zionism who in Palestine founded the Palmach, which became the nucleus of Tzahal (the Israeli Defense Forces). See his "Mayn Bakantshaft mit Hillel Zeitlin und Yosef Trumpeldor," *Di Goldene Kayt*, no. 5 (Winter 1950): 145–56.

8. To be explored in depth in a future accompanying volume to this book.

9. See his essay "Lev Shestov," *Ha-Me'orer* 2, no. 10 (1907): pp. 175–80, where Zeitlin remarks that "if I were asked who is the real successor of Friedrich Nietzsche, I would unhesitatingly answer: L. Shestov" (p. 177). See also his "Al Ha-hatira Ha-azuma shel Lev Shestov" (On the tremendous drive of Lev Shestov), *Ha-Tekufah* (Moscow and Warsaw) 20 (1923): 425–44, 21 (1924): 369–79. Republished as "Hipusheyi h-elokim shel Lev Shestov" (Lev Shestov's search for God), in Hillel Zeitlin, *Al gvul sneyi olamot* (On the borders of two worlds) (Tel Aviv, 1965), pp. 69–102.

10. See Menaham Brinker, "Nietzsche's Influence on Hebrew Writers of the Russian Empire," in *Nietzsche and Soviet Culture: Ally and Adversary*, ed. Bernice Glatzer-Rosenthal (Cambridge, 1994), pp. 393–413.

11. Shmuel Niger, introduction to Elchanan Zeitlin (Zeitlin's younger son, who was liquidated by the Nazis in the Warsaw Ghetto), *In a Literarisher Shtub* (Buenos Aires, 1946), p. vii; quoted by Moshe Waldoks, "Hillel Zeitlin: The Early Years (1894–1919)," (Ph.D. diss., Brandeis University, 1984), p. 95. This invaluable biographical monograph is a rich source of information.

12. See, e. g., Brenner's posthumously published essay "Al Hillel Zeitlin" (On Hillel Zeitlin) (1920), which begins with the words: "Thus spoke Hillel Zeitlin." *Pirkei Shifruth* (Literary chapters) (Tel Aviv, 1968), pp. 334–41. Thus the first modern Hebrew writer in Palestine, who was himself known for his admiration of Nietzsche, opens his highly impressionistic biography of his mentor with a paraphrase on the title of *Thus Spoke*

Zarathustra. This replacement of Zarathustra by Zeitlin was quite perceptive because it indicated to the readers that many of Zeitlin's intuitions were quite Nietzschean.

13. See Aaron Zeitlin, "My Father," *Jewish Spectator* (Summer 1974): 28–31, a concise version of his Yiddish "Mayn Foter," in his father's posthumous *Reb Nakhman Braslaver* (New York, 1952), pp. 11–47; and Elchanan Zeitlin, *In a Literarisher Shtub.*

14. The only available comprehensive Hebrew monograph on Zeitlin, that of Shraga Bar-Sella, *Between the Storm and the Quiet: The Life and Works of Hillel Zeitlin* (Tel Aviv, 1999), pictures Zeitlin's intellectual evolution as an organic and harmonious whole that adopted external sources (including Nietzsche) for promoting one cause: a revitalization of humanity and of the Jewish people (see, e.g., ibid., p. 10). This ideal picture does not take into account Zeitlin's stormy spiritual and existential crises, and his search for personal authenticity that made his evolution into a dialectical circle. On the other hand, those few early commentators on Zeitlin's thought and life who stressed his unwavering religiosity in his post-Nietzschean phase did not see fit to dedicate any space to the significance of Nietzsche's presence in his works. See, for example, Jacob Fichman's (1881–1958) short biographical introduction to Zeitlin's *Ketavim Nivharim* (Selected writings), vol. 1 (Warsaw, 1911), pp. i–xii. In contradistinction to these biased portraits, Fishel Lahover, two years after Zeitlin's return to the faith of his ancestors, provides us with a quite entertaining and Nietzschean picture of a Zeitlin who polemicizes "with a hammer," and who yearns to weave an inner harmony out of his conflicting inclinations by a synthesis that "instills Tolstoy's kind of love on the back of the Nietzschean 'Overman' and mixes Ibsen's heroic warrior with the ethic of the prophets and the purity of Hasidism." "Hillel Zeitlin," in *Reshafim* (Sparks) 1, no. 21 (1909): 21–32. Cf. also Joseph Klausner's short satirical essay on Zeitlin, "Jehudim Hadashim" (New Jews), *Ha-shilo'ah* 14 (December 1904): 95–96.

The culmination of a religious reading of Zeitlin's thought is found in one of the first extensive surveys of his life, written by Rabbi Simha-Bonim Auerbach in Palestine in 1944, under the auspices of the religious Moshad Harav Kook: "Megilat Hayav" (The saga of his life), in *Shefer Zeitlin* (The book of Zeitlin). ed. Yisajahu Wolfsberg and Zvi Harkavi (Jerusalem, 1944), pp. 9–75; reprinted as an independent pamphlet under the title *Hillel Zeitlin* (Tel Aviv, 1969). Unsurprisingly, Auerbach portrays Zeitlin as a person who was "thirsty for God" his entire life ("Megilat Hayav," p. 13). This account by a religious Jew is thoroughly apologetic, especially when it deals with Nietzsche's deep impact upon Zeitlin. In Auerbach's view "the Nietzschean period of Zeitlin was quite a short one" (p. 35). This tendentious downplaying of Nietzsche's role in Zeitlin's life and thought is quite biased, as the present chapter shows.

15. "Kizur Toldotai," *Ketuvim* (Works) (Tel Aviv) 2, no. 28–29 (4 April 41928): 1–3.

16. This also is Nietzsche's view in his parable of the "madman," the genuine atheist mocked by pseudo-atheists on account of his search for God. The madman once firmly believed in God and thus he found the disappearance of his belief to be cataclysmic, not only for himself, but for the entire culture. Only one who has had a father and has lost him can genuinely and profoundly experience this loss.

17. Auerbach, "Megilat Hayav," pp. 10–11.

18. "Ha-Zimaon: Hazon Lev" (The thirst: The heart's vision)," *Sifrut* (Literature) 4 (1910): 141–60.

19. Waldoks, "Hillel Zeitlin," p. 279 n. 175. Lewis S. Feuer, in his *Ideology and the Ideologists* (New York, 1975), p. 37, describes the "countless young Jews" who "listened to a master (Nietzsche) whose words rang with an unquenched sense of selfhood. For every German barrackeer who paraded with Nietzschean phrases, there was a ghetto Nietzschean who found his life kindled by Nietzschean images."

20. "Ha-tov ve-ha-ra" (the full name is "The Good and the Evil according to Sages of Israel and the Nations"), *Ha-Shilo'ah*, 5 (1899): 289–301, 395–405, 493–505; 6 (1899): 289–99, 397–404, 494–503; 7 (1901): 385–95, 497–509; 8 (1902): 201–11. References in the text are to this publication. Reprinted in book form in *Ketavim Nivharim*, vol. 1. Though Zeitlin's first mention of Nietzsche is in 1899, he knew about him well before then. In 1896, he gave Ahad Ha'am a manuscript for publication in *Ha-Shilo'ah*, "Torat Ha-Adam" (A theory of man). The article is no longer available but according to the testimony of his son Aaron (see note 13 above), it consisted of a string of Nietzschean aphorisms and was consequently rejected by Ahad Ha'am, who urged him (as he urged Berdichevski) to renounce this unstructured form in favor of a more rigorous and methodological treatment of specific philosophical themes. The result was "The Good and the Evil," and despite the rejection of "A Theory of Man" and Zeitlin's dismay at the lack of receptivity to Nietzsche's " philosophy of life" on the part of most of the Warsaw Jewish intelligentsia, he was unshaken in his devotion to Nietzsche, as the last section of "The Good and the Evil" testifies.

21. See also 6:497, where Zeitlin mentions "the confused thoughts of Rabbi Nahman of Braslav."

22. See vol. 7, pp. 497, 498.

23. One must reject Bar-Sella's contention that in this essay "the spirit of Schopenhauerian pessimism" has the upper hand (*Between the Storm and the Quiet*, pp. 55ff.), as well as the contention of Auerbach that "Schopenhauer is the great hero of this entire essay" ("Megilat Hayav," p. 38).

24. Zeitlin somewhat incorrectly refers to the second stage of Nietzsche's thought as that one in which Nietzsche attempted to attain absolute scientific Truth. Surely, his *Gay Science* is not exactly the product of a rationalist scientific philosopher. Zeitlin, however, was right in stressing Nietzsche's wish to reach "the highest level of self-knowledge" (8:203).

25. See above, p. 104, for Berdichevski's quote from Nietzsche: "*if a temple is to be erected a temple must be destroyed.*"

26. I cannot refrain here from a personal remark. I was pleased to realize that almost one hundred years before I delineated this distinction in chapter 5 of my *Nietzsche's Enticing Psychology of Power* (Ames, Iowa, 1989), another Polish Jew was indicating this very distinction in his perceptive interpretation of Nietzsche's mature philosophy.

27. *Baruch Spinoza: Hayav, Sfarav ve-shitato ha-philosophit* (Baruch Spinoza: His life, his writings, and his philosophical method), 2 vols. (Warsaw, 1900; 2d ed., 1914). References in the text are to the first edition.

28. While dealing with Spinoza's notion of *conatus* (ibid. pp. 98–99) as the will to perpetuate one's being, Zeitlin remarks that in this respect Spinoza preceded Schopenhauer, but whereas in the latter this will is a monistic drive, in the former it is only one of Nature's laws.

29. Nietzsche, *Ecce Homo* "The Untimely Ones," chapter 3, p. 281.

30. I could not locate this specific citation in Nietzsche's writings but a similar idea is expressed in his claim in SE I: "it is a painful and dangerous undertaking to tunnel into oneself and to force one's way down into the shaft of one's being. . . . A man who does it can easily hurt himself so that no physician can cure him" (p. 129). For discussion see my *Nietzsche's Enticing Psychology of Power*, pp. 114–19.

31. "Hirhurim" (Meditations), *Ha-dor* 1 (1900–1901), nos. 10:8–11, 16:12–15 21:9–11. This aphoristic essay is actually a critique directed implicitly against the "Jewish Nietzscheanism" of Ahad Ha'am's and Berdichevski's schools. In Zeitlin's eyes both those intellectual leaders were salon Nietzscheans, and Zeitlin continued to attack them in his 1905 monograph on Nietzsche. But already in these aphorisms Zeitlin adopts Nietzsche's antihistoricism, his stress on the present, his dislike of any abstract mode of thought and any school or ideological party—any "ism." He claims that by misusing Nietzsche for their ideological viewpoints and by founding schools of Jewish Nietzscheanism, Ahad Ha'am and Berdichevski are misappropriating Nietzsche's teachings and illegitimately enlisting them for the sake and the interests of the "mob." Hence they make the Nietzschean *Übermensch* into a new idol, into a new shadow of the dead God, whereas Nietzsche specifically overcame his faith in his God to destroy all abstract or historical shadows. One gains the impression that Zeitlin perceived the mobilization of Nietzsche for some kind of ideological battle as a real sacrilege, as a betrayal of the antidogmatic openness of Nietzsche's spirit, as a blow to the intimate feelings that Zeitlin cherished for him. Thus Zeitlin flatly states that Nietzsche should and must be appropriated solely for the sake of the Jewish *individual* here and now, and ought not to become a banner for some faction (the allusion is to Berdichevski's *Tzeirim*) or some cultural ideology (Ahad Ha'am). Clearly, Zeitlin, at this period, opts for individualistic Zionism: "Most of the Zionists aspire to create Jews as citizens, but I seek Jewish persons. . . . The conditions of life made us into slaves but we are aristocrats at spirit" (pp. 12–13). This individualistic and elitist view brings Zeitlin very close to Nietzsche's emphasis on the value of the individual for whom society must work in order to assist in the creation of the exceptional human being.

32. Hillel Zeitlin, "Friedrich Nietzsche: Hayav, shirato ufilosofioto" (His life, poetry and philosophy), *Ha-Zeman* (The time) (Vilna) (January–October 1905), vols. 1–3, pp. 113–24, 125–35, 131–41, 398–419, 423–31, (unfinished). Subsequent references are given in the text by page numbers only.

33. Lou Andreas Salomé, *Friedrich Nietzsche in seinen Werken* (Vienna, 1894).

34. Elisabeth Förster-Nietzsche, *Das Leben Friedrich Nietzsche's*, 2 vols. (Leipzig, 1895–1904).

35. It is highly probable that he means his *Friedrich Nietzsche: Der Künstler und Der Denker: Ein Essay* (Stuttgart, 1897).

36. See above, chapter 3, notes 56, 57, 58.

37. Anatoli Lunacharsky (1875–1933), a student of the German-Swiss philosopher Richard Avenarius, attempted the impossible intellectual venture of grafting the teaching of Zarathustra onto the socialism of Marx. Zeitlin deals critically with this undertaking in his "Kinyanei Ruah" (Spiritual assets) (1904), in *Ketavim Nivharim*, 2:5–87. In this essay, which bears the Nietzschean subtitle "Untimely Meditations," especially on pp. 26–31, Zeitlin deals ironically with Lunacharsky's attempt to forge a synthesis between Marxism and Nietzsche: "It is a great pity that the greatest master of intellectual syntheses, the literary critic and philosopher, Lunacharsky, employs his

sharp analytical acumen . . . his clarity of mind, and intellectual bravado. . . . to make such a blunder . . . and wishes to attach Nietzsche to Marxist scholasticism" (p. 27). It is well known that "Nietzsche hates socialism vehemently." Nevertheless, by *pilpul* (intellectual tricks) "one can combine everything . . . and one may even prove that the proletariat by means of his great war creates . . . the Overman" (p. 30). A concise and lucid portrait of this "leftist existentialist" is given in Isaac Deutscher's introduction to Anatoly Vasilievich Lunacharsky, *Revolutionary Silhouettes*, trans. Michael Glenny (London, 1967), pp. 9–25.

38. Which appeared in a translation by Bernard Martin in a collection: *Dostoevsky, Tolstoy and Nietzsche* (Athens: Ohio University Press, 1969), pp. 11–140.

39. Ibid., p. 72, 96, and elsewhere.

40. It suffices to quote here the last sentence of Shestov's essay on Tolstoy and Nietzsche: "We must seek God" (p. 140).

41. "Did Nietzsche really seek God? His passionate polemics against Christianity sufficiently testify to this" (ibid., p. 81; see also pp. 117, 133).

42. Shestov describes Nietzsche's tragic atheism as follows: "God is dead: this message . . . awakens in him a mystical horror (ibid., pp. 84–85). . . . All the comparisons that came to his mind appeared insufficient to impart to others the horrible inner feeling of devastation that he experienced when he saw and heard that God had been murdered (p. 86). . . . It is no longer given us to find without having sought. . . . We must understand all the horror of the situation of which Nietzsche speaks with the words of a madman" (p. 92). Surely this earthshaking experience of losing God, which Shestov emphasized in the case of Nietzsche and which Zeitlin himself had recently undergone, was another reason for the attraction that Zeitlin felt to Shestov's interpretation.

43. Zeitlin, "Friedrich Nietzsche," p. 127. This interpretation of Nietzsche as God-seeker was undoubtedly also inspired by certain passages from *Thus Spoke Zarathustra* (book 4: "Out of Service") that Shestov stresses ("The Good in the Teaching of Tolstoy and Nietzsche," p. 96): "O Zarathustra, with such unbelief, you are more pious than you believe. Some God in you has converted you to your ungodliness."

44. Ibid., pp. 128, 137. Shestov repeats this interpretation in another essay, written in 1903, only two years before Zeitlin's, "Dostoevsky and Nietzsche: The Philosophy of Tragedy," trans. Spencer Roberts, in *Dostoevsky, Tolstoy and Nietzsche*, pp. 141–322, where he states: "Dostoevsky and Nietzsche abandoned humanism for cruelty" (p. 319; see also p. 222).

45. See Shestov, "The Good in the Teaching of Tolstoy and Nietzsche," p. 23.

46. Hillel Zeitlin, "Adam Elyon o El Elyon" (Overman or Almighty God), in *Massu'ot* (Torch) (Odessa) 1 (1919): 237–58. Reprinted in *On the Borders of Two Worlds (Ketavim)*, vol. 2 (Tel Aviv: Yavneh, 1976), pp. 49–68. References in the text are to this republication. The quote is from p. 49.

47. For example, in an essay of 1905 (the same year that saw his monograph on Nietzsche) Zeitlin defends his support for the faction in the Zionist Congresses that was inclined to accept Great Britain's offer to establish a Jewish State in Uganda. "Hamasber: Reshimot Territoriali (The crisis: Notes of a territorialist), *Ha-Zeman* 1, no. 5 (August 1905): 259–95. Arguing against the lofty cultural Zionism of Ahad Ha'am, Zeitlin introduces his version of a personal Zionism for the authentic life of its followers, for those who "seek truthfulness of life" (p. 262). Only a land that is a

sort of *tabula rasa*, without any historical relics and shackles of the glorious but demanding past, may function well for the uninterrupted creations of new selves!

48. "Hipusheyi h-elokim shel Lev Shestov," p. 84.

CONCLUSION

1. As Karl Jaspers calls them in his *Philosophy*, trans. E. B. Ashton (Chicago, 1969–71), 2:178ff. See also my *In Search of Authenticity from Kierkegaard to Camus* (London, 1995), chap. 2.

2. *Alliance Israélite Universal*, a philanthropic Jewish-French Society founded in 1860 in Paris whose first president was Adolf Cremié.

3. Thus, B. Yack is quite right claiming in *The Longing for Total Revolution: Philosophic Sources of Social Discontent from Rousseau to Marx and Nietzsche* (Princeton, N.J., 1986) that Nietzsche shared with Kant the ideal of the realization of humanity in mankind that Kant's philosophy of freedom made possible (p. 311). Another of Nietzsche's recent commentators also stresses the point that the issue of "human perfection lies at the heart of Nietzsche's inquiries" and does not fail to notice that "modern ideas about knowledge, freedom, and mastery pervade and continuously shape his investigations." Peter Berkowitz, *Nietzsche: The Ethics of an Immoralist* (Cambridge, Mass., 1995), p. 2. But didn't these very ideas also pervade the ethos of the European Enlightenment?

4. This has also been perceived by other commentators; see Bruce Detwiler, *Nietzsche and the Politics of Aristocratic Radicalism* (Chicago, 1990), pp. 15–16; P. Bergmann, *Nietzsche: The Last Antipolitical German* (Bloomington, Ind., 1989), pp. 108–41; M. Warren, *Nietzsche and Political Thought* (Cambridge, Mass., 1988), p. 70.

5. For discussion see R. Hinton-Thomas, *Nietzsche in German Politics and Society 1890–1918* (Manchester, 1983) and the provocative work by Geoff Waite, *Nietzsche's Corps/e* (Durham, N.C., 1996) who delineates Nietzsche's "leftist camp," esp. pp. 139–66.

6. This is especially true if we realize that without Kant's thought (as I attempted to show in my *Nietzsche's Enticing Psychology of Power* [Ames, Iowa, 1989]), Nietzsche could not have arrived at his late philosophical tenets. This is also true of his early thought which was partly and initially derived from the metaphysics of Schopenhauer, who saw himself as a worthy successor of Kant. In a nutshell: without the thought of the Enlightenment (starting from Rousseau and Kant) it is difficult to grasp how Nietzsche could have become such a significant part of the history of Western philosophy and culture.

7. See also Nietzsche's other statement regarding "the man of Rousseau" "from [whom] there has proceeded a force (*Kraft*) which has promoted violent revolutions and continues to do so" (SE, p. 151). In social-political issues Nietzsche was far from being a radical revolutionary but believed (also in matters of personal transfiguration) in gradual evolution. This was virtually the position of mainstream Zionist activists and ideologues.

8. BGE, 30.

SELECT BIBLIOGRAPHY OF SECONDARY WORKS

Almog, Shmuel. *Zionism and History: The Rise of a New Jewish Consciousness.* New York, 1987.

Ansell-Pearson, Keith. *Nietzsche contra Rousseau.* Cambridge, 1991.

———. *An Introduction to Nietzsche as Political Thinker.* Cambridge, 1994.

Aschheim, Steven E. "Nietzsche and the Nietzschean Moment." *Leo Baeck Year Book* 37 (1992): 189–212.

———. *The Nietzsche Legacy in Germany: 1890–1990.* Berkeley, Calif., 1992.

Avineri, Shlomo. *The Making of Modern Zionism: Intellectual Origins of the Jewish State.* New York, 1981.

Band, Arnold J. "The Ahad Ha'am and Berdichewski Polarity." In *At the Crossroads: Essays on Ahad Ha'am,* edited by Jacques Kornberg, pp. 49–59. Albany, N.Y., 1983.

Ben-Horin, Meir. *Max Nordau: Philosopher of Human Solidarity.* London, 1956.

Bergmann, P. *Nietzsche: The "Last Antipolitical German."* Bloomington, Ind., 1989.

Berkowitz, Peter. *Nietzsche: The Ethics of an Immoralist.* Cambridge, Mass., 1995.

Bourel, Dominique, and Jacques Le Rider, eds. *DeSils-Maria à Jérusalem.* Paris, 1991.

Brinker, Menachem. "Nietzsche's Influence on Hebrew Writers of the Russian Empire." In *Nietzsche and Soviet Culture, Adversary and Ally,* edited by Bernice Glatzer-Rosenthal, pp. 393–413. Cambridge, 1994.

———. "Nietzsche and Hebrew Writers: An Attempt at a Synoptic View." In *Nietzsche and Hebrew Culture,* edited by Jacob Golomb, pp. 131–59. Jerusalem, 2002. (In Hebrew.)

———. "Nietzsche and the Jews." In *Nietzsche, the Godfather of Fascism? On the Uses and Abuses of Philosophy,* edited by Jacob Golomb and Robert S. Wistrich, pp. 107–25. Princeton, N.J., 2002.

Chowers, Eyal. "Time in Zionism: The Life and Afterlife of a Temporal Revolution." *Political Theory* 26 (1998): 652–85.

Conway, Daniel W. *Nietzsche and the Political.* London, 1996.

———. *Nietzsche's Dangerous Game.* Cambridge, 1997.

Detwiler, Bruce. *Nietzsche and the Politics of Aristocratic Radicalism.* Chicago, 1990.

Ellerin, Bruce Elkin. "Nietzsche among the Zionists." Ph.D. diss., Cornell University, 1990.

———. "Nietzsche et les Sionistes: Tableau d'une Réception." In *DeSils-Maria à Jérusalem,* edited by Dominique Bourel and Jacques Le Rider, pp. 111–19. Paris, 1991.

Feuer, S. Lewis. *Ideology and the Ideologists.* New York, 1975.

Förster-Nietzsche, Elisabeth. *Das Leben Friedrich Nietzsches.* 2 vols. Leipzig, 1895–1904.

Frankel, Jonathan. *Prophecy and Politics: Socialism, Nationalism and the Russian Jews, 1862–1917.* Cambridge, 1981.

Friedman, Maurice. *Martin Buber's Life and Work,* vol. 1: *The Early Years 1878–1923.* New York, 1981.

———. *Martin Buber's Life and Work: The Middle Years 1923–1945.* New York, 1983.

Gilman, Sander L. *Difference and Pathology: Stereotypes of Sexuality, Race, and Madness.* Ithaca, N.Y., 1985.

———. *Inscribing the Other.* Lincoln, Neb., 1991.

Golomb, Jacob. "Nietzsche on Jews and Judaism." *Archiv für* Geschichte der Philosophie 67 (1985): 139–61.

———. "Nietzsche's Early Educational Thought." *Journal of Philosophy of Education* 19 (1985): 99–109.

———. "Nietzsche's Judaism of Power." *Revue des études juives* 147 (1988): 353–85.

———. *Nietzsche's Enticing Psychology of Power.* Ames, Iowa, 1989.

———. "Nietzsche on Authenticity." *Philosophy Today* 34 (1990): 243–58.

———. *In Search of Authenticity from Kierkegaard to Camus.* London, 1995.

———. "Nietzsche and the Marginal Jews." In *Nietzsche and Jewish Culture,* edited by Jacob Golomb, pp. 158–92. London, 1997.

———. "Nietzsche's Positive Religion and the Old Testament." In *Nietzsche and the Divine,* edited by J. Urpeth and J. Lippett, pp. 30–56. Manchester, 2000.

——. "Buber's *I and Thou* vis-à-vis Nietzsche and Kierkegaard." *Existentia* 12 (2002): 413–27.

——. "How to De-Nazify Nietzsche's Philosophical Anthropology." In *Nietzsche, the Godfather of Fascism? On the Uses and Abuses of Philosophy,* edited by Jacob Golomb and Robert S. Wistrich, pp. 19–46. Princeton, N.J., 2002.

——. ed. *Nietzsche in Hebrew Culture.* Jerusalem, 2002 (In Hebrew.)

Hertzberg, Arthur, ed., *The Zionist Idea.* Philadelphia, 1997.

Kornberg, Jacques. *Theodor Herzl: From Assimilation to Zionism.* Bloomington, Ind., 1993.

——, ed. *At the Crossroads: Essays on Ahad Ha'am.* Albany, N.Y., 1983.

Kurzweil, Baruch. "The German Jew in Modern Hebrew Literature." *Leo Baeck Year Book* 6 (1961): 170–89.

——. *Our Modern Literature: Continuation or Revolution?* Jerusalem, 1971. (In Hebrew.)

Laqueur, Walter. *A History of Zionism.* New York, 1972.

Luz, Ehud. *Parallels Meet: Religion and Nationalism in the Early Zionist Movement.* Translated by Lenn J. Schramm. Philadelphia, 1988.

——. "Zion and *Judenstaat*: The Significance of the Uganda Controversy." In *Essays in Modern Jewish History: A Tribute to Ben Halpern,* edited by F. Malino and P. Albert, pp. 217–39. Madison, N.J., 1982.

Mendes-Flohr, Paul. *From Mysticism to Dialogue: Martin Buber's Transformation of German Social Thought.* Detroit, 1989.

——. "Zarathustra's Apostle: Martin Buber and the Jewish Renaissance." In *Nietzsche and Jewish Culture,* edited by Jacob Golomb, pp. 233–43. London, 1997.

Moseley, Marcus. "Between Memory and Forgetfulness: The Janus Face of Micha Yosef Berdichevsky." In *Studies in Contemporary Jewry,* vol. 12, edited by Ezra Mendelsohn, pp. 78–117. Oxford, 1996.

Mosse, George L. *German Jews Beyond Judaism.* Bloomington, Ind., 1985.

——. *Confronting the Nation: Jewish and Western Nationalism.* Hanover, N.H., 1993.

Nehamas, Alexander. *Nietzsche: Life as Literature.* Cambridge, Mass., 1985.

Neumark, David, "Introduction to the Teaching on the *Übermensch.*" *MiMizrahUmi-Marav* (Vienna) 1 (1894): 115–24. (In Hebrew.)

O'Flaherty, James C., Timothy F. Sellner, and Robert M. Helm, eds. *Studies in Nietzsche and the Judaeo-Christian Tradition*. Chapel Hill, 1985.

Reinharz, Jehuda. "Hashomer Hazair in Germany (I): 1928–1933." *Leo Baeck Yearbook* 31 (1986): 173–208.

Reinharz, Jehuda, and Walter Schatzberg, eds. *The Jewish Response to German Culture: From the Enlightenment to the Second World War*. Hanover, N.H., 1985.

Riehl, Alois. *Friedrich Nietzsche, Der Künstler und Der Denker: Ein Essay*. Stuttgart, 1897.

Roberston, Ritchie. "The Problem of 'Jewish Self-Hatred' in Herzl, Kraus and Kafka." *Oxford German Studies* 16 (1985): 81–108.

Rotenstreich, Nathan. *Jewish Philosophy in Modern Times: From Mendelssohn to Rosenzweig*. New York, 1968.

———. *Jews and German Philosophy: The Polemics of Emancipation*. New York, 1984.

Santaniello, Weaver. *Nietzsche, God, and the Jews: His Critique of Judeo-Christianity in Relation to the Nazi Myth*. Albany, N.Y., 1994.

Schaeder, Grete. *The Hebrew Humanism of Martin Buber*. Translated by Noah J. Jacobs. Detroit, 1973.

Schestov, Lev. *Dostoevsky, Tolstoy and Nietzsche*. Translated by Bernard Martin. Athens, Ohio, 1969.

Schilpp, Paul, ed. *The Philosophy of Martin Buber*. La Salle, Ill., 1967.

Schwarz, Leo W., ed. *Memoirs of My People*. New York, 1943.

Shapira, Anita. *Land and Power: The Zionist Resort to Force, 1881–1947*. New York, 1992.

———. "Ahad Ha'am: The Politics of Sublimation." *Studies in Contemporary Jewry* 11 (1995), edited by Peter Y. Medding, pp. 205–14.

Shimoni, Gideon. *The Zionist Ideology*. Hanover, N.H., 1995.

Simmel, Georg. "Friedrich Nietzsche: Eine moralphilosophische Silhouette." *Zeitschrift für Philosophie und philosophische Kritik* 107 (1896): 202–15.

———. *Schopenhauer and Nietzsche* (1907). Translated by Helmut Loiskandl, Deena Weinstein, and Michael Weinstein. Urbana, Ill., 1991.

Simon, Ernst. "Martin Buber and German Jewry." *Leo Baeck Year Book* 3 (1958): 3–39.

Sternhell, Zeev. *The Founding Myths of Israel: Nationalism, Socialism, and the Making of the Jewish State*. Princeton, N.J., 1998.

Strong, Tracy, B. *Friedrich Nietzsche and the Politics of Transfiguration.* Berkeley, Calif., 1975. Rev. ed., 1988.

Talmon, Jacob, L. *Israel among the Nations.* London, 1970.

Vital, David. *The Origins of Zionism.* Oxford, 1975.

Waldoks, Moshe. "Hillel Zeitlin: The Early Years (1894–1919)." Ph.D diss., Brandeis University, 1984.

Wistrich, S. Robert. *Socialism and the Jews: The Dilemmas of Assimilation in Germany and Austria-Hungary.* Rutherford, N.J., 1982.

——. "Theodor Herzl: Zionist Icon, Myth-Maker and Social Utopian," in *The Shaping of Israeli Identity,* ed. Robert Wistrich and David Ohana, pp. 1–37. London, 1995.

——. "Max Nordau, Degeneration and the *Fin-de-Siècle.*" in *Krisenwahrnehmungen im Fin-de-Siècle,* ed. Michael Graetz and Aram Mattioli, pp. 83–100. Zurich, 1997.

Witkowsky, Gustav. "Nietzsches Stellung zum Zionismus." *Jüdische Rundschau* 2 (1913).

Yovel, Yirmiyahu. *Dark Riddle: Hegel, Nietzsche, and the Jews.* Cambridge, 1998.

Zipperstein, Steven J. *Elusive Prophet: Ahad Ha'am and the Origins of Zionism.* Berkeley, Calif., 1993.

INDEX